AF375479

Living in Monaco

written by

Zsolt Szemerszky

Living in Monaco
- English edition -

First Printing: December 2015
Current edition: December 2020

ISBN-13: 978-2-493007-00-1

Publisher: Niche Media Monaco
                 17 Avenue Albert II, 98000 - The Principality of Monaco
                 http://NicheMedia.mc

Editorial lecture: Brandon Ivan Bohrn (2019) and Dorottya Novak (2020)

Distributed via IngramSpark

I would like to dedicate this book to my goddaughter Faye Martha. She is an exceptional little girl who taught me that money is not the prime asset in life. Family is what matters.

For many years I was living blindly. I almost let myself forget what unconditional love means, until this beautiful little girl came into my life and reminded me of the most important values in life.

I love you so much Faye!

Living in Monaco

Special thanks

I would like to say a special thank you to Michael Lanteri, who is one of my most loyal reader since the beginning.

Michael is the founder of the family owned Lanteri Partners Group in Melbourne, Australia, which is regarded as one of Melbourne's most successful independent Private Wealth Management firms.

A few years ago he decided to relocate to the Principality of Monaco. He read my book and contacted me directly.

Since then, Michael has successfully applied for Monaco residency and he has also established a consulting office in the heart of the Principality.

Michael, I greatly appreciate your loyalty and support towards my „Living in Monaco" book series.

One big thank you goes to Maya Ivdra (real estate broker at Monaco Villas) and Olivier Milliex (the founder of OMYS Monaco). They are a wonderful couple with great passion towards their professions as well.

In this book I am often referring to Olivier in the financial areas, since he is one of the top experts in the Principality when it comes to high value acquisition, construction and ownership optimization.

Thank you for both of you for being part of the "Living in Monaco" project. And thank you for being such valuable persons for the family of Monaco residents.

I also want to mention here Jamal Qureshi, founder of Svalbarði Polar Iceberg Water. Jamal is not a resident of Monaco, but we have been working together closely for three years because he creates amazing initiatives that are valuable for the Principality.

Jamal's work on polar iceberg water is highly valued because it stems from his passion to help save his arctic home. By collecting iceberg water from the Norwegian island territory of Svalbard that would otherwise be lost and contribute to sea level rise, he is able to use revenues from the product to save a hundred times the ice gathered. He has created a luxurious, gourmet, carbon-negative product from icebergs, which is redefining the very notion of drinking water.

It is a great please to work with you Jamal and I am entirely honoured for all your enthusiasm towards Monaco. I just hope that more people like you will be part of our small but unique community.

Last but not least, I would like to thank my very best friend who always believed in me and never let me give up on my dreams.

Thank you Dodo Newman for the journey we have made and shared together during more than 20 years of friendship.

Thank you for all of your support and belief in me. No matter what I decided to accomplish in my life, you were always there to push me further.

Special thanks

Living in Monaco

Living in Monaco

Table of Contents

Contents in details

Table of Contents

CHAPTER 4:

RELOCATION AND WHAT IS TAKES — 95

CHAPTER 7:

YACHT REGISTRATION AND CHARTERING 215

CHAPTER 8:

ADMINISTRATIVE ASSISTANCE 233

CHAPTER 9:

SCHOOLS IN MONACO 239

CHAPTER 10:

TAXATION 263

CHAPTER 11:

TYPICAL ADMINISTRATIVE CHALLENGES 273

CHAPTER 12:

LEGAL PROTECTION 289

CHAPTER 15:

THE LOCAL INVESTMENT SCENE   413

CHAPTER 16:

DUE DILIGENCE / WHO TO TRUST?   455

CHAPTER 17:

TRAPS AND FRAUD ALERTS   479

Living in Monaco

Living in Monaco

Preface

Acknowledgements

I would like to say thank you to all of the people, companies and institutions that guided me during the writing of this book. Since its very first version back in 2013, the "Living in Monaco" book developed into one of the most comprehensive guide on the Principality of Monaco. During this Monaco journey I met with some truly exceptional people and businesses who were able to offer unparalleled value to this book.

First of all, I have to give a special thank you to the Government of the Principality of Monaco and to the Institut Monégasque de la Statistique et des Études Économiques. Without their kind cooperation, their detailed statistics and internationally translated materials, I could not have written this book with such depth and precision.

Institut Monégasque de la Statistique et des Études Économiques
9 rue du Gabian, 98000 Monaco
Phone : (+377) 98 98 98 88
Fax : (+377) 98 98 87 59
http://www.imsee.mc

In many parts of the book, I also received an immense amount of guidance from Mr. Régis Bergonzi, who is in my opinion among the most excellent Avocats-Défenseur in Monaco. Actually it is not only based on my opinion, since his company the Bergonzi Law Firm was named "Law firm of the year – Monaco" at the Citywealth IFC Awards in 2020.

Between January and March 2014, Mr. Bergonzi gave me his professional inputs and suggestions on several topics I aimed to cover. His professional and personal experiences, including over ten years of legal practice in the Principality of Monaco, contributed a lot to my research on Monaco. I believe our time together truly increased the value of this book.

Thank you, Régis! I honestly appreciate everything you have done for me.

I would like to clarify in advance that Mr. Bergonzi conveyed his views to me as a friend to another friend, not as a professional advice. The content of this book represents my own personal views and my own interpretations of topics about the Principality of Monaco.

Therefore, I highly recommend and encourage you to seek professional advice if you are interested in acquiring more detailed information about any topics presented in this book. Also, naturally, regulations can change over time.

If you seek legal advice, my recommendation would be Mr. Bergonzi, who is currently also the President of the Monaco Bar Association.

Cabinet Bergonzi
37 Boulevard des Moulins, 98000 Monaco
Phone: (+377) 93 30 89 89
Fax: (+377) 93 50 89 30
http://www.regisbergonzi.com

During the writing of "Living in Monaco", I also learnt and developed knowledge from the representatives of the Direction de l'Expansion Économique, or as they are called in English, the Monaco Welcome Office. I received trustworthy, recommended contacts, and endless support in answering all of my questions. Thank you for this!

Direction de l'Expansion Économique
9 rue du Gabian, 98000 Monaco
Phone : (+377) 98 98 98 00
Fax : (+377) 92 05 75 20
https://service-public-entreprises.gouv.mc/Fiches-par-entites-administratives/Demarches-et-Informations-Direction-de-l-Expansion-Economique

I would like give a special thanks to Mr. Aymeric Pazzaglia and the Direction de l'Expansion Économique. Back in 2013, I spent days with him clarifying all of my questions, and he was always exceptionally helpful, resourceful and, more importantly, incredibly patient with me.

In the book, I also used several internet resources with the concept of Fair Use. (See them detailed in the chapter called "Resources"). Thank you Google and WikiPedia for the amazing abundance of knowledge. Also, I appreciate the information I gained from the companies, blogs and private individuals I listed under the same chapter. Much of the content was used under the term of Fair Use and Creative Common. Copyright Disclaimer Under Section 107 of the Copyright Act 1976 grants permission to use information and images for educational purpose that might otherwise be infringing. Additionaly, I always ensured the photo credits and names of their sources if they were available.

Special thanks to Monte-Carlo Société des Bains de Mer (Monte-Carlo SBM) for the beautiful and historic photos of the Principality of Monaco and selected personalities. For those who are interested in the old Monte-Carlo, I highly recommend checking out the "Monte-Carlo Legend" project which is a beautiful commemoration of the heritage of Monaco.

Also a huge shout out to Brandon Ivan Bohrn, who helped me proofread the 2019 version of my book. Thank you Brandon for all your energies.

Last but not least, I would like to thank Dorottya Novak, who helped me proofread the 2020 version of my book. Thank you for your kindness.

Preface

Living in Monaco

Introduction

I am a National Quality Prize winner (2006), revenue specialist and the author of multiple internationally published books.

I am a passionate admirer of the Principality of Monaco and I am committed to promoting its core values, including its family-oriented and cultural heritage. From my vast experience, my aim is to provide a compelling review on the heritage, lifestyle and administrative challenges of Monaco, bringing together the past and present. In essence, my book is dedicated to those who are looking to relocate to the Principality of Monaco by offering them reliable information and trusted service providers.

In my professional work, my aim is to help individuals and corporations achieve their highest ambitions. Being an author of multiple books, published in over 50 countries world-wide, helped me create business values for people and to guide them in the road towards their aims.

One of my most quoted sentences is:

> *"Every mountain can be climbed – you*
> *just have to find the appropriate way to do it.*
> *If you do not achieve your goal,*
> *then you have not done everything to achieve it.*
> *The secret of success is persistence!"*

To discover more: zsoltszemerszky.com

Living in Monaco

written by

Zsolt Szemerszky

Foreword

I still clearly remember that back in 2013, before I started writing this book, many people thought I was crazy. My friends and business partners repeatedly asked the same question:

"Why I am writing another book about Monaco?"

My answer was quite simple, because none of the tourist guides answer the really important questions. And frankly I wanted to give an honest, first-hand opinion to all of the people who are aiming to relocate their personal or business life to Monaco. Since 2010, I am managing and am the founding member of MonacoWealthManagement.com, an unbiased business itinerary, which has helped hundreds of Monaco residents to relocate and launch businesses in Monaco. I felt that based on the experience I have gained during these years, I am entitled to write an honest book about the Principality of Monaco.

The truth is that when you are thinking about relocating to the Principality of Monaco or opening and extending your business venture in Monaco, you are no longer interested in sightseeing. And that is exactly the point when you will face the really important questions. These are decisions that can cost you tens of thousands of euros in extra costs, if you are not prepared. However, this book can provide the information needed to save you money and energy. Because at the end of the day none of us want to waste valuable time and money.

If you are looking for a tourist guide, then close this book immediately because then this book is not for you. All you will find here is the most important information needed to create a better quality of life for yourself and your beloved ones in the heart of the Principality of Monaco.

This book was written to provide a collection of my own personal experiences and materials to use as a reference or starting point, not as official advice.

This book is also intended to be your own practical guide, and thus includes the main contacts you might need to proceed further with your aims and goals. Yes, your read that right. I will mention the most important authorities with their contact information (address, phone, fax, e-mail if possible) in order to shorten your path to achieving your highest ambitions in Monaco.

No matter whether your aim is to retire in Monaco as a millionaire, work there as an employee or to operate your own business, you will definitely need a good base of knowledge to make your dreams happen, and to do it as smoothly as possible. Believe me, the Principality of Monaco cannot be compared to any other country. There is a different set of rules, and unlike most places, in Monaco, money by itself is not enough to accomplish your goals.

Before writing this book, I had a great desire too: I wanted to hunt down the myth around Monaco and go beyond the gossip. Monaco has a glorious, but shady past too.

People often refer to the Principality as a "sunny place for shady people", however the truth is much more complex and you have to dive into its culture and heritage to really discover its beauty. So can you learn something from my journey? I am confident that the answer is yes.

Last, but not least, my other aim with "Living in Monaco", is to support local businesses and help them to connect with high-net-worth individuals, investors and business owners from outside the Principality, which is often difficult due to the similarities between the French and the Monegasque legal systems (I will explain this later in detail). Therefore, I also dedicate this book to the businesses, business leaders and owners in the Principality of Monaco.

As you will see, this book will raise attention to the most typical frauds and moral hazards committed by non-Monaco-based gold diggers and fortune hunters. They often target and mislead wealthy individuals who are aiming to invest or relocate in the Principality without having the proper time or knowledge to understand the local business scene and regulations.

I love Monaco and its community, therefore, I could not stand not to write this book. I am not the type of person who gives up and says "That's life..." when something unexpected happens. I am the guy who goes after it and tries to find out the reasons behind it. Why? Because we can always learn from the mistakes of the past. This is the only way to develop and make things better.

It goes without saying that my own experiences should not influence your own choices. Do not take what I say for granted! Based on my experience, it is very important to have a basic understanding about things before you start to pay an hourly fee for an advisor.

Nonetheless, if you really want to implement any aspect of this book into your personal life, I highly recommend you contact professionals who are authorised to advice you on it. Check and question all of the information and dare to ask for professional help and guidance.

See every obstacle as an opportunity to increase the quality of your life. The Principality of Monaco offers various sources to protect you but if you fail to do sufficient research, it cannot protect you.

I hope you will find this book and my own personal life experiences a good eye-opener for better and safer decisions in your life, especially when you are relocating to the Principality of Monaco.

Good luck with everything,
Zsolt Szemerszky

Monaco in a nutshell

Monaco in a nutshell

The very first impression of the Principality of Monaco is that it is breathtaking without a doubt. It is an incredibly small country, the second smallest country worldwide (after the Vatican City) and its population is around 37,900 people. Nonetheless, the Principality has capitalised well on its own potential.

Monaco is an independent sovereign state, ruled by the Grimaldi family since 1297. As glamorous as it is from the outside, it can be just as difficult from the inside. Yet, one can find a real multi-cultural environment made up of many nations, which makes the whole place very interesting and lively.

Access to Monaco is very easy by air, road or train. The airport in Nice is a 20-40 minute drive, depending on traffic or an 8 minute helicopter ride. It is also very rarely closed because of lack of adverse weather conditions. Italy is within a 30 minute drive and there are ski resorts within a range of 1.5 to 2.5 hours of driving (or 20 minutes by helicopter).

Many people say that it is about luxury and wealth as well. However, I discovered another side of Monaco as well, which is the very friendly Mediterranean side of the Principality where you can find lovely small streets on the Rock or can discover the view of endless orange trees standing in a row besides the main roads or the small chapels.

Living in a zero debt, green and wealthy country is quite a privilege. The cultural and artistic influence of the Principality of Monaco is worthy of the greatest European capitals.

It is good to know that Monaco is part of the European Monetary Zone, the European Union's Schengen, but it is entirely independent from the European Union. Therefore the laws that apply in the EU, will not necessarily apply in the Principality of Monaco.

The standard of living in the Principality is excellent, the life expectancy is 89.5 years, the lengthiest in the world. Monaco has first class medical facilities in all aspects of medicine.

Also an interesting fact is that the Principality of Monaco is voted to be one of the happiest places to live on earth. An air of positivity, peace and luxury shines throughout the country and its culture each day.

The whole environment is such as to make a positive day for you. Monaco offers almost 300 sunny days during the year with an annual average temperature of 16.6 °C. The temperature rarely goes lower than 10 °C in winter.

The Principality of Monaco is one of the most secure places in Europe with the world highest police to population ratio. Even the celebrities who are frequent visitors in Monaco are able to walk through without their bodyguards.

The country has a very good reputation when it comes to education. Furthermore, because of the general safety, most children take the bus to school unaccompanied.

The fiscal climate is of course very favourable, with no local income (including dividends) or capital gains tax. For example zero percent inheritance tax applies for first level inheritance. Although commercial entities in Monaco are subject to corporate tax, there are fairly substantial allowances for directors/shareholders' remuneration before tax.

Having said all this, Monaco is not perfect. It has its challenges when it comes to topics such as "finding a home", tourism and traffic or air quality.

We can say that the Principality of Monaco is one of the most densely populated independent country in the world. It also has a consequently competitive housing market with the average property only changing hands every 37 years.

As an interesting contrast, Monaco has the most expensive real estate market in the world, yet given the lack of space, apartments are generally much smaller than elsewhere.

The Principality of Monaco can be quite noisy during the daytime with heavy traffic during the tourist season, roadworks and new building works. Due to this, during the height of the tourist season air quality can be poor by Monaco standards.

Finally let's talk about money. It is a known fact that 1 in 3 people are millionaires in Monaco (estimated 40% of the population), and 1 in 52 are considered as ultra-high-net-worth, which means their total asset exceeds the 20 million Euro (17.5 million GBP or 21.6 million USD or 21 million CHF).

When we reverse these statistics, we can also observe that approximately 60% of the Principality is composed by regular people. Most people enjoy a high level of living quality, but not everyone is a millionaire in Monaco. Despite its luxurious environment, the average monthly net earnings hardly go over the estimated average of 4,200 Euro (3,680 GBP or 4,540 USD or 4,450 CHF).

Monaco and the European Union

Talking about the Principality of Monaco, I would like to highlight six questions nobody talks about when it comes to the relation between Monaco and the European Union. With most of these topics you will find more detailed information in the upcoming chapters, but it is always interesting to have a quick overview of the effect of the European Union on the Principality of Monaco.

Is Monaco part of the European Union?

No. The Principality is part of the European Union's Schengen zone and its monetary zone, but Monaco is not part of the European Union yet.

If you can enter the European Union, then you are also allowed to stay in Monaco for up to three months without having to apply for any kind of residence permit.

Does Monaco enjoy EU customs benefits?

Yes. Monaco is part of the EU customs territory through an agreement with France, and is administered as part of France.

It is actually a pretty big thing if you consider countries such as Liechtenstein, San Marino and Andorra. For instance, Liechtenstein is a member of the EEA and it is within the EU internal market and applies certain EU laws. San Marino and Andorra are in a customs union with the bloc.

Does the GDPR has any impact in Monaco?

In principle GDPR should not affect business in Monaco.

GDPR is now in force in the European Union. However, even if Monaco has entered into specific treaties with the EU - in particular on financial matters - the Principality is not a member of the European Union. It is good to know that GDPR is out of the scope of such treaties.

However, things can change if a Monaco based business deals with clients from outside the territory of the Principality of Monaco. In that case businesses have to comply with both Monaco data protection laws and GDPR.

A new law in Monaco amending the current data protection legislation is soon expected. This change in legislation is also required to obtain the long-awaited "adequate level" of protection for the Principality of Monaco, which will facilitate data transfers from an EU controller.

Can a Monaco made product be labelled as "Made in EU"?

No. Monaco is a de facto member of the Schengen area since its borders and customs territory are treated as part of France, and it officially uses the Euro as its sole currency.

However, this relationship does not extend to external trade. Therefore, Monaco may not claim EU origin in this respect.

Is Monaco heading to join the European Union?

Maybe. Theoretically EU membership for the Principality of Monaco is unlikely as, aside from its size, unlike the constitutional monarchies within the EU, the Sovereign Prince, H.S.H. Prince Albert II of Monaco has considerable executive powers and is not merely a figurehead. The Principality of Monaco is an independent country with respect to the European Union.

Since 18 March 2015, the Principality of Monaco has been officially engaged in negotiations with the European Union (EU), aimed at reaching a balanced agreement. This will allow Monaco to participate as fully as possible in the EU's internal market, while ensuring respect for the Principality's vital interests, taking into account its unique geographical, demographic and economic features.

On 13 March 2019, the European Parliament adopted a report on the Association Agreement between the EU and Monaco. This document contains a number of recommendations addressed to the Council and the Commission on the conduct of the negotiations, in particular with regard to taking into account the specific characteristics of the Principality.

It seems Monaco has strong perspectives on the integration of the Principality into the European Union. Yet, and to be realistic it will take a long way of negotiations if it ever happens.

Is there any Mobile Data Roaming fee in Monaco?

Yes, because the European roaming freedom does not apply in the Principality of Monaco. As a tourist, visiting Monaco you have to expect to pay significant roaming fees.

There are thousands of tourists visiting the Principality of Monaco every day and most of them are not prepared and well-informed about the roaming charges in Monaco. The majority of people do not even notice that their smartphones have automatically selected a non-French network.

This effects not just the phone calls, but also data services are charged automatically instead of the monthly data allowance being used.

Be aware that roaming fees apply for visiting tourists.

CHAPTER 2

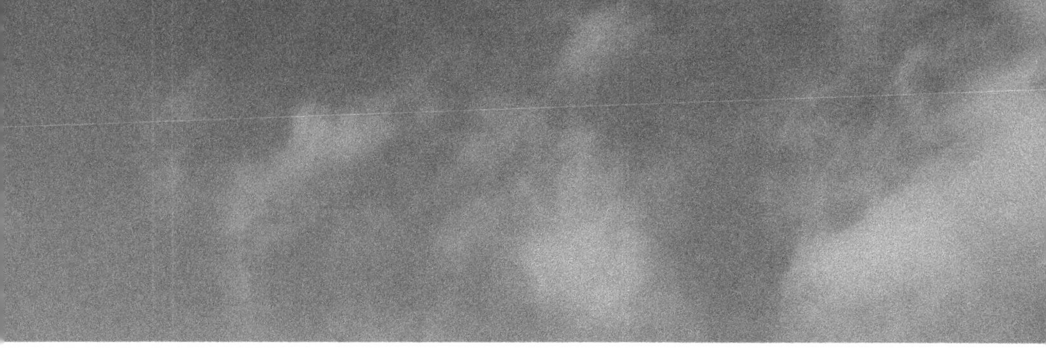

Top private reasons to relocate

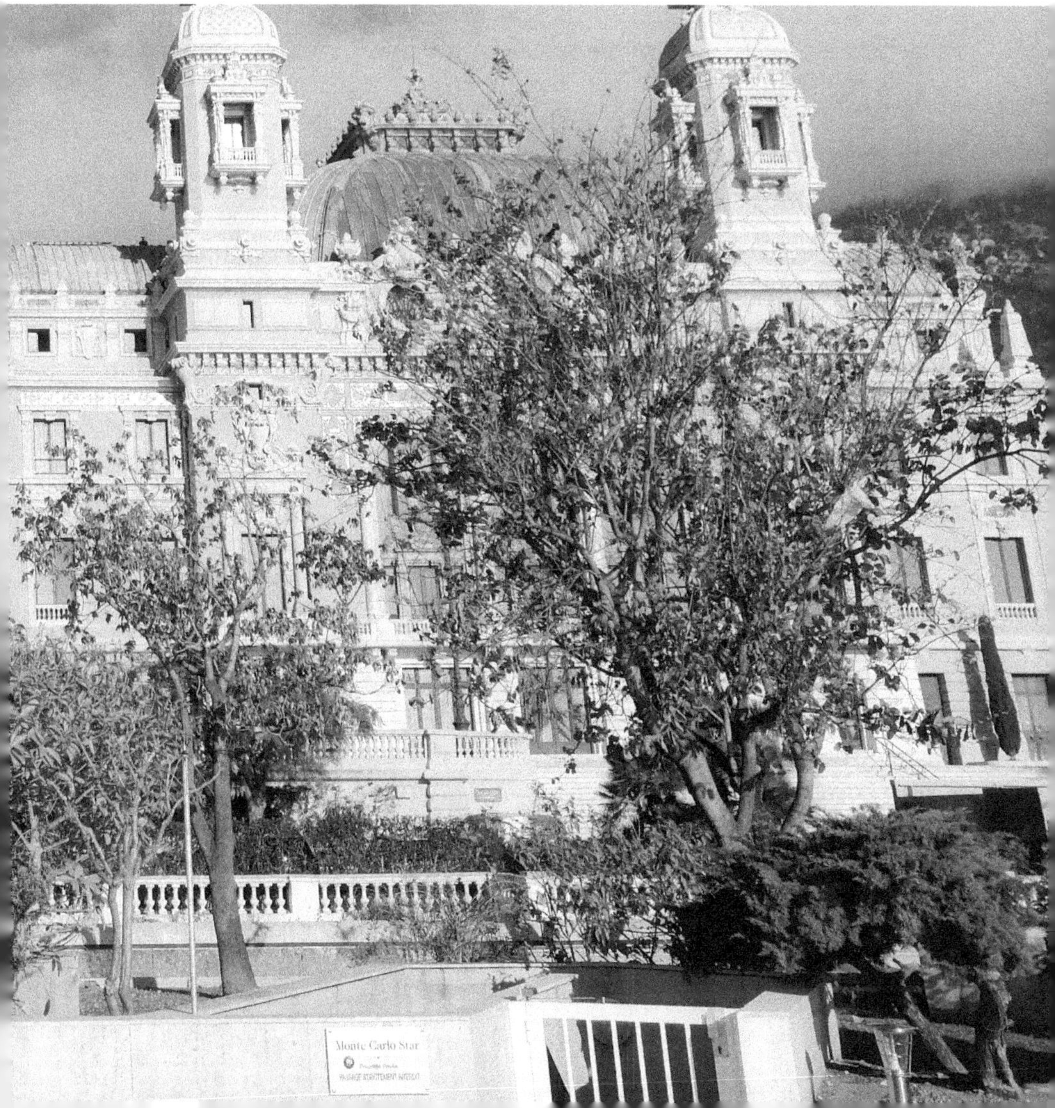

Top private reasons to relocate

People often misinterpret Monaco. The most common three thoughts in people's mind regarding Monaco are usually "Tax haven", "Luxury" and "Prince Albert II." However, and more interestingly, for most of its residents, Monaco is much more than that. It is more about the safety, the living quality and the highly supportive community of internationally accomplished people.

It is very frustrating to often read in the press and in various media sources that Monaco is an offshore country, when it is not. Those people are the ones who misjudge Monaco, like judging a book based on its cover. They never take the energy to see what the country really is/offers.

There are many countries around the globe offering taxation benefits or acting as a complete tax haven. And despite all the misbelief, Monaco is not even tax free. The only advantage it has is a zero-income tax. In many other aspects, there are stronger requirements. For example, local businesses are obliged to pay an annual tax. From a heritage perspective, Monaco also offers zero tax on first-line inheritance. However, in every other case, even Monaco's neighbour, Italy, offers better conditions.

The competition for taxation benefits is high, however, Monaco has a very sexy prosperity which is clearly reflected by the fact that there have never been so many resident requests before. However, taxation is not the only reason why the Principality attracts these established groups of people.

The Principality of Monaco is an exceptional place to colourise your life if you are sick of the usual black and white. It is a land just under the rainbow of the coast of the Mediterranean sea where people usually come to live their dreams, even if it is just for a day. However, if you allow yourself this dream, then it is able to provide much more. It can be your true reality and offer an exceptional quality of life for you and your loved ones.

Monaco offers a combination of unique advantages in a very integrated way which makes the Principality a special place in Europe. The size of the Principality of Monaco and its Monégasque territory is 1.98 km². Yes, it is smaller than an average district in a bigger city in other countries. Even if it is a tiny pearl with its small location, it offers ultra-high security, a profitable fiscal system, political and economic stability, as well as exceptional weather conditions during the whole year.

In the eye of the world, the Principality of Monaco has always represented the elegance and luxury rooting back hundreds of years. Monaco also has an important international presence, since it takes part in multiple international events. Once you relocate to Monaco, you will notice that almost every week there is a new and exciting event, so you can always find something that meets your taste. In between the events, you can also observe the enormous efforts that Monaco makes with its various commitments at the international level.

What makes Monaco exciting are the advantages it offers to its residents, even if the Principality is strongly influenced by its relationship with France.

Monaco and France have always worked hand in hand throughout history, and often France provided protection for the population of this tiny country. This French-Monégasque relationship was also built on very strategic pillars. Due to its location between the borders of Italy and France, Monaco always played an important strategic role.

However, we have to emphasise that the Principality of Monaco is not a French county or a French territory. There are many differences between the two cultures, even if they share some of the social backgrounds and economic aspects. Monaco's small population has always been isolated by the sea and the surrounding mountains. Monaco's natural boundaries provided great isolation and protection from external influences.

Since 1993, the Principality of Monaco is a member of the United Nations, which has also helped it to develop and build up mutually beneficial links with key international organisations.

Monaco is also part of the European Monetary Zone, called the Eurozone. However, Monaco is not a member of the European Union. The European Union respects the identity and the rules of the Principality, and it allows harmonious economic development for the benefit of both parties. Therefore, it is an important fact that the Principality of Monaco never agreed to transfer sovereignty to the European Union.

This independent environment and vibrant, multi-cultural community has attracted many foreigners from hundreds of nations. Smartly, Monaco did not jeopardise its uniqueness, in particular, its specific right of establishment and the preference given to its citizens.

Economically, Monaco is a full participant of the world, and the European Union is a stage for Monaco where its standards are going to become more and more precise. The Principality also has a very specific real estate market making Monaco the number one real-estate investment territory in Europe. It also provides great business and investment conditions.

However, in the past years we can also observe some major changes between the European Union and the Principality of Monaco. While both embody the changes, one can feel the tension in the European Union. Due to various political and economic factors in the European Union, many people think they have to choose between their identity and economic survival.

While Monaco never intended to merge peoples' cultural diversity, it just creates a platform to unite diverse interests. This clearly reflects the fact that Monaco's two square kilometre territory includes 139 nationalities composed by only 37,308 residents. This makes the Principality of Monaco a kind of pearl on the southern shore of Mediterranean Europe.

Competitive for your family

One of the most positive aspects of the Principality of Monaco is the care and the security that it offers its residents. It is among the main key factors for many people who come to Monaco from unsafe environments. Once they realise all that Monaco offers for its residents, they are willing to pay higher initial fees to find a secure and pleasant place for themselves and for their beloved family.

Why? Personally, if there is one thing I have learnt, it is that money is not the prime asset in life. Once you understand that love and care cannot be justified by money, then you will start to seek different qualities for yourself and your loved ones.

Maybe you have heard about Monaco's extraordinary skyscraper the Odeon Tower (Tour Odeon) which is actually one of the largest skyscraper in Europe at 170 meters high. It was built by the Marzocco Group which was founded in the 1960s by Domenico Marzocco, and is currently one of the leading real estate development companies in Monaco.

The Marzocco family is an Italian family, and Domenico Marzocco has a son named Claudio Marzocco. In 1988, the young Claudio was kidnapped by the Calabria-based mafia, Ndrangheta ,and they demanded a ransom from the Marzocco family.

The deal for the ransom never took place, because luckily Claudio managed to escape after 15 years of abduction. Just a week later the whole Marzocco family moved to the Principality of Monaco where they found security for both themselves and their business.

Nowadays, there are many ways to protect our loved ones. The ultra-rich go to such extremities as to placing GPSs into the teeth or underneath their skin of their children. However, by living in Monaco you can reduce the unnecessary risks and enjoy an undisrupted, high quality of life with your family.

The Principality of Monaco forms a part of our self-ideal. In Monaco, you can find all of the qualities and attributes of other people you may admire. Perhaps you have not always lived your best life, but if you are striving to be better in different areas of your life, this environment can motivate you and your family to achieve whatever your desires may be.

What is also unique to see as a foreign person is the strong respect and mutual support that the Grimaldi family and the Monégasque people care for each other. It is very rare to find a bond like this in other countries, especially a bond which has remained so strong throughout the past centuries. This is one of the factors, which will definitely change your life philosophy once you become a long-term resident of the Principality of Monaco.

As an interesting remark, I would also like to highlight that the members of the Monaco Princely Family often marry commoners. And this trend did not even start with Grace Kelly, since Princess Grace was not even the first American citizen married in (location)/married into (family) the Principality of Monaco. Actually, the first American-born princess was Marie Alice Heine who wed H.S.H. Prince Albert I in 1889, becoming Her Serene Highness Princess Alice of Monaco. So the bond with commoners is there at every level.

After spending only a few months in Monaco, you can realise how competitive it is for you and your family. This is because Monaco offers values for each member of a family without age limitations. And the perfect thing is that a person who speaks English or Italian can deal with the local administration without learning French.

The Principality of Monaco is also very strong in cultural values. In its multi-cultural environment the Principality offers high quality, internationally-recognised education for your children.

In this multi-language environment, where the three most commonly used languages are French, Italian and English, you can find an exceptionally rich cultural atmosphere. This is a major difference when you compare Monaco to other countries which also offer taxation benefits. The thing is, for example, in the Cayman Island or Bahamas, you can go and play golf, but that' is basically it. Many offshore jurisdictions are limited in activities, however, in Monaco, you can have countless programs during the whole year, starting from Opera and Ballet to various concerts, charity functions or exhibitions.

Although Monaco's official language is French, sometimes you can also hear the traditional national Monégasque language of the Monégasque people. Monégasque was threatened with extinction in the 1970s, but luckily the language is now being taught in schools and its continuance is considered secure. It is a very interesting fact and sign of safeguarding the Monégasque language that in the old part of Monaco, the street signs are marked with Monégasque in addition to French.

The multi-cultural environment and the possibility to learn and practice three to four languages in the same small environment is a great and motivating aspect. It also provides the benefit of better future possibilities for the young generation who grow up within the territory of the Principality of Monaco.

Obviously, the Principality is also competitive for the elder generation by offering a very flexible business environment. What is very interesting in Monaco is that after three years of a business operation, the Government taxes you based only on your business profit. Therefore, you will have an abundance of support and motivation, which will allow you to focus on your business development.

It is a mutual interest in Monaco between the business owners and the Princely Government. Obviously if you are getting more and more wealthier it enlightens the prestige of the Principality as well. Common goals and common efforts make this environment very special.

Show-off or lifestyle?

Perhaps one of the most common negative labels of Monaco is that it is a "show-off" environment – a place where everyone is driving Ferraris and Bugatti's, the Port is fully packed with ultra luxury yachts and where rich old people go to play every night in the Casino, while their trophy wives are enjoying cocktails at the luxury bars.

Monaco has an image, which is undoubtedly equated with high-end luxury, and this world comes with a bold price tag as well. But who has the right to judge whether it is superficial or not?

As I always say to myself and to my friends and business partners, do not judge something from first impressions; try to look under the surface. The Principality offers a luxurious lifestyle and its residents are among the wealthiest people on earth, but most of them live in a very quiet way. To be honest, most of the billionaires do not even socialise with other people.

After spending a year in Monaco, you will realise that even if it offers an exceptional quality of life, the people in Monaco are different from what you may have originally expected.

You will see that most of the show-off people are those who come to Monaco for a short period, just to present or pretend their wealth. Many of them come only for a few days, they rent a Ferrari or another sports car, revving loudly on the main roads, and at the end of the week, they leave silently.

I believe that the louder someone is in Monaco about his or her wealth, the less reality there is behind it.

To be completely honest, I also arrived to Monaco in 2010 with a great misconception in my head. I still remember that on the first day, I walked around and wore my "Fuck the Crisis" T-shirt. I was so proud to be in Monaco, and honestly it took some weeks for me to understand and experience on my own that in Monaco, money cannot buy things, only connections, trust and credibility which takes time and serious effort to build up. The Principality is built on different kinds of values.

After spending some weeks in the Principality, you will realise that it is more like a small village or a small club. Most of the residents know each other, and they maintain a mutual respect since they all share the same privilege: to be residents of the Principality. It is like a prestigious club for the accomplished and wealthy.

For example, on a typical morning, while you are heading to the Carrefour shopping centre in Fontvieille, all of a sudden you might see David Coulthard, the former Formula One racing driver with his bicycle riding alone. Nothing fancy, just a great man making a little bit of morning sport. No bodyguards or any kind of security, just the man himself.

In Monaco, you will soon realise the bold difference between the social(ite) events during the evenings and the daily life cycle. During the daytime, even the ultra-rich residents enjoy a relaxed life style than they have in other countries.

Obviously, they are entitled to do it since the Principality takes good care of them. Monaco has a zero-tolerance policy for paparazzi, therefore, many celebrities and well-known people walk around without bodyguards.

Flying a drone in the Monegasque territory without a permit is also forbidden. It makes sense since drones are also recording pictures and videos which might infringe on individual privacy rights.

It is easy to see that Monaco is a combination of luxury lifestyle and something unique that one can experience only here. I would call it peace.

Obviously, those who say that the Principality of Monaco is a place of show off, then they are right as well. It is part of the luxury world. But it is important to first understand who you have seen before you make your opinion: a resident or a visitor? I would also raise my concern as to whether it is possible to judge something based only on a few days of experience.

However, talking about luxury and quality of life, I have to mention that Monaco has some world-class programs. To be more precise, Monaco has more than 700 events in a year.

The Principality of Monaco is also a paradise for shopping lovers. Just take a walk around the Formula One track line and you will immediately understand and discover that almost all the greatest names in the fashion and lifestyle industry are represented in Monaco. During a 30-minute walk, you can see brands like Chanel, Céline, Christian Dior, Gucci, Hermès, Ichthys, Louis Vuitton, Prada, Rive Gauche, Saint Laurent and many more in a small, concentrated, but exceptionally luxurious area.

There are historical shopping places such as the Metropole Monte Carlo, however, Monaco also opened recently (in February 2019) the ultramodern One Monte-Carlo, which is home to the most exclusive luxury brands. One Monte-Carlo is located right next to Hotel de Paris and it is a comprehensive luxury experience similar to the legendary Place du Casino. The reason why I also mention One Monte-Carlo is because it features the Promenade Princesse Charlène, a new pedestrian area lined with trees and 7 buildings where transparency and vegetation are given pride of place.

Prestige

Living in the Principality of Monaco is always considered prestigious for you, your family as well as your business. Just see the first impression you get when people hear that you are relocating to Monaco… You will definitely experience the "wow factor", or a slight sign of envy.

Living in a green and wealthy country with zero national debt, is quite a privilege. It is something which will motivate you to create and maintain a high quality of life for yourself and your beloved ones.

However, this prestige comes with a bold price tag as well. For one million euros (approximately 875,000 GBP or 1,080,000 USD or 1,055,000 CHF) one can buy only 17 square metres of property in the Principality of Monaco. This definitely creates a playground for the rich and famous.

To be honest, the real estate prices are extremely high in Monaco, however, you can find similar prices in other well-known destinations for the world's super rich, such as Hong Kong, London, New York or Singapore.

Of course, Monaco also aims to serve you, and therefore you can take advantage of its many opportunities. Most wealthy people are even moving and relocating a part of their businesses to the Principality in order to benefit from its well-branded name.

The cultural and artistic influences of the Principality of Monaco are worthy of the greatest European capitals. Offering diversified cultural programs from ballet, opera, art, sport and prestigious exhibitions attract people throughout the whole year.

And do not be confused with the size of the Principality of Monaco, because it might change soon. The thing is that Monaco was always somehow the symbol of prestige and luxury and to maintain this status, the Principality of Monaco always aims to renew itself.

When we talk about prestige and luxury in the Principality, Monaco has to think about the needs of its own residents as well. Monaco offers one of the leading Luxury MBA programs at the International University of Monaco. For these reasons, the quality of life plays a key role in the necessity for Monaco to maintain its prestige.

Monaco already recognised that its residential surface has some limitations. However, Monaco also understands that it is necessary to maintain its luxury, because over 500 new residents are arriving in the Principality every year. Monaco needs to maintain housing needs and provide luxurious living spaces. Therefore, one of the most interesting ongoing topics is the long-awaited land reclamation.

Monaco's aim is to extend its borders towards the sea. This complex project has required very careful planning. In recent months, the project got the green light, after the government and town representatives unanimously approved the land extension.

Of course, a transformational project such as Monaco's land extension will take time. It will be at least 10 years until residents will be able to enjoy the new district with all its urbane developments, including housing, shops, marina and beautiful garden areas. The first steps were taken at the end of 2016, with the removal of the protected marine species, which were relocated carefully in nearby natural reserves.

What makes this extended territory also special is that Monaco, one of the smallest country in the world is reclaiming new land peacefully. Truth to be told, there are not many countries that can expand their borders without war. So a big applause for this ideal solution.

The name of the new district will be "Anse du Portier" which means Portier Cove.

With this approximately 60,000 sqm development, Monaco will be able to maintain its sustainable development and also offer new, high-end luxury standards to its residents. There are new apartments planned for over 700 people.

Also, the famous Grimaldi Forum, the location of some of the most important conferences in Monaco will be extended during the upcoming years. Additionally, a new waterfront promenade will provide a spectacular view of the Rock and Monte-Carlo.

The new land extension is luxury and business as well. It is a fascinating fact that the two billion euro project will be completed at no cost to Monaco. Yes, it is free for the Principality. The project is sponsored by the involved companies and entirely financed by the private sector.

So what can be more prestigious than living in a country where the people simply finance their own country's development. That shows a level of well-being for sure.

Monaco is sexy

Monaco offers a Mediterranean atmosphere with mild winters and summers. Every morning, it is a great blessing to have good weather. The whole environment is there to make a positive day for you. Monaco offers almost 300 sunny days during the year with an annual average temperature of 16.6 °C.

	Average temperature	Precipitation days	Days with snow	Daily sunshine
London	10,3°C	236 days	39 days	4,9 hours
Paris	12,4°C	193 days	14 days	9,0 hours
Milano	11,4°C	87 days	165 days	10 hours
Monaco	16,5°C	41 days	1 day	9,7 hours
Wien	11,4°C	43 days	49 days	5,1 hours
Zurich	9,3°C	123 days	107 days	9,6 hours

On most mornings, you can wake up to sunshine since Monaco offers beautiful sunny weather in all seasons of the year. Then when you open the windows or doors to your terrace, you can smell the salty air that the slight wind brings over to you. Then you can take in a glimpse of the morning reflections of the wavy sea.

Later on, heading to the streets, you will start your day walking in the fresh air under countless orange trees. I simply love the view and the feeling of the small cosy streets with endless orange trees. For me, the oranges are like small little balls of sun with their vibrant colours smiling upon you.

It is interesting that while I am writing these lines, it is the season of collecting oranges after the cold winter period in Monaco. The workers of the Department of Urban Amenities have already collected over 18 tons of oranges during the annual pruning of the bitter orange trees that line the main roads. It is an incredibly large amount, so you can imagine the view of those little orange balls rolling up and down the streets.

The Principality has over 700 citrus trees and part of the oranges are given away free to anyone who would like them. It is great to vitalize your day with some fresh fruit. Therefore, my morning walks under these orange forests are always a colourful dream for me, and it puts me in a good mood for the start of the day.

Finally, you will arrive at your favourite coffee place probably just at your corner, where you can enjoy your strong espresso with a freshly baked, crunchy croissant. Meanwhile you will be noticed and greeted by many of your acquaintances and friends, who send you the sign that you are not forgotten in a multi-million city. You are somebody here, a part of the unique Monaco family. No matter how you will spend the rest of your day, this uplifting start is always guaranteed.

What you will also notice in Monaco is the level of positivity. The Principality is a very positive place where people are still ready to smile or talk to each other just as our grandparents did hundred years ago.

Monaco is a very vibrant country but I would never label Monaco as a busy and stressful place. Comparing Monaco to other big financial cities is not possible. You cannot find the same busy and stressful atmosphere that you see in big cities such as New York. Monaco offers a very laid-back life-style for its residents. It whispers in your ears that you have arrived, and that you have reached something in your life – something great.

In my personal experiences, almost every single night, I go out to enjoy the night scene of the Principality. I do not go out to a club, but rather enjoy the night view and the fresh air. I often light a big cigar and I walk hours during the evenings enjoying the lights reflecting on the sea. The port is beautiful during the night, especially with the recently-built Monaco Yacht Club. It is a gorgeous construction shaped like a huge ship.

Meanwhile, I enjoy the taste and the smoke of my Pleiades. It is always a great privilege to look up on the Rock where the Princely Palace stands and see the tiny lights of Monaco-Ville, the oldest part of the Principality of Monaco. Having this view, I always feel respect, acceptance and appreciation to be here.

Often, I also gaze at the sky, which is usually clear and full of stars. It is a beautiful view, and for me, it is breathtaking to see the clear sky in such beauty. I came to Monaco from Berlin, Germany which is a much bigger city. The street where I lived were almost twice as long as the whole country of Monaco, and because of the countless city lights, it is nearly impossible to see the stars as bright and clear as you can observe them above the skies of the Principality.

Walking further, my midnight stroll often goes around the Casino, which has its special magic during the night.

You can also have this feeling when big events take place such as the Formula One Grand Prix, the Monaco Yacht Show, the Tennis Rolex Masters, the Top Marque, the Opera Bal, etc. In Monaco, each and every event you are part of is something unique watched by the rest of the world.

As you can see, the Principality of Monaco is exceptional for me also because often the old and traditional is mixed with the new and modern. One of the greatest example one can observe of this, is in the architectural scenery of the Principality.

Last year I took a beautiful photo showcasing this contrast. It is one of my favourite one, because it features an old classical villa right next to the magnificent, ultra-luxurious Tour Odeon. The difference between them is spectacular, yet they both represent the luxury from their respective eras.

Living in Monaco is a kind of a sexy feeling, especially if you open your eyes and soul to observe the hidden beauties of the Principality.

The L'Orangerie story

As I mentioned before, I love the orange trees in Monaco, and how smart and generous it is of the Government that oranges are given away to anyone who would like them.

One of the local guys also found this concept impressive, and back in 2017, he started to build a business out of it. Shortly thereafter, he founded the L'Orangerie Liqueur de Monaco, the first premium orange liqueur from Monaco.

Mr Philip Culazzo produces a 100% Monegasque artisan liqueur, handmade from unprocessed bitter oranges picked from the trees that line the streets of the Principality. How cool is that?

He also created a cocktail called Monaco Spritz to embrace the fact that it is a local good.

Personally, I love this product because it offers a truly genuine taste of Monaco. Because of this in 2019, I decided to have a book dedication in this unique location.

Le Monaco Spritz
L'Orangerie Liqueur de Monaco

Ingrédients:
4cl of L'Orangerie
Topped up with Prosecco
Orange zest, or a slice of fresh strawberry.

Not so many people know that a long time ago, before casinos, tourism, yachting and Grand Prix, the Principality of Monaco was an agricultural land.

Nowadays, you still have the annual lemon festival in the neighbourhood Menton, France, but as the country developed, it lost its true citrus fruit farms. The only thing that remains of the history are those beautiful lemon and orange trees all around Monaco.

Therefore, I truly applaud this product, because it is a smart combination of of past and present.

Book dedication event in July 2019

Protective

When you relocate to the Principality, it can be a very positive advantage for you that Monaco enjoys extraordinary security. With its over five-hundred police officers in 1.98 km², Monaco has the largest police presence in the world on both a per-capita and per-area basis. Not to mention, Monaco has more than 520 surveillance cameras.

First, it might seem weird to see a police officer in almost every direction, but it provides a great feeling of safety. In Germany, when you need a police officer, you call the central phone line and have to wait until they send someone, while in Monaco they are there without hesitation if the situation requires it.

You can also notice the police presence as well as the surveillance cameras on every corner of the street. They all send a message that the security is under control, protecting you and your loved ones.

Obviously, this protection is not limited to criminal activities. The Principality offers all human and technological resources for general surveillance of its territory to protect both objects and people at the same time.

The Principality of Monaco is very protective of its residents. For example, without a police interview, you cannot even apply for a residence permit. The constant protection has developed a way of thinking as well, which is shared by many people from the past. This is the care and respect for others and other's properties.

It is the same with the commercial ventures and business entities. Monaco carefully protects its circles, and there are times when money and wealth become secondary.

Even if you believe you can buy the rules with your wealth, you will face the reality that you have to adopt and respect the rules of the Principality. It is a very protective environment.

Family oriented

One of the things that people rarely talk about is how family-oriented the Principality of Monaco is. It may be obvious that an ultra-rich environment offers various ultra-luxury and lifestyle services, but it is also important to see that Monaco offers exceptional care for families as well.

Despite its small size, Monaco has many small baby clubs, that your child can attend at an early age. I had some experience with the toddler club, and I have to say it is also a great place to meet with international people. While your toddler plays with other children, you can enjoy some tea, coffee and the good and interesting international company of the parents.

Most of these toddler clubs offer occasional entrance as well, therefore, if you are just visiting Monaco, you can still go there to get some inside experience about the Principality and its residents.

Of course, Monaco has many possibilities for education in local or private schools as well. Not to mention, most of the schools offer a multi-language education. When the time comes for university, the International University of Monaco offers well-recognised education and MBA programs.

I believe by relocating to the Principality of Monaco, you will be able to offer a good start for your children through strong start-up knowledge and credit for their aims.

There are various sport activities as well. Football in Monaco is highly cultivated, and AS Monaco is among the greatest football teams in Europe. Monaco also offers many sport activities for children such as basketball or swimming. The popularity of swimming is also growing, since H.S.H. Princess Charlène and her team came in fifth in swimming at the Sydney Olympic Games in 2000.

In the same year, the Princess won the gold medal for the 200m backstroke event at the "Marenostrum" international swimming meeting in Monaco. This is when she met Prince Albert II for the first time. He was presiding over the international competition.

And still nowadays, the Princess of Monaco holds many swimming lectures for the young ones, just as she also supports swimming education in her home country, South Africa. Basically, the Princess of Monaco launched her foundation in 2012 with the primary objective to save lives by putting an end to drowning.

Monaco also carries exceptionally equipped hospitals and medication centers, as well homes for elderly people.

However, what is really exceptional is the way that the Principality handles the question about heritage. In Monaco, the focus is always on your children. In the Principality, they are the biggest beneficiaries of your wealth and assets, not your spouse. You can also see that the legal system within the Principality protects your family and serves the best interest of your children in every respect.

And for those who did not believe in this, a few years ago, one can see a completely transformed Princely couple. Since 10 December 2014, the birth of the Princely twins, H.S.H. Princess Gabriella Thérèse Marie and H.S.H. Prince Jacques Honoré Rainier, family values are becoming more and more of a focus in the Principality of Monaco.

By having their new family, the twins not only strengthened the Princely couple's love, but also their appreciation towards each other and other families in the Principality.

The craziest people to approach Monaco

I have a true story to share with you. It was a time when I definitely moved out of my comfort zone; however, it shows how friendly Monaco and its Princely family are.

I remember back in January 2012, I decided to go up to the Prince's Palace of Monaco without an invitation because my friend Dodo Newman and I had a vision.

Dodo is an artist who created a beautiful commemorative project for the 100th Anniversary of the Titanic. The project was interesting because it celebrated both 100 years of cultural changes and provided individual memorabilia artworks for 600 selected passengers. So why was this interesting in Monaco? Well, because one of the passengers of the Titanic ship was actually a Monaco resident.

Our aim was to introduce this project to H.S.H. Princess Charléne of Monaco and also to donate one of the Swarovski Crystal surfaced memorabilia to her. So what would be easier than simply going up and ringing the bell?

Of course, everyone around me thought we would never make it and then asked the same question: "Are you stupid?" And everyone told us that it is impossible to just go up to the Palace. There is a hard protocol, formalities, official procedures and, of course, you have to ask for an appointment. Even a friend who is a fashion designer and has been a resident of Monaco for many years could not arrange a meeting with the Princess.

So why did we decide to dream and make it happen? Because I thought we had nothing to lose by trying, and it is exactly the crazy things that usually work.

Life is about movement, about trying out different things, taking risks and taking up new challenges. Things that are stagnant and stick to the status quo eventually disappear. Therefore, Dodo and I decided not to wait for something magical to happen, but instead to go for it and to enjoy the movement of life.

In the following days, we were driving to Monaco with a rented Mercedes and with Dodo's Swarovski surfaced Titanic memorabilia in the trunk.

By that time, I knew that no foreign cars were allowed to enter Monaco-Ville, which is the area leading up to the hill, where the Prince's Palace of Monaco stands tall. As expected, the security guard immediately stopped me at the bottom of the hill.

Was I crazy to make the 1,300 km drive from Berlin, Germany to Monaco-Ville, Monaco? Perhaps so, but at the same time I had a strong gut feeling that I would get overcome the obstacles.

I told the security guard that I was bringing a gift for the Princess all the way from Berlin, Germany. He seemed confused, because it was so unusual. He had never encountered a situation like this before. As you can imagine, it is not normal for someone to simply "drop in" at the Prince's Palace. Most likely, as a result of this special circumstance, after some discussions with his colleagues up in the Palace, he allowed us to continue our journey. Once up by the main entrance of the Palace, we were confronted with the second obstacle.

When we arrived at the Palace, the guards stopped us and we had to explain our intent. The gift was so unique that the concierge helped us to reach the private secretary of the Princess, who was open to meet with us.

Later, during our future visits to the Palace, the private secretary of the Princess also gave us a private tour, and we had the chance to see the work place of H.S.H. Princess Charléne of Monaco.

My mission was accomplished.

But as you know… What worked once will work twice as well…

A few weeks later, Dodo got a surprise e-mail from the Prince's Palace of Monaco, which started a larger and extended line of communication. During our visits to the Palace, she also got to know that the favourite colour of the Princess is purple, which made me think on something new.

In that time, Dodo was four months pregnant with her baby girl Faye Martha; still, she decided to create something special for the Princess. She envisioned a 3-meter-long diamond and Swarovski-covered artwork. It became an artwork full of symbolic elements. Dodo first split the piece into two halves and included many interesting materials in it.

Dodo included two original coals recovered from the ship wreck of the Titanic, which represented the past. She placed thousands of Swarovski Crystals in it representing the light and stars of our life. And she also placed diamonds in it representing the hope of new life that changes bring to us.

The concept was ready in her head, but Dodo knew that she wanted to do something special. Understanding the Princess's passion for swimming and water, Dodo decided to create a special wave cut that separates the artwork into two pieces. It became the symbol of many elements, such as the loving bond of the Royal couple, the Monaco-South African bond, as well as the projection of two children in their life.

When the artwork was ready, we decided to go up again to the Palace, taking one half of it up myself. That was the time when people started to refer to myself and Dodo as "the craziest people in Monaco". On our next trip to Monaco, we were even more confident than during the trips, and we successfully managed to deliver Dodo's gift.

This story shows that people in Monaco are protective, but also very helpful and kind. If you approach people with respect, usually you can find your way in Monaco. When you have a deep desire and do not give up, when you have passion for it and know it belongs to only you deep inside, then even the craziest ideas have the potential for great success.

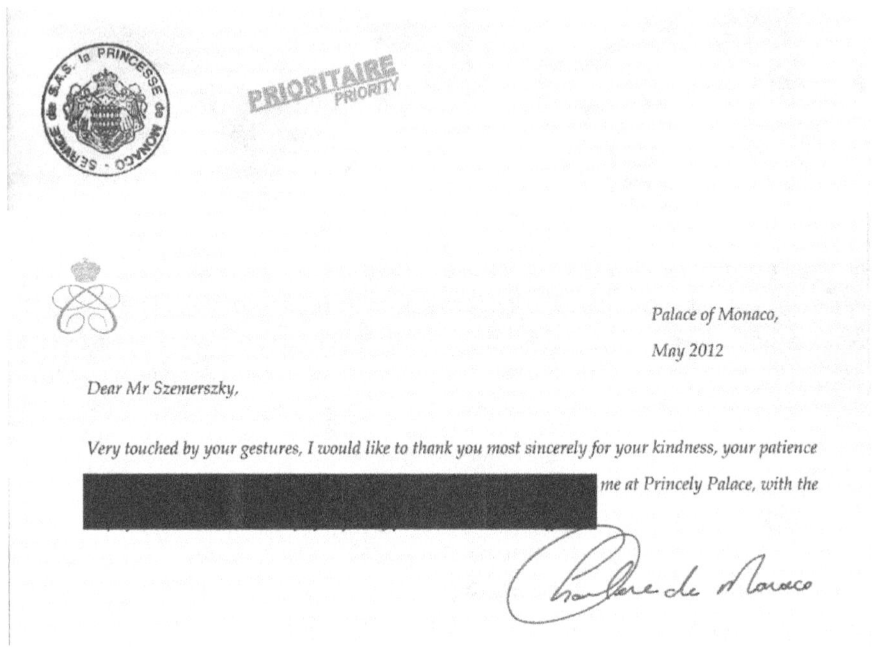

And just to prove how crazy ideas work, in January 2014, this Princely artwork was selected into the TOP 100 Ultra Luxury trends in 2013. One of my favourite press article referred to Dodo's artwork as priceless art symbolising the value of precious love.

Almost two years have passed since Dodo's prediction, and in December 2014, the Prince and the Princess became proud parents of their new born twins. Prince Jacques and Princess Gabriella had arrived. It was a reminder for us of the importance of the new things in our lives and of the courage that moves us to go beyond our comfort zones.

To be honest, I have serious doubt that we could ring up Buckingham Palace in to bring a gift to the Queen. It probably would not work. The benefit of Monaco is that due to its small size, people still trust and assist each other if they can.

A little bit of Royal life

He was an owner of a small business company and he wanted to create his annual event in the Principality. He knew for sure that this year he wanted something special, something unique. Since many months now there was this little idea in his head but he always considered it something impossible. "Why would they do it for me?" "Who am I to gain this respect and attention?"

He was swirled with doubts for many weeks, but today he decided to make that call. His hands were shaking while he lifted up his mobile and dialled the number. Between dialling, he started to feel the heat in his body and the pressure inside his head. When he finished the dialling, he started to sweat, and between the ring tones, tiny water pearls fell down on his forehead. Every ring on the phone felt like long minutes for him and his heart pumped in a way he could not control.

After four rings, someone picked up the phone on the other end. A very kind voice welcomed him, but he started to sweat even more when he asked the big question with his shaking voice. The answer was quite surprising for him:

- So you are asking about the Prince of Monaco generating some buzz for your event by his appearance, right?
- Yes. - he answered with a shaky vibration and full of fear from rejection in his voice.
- No problem we can forward to the Prince your kind invitation and approach.
- And how much will it be? - he asked the standard question.
- It is FREE. If the Prince is available he will definitely consider your request.

They changed contact details and they said good bye to each other. The next day, he received the answer and the confirmation for his request.

It is always surprising to see how flexible H.S.H. Prince Albert II is when you are aiming to involve him into an event, which also strengthens the name and the value of the Principality of Monaco.

Especially with events which are related to the aims of his Foundation – the Prince Albert II of Monaco Foundation – which aims to protect the environment and to encourage sustainable development.

The Sovereign Prince is also a great humanitarian and is often involved in events, which are related to various humanitarian projects.

If you are lucky, you can also meet with the Prince on many occasions where he is very direct with all the guests. Even if close friends of the Prince suggest that he does not really like it, you can take a photo with him, shake his hand, and you can also have a very nice conversation with him. He is always curious about the new and exciting things, and is happy to carry on good conversations. I would consider him a perfect "host" of his beloved home country.

As I mentioned before, the Princely family maintains a relatively close relationship with the Monégasque people and the Monaco residents.

During the past years, I had a chance to talk with many Monégasque people who were born and raised in the Principality. Most of them also refer to H.S.H. Prince Rainier III (Rainier Louis Henri Maxence Bertrand Grimaldi; 31 May 1923 – 6 April 2005), the father of H.S.H. Prince Albert II, as the grandfather of Monaco. Some locals even called him "le patron", which basically means "the boss". This also shows the mark that this exceptional Princely relationship has left on the hearts of the people.

Personalities

People often visit Monaco to realise their dreams, even just for a day. For hundreds of years, this exceptional place has attracted not only tourists, but the most colourful personalities. Many of the residents of the Principality of Monaco work with each other in the community where they make positive global change.

Monaco does not just merge cultural diversity, it also creates a platform to unite diverse interests. This is clearly reflected by the fact that Monaco's two square kilometre territory is the home to 139 different nationalities. This makes the Principality of Monaco a multi-national hub on the southern shore of Mediterranean Europe.

As I described before, Monaco offers a combination of unique advantages in an integrated way, which makes the Principality a special place in Europe. This tiny country, with its small population, offers exceptional security and safety, a profitable fiscal system, political and economic stability, as well as exceptionally good weather conditions throughout the year.

Few people know that Monaco is not just a pioneering region in the field of sustainability, but it has always had a strong role in the innovation sector.

1910 - Aviation in Monaco | © Courtesy of Monte-Carlo SBM

It is widely known that Monaco was a pioneer in the history of the casino industry, but it is much less known that Monaco was a key site that attracted numerous innovators of the aviation world.

This started in 1908, when Camille Blanc suggested to Prince Albert I of Monaco that they should organise a major flying competition in the Principality. In 1911, Henri Fabre flew over the Port of Monaco in his seaplane, putting on a unique show for spectators who had flocked to the Casino terraces, before his plane unfortunately crashed on the rocks. Later in 1914, Monaco was the arrival point for the first air rally, inspired by automobile rallies.

In 1921, Monaco held its last flying competition. The activity was abandoned due to the lack of space to accommodate the ever-growing crowds of spectators. Monaco was proud to have played an important part in aviation history for a decade.

More recently, the Palace has turned its hand to marine protection, evolving a green and sustainable environment. In June 2006, H.S.H. Prince Albert II established his foundation (Fondation Prince Albert II de Monaco) with the purpose of protecting the environment and encouraging sustainable development. Noting the remarkable efforts of the Prince, many Monaco-based companies are committed to following in his footsteps. The decision to drive cleaner vehicles, create solar energy, and build waste-water treatment plants, all

1913 - Aviation in Monaco | © Courtesy of Monte-Carlo SBM

1920 - Aviation in Monaco | © Courtesy of Monte-Carlo SBM

represent key aspects of a modern and sustainable region. Monaco's green environment and its global efforts attract millions of people from around the world.

The Principality of Monaco motivates people to change at the global level. And what is very interesting to see is that Monaco helps its residents maintain their self-expression and personal identity.

For example, not so many people know that Princess Stephanie did a single with Michael Jackson or that Monaco royals like tattoos.

H.S.H. Princess Stephanie always tried to stand out from her brother, H.S.H. Prince Albert II and sister, H.R.H. Princess Caroline. The Princess released two music albums and her song "Ouragan" - released in 1986 - is one of the best-selling singles in France of all time.

The Princess even had a single with the "King of Pop", Michael Jackson. The song "In the Closet" was released on April 9, 1992 as the third single from Michale Jackson's eighth album, Dangerous (1991).

It became a worldwide hit and reached the top 10 in the United States. At the time of the release, the song's female vocal was originally labeled as "Mystery Girl". H.S.H. Princess Stéphanie's involvement was not revealed until a few years later.

She was a cover girl on Vogue and Vanity Fair. She also launched her own swimwear collection and perfume fragrance.

H.S.H. Princess Stephanie, has also frequently put her tattoos on display over the years, including a dragon inking on her back. The Monaco royal also has a floral tattoo on her wrist, as well as two jumping dolphins on her ankle.

Her daughter, Pauline Ducruet, has followed mother H.S.H. Princess Stephanie's lead, and has a flower inked onto her arm.

Self-expression and being proud of who we are is part of the everyday life of the Principality. This is also the reason why many celebrities, professional athletes, and accomplished people choose the Principality; it is a space where they can truly be themselves.

Glamour and fascination

The Principality of Monaco has always represented elegance and luxury dating back hundreds of years.

At the beginning of the 20th century, Monaco was an attraction for Russian nobility. The Principality's prosperity, and particularly that of the casinos, was in large due to the Russian community.

Since 1909, the Principality of Monaco has hosted its world famous "Russian Ballet". Since then, it has been through several rebirths to maintain its notability, and with the arrival of Jean-Christophe Maillot in 1993, the Ballets de Monte-Carlo joined the ranks of the world's most renowned ballet companies.

The Place du Casino in Hollywood in 1922 | © Courtesy of Monte-Carlo SBM

One of the most amazing fascinations of the Principality was glorified by actor and director Eric von Stroheim, who built a perfect replica of the Place du Casino in Hollywood at the Universal Studios in 1922. His attention to detail thoroughly captured the atmosphere of Monte Carlo for the movie Foolish Wives (Folies de femmes).

The movie stirred up an American fascination with Monte Carlo, thirty years before the legendary royal marriage linked the two nations in April 1956. The marriage which was Monaco's own fairy tale.

Since then, Monaco has become the location of choice for many film directors searching for genuinely dreamlike and elegant settings.

Yves Montand, scene from the movie "Grand Prix" in 1966
© Courtesy of Monte-Carlo SBM

The Principality has had a long relationship with the brightest celebrities and sports personalities.

The building of the legendary Monte Carlo Country Club was inspired by Suzanne Lenglen, who was the number one ladies' tennis player in the world in the 1920s, dominating the sport by having only lost 4 sets during her 7-year career.

Suzanne Lenglen in Monaco in 1921 | © Courtesy of Monte-Carlo SBM

And the Principality cares for its celebrity visitors. Josephine Baker was one such recipient, who was a huge star and possibly the world's first African-American celebrity.

Grace Kelly and Josephine had a strong friendship, which began in 1951, when the future princess of Monaco bore the title of a rising star of Hollywood.

The meeting of Josephine and Grace took place in the glamorous Stork Club restaurant in New York. Josephine Baker returned to the States, where the National Association for the Advancement of Colored People (NAACP) named her the Woman of the Year.

Ironically, Josephine's visit to New York was marred by an incident: the Stork Club staff refused service to the famous dancer. Being a witness to the outrageous scene, Grace Kelly unceremoniously left the restaurant with the black star and never returned there.

Even after Grace married Prince Rainier III, becoming the princess of Monaco, their relationship remained the same.

After great success, Josephine had greater bad-luck and racial issues and by the mid-1960s, she had used up her entire fortune.

Josephine Baker in 1932 | © Courtesy of Monte-Carlo SBM

A period of dark days overwhelmed her and her children, when Brigitte Bardot and Princess Grace personally came to her help.

Bardot helped her financially, and following that Princess Grace invited her to Monaco, helping with funds raised at galas held in the Principality, offering her a home for life.

Josephine's Parisian concert dedicated to the 50th anniversary of her career was financed by the Prince of Monaco, Jackie Onassis and Princess Grace.

Josephine died a few days after her last concert from a brain hemorrhage. After the ceremony in Paris, she was buried in the cemetery of Monaco.

Princess Grace also attended the funeral of Josephine, who found her final resting peace in the Principality of Monaco.

Amongst the most famous and internationally recognised people to be connected to the Principality was Sir Winston Churchill, who loved Monaco and visited it often. As early as 1945, he regularly enjoyed staying at the Hôtel de Paris for Monaco's famous New Year festivities.

Sir Winston Churchill in Monaco in 1958 | © Courtesy of Monte-Carlo SBM

What I love in Monaco

Having spent ten years in and out of the Principality of Monaco, I still enjoy the sunshine, the sea, and the view of those beautiful orange trees. Although, I have to confess that even though I spent my first months in Monaco, later on, I decided to reside in Beausoleil, France which is the town around Monaco.

For those who do not know, the Monaco-Beausoleil relation, they are "breathing" together. The locals basically call Beausoleil "upper-Monaco".

When you walk on the border of Monaco, the right side of the one-way street is Monaco and the left side is Beausoleil. The distance between them is just 3 meters (and of course the jurisdiction to which they apply).

For me, it was an easier choice to stay in the European Union, and the three steps I needed to to cross the street, made this decision much easier. Still, I can spend all my daytime in the heart of the Principality of Monaco.

I also love that I am in a place, which motivates me to create a better quality of life myself. Seeing so many successful people allows you to learn from them and to get inspiration to move forward and to achieve your own ambitions.

I always believed that the environment where we live strongly influences us. Without even realizing it, we are able to develop habits based on the people surrounding us, and sometimes it can bring us back to our aims. However, living in an environment, which motivates us and shows us things we are aiming to accomplish can give a whole different vibe.

Yes, changing environment can be crucial because you leave your comfort zone. But is it really a bad thing? I do not believe so. Comfort zone means things based on our daily routines. It seems to offer safety and stability, but never significant improvement. All the magic happens outside of your comfort zone, because that is where you can find the contrast and the motivation. When you are able to challenge your comfort zone, you will also find the possibility to turn your dreams into reality.

At the moment you make your foothold in the Principality of Monaco, you will see that Monaco really appreciates creative people, new ideas, and out-of-the-box views. You will also appreciate that it is not as superficial as you may have thought it to be, before you finally decided to relocate. You can find great communities based on your deepest desire, and investors and patrons to fulfil your visions and dreams.

For me the infrastructure of Monaco is also fascinating. If you ever walked on the little mountain called the "Rock" you can discover the amazing Monaco-Ville with its tiny old streets and beautiful buildings. It resembles a small-scale Venice, just without the water and gondolas.

I also get many inspirations from the Japanese Garden, which I believe holds a special atmosphere. It is one of the sources of my creations as well.

However, for many years, Monaco has been undergoing massive modernisation.

It is truly impressive to see the contrasting scenery, specifically the old historic villas next to the ultra-modern buildings. It is an impressive mix of traditional and modern luxury, as the history blends into the future.

I kindly advise everyone to spend more time to discover the small and even more amazing details of Monaco, because the Principality is more than a Formula One Grand Prix race track or a casino with sport cars. The more you discover, the more magic happens…

Some disadvantages…

Yes, magic always happens, but before you start to believe that this is a book that only showcases the glorious things about Monaco, I have to confess that it is not. It is about my own perspective and my own experiences, which sometimes provides a different side of the imagined world.

Frankly, I had and continue to have countless great moments in the Principality, but during the time I spent in Monaco, I encountered some misunderstandings – or let's say different viewpoints – on some local topics. People say that Monaco is just competitive, however, I find that some situations seem to be full of contrasts, which can be frustrating or at least confusing for foreign people.

I believe as a person coming from another country and a different type of environment, I had a more diversified view on things than some of the people who had been living in Monaco for ages. It is normal, since in many cases we cannot observe little things around us which are usually obvious for people coming from outside of our world.

Periodic things often become routines and we can easily get used to things without questioning or challenging their impacts on our life. In my business field, this is also the reason why I usually approach external advisors. Usually, they have a different, and in some cases, a fresh and out-of-the-box view.

I have to admit that Monaco has a very strong economy compared to its surroundings. Even in Europe, not many countries can compete with the stabilised economy that the Principality of Monaco has maintained for decades.

The Principality is also a great place to live, especially if you have the requested fund to settle down here. However, if you are coming to Monaco with the hope of finding a new job position and to settle down by hard work, it can have some difficulties for you.

Despite its luxurious environment, the average monthly net earnings hardly go over the estimated average of 4,200 Euros. It may seem like a nice salary, but I would say it does not even cover the monthly rent of a one-bedroom apartment. It may sound brutal, but it is good to understand why Monaco is so unique concerning its living costs.

Of course, in some sectors, such as private banking and wealth management, Monaco offers exceptionally good salaries which may vary considerably from the average. However, these positions are rare, and still the biggest obstacle is not the salary at all.

In the Principality of Monaco, any job position by regulation is first offered to the Monégasque people. No exceptions. In the second round, the residents are considered, and in the third round the people from the surroundings who have worked in Monaco before are taken into account. Foreign individuals are only considered after the previous three selection rounds have failed. And here comes the crude reality…

Even if you have a chance to get a job position offered in the Principality of Monaco, the Employment Office has the power to refuse the employer's choice and to deny the issuing of the work permit no matter how much you could contribute to your possible employer.

From my personal point of view, and as an outsider, I believe it can easily raise a concern about the competency of some people's skills and knowledge. While the Principality of Monaco has a competitive economy, sometimes an employer has to choose the candidate offered by the Principality instead of the one who is really capable to get the requested job done. It is a pity.

When you as a foreign nationality are aiming to get a job based in the Principality of Monaco, always try to negotiate and settle your conditions first. To avoid any unpleasant surprises, it is highly recommended to get every work permit before you arrive in Monaco. Otherwise, even if you have already rented an apartment, you might not be eligible for a residence permit.

Getting a work permit in Monaco is hard. Never underestimate the government hierarchy for job applicants, because as a foreign national you belong to group 4, which is the last choice.

Therefore, even if you are an expert in your field with a proven track record (diplomas, MBA and other certificates), it is still not easy to get a foothold in the Principality. However ,when someone succeeds, she or he will enjoy all the benefits of Monaco. These benefits are sometimes very surprising ones.

You can also find these contrasts in your everyday life. For example, when we are talking about daily living costs, you can see the ultra-expensive, but exceptionally high quality restaurants, the luxury bars and clubs. However, you can also find the discount chain Carrefour or Marche to provide to your daily needs at a lower price. Monaco offers you both exclusivity and affordability.

I know that many people say that Monaco is one of the most expensive countries in the world, but in my opinion, the price is not the main obstacle in Monaco. Just think about it, Moscow, New York, London, Zurich or Singapore are also expensive.

The important question you have to realise is not the money or the living expense; it is the size. To be honest even if the real estate prices are going up, Monaco cannot increase its prices to a higher level. For example, Switzerland is different. If prices go up in an extreme way in Monaco, then people would leave and go to the surroundings. This would be a huge mistake for Monaco.

Once you have successfully settled, the main challenge is to be accepted in this closed circle – to be adopted into the Monaco family. And believe it or not, without a good moral, no matter how wealthy you are, money cannot buy you the residence permit. To be welcomed in Monaco as a long-term resident, it often relies on the balance of wealth, contribution and personal values.

Being accepted in most of the circles of the Principality can take serious time and effort, which may seem much more difficult than in any other European country. So get ready…

But to close these thoughts with a positive conclusion, I would remind you of the most well-known quote of mine:

"Every mountain can be climbed – you
just have to find the appropriate way to do it.
If you do not achieve your goal,
then you have not done everything to achieve it.
The secret of success is persistence!"

Therefore, do not forget that there is no such thing as impossible, and if you are persistent enough, the reward can be exceptional. In life, we have a greater appreciation for the things which we gain through fighting, because they are more than simple objects, they are symbols of our individual victories, and they all remind us that we are capable of achieving big and important things in our life.

Hommage des Colonies Étrangères
à S.A.S. le Prince Albert I
à l'occasion de ses XXV années de règne
La science découvrant les richesses de l'océan
Inauguré le 13-IV-1914
Oeuvre de Constant ROUX

CHAPTER 3

Facts and figures

Monaco

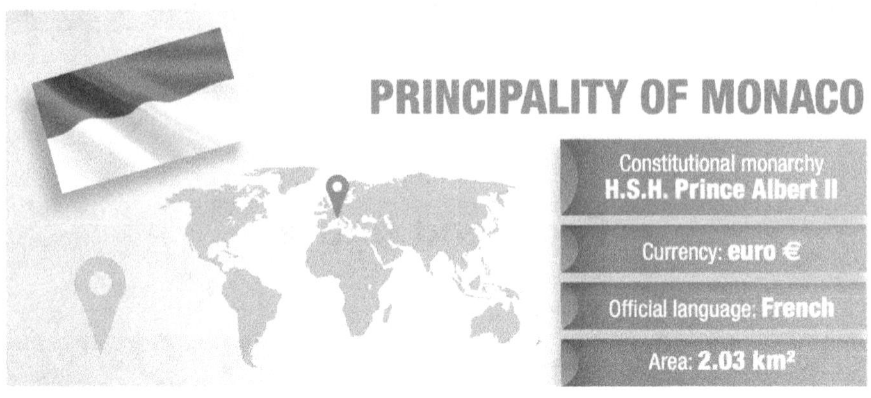

POPULATION

Breakdown by age group

Age group	
Under 18	15.9%
18 to 35	16.9%
36 to 49	18.8%
50 to 64	22.5%
65 and over	25.9%

STATE BUDGET

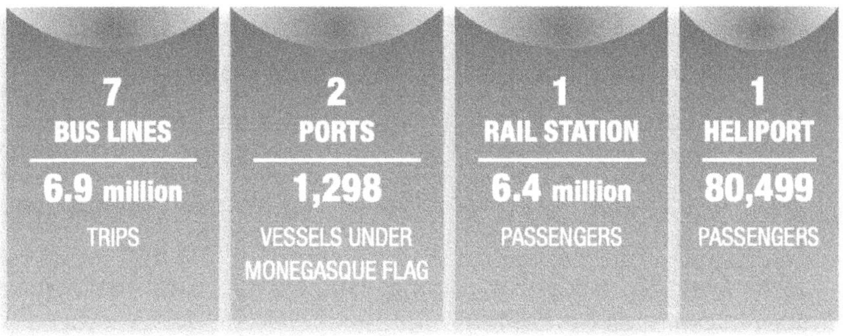

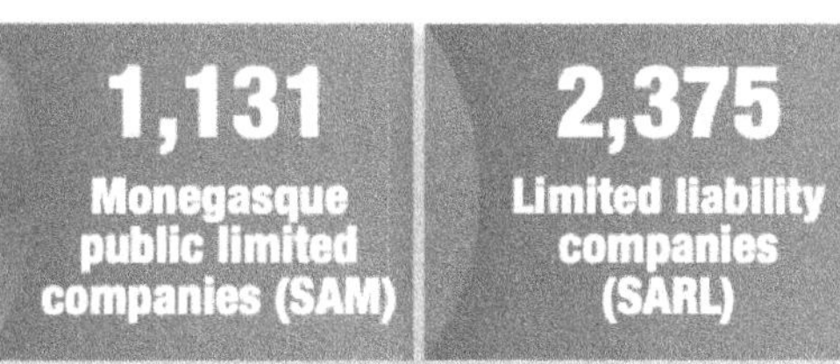

Source: Institut Monégasque de la Statistique et des Études Économiques (2019)

The Principality's historical landmarks

- » 1297 January 8: François Grimaldi took over the fortified castle by deception and occupied the Rock of Monaco.
- » 1911 January 5: Prince Albert I promulgated the first Monégasque Constitution.
- » 1962 December 17: Promulgation of a new Monégasque Constitution.
- » 1993 May 28: Accession of the Principality to United-Nations membership, as permanent member.
- » 1997 700th anniversary of the Grimaldi dynasty.
- » 2004 October 5: The Principality of Monaco became a member of the Council of Europe.
- » 2005 July 12: Accession of H.S.H. Prince Albert II.
- » 2006 June 27: Establishment of the Prince Albert II of Monaco Foundation.
- » 2010 March 29: Mr. Michel Roger took the oath before H.S.H. Prince Albert II and became the first Minister of State chosen by a Sovereign Prince of Monaco.
- » 2010 June 23: Announcement of H.S.H. Prince Albert II's betrothal with Miss Charlène Wittstock.
- » 2011 March 18: Death of Princess Antoinette.
- » 2011 July 1 and 2: Marriage of H.S.H. the Prince and Miss Charlène Wittstock.
- » 2012 December 17: Fiftieth anniversary of the 1962 Constitution - Throne Room.
- » 2013 April 3: Official visit to Monaco by United Nations Secretary General H.E. Mr Ban Ki-moon.

The Principality's geography

Attitudes

Palace Square	62.20 meter
Highest point at ground level (Access to Patio Palace on D6007)	164.44 meter

Oceanographic Museum

Latitude	43°	43'	49"
Longitude	7°	25'	36"
Solar time difference with Greenwich	22'	42"	4
Solar time difference with Paris	20'	21"	6

Surface of the Principality

Surface of the Principality (New Dike included)	202 hectares

Length of land border

Length of land border which is divided as follows:	5,469 meter
Cap-d'Ail	1,341 meter
La Turbie	390 meter
Beausoleil	3,274 meter
Roquebune-Cap-Martin	464 meter

Length of coastline

Length of coastline Outer boundary line of ports and beaches	3,829 meter
Greatest length	3,344 meter
Greatest width	1,140 meter

The Principality's climatology

This climatogram was established from the climate normals between 1981-2010 for the precipitations and the temperatures.

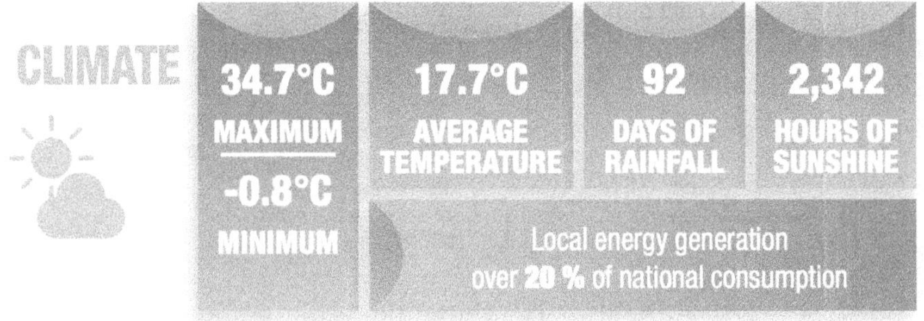

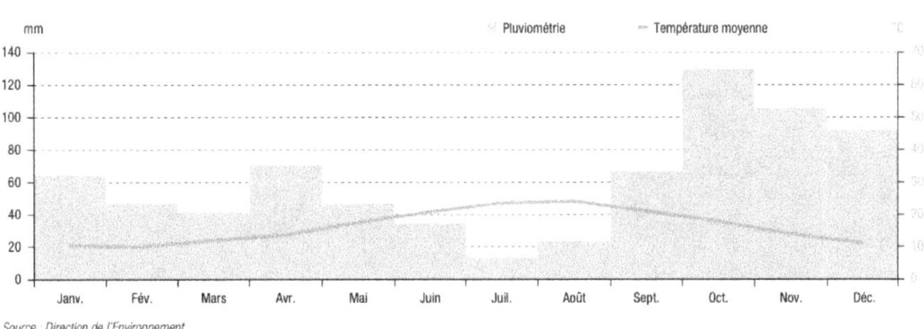

Source : Direction de l'Environnement

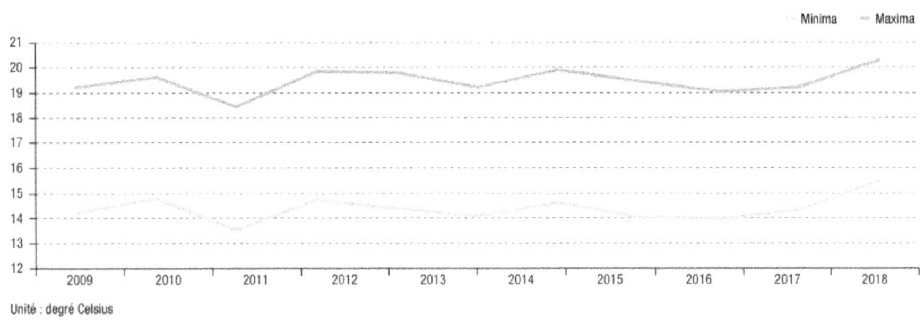

Unité : degré Celsius

Source : Direction de l'Environnement

Monégasque National Anthem

Monaco's national anthem is called "Hymne Monégasque" or "Monégasque Anthem".

Théophile Bellando de Castro wrote the original lyrics in French and composed the music of the 1st edition of Hymne Monégasque in 1841, later Castil-Blaze modified the melody and made several other minor changes.

Original Lyrics in French

Principauté Monaco ma patrie,
Oh! Combien Dieu est prodigue pour toi.
Ciel toujours pur, rives toujours fleuries,
Ton Souverain est plus aimé qu'un Roi.

Fiers Compagnons de la Garde Civique,
Respectons tous la voix du Commandant.
Suivons toujours notre bannière antique.
Le tambour bat, marchons tous en avant.

Oui, Monaco connut toujours des braves,
Nous sommes tous leurs dignes descendants.
En aucun temps nous ne fûmes esclaves.
Et loin de nous, régnèrent les tyrans.

Que le nom d'un Prince plein de clémence,
Soit répété par mille et mille chants.
Nous mourrons tous pour sa propre défense,
Mais après nous, combattront nos enfants.

Original Lyrics in English

Principality of Monaco my country
Oh! How God is lavish with you.
The sky always pure, the shores always blooming [with flowers],
Your Monarch is more revered than a King.

Proud Companions of the Civic Guard,
Let us all respect the voice of the Commander.
Always follow our old banner.
The drum beats, let us all walk ahead.

Yes, Monaco always had brave men,
We are all their worthy descendants.
Never were we slaves.
And far from us the tyrants ruled.

That the name of a merciful Prince
Be repeated by a thousand songs.
We shall all die in his own defense,
But after us, our children will fight.

In 1848 the National Guard created by Prince Charles III, adopted Bellando's song and it became the March of the National Loyalists.

In 1896 Charles Albrecht composed a new arrangement for piano, published by Tihebaux in Paris and called Air National de Monaco; in 1897 Decourcelle of Nice, printed an edition called 429 Hymne National de Monaco for piano.

Years later, François Bellini orchestrated the song by Albrecht; this new arrangement for a trio was judged to be too long for people in 1900 and ceased being played.

The modern version was created by Léon Jehin in 1914 and was played for the first time during the 25th anniversary of the beginning H.S.H. Prince Albert's reign.

Full Monégasque Lyrics

Despoei tugiù sciü d'u nostru paise
Se ride au ventu, u meme pavayùn
Despoei tugiù a curù russa e gianca
E stà l'emblema, d'a nostra libertà

Grandi e i piciui, l'an sempre respetà
Oila cü ne toca!
Oila cü ne garda!
Fo che cadün sace ben aiço d'aiçi:

Riturnelu:
Amu avü sempre r'a meme tradiçiùn
Amu avü sempre r'a meme religiùn
Amu avüu per u nostru unù
I meme Prìncipi tugiù
E düsciün nun pura ne fa scangia
Tantu ch'au celu, u suriyu lüjerà;
Diu n'agiüterà
E mai düsciün nun pura ne
fa scangia
düsciün.

Nun sëmu pa gaire,
Ma defendëmu tüti a nostra tradiçiun;
Nun sëmu pa forti,
Ma se Diu voe n'agiütera!

Oila cü ne toca!
Oila cü ne garda!
Fo che cadün sace ben ailo d'aili:

Riturnelu

Full Monégasque Lyrics in English

Historically, the same flag
Floats happily in the wind of our country
Always the colours red and white
Have been the symbol of our freedom

Great and small have always respected it!
Greetings, you who are our neighbours!
Greetings, you who are watching us!
It is important that everyone remembers the following:

Chorus:
We have perpetuated the same traditions;
We celebrate the same religion;
We have the honour
To have always had the same Princes
And no one can make us change
As long as the sun shines in the sky
God help us
And no one can ever
make us change
No one.

There are not very many of us,
But we all strive to defend our traditions;
We are not very powerful,
But if he wants to, God will help us!

Greetings, you who are our neighbours!
Greetings, you who are watching us!
It is important that everyone is well aware of that!

Chorus

Finally, in 1931, Louis Notari wrote the lyrics in the Monégasque language. Only the Monégasque lyrics are official, reportedly dating back to a request from The H.S.H. Prince.

Current Official Monégasque Lyrics

Despoei tugiù, sciü d'u nostru paise
Se ride aù ventu, u meme pavayun
Despoei tugiù a curù russa e gianca
E stà l'emblèma d'a nostra libertà
Grandi e piciui, l'an sempre respetà

Current Official Monégasque Lyrics in English

Forever, in our land,
One flag has flown in the wind
Forever, the colours red and white
Have symbolised our liberty
Great and small [people] have always respected them

The current official lyrics contain only one verse, sung at the start of the song and repeated again near the end after an instrumental interlude in the middle.

The national anthem is rarely sung aloud if at all in Monaco, except at official occasions.

Population census

The most recent census in Monaco took place from 7 June to 29 July 2016, and it was made by the Monegasque Institute of Statistics and Economic Studies (IMSEE).

The census, carried out on average once every ten years, allows the population to be counted and provides an understanding of Monaco's resident population and housing stock. It covers everyone living within the Principality's territory.

Population

As at 7 June 2016, Monaco's resident population was estimated at 37,308, (representing 139 different nationalities) which is an increase of 5.5% compared with 2008.

Change in resident population

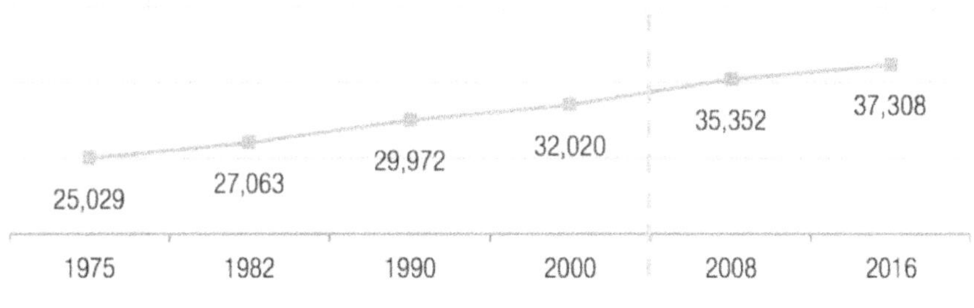

Source: Population census

It is also interesting to see that the Principality of Monaco has a female-male breakdown of 50.1% for the females and only 48.9% for the males.

The average age in Monaco is 46.5 years old, 45.5 for the males and 47.4 for the females.

A total of 139 different nationalities were recorded among residents.

Proportion of Monegasques

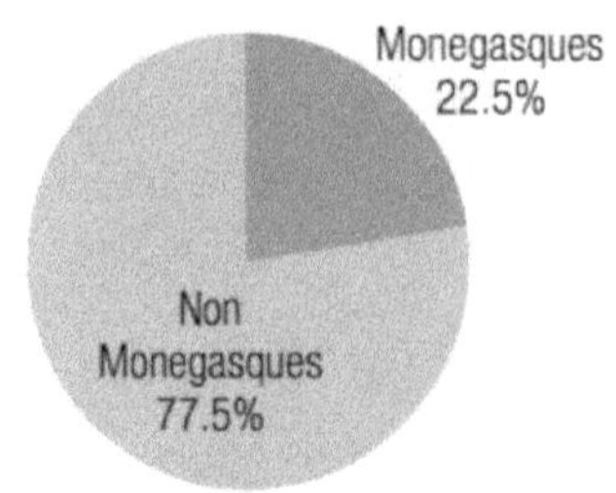

Source: 2016 population census

Breakdown of other nationalities

	Number	% of pluri-nationalities
French	9,286	12.3%
Italian	8,172	13.8%
British	2,795	14.6%
Swiss	1,187	22.9%
Belgian	1,073	8.1%
German	907	14.7%
Russian	749	12.5%
Dutch	555	10.5%
Portuguese	523	6.5%
Greek	401	6.6%

Source: 2016 population census

Furthermore, the census recorded 8,378 residents of Monegasque nationality. This means 77.5% of the Principality is formed by foreign residents.

Male–female breakdown

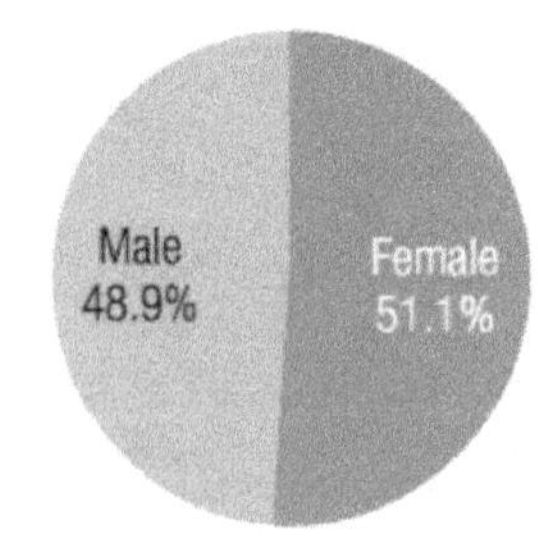

Source: 2016 population census

Change in age pyramid

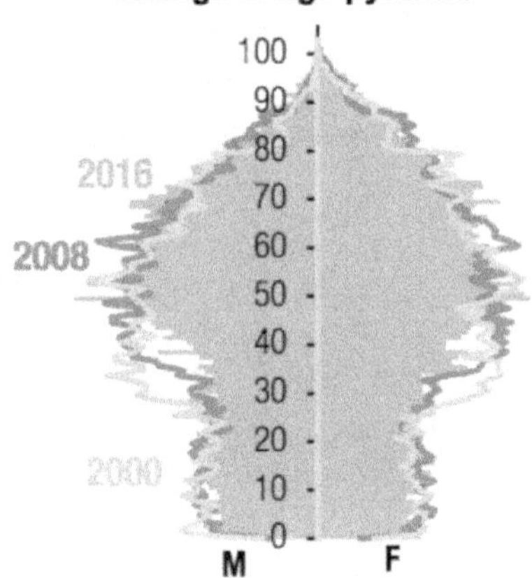

Source: Population census

Breakdown by age group

Less than 18		15.9%
18 to 35		16.9%
36 to 49		18.8%
50 to 64		22.5%
65 and more		25.9%

Source: 2016 population census

Average age of residents

Average age	46.5
Male	45.5
Female	47.4

Source: 2016 population census

More interestingly a quarter of all residents in 2016 had moved to the Principality of Monaco during the last eight years.

The majority of residents aged 17 or over live with a partner. More than half of residents live with a spouse.

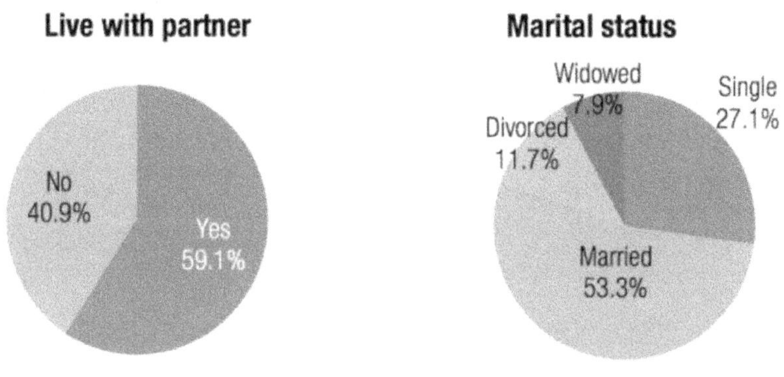

Source: 2016 population census

Source: 2016 population census

Employment

Monaco attracts an educated population: 23% of those aged 17 and over hold the equivalent of a master's degree (bac+5) or higher, and this figure increases to nearly 33% among residents who arrived in the Principality between 2008 and 2016.

Main employment situation

Source: 2016 population census

In 2016, nearly one in two residents aged 17 or over was employed, and one in three was in retirement or retired from business. The level of unemployment among the population aged 17 and over was 2%. Among those in employment, 58% were men.

Main place of work

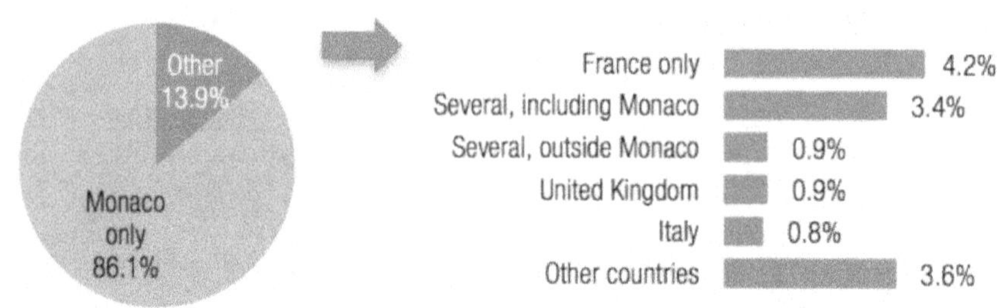

Source: 2016 population census

Almost 90% of residents who work are employed in the Principality. While in 2016, self-employed workers and company directors represented more than a third of the working population.

Housing

The total number of residential units in Monaco was estimated at 19,534 on 7 June 2016, of which 89% were main residences.

Sixty-three percent of main residences are occupied by at least one tenant or subtenant.

The Monte-Carlo district has the highest number of residences, while Monaco-Ville has the lowest.

The average number of rooms in a main residence in 2016 was 2.9.

Three-room homes are the most common type of main residence in the Principality. And 25% of households in main residences have at least one pet.

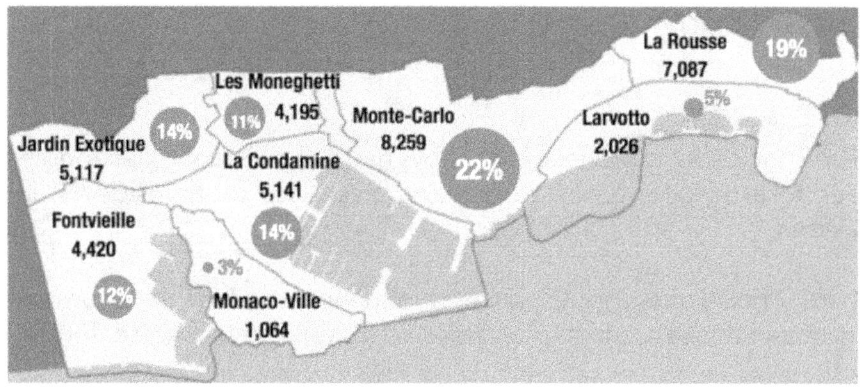

Source: 2016 population census

Breakdown by type of residence and by district

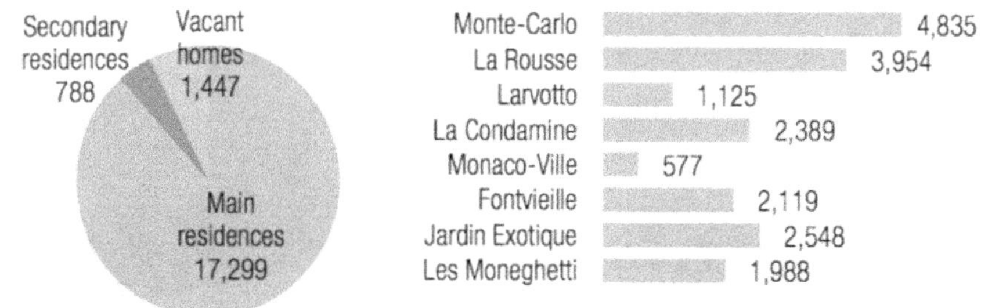

Source: 2016 population census

Breakdown by number of rooms

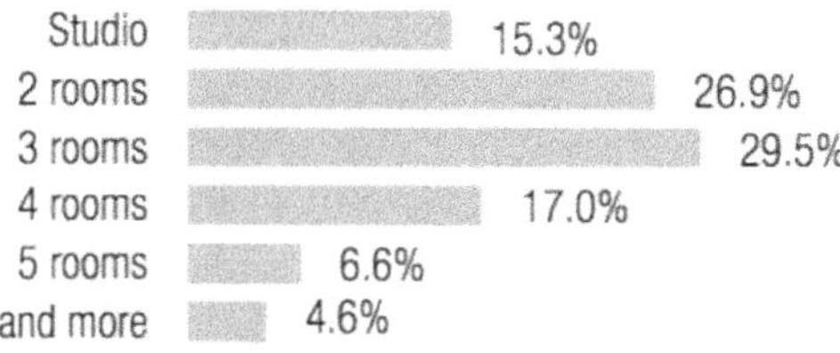

Source: 2016 population census

Gastronomy

The Principality of Monaco has always had a rich history in gastronomy, due to a national desire to provide excellence to its residents and visitors.

Traditional Monegasque cuisine is influenced by French culture and its main recipes are based on fresh vegetables, rice, and seafood.

Barbagiuan is a pastry considered a national specialty of the Principality of Monaco, produced from rice, cheese, leek, and pumpkin or spinach. Most local appetisers in the Principality of Monaco are made from either fruits or vegetables.

One of France's most popular and delightful desserts, the "Crêpe Suzette" was evolved in the Principality at the end of the 19th century.

The recipe of this delightful pancake soaked in Grand Marnier was invented by chance at the Café de Paris during one of the visits of the Prince of Wales, later to become King Edward VII of England. He was a frequent and enthusiastic visitor of Monaco and whilst having lunch one day at the Café de Paris, Chef Carpentier was preparing pancakes with a liqueur when suddenly the contents of the frying pan burst into flames.

The Prince of Wales was enchanted by the spectacle and asked the chef what the recipe was called. Caught off guard but coming quickly to his senses, the chef admitted that the recipe had been invented for the occasion, but suggested off the cuff that the pancakes be called "Princely Crêpes".

In a gesture of gallantry, the Prince of Wales proposed that the dessert be named after the charming young woman he had invited to lunch, whose name was Suzette.

The Principality of Monaco has always attracted entrepreneurs, whose desire and ambitions drive them to achieve more to prove their commitment and excellence in their own fields, a great example being Alain Ducasse, one of the greatest chefs in the world. In 1987, the late H.S.H. Prince Rainier III requested Alain Ducasse take over the management of the kitchens at the Hôtel de Paris, the prestigious establishment owned by Monte Carlo SBM. Alain Ducasse's assignment was to achieve three stars in the Michelin Guide for the hotel's main restaurant. Thanks to commitment and passion with his Mediterranean cuisine and being inspired by excellence at the highest level, the Restaurant Louis XV, run by Alain Ducasse, was awarded its third Michelin star in 1990.

This was the first step towards a gastronomical change in the Principality of Monaco.

Alain Ducasse's Mediterranean-inspired cuisine became his signature by the end of the 20th century, and it still strikes a subtle balance between location, tradition, and innovation.

Alain Ducasse brought culinary class to Monaco, and the bar has been rising ever since with other great gastronomical geniuses building on these foundations.

And a gastronomical revolution still lives on thanks to numerous other Michelin star chefs, who strive to push the boundaries of what can be achieved and who are cultivating the Principality with their excellence.

To further develop this growth, the Principality of Monaco hosts various gastronomical events each year to showcase its culinary heritage and to offer a platform for innovation to develop.

One of my favourite local chefs is Marcel Ravin. I believe he is not only a great chef, but an artist in his heart, and his meals are immediately tied to his identity. No wonder why he was awarded a Michelin star.

Chef Marcel Ravin has managed the kitchens at Blue Bay, located at the Monte Carlo Bay Hotel & Resort, because of its inauguration with his innovative culinary style and tremendous skills.
Inspired by his Martinican origins and experiences, Chef Ravin has developed a fusion of Caribbean and Mediterranean influences from his native French West Indies with the treasures offered by the land and sea of his newly adopted Mediterranean home.

Chef Ravin also has another restaurant championing local produce and creating genius flavour combinations. It is located at the One Monte-Carlo and called Mada One. Interestingly, the name, Mada One, is inspiring by chef Ravin's homeland, Martinique or Madininia/Madiana, the island's former name, meaning "mythical island".

If you ever have the chance just to see his creations (even on Instagram) you will immediately understand my fascination. Pure art on a plate.

„Mr Goodfish" campaign

Talking about gastronomy, the Prince Albert II of Monaco Foundation is the South East regional coordinator for the "Mr. Goodfish" campaign to promote the responsible consumption of seafood.

In association with the Mare Nostrum Aquarium and the Oceanographic Museum of Monaco, the Prince Albert II of Monaco Foundation is making hotel professionals, chefs, fishermen, and restaurant owners aware of the issue of sustainability. They propose and clearly indicate which seafood products are preferable for selection and consumption.

The goal of this initiative, which is already hugely successful in the Channel and North Sea areas, is to offer an alternative to consumers by encouraging them to try new species selected from a list established by the "Mr. Goodfish" campaign.

The selection of suggested fish is planned at each change of season according to the region, the state of the resource, the size, and the status of the species (protected or not). The incentive enables followers to purchase fresh fish and at the same time preserve the resources of the sea.

Many iconic chefs and restaurants follow the commitment of the Prince Albert II of Monaco Foundation, which concerns itself with global sustainability and the environment.

Committed since its creation to the preservation of endangered marine species and in particular the Bluefin Tuna, the Prince Albert II of Monaco Foundation coordinates the development of the "Mr. Goodfish" campaign along the Mediterranean coast.

The WWF recently congratulated Monaco for being the first territory in the world to achieve Bluefin-free status as all restaurants, retailers, and chefs in the Principality of Monaco have removed endangered Atlantic Bluefin tuna from their shelves and menus until stocks of the fish have recovered, and the fisheries and trade are managed in a sustainable way.

Monegasque Barbagiuan

Monaco's national dish is the Barbagiuan – a delicious pastry mainly found in the eastern part of the French Riviera and northern Italy. The Barbagiuan (or Barbajuan) is a fritter stuffed with Swiss chard and ricotta, amongst other ingredients. It is especially consumed on the National Day, 19 November. The word means Uncle John in Monégasque.

Recipe (makes 20 portions)

Ingredients for the pastry:

200g plain flour dash salt
50ml olive oil
1 egg, beaten 50ml water
Vegetable oil for deep frying

Ingredients for the filling:

15ml olive oil
30g onion, finely chopped
3og leek (white part only) finely chopped
2 Swiss chard leaves (green parts only), shredded and chopped
50g fresh spinach, chopped
pinch dried oregano, crumbled
50g ricotta cheese
30g freshly-grated Parmesan cheese
1 egg white, beaten

Prepare the pastry:

» Sift the flour and salt into a bowl

» Add the olive oil and half the egg white and blend with a fork. Reserve the rest of the egg for the filling.

» Add just enough water to bring the pastry together as a firm dough.

» Turn this out onto a lightly-floured surface and knead until smooth and elastic (about 5 min)

» Wrap in plastic wrap and chill in the fridge for 30 minutes.

Prepare the filling:

» Heat the olive oil in a shallow pan over medium heat and add the onion and leek and fry until golden (about 5 minutes)

» Add the chard, spinach, and oregano and fry until the chard is tender (about 10 minutes)

» Transfer the contents of the skillet to a bowl and then mix in the cheeses and the leftover egg from the pastry.

» Season with salt and pepper and set aside to cool.

Final preparation:

» Roll the dough out on a lightly floured work surface to about 2mm thick.

» Use a floured 6cm round pastry cutter and cut into as many rounds as you can.

» Gather the scraps, re-roll out and cut again. You should end up with about 20 circles.

» Place 1 tsp of the filling in the centre of each pastry round and brush the edges with the egg white.

» Fold the dough over to form a semi-circle and press the edges with the ends of a fork to seal.

» As you complete each pastry, transfer to a baking tray lined with foil.

» Note: at this stage, you can freeze the pasties and then thaw before cooking, or you can cook them right away.

» Pour vegetable oil into a deep pan (you need at least 4cm) and heat to fry.

» Working in batches, add the pasties to the oil and fry until brown and crisp (about 5 minutes).

» Transfer to a plate lined with kitchen towels using a slotted spoon.

Monégasque holidays

There are twelve National holidays in the Principality of Monaco.

1. New Year's Day (First Monday if 1st January is Saturday or Sunday)
2. Saint Dévote's Day
3. Easter Monday
4. Labour Day
5. Ascension Day (40 days after Easter)
6. Whit Monday (7th Monday after Easter)
7. Corpus Cristi (Second Thursday after Whistsun)
8. Assumption Day (Assumption of Mary)
9. All Saints Day
10. H.S.H. The Sovereign Prince's Day (Monaco National Day)
11. Immaculate Conception Day
12. Christmas Day

Saint Dévote's Day

Saint Devota (French: Saint Dévote) is the Patron Saint of Monaco (and Corsica) and her feast day in the Catholic Church is 27 January.

According to tradition, Devota was born in Corsica in about 283 AD. She was a Christian and had decided to devote herself to the service of god.

Devota was imprisoned and tortured for her faith during the Diocletian persecution of the Christians and was martyred for her faith by either being stoned to death or racked in 303 AD.

Following her death, the governor of Corsica ordered that her body be burnt so that her remains would not become venerated. Her body was saved from the fire by Christians and put on a boat bound for Africa where she would receive a proper Christian burial. During the journey, there was a raging storm and it is said that a dove appeared to guide the boat to the coast, landing safely in the Principality of Monaco on the 27 January.

Over the centuries, the tale of Saint Devota has become one of the oldest and best-loved traditions in Monaco, and it is believed that Saint Devota has protected the Principality in its times of need.

Ascension Day (40 days after Easter)

Ascension Day is the 40th day of Easter, and commemorates the ascension of Jesus into heaven 39 days after resurrection on Easter Sunday. It is celebrated by putting out an Easter (Paschal) candle.

This Christian festival is also known as The Feast of the Ascension, The Ascension of Jesus, Ascension Thursday or Holy Thursday.

You will find the Biblical accounts of the Ascension in Matthew 28:16-20, Mark 16:19-20, Luke 24:50-53 and Acts 1:6-11.

During the forty-day period before he ascended into heaven, it is believed that Jesus preached and intermingled with his apostles and disciples.

According to tradition, Ascension Day was first celebrated in 68 AD, however, the first written evidence of the Ascension Day Feast occurred in 385 AD.

Today, Ascension Day is celebrated primarily by Catholics and Anglican Christians. According to the Western Christianity methods of calculating the dates of Easter, the earliest possible date for Ascension Day is 30 April, the latest possible date is 3 June.

Whit Monday (7th Monday after Easter)

Whit Monday, also known as Pentecost Monday is a public holiday in several countries on the Monday after Whitsunday, also known as Pentecost. Whitsunday is observed fifty days after Easter and ten days after Ascension. This marks the end of the Easter cycle that began 90 days before with Ash Wednesday at the start of Lent.

The name "Whitsunday" is now generally attributed to the white garments formerly worn by the candidates for baptism on this feast.

The day commemorates the coming of the Holy Spirit in the form of flames to the Apostles, as recorded in the New Testament in Acts, 2.

The Holy Spirit allowed the apostles to speak in other languages, and they started preaching the word of Jesus to the Jews who had come to Jerusalem for the feast of Shavuot (Pentecost) and many Christians recognize this event as the birth of the Church.

The following day, Whit Monday (Pentecost Monday), is celebrated as a holiday in many European countries.

Interestingly, in France (Monaco has a very close historical relationship with France) the whole of Pentecost week used to be a holiday, but after the 1789 revolution, only the Monday remained a public holiday.

In 2003, France suffered a heat wave, which resulted in almost 15,000 deaths, mainly elderly people. This prompted the idea of how to increase the funding for additional care for the elderly. In 2005, it was decided to encourage workers to give up one day's holiday – and Lundi de Pentecôte was selected.

At first, an encouraging 44% of people gave up the holiday, but this amount diminished over the years – so much so that it was reinstated as a public holiday in 2008. Instead, the idea now is that each French worker has a "solidarity day". They can give up a holiday, a vacation day, a compensation day or even seven hours divided up all through the year.

Corpus Cristi (Second Thursday after Whistsun)

The Feast of Corpus Christi is a catholic festival celebrated on the second Thursday after Whitsun. Corpus Christi means the Body of Christ and refers to the elements of the Eucharist also called the Holy Communion, Last Supper or Lord's Supper.

The emergence of Corpus Christi as a Christian feast did not happen until the second half of the thirteenth-century with the efforts of a nun called Juliana of Liège.

Since childhood, Juliana had been claiming that God had been telling her that there should be a feast day for the Eucharist and eventually she petitioned to the Bishop of Liège. In those days, bishops could order feasts in their local dioceses. The bishop agreed to the feast and convened a synod in 1246 and ordered that a celebration of Corpus Christi should be held annually.

The Corpus Christi celebration only started to become more widespread after both Juliana and the Bishop had died. In 1264, Pope Urban IV issued the papal bull Transiturus, in which Corpus Christi, was made a feast throughout the entire Latin Rite.

Corpus Christi is primarily a Roman Catholic feast, but it is also acknowledged in the calendar of a few Anglican churches, most notably the Church of England. It is also celebrated by some Western Rite Orthodox Christians. Across many parts of medieval Europe, Corpus Christi was a popular time for the performance of mystery plays.

Assumption Day (Assumption of Mary)

The holiday is celebrated annually on the 15 August, and many parts of Europe celebrate it as the Feast of the Assumption of Mary.

The Feast of the Assumption of Mary is a very important day in the Catholic religion, and it is the principal feast of the Blessed Virgin, the mother of Jesus Christ.

This feast commemorates two events: the departure of Mary from this life and the assumption of her body into heaven.

The church's official doctrine of the Assumption says that at the end of her life on earth, Mary was assumed, body and soul, into heaven.

Some mistakenly believe Mary "ascended" into heaven, which is incorrect. It was Jesus Christ who ascended into heaven, by his own power, but Mary was assumed or taken up into heaven by God.

Pope Pius XII, in 1950, defined that Mary "after the completion of her earthly life was assumed body and soul into the glory of Heaven." Her body wasn't allowed to corrupt nor was it allowed to remain in a tomb. However, there are claims by some cities about possessing her temporary tomb.

In the early Christian centuries, relics of saints and those who gave their lives for the faith were jealously guarded and highly prized. While many cities claim the mortal remains of saints, both famous and little-known, there are no records of Mary's bodily remains being venerated anywhere.

All Saints Day

All Saints' Day is celebrated on 1 November as a commemoration day for all Christian saints and it is also known as All Hallows' Day, Solemnity of All Saints, Hallowmas, or Feast of Saints.

The origin of All Saints' Day may date back to a Greek Christian tradition from the 4th century, when a festival was held to honor saints and martyrs on the Sunday following Pentecost.

The first recorded All Saints' Day occurred on 13 May 609 CE when Pope Boniface IV accepted the Pantheon in Rome as a gift from the Emperor Phocas. The Pope dedicated the day as a holiday to honor the Blessed Virgin and all the martyrs.

In 835 CE, during the reign of Pope Gregory III, the festival was moved to 1 November and was expanded to include the honoring of all saints. It is likely that the 1 November was intentionally chosen to replace the pagan feast of the dead, Samhain. The night before Samhain was a time when evil spirits roamed the land looking for humans, and to confuse the spirits, people would dress up as creatures. This tradition carried on after the 1 November to become a Christian festival, hence the name of Halloween – which is a shortened version of All Hallows' Eve.

The day survived the Reformation, though the Protestants combined it with All Souls' Day, which was on 2nd November.

The day was abolished as a church festival in 1770 but is celebrated by many churches on the first Sunday in November.

In Roman Catholicism, All Saints' Day is a Holy Day of Obligation. This means Catholics must go to Mass on the day unless there is a good reason not to attend, such as illness. The holiday is typically observed with a reading of the Beatitudes, eight blessings given in Jesus' Sermon on the Mount as recounted in the Gospel of Matthew.

In recent years, it has become common in many churches to commemorate those who died during the year on the day itself. The tradition of placing candles on the graves the evening before All Saints' Eve is becoming more common.

H.S.H. The Sovereign Prince's Day (Monaco National Day)

This public holiday in Monaco is celebrated on the 19 November, and if this falls on a Sunday, the public holiday will be observed on the following Monday.

Also known as "H.S.H. The Sovereign Prince's Day" or "La Fête du Prince" in French, this holiday is the National Day of Monaco and marks the official ascension of H.S.H. Prince Albert II to the throne on the 19 November 2005.

The tradition of a Monégasque National Day began during the reign of H.S.H. Prince Charles III in the second half of the nineteenth century. The date for the National Day could change depending on the reigning Prince and the day of the saint they were named after.

When H.S.H. Prince Albert II succeeded his father in 2005, he decided to honor his father and maintain the National Day of the 19 November, St. Rainier of Arezzo's day. The 19th of November is a fitting date as it is also the same day of H.S.H. Prince Albert II's official ascension to the throne in 2005.

H.S.H. Prince Albert II is a member of the House of Grimaldi which has ruled Monaco since 1297.

Immaculate Conception Day

This national holiday is observed in several Catholic countries and regions and celebrated on the 8th of December.

It is a day that celebrates the belief that Mary, mother of Jesus, was preserved from original sin all of her life.

For Roman Catholics, it is observed as a day of obligation with required church attendance.

The Immaculate Conception is a Holy Day of Obligation whose meaning is often confused.

By the sounds of it, one would think we would celebrate the day Jesus was conceived. On the contrary, it is the day that the Blessed Mother Mary was conceived.

Mary's mother was St. Anne and her father was Joachim. While they are not mentioned in the bible, their names appear in some very early Christian texts. Anne and Joachim had been a childless couple until an angel appeared telling Anne that she would give birth to a child that the world would honor. Anne became a saint as she offered her child to god's service.

This day has been celebrated since at least the eighth century, but the idea that the word immaculate means that Mary was born without original sin divided many theological scholars over the centuries. It was not until 1854 that the argument was decided when Pope Pious IX proclaimed this belief to be an essential dogma of the Roman Catholic Church.

Christmas Day

Monégasque Christmas is celebrated with a special family tradition.

Christmas Eve is the occasion when all the members of a family would gather at their parents' home to perform as a preliminary to the evening meal, the rite of the olive branch.

Before sitting down, the youngest of the guests, or the oldest, soaked an olive branch in a glass of old wine. They would then approach the fireplace where a great fire of pine and laurel branches burned, and with his little branch traced the sign of the Cross while pronouncing a few words on the virtues of the olive tree, a source of all kinds of good things.

After this, everybody in turn wets their lips in the glass of wine serving as an aperitif. Before the gala dinner whose main dish is an enormous "brandamincium" a Monégasque dish of salt cod pounded up with garlic, oil and cream, surrounded by "cardu", cardoon in white sauce; "Barbagiuan", stuffed fritters and "fougasses" flat crunchy biscuits sprinkled with sugared aniseed colored red and white, flavored with several drops of rum and orange-flower water.

On the table covered with a splendid cloth lay a round loaf of bread "u pan de Natale" (the Christmas loaf) on which four walnuts formed a cross surrounded by several olive twigs.

From this Christmas of olden times, some elements are still in existence, besides Midnight Mass in the Cathedral, "Barbagiuan", "fougasses" and "u pan de Natale" can be found at some bakeries in the Principality.

On the 24th of December each year, the Principality offers the U Pan de Natale (Monaco's Traditional Christmas Bread). On this day, the Committee for the preservation of Monaco's Traditions requests all bakers whose bread is baked in the Principality to sell "U Pan de Natale", Monaco's Traditional Christmas Bread, on the days before Christmas in accordance with recipe and presentation instructions left to us by Lazare Sauvaigo, a late Monégasque poet, historian, public-speaker and former vice-president of the above committee.

Facts and figures

Chapter 4

Relocation and what is takes

Relocation to the Principality

There is a possibility to stay and live in the Principality of Monaco for a maximum period of three months in a year without any residency permit or VISA. During this time period, you are considered a tourist.

Based on the regulations, any person of foreign nationality who wishes to enter Monégasque territory and stay there for a period not exceeding three months must have the document (passport, travel, or identity document) required. Any travel document accepted which is valid for entry into French territory.

It does not matter whether you arrive for a one-day visit or for a longer time period of up to three months, the basic principles are the same.

Usually this three months period is enough to get a glimpse of the quality of life that the Principality of Monaco offers. You can also get a great impression of the country, the events, the people, and the whole atmosphere. If you are smart enough, you can discover many social clubs and networking places. Furthermore, you can already build up some valuable connections by the end of the third month.

Conditions required for entry and residence in the Principality for a period not exceeding three months:

» Any person of foreign nationality who wishes to enter Monégasque territory and stay there for a period not exceeding three months must have the document (passport, travel or identity document) required for entry into French territory.

» French subjects must merely be holders of the national identity card.

No other formality is required for foreigners who wish to travel to Monaco, which is a great thing.

Many visitors use this initial three-month period to see how they can adjust their daily routines to the new life offered by Monaco. After three months, they need to make a decision whether to stay longer or not, since the Principality of Monaco requires a residence permit (Carte de Sejour or often referred as Carte de Residence) if one is willing to extend their stay for a longer period.

Resident permits are not issued to minors under the age of 16. In some cases, a travel document for a foreign minor may be issued to enable overseas travel.

If you leave Monaco permanently, you must surrender your residence permit.

How can you be a resident in Monaco?

There are multiple companies offering their supporting guidance for you and your family regarding relocation to the Principality. Administration assistance and relocation services are some of the flowering businesses in Monaco, however you should never forget that the Monaco Welcome Office offers its free advisory services for new residents.

The Monaco Welcome Office even holds regular event both in French and English languages, interestingly copying the name of my book: "Living in Monaco informational night". Since I published my Living in Monaco book years before their first event, I feel this is a secret admiration and acknowledgement towards this book.

Usually there are four ways to relocate to the Principality of Monaco:

» By having the ideal (requested) wealth to afford the living quality in Monaco

» By having a sponsor/guarantor for your living costs

» By getting a job in Monaco

» By opening a new business entity in Monaco

As you can see above, you do not have to be super rich; only one of the four ways is built on your financial statements.

However, what is common in all the four ways is that any foreigner, except French subjects, who wishes to live in Monaco for a period longer than three months or establish a residence in the territory of the Principality of Monaco must be the holder of a settlement visa.

The next important step is to find your desired apartment to live in, because without a physical address in the Principality, you cannot apply for a residence permit.

It is highly important to be aware of the housing requirements in Monaco. Each home must have enough rooms to accommodate each adult living there. Therefore, if you are aiming to relocate to

Monaco as a couple with a child, you cannot apply for a residence permit by renting or buying a studio apartment. For the application to be successful, you must have a separate room for your child and for you and your spouse.

There are four ways you can prove your Monaco based address:

» Being the owner of a house or apartment

» Being the director, or unit holder of a company which owns a house or apartment

» Renting a house or apartment; or

» Staying with a close relative, your spouse, or partner with whom you are living as a couple

Based on the general rule, every foreigner over sixteen years of age is required to request within eight days of his/her arrival in the Principality of Monaco a resident's card (Carte de Resident) or residence permit (Carte de Sejour) from the Foreigners' Section of the Directorate of the Police Service. Do not be confused because the resident's card and residence permit are actually the same thing, but many people refer to them with both names.

Unlike other countries offering residency programs, applying for residency in Monaco does not require the applicant to "invest" a specified sum of money in Monaco, nor is it compulsory to purchase a property, as renting accommodation is sufficient.

The cost of applying for residency in Monaco mainly relates to the expense of renting an apartment, added to the general cost of living in the Principality.

Following your case approval, your residency permit will be available for you to collect from the Residents Section office within a maximum of 8 weeks if you are a European Union passport holder. For non-EU passport holders, the administration process can take up to 16 weeks due to the settlement visa request from the French Embassy in their country of residence.

Types of resident cards

It takes a minimum of ten years to secure a long-term residency permit in Monaco. Though you can get your temporary residence card relatively quickly, the whole process takes a really long time. During these ten years, the Monegasque Government and the Monegasque Police will double check and review your request multiple times.

The first step is to gain the temporary residence card issued for one year only. The card is called a "Monaco Carte de Resident, Temporaire". You can immediately receive this temporary residence card, and start your relocation into the Principality of Monaco without any delays.

However, you should never forget that the temporary residency permit is usually granted for one year only. So, if you relocate for taxation reasons, be aware of this.

Once your application for the temporary residence permit has been submitted to the Monégasque authorities, you are eligible to request the temporary residence card. The fee for this card is 10 euros. Basically, the "Monaco Carte de Resident, Temporaire" is the resident card for first-time residents.

After the expiration of the one-year period, you need to request an extension. The card must be renewed each year for the first three years before the twelve-month expiration date.

In the fourth year of your continuous residency in the Principality of Monaco, the "Monaco Carte de Resident, Temporaire", the temporary residency cardholder will then be issued a three-year card, known as the "Monaco Carte de Resident, Ordinaire". These cards are valid for three years, and until you exceed the ten years of continuous residency in the Principality of Monaco, you are entitled for three years of residency extensions.

In year ten, the holder of a Monaco residency may apply for the long-term residency card, known as "Carte Privilege". It is valid for ten years.

The long-term residency card is granted at the discretion of the Monaco authorities, however, it is not automatically granted. In the case of rejection, the applicant will continue to receive the three-year Monaco resident's card.

So, to summarise it, there are three general types of residence permits, and an additional fourth type:

» A "temporary" (**temporaire**) permit can be issued with no minimum requirement period for residency in Monaco. It is therefore applicable to first-time residents. It is valid for one year and the issuing costs are 10 €

» An "ordinary" (**ordinaire**) permit can be issued to people who have lived in Monaco for three years. It is valid for three years and the issuing costs are 15 €

» A "privilege" (**privilégié**) permit can be issued after ten years of residence in Monaco. It is valid for ten years and the issuing costs are 30 €

» A "spouse of a Monegasque national" (**conjoint de monégasque**) permit can be issued to any foreigner who is a spouse of a Monegasque national and who has lived in the Principality for at least one year. It is valid for five years and the issuing costs are 20 €

What is really interesting to obverse is the way that Monaco bends its own rules based on its personal preferences. Actually, they are quite selective with the residents.

For example, the ten-year residency requirement can be reduced to one year in special cases, therefore some people will be eligible for the long-term residency card, the Carte Privilege, after only one year in Monaco.

On the other hand, there are no guarantees that you will be eligible for the long-term residency, even if you have spent over ten years in the Principality of Monaco. Remember, the long-term residency card is granted at the discretion of the Monaco authorities and is not automatically granted.

General prerequisites

To successfully apply for the Monaco residency card, there are several prerequisites to fulfil. These prerequisites are reasonably straightforward and if the applicant can provide all of the required documents, there should be no general reason why the applicant would not be granted Monaco Residency and receive their Monaco residency card.

It is good to know that each of these evidences and supporting documents have to be presented in an original form and accompanied by a certified French translation.

Identifications

For general identification, the Monégasque Government requests valid passports and birth certificates from all applicants.

You will not be granted a Monaco passport during your first year of residency due to the Monaco Carte de Resident, Temporaire (temporary residents permit), therefore your passport has to be valid for the period of your Monaco residency.

Good character

One of the most important prerequisites for a residence permit is proving that you are of good character. The Monégasque Government will require a certificate of good conduct, namely a criminal record check (Certificato penale) information from the country or last two countries in which you have resided in the five years prior to your arrival in Monaco.

This Monaco residency security check is required for each member of your family who are also applicants for a Monaco residence permit. In the Principality, an adult is anyone over the age of 18 years for this purpose. The police certificate should not be more than three months old at the time of application for the residency.

Family status

For your application for a Monaco residence permit to be successful, you also need to provide information on your family status.

If you are married, you need to provide your marriage certificate. In the case that you are divorced, an official divorce certificate or a certificate of legal separation will be requested by the Monégasque government.

If you are a widow, then you need to provide a death certificate of your spouse who is deceased.

Your marital status is also important for opening a bank account. Even if it is not an official requirement, the bank might request to have a signed prenuptial agreement, known as a marriage contract. Furthermore, if you have children under the age of 16, you need to provide the passport or identity card for each child, proof of custody of minors, (proof of adoption, if applicable) as well as proof of schooling for children educated outside Monaco.

Accommodation

A physical address in the Principality of Monaco is a prerequisite for the application. In addition, it is highly important that the property has sufficient bedrooms to accommodate the number of persons applying.

If you buy an apartment in the Principality, you need to provide a notarised property deed to prove that you are the rightful owner of the property.

If you are renting an apartment, you need to provide the tenancy agreement registered with the Department of Tax Services.
When you rent an apartment, you must be aware that your tenancy agreement for the property is subject to registration duty tax and the leasehold duty tax, which is always covered by the tenant.

The leasehold duty is calculated at a rate of 1% of the rent amount, and this includes the costs corresponding to the entire period in which the tenant occupies the property. You must pay the leasehold duty in full when you register your tenancy agreement contract.

You must register your tenancy agreement within the first three months that follow the signing of the contract to avoid penalties. You will also need this proof for the application of the Monaco residence permit application.

If you are staying with someone, you will need to present a certificate of free accommodation signed by the person you are staying with. It is important to know that friends cannot stay together, only families. For example: a close relative, your spouse, or partner with whom you are living as a couple.

You must also provide the tenancy agreement of the person you are staying with who rents their home, or the property deed if the person you are staying with owns their home.

In every case, you also need to provide a new electricity contract for your Monaco apartment and the most recent electricity bill if there is any.

Health report

A health report is requested for applicants of 70 years and over.

Financial status

All applicants must show evidence of sufficient funds in which to live within the territory of the Principality of Monaco.

There are six different ways to be accepted for a Monaco residence permit:

1. If you are self-employed or the manager or director of a company, you need to provide a copy of the relevant Trade and Industry Register entry.

2. If you are setting up a business in Monaco, you need to provide a receipt from the Business Development Agency confirming the

admissibility of your application to start a business.

3. If you are an employee in Monaco you need to provide a certificate from the Employment Office authorising employment in Monaco appropriate to individual circumstances, namely an undertaking of employment, an application for permission to hire, or your work permit and most recent pay slip.

4. If you are retired, a proof of pension.

5. If you are being supported by someone else, a letter from the third party, namely a relative, spouse, or partner with whom you are living as a couple, confirming that they are fully supporting you. Also, documentary evidence of that person's financial resources as appropriate to their circumstances.

6. For all other cases, a reference from a Monaco-based bank confirming that you have sufficient funds to live in Monaco. It might also be helpful if you can provide any other documentation to the Monégasque Government that establishes you have sufficient financial resources to live in Monaco.

Police interview

To complete the Monaco residency process, an official residency interview will be arranged, during which all of the required documents are to be submitted. This usually take place in the Residents Section of the Directorate of Public Security (Direction de la Sûreté Publique).

Following this, your Monaco residency application will be processed, and if all documentation and prerequisites are fulfilled, it will be authorised. All of the documents must be completed, duly signed, and translated to French.

There are slight differences between the European Economic Area Nationals (Germany, Andorra, Austria, Belgium, Bulgaria, Croatia, Cyprus, Denmark, Spain (including the Balearic and Canary Islands), Estonia, Vatican City, France (Guadeloupe, Martinique, French Guiana, Réunion), Finland, Greece, Hungary, Ireland, Italy, Iceland, Latvia, Liechtenstein, Lithuania, Luxembourg, Malta, Norway, the Netherlands, Poland, Portugal (including the archipelagos of Madeira and the Azores), Czech Republic, Romania, United Kingdom (England, Scotland, Wales, Northern Ireland, Gibraltar), San Marino, Slovakia, Slovenia, Sweden, Switzerland.) and non-EEA Nationals.

One of the most important changes is that non-EEA Nationals must first apply for a settlement visa from the French Consulate in their home country.

Minimum fund to live in Monaco

There are many legends, rumours, and gossips related to the minimum fund you need to have to relocate to the Principality of Monaco. Some of them might tell you that it is a minimum of five million euros or even higher.

Many people believe that people who live in Monaco are all part of a big tax evasion fraud scheme. So, let's clarify this in black and white: Tax evasion is a crime in many countries, however tax avoidance is not.

Tax avoidance means that it is within your rights to pay only the amounts required by law, and nothing more. Therefore, by choosing the Principality of Monaco as the place of your residency, you will be obliged to pay your tax based on the Monegasque law (which we all know offers zero personal tax, but requires other taxes).

The common belief is that you have to have at least one million euros to open a bank account in Monaco. This is not exactly true, because you can apply for residency for less than 20,000 euros, even if you do not have a job.

There are different ways to relocate to Monaco with or without money. Situations can arise where if you have a strong financial background, your application may not be granted. It is good to be clear in advance that the Principality of Monaco is not really a good place for commercial banking, even if a few banks offer these solutions.

However, the problem is not truly the financial part, it is the real estate prices. The biggest challenge is to prove that you can pay your rent in the long term.

Monaco does not draw any line on how much funds you need to relocate and to live in the Principality. Despite all the expectations, it has never been regulated. The only thing that the government requests is a visible proof that you will have enough funds/income to maintain your living costs and residency once they accept your residence request.

This basically allows local banks and wealth managers to develop tailored approaches for individuals looking to relocate.

However, in May 2017, The Association Monégasque Des Activités Financières, or AMAF association, in Monaco recommended that its members ask for a minimum deposit of 500,000 Euro.

Many banks in Monaco are part of the AMAF, so these partners are most likely to ask for this 500,000 Euro minimum deposit.

The amount of capital required to relocate to Monaco can vary from the amount requested from banking institutions to open your bank account. The Monégasque Government requests visible proof from your bank that you have sufficient funds and income to maintain your living costs and residency once they accept your residence request.

Since Monaco highly respects the privacy of its residents, they will never ask how much money you have. They entrust the bank to declare (without disclosing your wealth) that you can pay your stay during the period of your Monaco residency.

Some banks are very selective, and they do not prefer smaller clients. The usual practice for big banks is 500,000 Euro, however some banks accept significantly smaller amounts as well. It is recommended to bring an independent advisor who represents your personal interests to partake in these negotiations.

I know some people who are living in Monaco with a very low income, paying less than 3,000 Euro per month. However, there is a big difference between living and LIVING in Monaco. You have to face the sad truth that a small budget will never allow you to fit into the high society.

Usually, it is said that you should consider moving to Monaco only when you can afford to spend 2,000 Euro for your monthly living expenses. This is also a main reason why Monaco usually welcomes individuals who have at least the minimum of 10 Million Euro in wealth. But again, the requested fund to live in Monaco is not regulated.

In the Principality of Monaco, 1 in 3 people are millionaires. This means the 66% of the country are from an average demographic.

This is a very important fact because it is easy to forget that Monaco is not just a playground for the millionaires, it is much more than that.

Usually people are relocating via two ways:

» by being employed by a Monaco-based company, or
» by having enough money to live without work

The first one is quite obvious. However, the second one is a truly really exciting topic, since 99% of the residents do not come to Monaco to work, but to enjoy its multiple benefits.

In the Principality, you can fin almost one hundred banks and wealth managers. Most of them offer different conditions and services for you, most importantly, the handling and managing of your money. What is interesting, but not commonly known, is that you always have the power to negotiate your own conditions. Many banks and wealth managers are flexible when they see their interests in you.

Therefore, you might be able to open a bank account even from 150,000 Euro, down from the average of 500,000 Euro. However, the most important thing is that you need to convince your bank to ensure proof for your residence. The declaration for the residence proof should be a main decision criteria for you; otherwise, you can face some unpleasant surprises.

The bank proof for the Government never states the actual amount you have, just a note that you have a good financial condition to live and relocate to the Principality of Monaco. Since the Government is not interested in your financial status, you have great potential to create a perfect foundation to enter negotiations with your bank.

Obviously, you have to be careful with the differences and the values they offer you.

For example, there are banks that open bank accounts from 150,000 Euro, and for this amount they are ready to give you the financial proof for your residency. However, what you might realise later is that they can block your amount for payment security purposes until you leave the Principality. Therefore, you cannot use the amount for at least a year.

Many banks offer you possibilities of opening a bank account from 250,000 to 500,000 Euro. They also have their own limitations, which is usually something related to the service or the flexibility.

The big banks often welcome you with a minimum opening amount of 1,000,000 Euro. However, they rarely lock your amount; furthermore, many of them even prefer that you sign a clausal in your contract giving them the power of attorney, specifically that they are allowed to manage and reinvest your fund.

There are many small differences between services, therefore it is always beneficial to negotiate your own conditions. Many big banks will try to advertise their products and additional services to you, but at the end of the day, they can be really flexible in order to keep you and your wealth in their bank.

I would also be careful with the small opening amounts. Many banks have had negative results during the last years, therefore, if you remember my example about the "tree and its roots", you have to see beyond the shining surface. I know it is weird but it is like gardening and producing juicy fruits... You cannot expect perfect fruits on your tree if the roots are damaged, rotten, or just simply unstable.

Dare to ask the bank to disclose their financial results (which is usually considered to be public information). After reviewing the financial indicators from the last three years you will have much better confidence to choose a bank. You do not have to be an accountant but you can clearly see the end results at the end of the years as well as the number of the clients they handle. These indicators can easily show you whether they are making increases or decreases in their activities.

I believe choosing a bank is a highly important decision since they will handle your savings which you earned by many years of hard work. And probably you do not want to open a bank account to lose your savings, but to increase it. Therefore, if they were unable to create results in the past for their current clients, then you have no guarantee at all that they will be the right partner for you.

I would really say that relocation is not just a matter of your wealth, but the choice of the right financial partner.

Relocating with sufficient funds

One of the most important steps is to open a bank account in Monaco in order to manage your daily living costs and also to successfully apply for the residence permit.

Opening a bank account can be done through a bank or wealth manager, if you have sufficient wealth. Alternatively, you can also open a commercial bank account, if you are employed by a Monaco-based company.

The Monégasque government does not check how much wealth you actually have, however, it requires a declaration – a written statement from your chosen bank that you have sufficient financial resources with which to live in the territory of Monaco.

Sufficient financial resources, by means of:

» A salary; or professional income (independent commercial activity or through a company); or

» Sufficient savings (the sum which is judged sufficient depends on the banking establishment in Monaco providing the reference); or

» Being supported by a relative, spouse, or partner with whom you are living as a couple

You might say that getting residency in Monaco is all about the bank certificate for which your wealth is a key factor. However, your wealth is not the only factor for a successful application.

One of the most important prerequisites needed to secure a residence permit by the Monégasque government is the 'Certificate of good conduct', widely known as good morality and a clean criminal record.

This is also the reason why when you move to Monaco, you are eligible only for a temporary residence permit. Normally within 3 months of the residency application request, the Monégasque government will double check your submitted documents and conduct an investigation into international criminal records. Also, during the first 3 months, the Monégasque Police initiates an interview with you as a potential new resident.

For many years, the Principality of Monaco has taken serious steps and led an active fight against money laundering, corruption, and terrorist financing. These steps often reach international levels as well.

The Principality of Monaco has created its own Financial Investigation Unit, called S.I.C.C. FIN (Service d'Information et de Contrôle sur les Circuits Financiers). The S.I.C.C. FIN works together on an international level with more than 130 countries around the globe. Its role is to suspend financial transactions carried out by professionals who are subject to legal matters.

Understanding the meaning of deposit

If you relocate to the Principality of Monaco based on your wealth and without working in a Monaco-based company, there is a highly important step you need to take; this is the opening amount, or as many banks refer to it, the security deposit.

It is a common standard that the banks and wealth managers in Monaco will require a form of deposit to secure your financial status for residency. This bank deposit is usually the amount you need for your residence permit, normally anything between 500,000 and 1 million Euro.

However, what many banks do not make clear is that this deposit amount cannot be accessed during your residency. They simply expect you to understand the "small text" in your contract, and since you need to wait at least 10 years before you can apply for a permanent residence permit, it means that your bank deposit cannot be touched for at least 10 years, except if you decide to leave Monaco.

Therefore, if you open a bank account with 500,000 Euro, you most likely cannot access this amount during the period of your residency. It is like a form of guarantee.

In practical reality, if one rents out an apartment for 10,000 Euro a month, then he/she needs the 500,000 Euro bank deposit as well. Financially, the opening amount the bank will be looking for is 620,000 Euro for the first year, (500,000 Euro as deposit and proof of 120,000 Euro for the annual rent). This is the point where choosing the right bank is crucial.

In addition, some contracts contain a clause stating that you automatically approve that during your residency the bank can manage, use, and reinvest your deposit without limitations. It goes without saying, that by allowing the bank to reinvest your security fund, it is not guaranteed that you will see that amount back.

The problem with these types of bank contracts is that if the bank loses your deposit, then you will be asked to top it up at least to the original amount, or you might lose your residence permit. This is because the bank may not guarantee the requested statement for you anymore.

What is interesting but not commonly known is that you always have the power to negotiate your own conditions before opening a bank account. Therefore, if you aim to be a long-term resident in the Principality of Monaco, be very cautious with your banking and wealth management contracts.

Ask for independent and professional help to avoid some expensive surprises.

The 20k trick

Obviously, there are a few shortcuts as well; maybe some would refer to them as administration holes. One of these makes the process way longer, but it can significantly reduce your initial relocation costs.

For example, if you are employed in Monaco then you do not need the big starting fund to open a bank account. Therefore, in most cases, those who are employed do not necessarily have high net-worth assets.

In the case that a Monaco-based company employs you, you do not need to pay a deposit to open a bank account. As an employee, you will be able to relocate to the Principality of Monaco without any financial conditions or bank confirmation of your personal assets value. Therefore, you can open your Monaco bank account with zero euro.

However, if you are wealthy enough you do not want to be employed.

And here is the hole you can take advantage of: once you successfully apply to form a business corporation, or even just to form an administration office for your existing business, you can be eligible for residency. For example, many people gain residency by forming a limited liability company (S.A.R.L.)

To form a S.A.R.L. you can do it for less than 20,000 Euro (S.A.R.L. needs only 15,000 Euro as base capital). Once you are accepted you can use the base capital freely. So, sometimes it is more beneficial to form a company and to employ yourself.

Of course, it requires more administration and a longer approval time, and it is not easy to be approved. It depends on the value that your business can bring to the Principality of Monaco.

However, at the end of the day, no matter which way you relocate to the Principality of Monaco, once your residence permit is accepted, you can enjoy all the benefits of the Principality, including, but not limited to, the no income tax benefit.

But there is another advantage to forming a company in Monaco, which attracts the millionaires as well.

Living in Monaco without depositing a relatively large sum is a highly significant difference, and many people, even with a strong financial background, consider the option to be employed. Understandably, if you have significant wealth and prestige, you do not want to be employed by any other company.

One of the most common solutions for high net worth individuals is to set up their own family office and to be employed in it. Financially, it has many benefits, because once your new company has been accepted, you can use the base capital freely. In many cases, it is more beneficial to form a company and to employ oneself. As the population census highlights, almost 90% of residents who work are employed in the Principality.

Of course, everything depends on your time schedule, since by having sufficient funds to live in Monaco, you are ensured a temporary residence permit the same day you open your bank account. Opening a family office or any other business form in Monaco requires more administration and longer approval times, which can take up to 6 months.

What is important to realise is that even if the Monégasque law allows you to have multiple options in which to receive a Monaco residence permit, you should never forget that maintaining a certain quality of living in the Principality requires a certain minimum level of wealth.

Nationality challenges

Advisors speak about various taxation benefits and the lifestyles of the Principality of Monaco, but they hardly speak about the difficulties that some nationalities face.

Any foreigners, excluding French nationals, who wish to reside in Monaco for a period longer than three months, or establish a residence in the territory of the Principality of Monaco, can apply for a settlement visa.

In practical reality, it is not that simple, since even US Nationals can face extreme difficulties during their application for a residence permit.

The Principality of Monaco maintains a strong partnership with France and this is the reason why French nationals can face the strictest rules.

History tells us that Monaco's strong bond was in a very fragile state in the early 1960's when France created a blockade around the Principality causing very heavy political tension between the countries. H.S.H. Prince Rainier resolved the tension, through implementing new fiscal reforms.

Since then, the Franco-Monégasque treaty imposed by General de Gaulle in 1963. It states that all French nationals are due to pay tax in France as well.

This mutually-signed agreement states that French citizens with less than five years of residence in Monaco, and companies doing more than 25 percent of their business outside the country, would be taxed at French rates. This is without a doubt a huge burden for both private individuals and business entities, since they are not allowed to enjoy some of the major advantages of the Principality.

This Franco-Monégasque treaty was against the image of the Principality of Monaco. H.S.H. Prince Rainier said in an interview to France Soir, that "direct taxation would harm the very roots of our sovereignty".

However, it is hard not to mention that since the Franco-Monégasque treaty, there has been no real border between Monaco and France, which creates great positive advantages for the residents.

In 2014, a minor amendment was implemented affecting the long-term French residents of Monaco. France's Council of State ruled that French nationals born in the Principality, who have lived continuously in Monaco, will no longer be subject to French income tax. A strong contingency was included to the amendment stating when they leave the Principality they will be immediately subject to French taxation rules.

To avoid the same difficulties that happened in 1962-1963, Monaco created a taxation transparency agreement with other countries as well.

To maintain the good relationship with France, Monaco does not allow French residents to enjoy the country's benefits. Should a bank account be opened by a bank or wealth manager for a French national, it is doubtful that they will ensure the necessary papers for the residence permit.

American citizens would most likely receive no benefits from a tax perspective from residing in Monaco. Furthermore, Eritrean and Philippine citizens are two other countries required to pay taxes on a worldwide basis.

It is important to understand that the Principality of Monaco is not an offshore jurisdiction, and taxation is a serious thing in Monaco. Yet, the basic principle is that Monaco has zero personal income tax; however, in some cases the Principality may suggest basing the taxation on the country of citizenship. This means that as an American citizen, you might be eligible for residency and a second Monégasque passport; however, you will be still obliged to make your annual taxation based on the US tax rules.

As a possible solution, one might say that new residents can renounce their citizenship to eliminate their worldwide tax burden, but that would not work either, due to laws that require filing and continued taxation for a certain period. With this strategy, the Principality forms a basis for legally minimising avoiding tax in other countries.

The problem of long staying residents

One of the untold problems in the Principality is the lack of long-term residents. It is a genuine problem since a quarter of all residents (in 2016) had moved to the Principality of Monaco during the last eight years.

When people are relocating to the Principality of Monaco, they often miscalculate the living costs, which is much more than a monthly apartment rental fee. In other cases, people come to Monaco to "get rich", which rarely happens from one day to another.

It is a sad fact that a very significant amount of young residents leave Monaco during the first three years. This problem strongly effects the society and the economy as well. I consider this among the very first reasons why it is so hard to build up trust as a foreign individual in the first years.

People in Monaco want to be sure that you are capable of staying longer and that you are not just a fortune hunter. Frankly, I can understand this because any partnership should be a commitment for long0term and mutually-beneficial activities, which is not possible if someone leaves the next year.

A few years ago, as an after effect of the global economic crisis, Monaco lost more residents than usual. This was because the market seriously affected the savings of some of the residents.

There is a reason why people often say that "Monaco is the playground of the super-rich". If you have the desire to relocate with your family to Monaco, always consider how long you can afford the lifestyle that the Principality requires.

Currently, Monaco is gaining back more and more residents, but still it is an open question how long they can afford the lifestyle that Monaco requires.

Future problems with your country of origin

Once you are able to successfully acquire your residency permit, which is granted for you and your family, you will have many great benefits in the Principality. However, one of the most important things you need to consider is the way of proving that you are actually living for more than six months a year in the territory of Monaco from the date of the issuing of your permit.

Since Monaco offers a zero-personal income tax, the Government does not check the period of your stay during the first ten years. Obviously, they have no reason to do that, since it does not matter how much time you spend in the territory of the Principality of Monaco; your personal wealth is tax-free.

However, in many cases your country of origin requests hard evidence regarding the days you spend in Monaco. It is an obvious process because your wealth is an important tax source for your country of origin. Therefore, they might try to prove that you are not living in Monaco for over six months in a year.

This could be also important for you if you would like to relocate to Monaco and find your final home in the territory of the Principality. Even if Monaco authorities do not really check the period of your stay in the first years, it could be really crucial after ten years when you will apply for a long-term residency for a naturalisation. Always take this into consideration.

After ten years, the Monégasque authority will check the whole period of your stay. There are many methods for this, but one of the basic ones is that they check the meter tendency of your water and electricity invoices going ten years back. This provides an initial indicator for the authorities regarding when your apartment was really used for living.

In many cases your final residency permit depends on the way you can prove your long-term stay in Monaco. It is something you have to consider when you are acquiring residency in the Principality of Monaco.

As a side note, I often hear stories that some people pay for others to go to their home to open the water and to use the electricity while they are not in Monaco. It usually happens through the maids and the cleaning ladies who go there anyway to water the flowers and to maintain the cleaning condition of the apartments. However, I have also heard that if the authorities catch you with this, they will restart your ten-year process towards the long-term residency.

How can you become a citizen of Monaco?

Many people's dream, including myself as well, is to become a citizen of Monaco. It is not about loyalty or a passport; it is more about being a part of an ideal community.

There are many possibilities for gaining citizenship, however, in many cases the process can be extremely hard since naturalisation is granted only by sovereign ordinance. And once the Prince has made his decision, it is incontestable.

Decisions of rejecting or deferring the request are not subject to appeal, and it can happen that your request is always rejected, even if your request satisfies all the pre-conditions laid down, as these merely confer the right to make the request for naturalisation.

It may seem very personal… well it is.

In general, any person who has been ordinarily a resident in Monaco for at least ten years after reaching the age of eighteen may apply to H.S.H The Sovereign Prince for naturalisation as a citizen of Monaco.

The Department of Justice is responsible for examining applications for naturalisation and presenting a report to H.S.H. The Sovereign Prince in accordance with the provisions of the organic law of 9 March 1918.

During the examination phase, a number of other authorities are consulted, in particular the Minister of State.

Monégasque citizenship is generally granted to those who fulfilled one of the following criteria:

» Individual with family ties to the Monégasque community

» Individual who is well integrated into the economic, social, or cultural life of the Principality

» Individual deemed worthy of this favour by H.S.H. The Sovereign Prince

The French authorities are consulted on all applications that have received a favourable response from H.S.H The Sovereign Prince prior to the publication of the Sovereign Ordinance.

Once your nationality has been successfully granted, a certificate of nationality will be provided to you, which is required for certain administrative documents in Monaco. In such cases, you can request that the Town Hall Nationality Department send the certificate directly to the relevant department.

Acquisition by marriage

Marriage certificates apply to anyone who marries in Monaco, however, a marriage certificate does not automatically grant you the Monégasque citizenship. Unlike many other countries, in Monaco there are no "green-card" marriages, maybe only "good life" marriages.

The marriage of a Monégasque national has no effect on nationality.

For many decades in the past, there was a common rule that only a Monégasque man was able to acquire citizenship. Therefore, if a foreign man married a Monégasque woman, he was not entitled to acquire the Monégasque nationality.

It seemed too harsh for the man and gave an almost unfair advantage to the women. Currently, the rules are not as binding as before, but still any foreign man needs to be married at least ten years before he can apply for the naturalisation. Therefore, marriage does not change the overall naturalisation conditions for men.

A foreign woman, who marries a Monégasque is able to acquire the Monégasque nationality. Once it is granted, she will have the Monégasque passport and nationality, however, she does not become an elector or eligible to be a candidate in elections until a period of five years has passed since the date of the marriage. Therefore, foreign women still have a minimum five-year advantage over foreign men.

A Monégasque woman who marries a foreigner man retains her Monégasque nationality unless she expressly states that she wishes, in conformity with the arrangement of the national law of her husband, to acquire the nationality of the latter.

This declaration must be made at the time of the celebration of the marriage in order to answer the questions posed by the Registrar, otherwise, it is invalid; such a declaration is to be noted on the marriage certificate.

If the marriage is celebrated abroad, the declaration must be made before the marriage is celebrated, specifically before a diplomatic or consular representative of the Principality of Monaco; otherwise, it is invalid.

Acquisition by declaration

By reason of birth

During the year following his majority, any person listed below may acquire Monégasque nationality by means of a declaration made before a registrar, provided that he lives in the Principality and proves that he has had his legal domicile or habitual residence there during his minority:

» Any person born in Monaco of a parent born as a Monégasque, even if this person has lost this nationality;

» Any person born in Monaco of a Monégasque parent and of whom one of the ancestors of the same branch was born Monégasque, even if the parent or ancestor has lost this nationality.

This right is also open, without conditions as to the place of birth or habitual residence or legal domicile to a minor, born before 11 July 1975.

By reason of adoption

A foreigner who has reached his majority and has been adopted by a Monégasque may acquire the Monégasque nationality by means of a declaration made before the registrar, provided that he proves loss of his previous nationality and has established his domicile or habitual residence in Monaco for at least ten years.

If the adopted person is a minor, it is his legal representative who acts in his name. In the year following his majority, the minor whose consent was not sought has, however, the opportunity to repudiate his Monégasque nationality.

In the case of a Monégasque adopted by a foreigner, he retains his nationality if he does not acquire that of the person adopting him.

Municipal rule

The person obtaining the Monégasque nationality does not possess political rights, that is, may neither be an elector nor present himself as a candidate, until the fifth year following the date on which he acquired this nationality.

Acquisition by naturalisation

The person who wishes to acquire the Monégasque nationality must prove:

» That taking the Monégasque nationality will cause him to lose his previous nationality;

» That naturalization will definitely relieve him of the obligation to perform military service abroad;

» That he has resided ten years in the Principality after reaching the age of twenty one; this residence must be unbroken and in effect at the moment the request for naturalization is made and not be mere residence at an earlier period.

The following are exempt from fulfilling the condition of requiring ten years residence:

» A foreigner whom the Prince judges worthy of this favor;

» A woman married to a foreigner, whose husband requests naturalization or who has already obtained it;

» Children, who are still minors, of a naturalized foreigner, provided that they reside in Monaco at the moment of their request.

The request must be addressed, on stamped paper, directly to the Prince.

Monégasque nationality is granted automatically to children who are minors of a father or a mother surviving her husband (in the event of the death of the latter) who obtains naturalization.

These children have, however, the opportunity to renounce their nationality by making a declaration before the registrar in the year which follows the date on which they reach their majority.

In all other cases naturalization is granted by sovereign ordinance. Decisions rejecting or deferring the request are not subject to appeal; the request may always be rejected, even if the person making the request satisfies the conditions laid down, as these merely confer the right to make the request for naturalization.

This also means that even if you had ten years of residency with all the requested wealth to live in the Principality of Monaco, your naturalisation could be refused. You can be entitled for long-term residency, but to successfully acquire a Monégasque passport, you have to prove that you are a valuable member of the society. What you personally bring to Monaco is always considered a major decision factor.

Recommended partners:
MONACO VILLAS
REAL ESTATE
OMYS
CONSULTING

CHAPTER 5

Finding your home, Monaco's real estate scenery

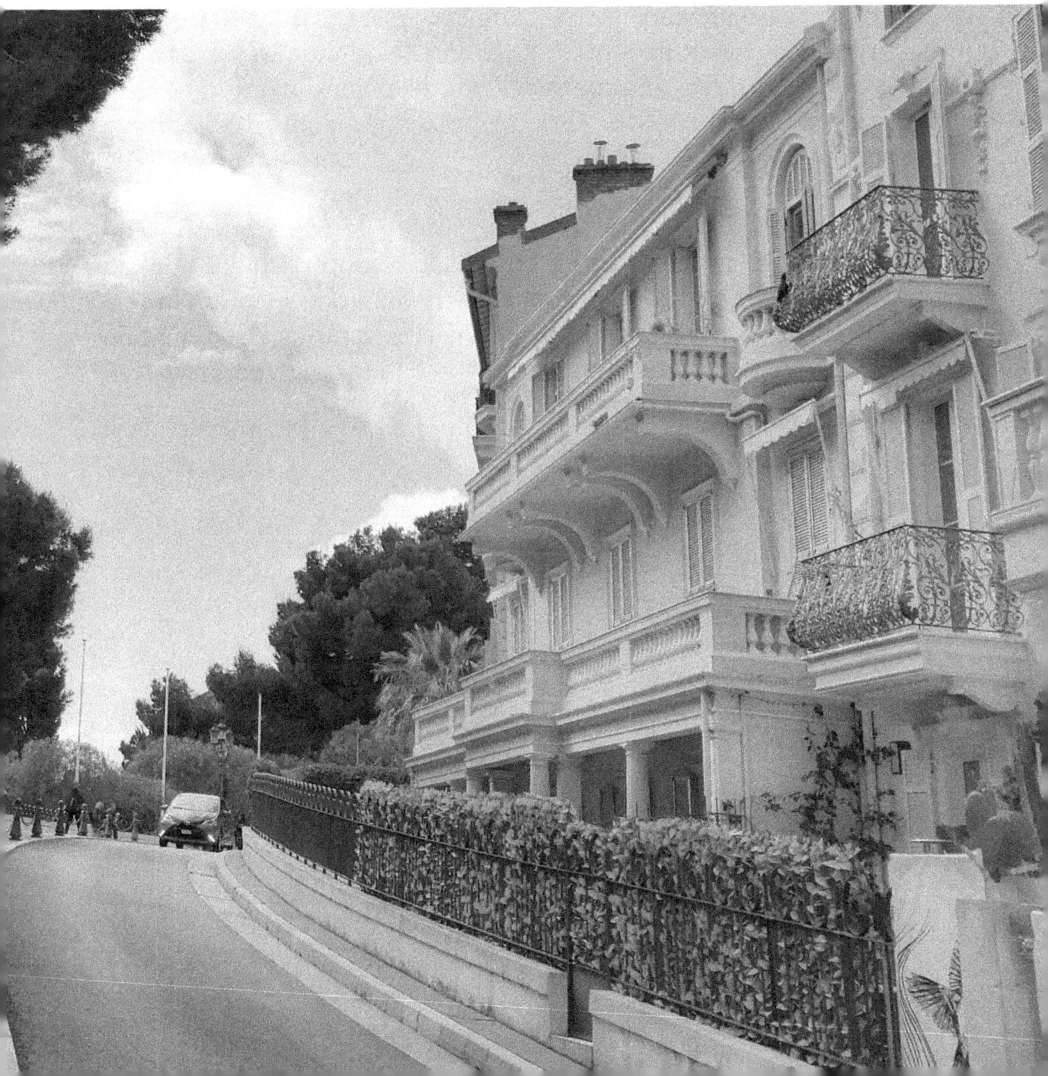

Finding the perfect home

Let's summarise Monaco again briefly. The Principality of Monaco is an independent sovereign state located in the south east of France, close to the Italian border. Its great location and exceptional climate makes Monaco a highly comfortable place to live throughout the year. Winter is mild and summer is very sunny.

The Principality of Monaco is surrounded by nature, on one side you have the deep blue Mediterranean Sea, and on the other side, the mountains with their vibrant green vegetation.

Monaco offers a balanced lifestyle; one can walk around and discover the amazing tiny old streets of Monaco-Ville, and then venture to the other side of Monaco to experience the excellent luxury buildings including the fabulous Tour Odeon housing the most expensive apartment in the world.

The traditional language of the Principality is Monegù and the official language is French, although Italian and English are spoken by a large number of people. Monaco benefits from an international environment with more than 139 nationalities for a total population of only 39,000 inhabitants. The territory of Monaco covers only 1.98 km², of which 20% were reclaimed from the sea.

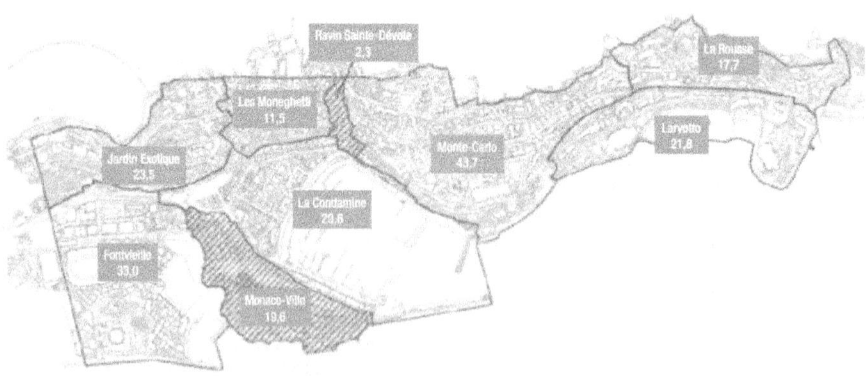

Unité : hectare

Source : Direction de la Prospective, de l'Urbanisme et de la Mobilité

It may seem easy to understand Monaco by numbers and facts, however, its real estate market is much more difficult and the demand is extremely diversified.

When I first arrived to the Principality of Monaco back in 2010, I heard many rumours about the condition of the apartments. Some of the residents complained about the old pipes and electricity systems. Even if this seemed quite obvious to me since Monaco is full of old, historical constructions, I could not really adjust these complaints with the image of the Principality.

Talking a lot with my great friend, a real estate agency owner, I realised that Monaco spends incredible amounts for the reconstructions and renovations. I also got to know that many of the "bad" locations have already been renovated during the past years. Therefore, it is always important to see the past and the future city development plans before you accept any opinions or rumours. To do that, one of the best starting points is the environment and urban development project, which is a special role of the Ministry and its departments.

In order to make a proper real estate decision/investment in the Principality of Monaco, it is always good to understand the characteristics of the different districts and to take a short visit to get a glimpse of their feelings.

Because no matter what some people say, the real estate market is booming in Monaco. 2018 was an exceptionally good year too. Just to give you a brief insight, approximately 2.7 billion euros were exchanged on real estate transactions in 2018. The number of transactions was +11% in existing apartments, and there was a record number of sales for new apartments.

In 2018, prices have been up +18.1% on average from 2017. Mean value in Monaco is now 48,799 Euro per square meter, which is a new record; this is almost two times the average price of 2009.

Regarding areas, Monte Carlo is still the place to be combined with La Rousse, these two areas represent 60% of the number of transactions completed and 66% approximately of the amount exchanged. Prices have been up everywhere except Larvotto. There is a large gap between the Monte Carlo average of 56,000 Euro per sq. meter and the less expensive Moneghetti at 36,000 Euro per sq. meter.

In the new property market, mostly one bedrooms have been sold. In the resale market, we have seen a decrease in studios transactions due to tighter restrictions on residence card applications regarding minimum living spaces. One, two and three bedrooms have been sold more than the previous year.

Many renovations by property developers are currently underway, providing better quality or upgraded properties in the market. New projects such as the sea extension will be a good advertisement for Monaco and will provide modern, high-grade residences.

Districts of Monaco

By characteristics the Principality of Monaco is composed of ten wards and divided into five districts.

The five districts and the ten wards are (the numbering is for illustration purposes only):

Monaco-Ville:

    1. Monaco-Ville

Monte-Carlo:

    2. Monte-Carlo / Spélugues

    3. La Rousse / Saint Roman

    4. Larvotto / Bas Moulins

    5. Saint Michel

La Condamine (including Jardin Exotique):

    6. La Condamine

    7. La Colle

    8. Les Révoires

Les Moneghetti:

    9. Moneghetti / Boulevard de Belgique / Ravin Ste Dévote

Fontvieille:

    10. Fontvieille

Monaco is also in the middle of a land extension project. By 2025 the new district called Anse du Portier will be completed.

Monaco-Ville

The oldest district in the Principality of Monaco is Monaco-Ville, which is located on the "rock". Monaco-Ville is the historical town of Monaco; here stands the cathedral, the Prince's Palace, and the famous Oceanographic Museum. Monaco-Ville is often referred to by the locals as Monaco City, Le Rocher or simply the Rock of Monaco.

It is a distinctive area full of history like no other place in Monaco. This old city district prominently extending into the Mediterranean provides an exceptional panoramic view for the people living there.

The daytime brings an abundance of tourists who venture there to visit the Prince's Palace or the Oceanographic Museum. However, since this is the home of the Princely family, it is also a very highly protected district.

There are permanent police officers who control access for vehicles driving to the historical town, and principally give access to vehicles registered only in Monaco or in the "Alpes Maritimes", a French department close to the principality.

Monaco-Ville is a very charming place with rigid streets that are typical of traditional French and Italian villages. It is a sought-after tourist location all throughout the year, but a very calm place in the evening. It also offers approximately 50 small boutiques offering souvenirs, local arts and crafts, as well as charming restaurants with a large selection of regional cuisines. Most inhabitants in this district consider this aspect as a significant advantage to living on 'the rock'.

In the street of Emile-De-Loth, which is in the center of Monaco-Ville, prices of apartments range from 35,000 to 45,000+ Euro per square meter. However, availability of apartments with a beautiful view on either side of the rock is very rare. People who want to invest in Monaco-Ville should be patient to find the property of their dreams and should bear in mind that parking spaces are also very limited in the area.

According to real estate professionals, one must know if the apartment that you are purchasing is under the Monégasque "Sous le loi 1291", because this law stipulates the amount in which you can charge to rent out your apartment. Therefore, investors should be careful in purchasing an apartment in this district, as most of the apartments in Monaco Ville are under this law (Sous le loi 1291.)

It is also an interesting fact that the two sisters of H.S.H. Prince Albert II of Monaco do not live in the Prince's Palace. H.R.H. Princess Caroline lives in Monaco-Ville at the Villa Clos St Pierre with her family, and H.S.H Princess Stéphanie lives with her family just next door to her sister's home at Villa Clos Saint-Martin.

Monte-Carlo

No doubt, Monte-Carlo is the most prestigious district in Monaco, home to the Place du Casino, famous hotels, and it contains the largest concentration of luxury stores such as the Metropole Shopping Centre.

Since 1870, during the reign of Charles III, Monte-Carlo has been considered the principal residential and resort area of Monaco, which includes the famous Monte-Carlo Casino and Hotel de Paris among other landmarks.

The most famous and most expensive area inside Monte-Carlo is the "Carré d'Or/Golden Square" which was founded in the middle of the 19th century by Prince Charles III, this district is known as having the most expensive real estate in Monaco.

It is very rare to find an apartment for less than 52,000 Euro per square meter in this area. In some renowned buildings such as the Mirabeau, the Floralies, the Park Palace, the Sun Tower, or the Monte-Carlo Star, the price per square meter is much higher.

Due to Monte-Carlo's historical prestige, it remains the "investors" first choice in finding an apartment to purchase.

Close to the Hermitage Hotel is the "Boulevard de Suisse." This boulevard is composed of beautiful villas that have a wonderful view of the castle and sea.

A typical villa at the Boulevard de Suisse can easily exceed 90,000,000 Euro in selling price. This boulevard also includes modern constructions such as the "Saint André"; unfortunately, there are only a few apartments in "Saint André" that have a sea view. This factor can be a significant inconvenience when seeking property in such an expensive price range. On the other hand, this building has a prestigious location and luxurious facilities, and it is only few minutes' walk to the heart of Monaco. It also includes several levels of parking, which is at a premium in Monaco.

Monte-Carlo has various styles of constructions; the 'Boulevard des Moulins' is composed of various bourgeois-style buildings, and the price of apartments here is more affordable than the apartments located in the "Carre d'Or." The reason behind the affordability in this area is because there are very few apartments that have a panoramic view, and many residents do not take advantage of their terrace because of the noise generated from the street below.

The "Boulevard des Moulins" is also one of the main streets in Monaco and is highly frequented because of the presence of various stores and activities in the neighborhood, and residents are well located for daily shopping and have easy access to Larvotto and the Casino.

Larvotto is one of the wards of Monte-Carlo, built in the 1960s, and located on the east side of Monaco.

Larvotto and Larvotto Beach is often seen on Monaco postcards, with its beachfront properties, immediate proximity to the beaches, Jimmy'z, the Grimaldi Forum, waterfront restaurants and bars, makes this an extremely popular area when renting or purchasing a property in Monaco.
This area is mainly composed of modern buildings of a relatively high standard. Among others, here you will find 21 Princesse Grace, the Vallespir, the Columbia, and slightly back from the sea front, the Florestan.

The core problem for potential investors looking for an apartment on "Princess Grace Avenue" is the limited number of buildings that are available for sale. The only two apartment buildings that an investor can purchase in are "La Reserve" and "21 Princess Grace."

In the La Reserve residence, the price per square meter is approximately 60,000 euro per square meter and can even reach upwards of 90,000 euros per square meter for apartments with a beautiful panoramic view of the sea.

Most of the properties in Larvotto are privately owned and managed by the Pastor Group, and many apartments in this area are only available for rental purposes. There is a large demand for these apartments because of the beautiful view and their location, which is very close to the beach.

Although the "21 Princess Grace" does not benefit from a total sea view because of its location in front of the "Grimaldi Forum", this residence remains one of the most expensive apartments in Monaco. When apartments become available in this building, the prices range between 42,000 and 90,000 Euro per square meter.

The main complexity when looking for an apartment in the highly demanded district of Larvotto is the scarcity of apartments. People who desire to live close to the Larvotto district generally go to the area of Saint Roman where prices are lower, but accessibility to Larvotto is excellent.

Residents will find they have easy access to Larvotto beaches and the city centre thanks to the various elevators and frequent buses in and around Monaco. The residential buildings with the highest demand are the "Park Saint Roman", "Monte-Carlo Sun" and the "Villas del Sole". In those residences, the prices range per square meter from 38,000 to 45,000 Euro and can even reach 52,000 Euro per sq meter for apartments with a beautiful panoramic view.

One should always take into consideration and check with local advisors if there is any possibility of future construction of new buildings in the neighborhood, because there have been numerous apartments in Monaco that lost their wonderful panoramic view due to a new building construction.
Indeed, the view cannot be guaranteed especially now with the new land extension which will become Monacos new district, Anse du Portier.

As an example, "21 Princesse Grace", an apartment building in Larvotto used to have a great sea view, however due to the Grimaldi Forum construction, the residence's sea view has now been ruined, affecting property prices at the same time.

As an investor or future resident, you can always call the Monaco State "Direction de la prospective de l'urbanisme et de la mobilite" to verify if there is any future construction plans around the building or area in which you are looking to purchase.

La Condamine

The La Condamine district covers the northwest section of Monaco, which includes the port area and the Exotic Garden, known as Jardin Exotique de Monaco.

La Condamine is the oldest commercial quarter of the Principality of Monaco, known for its Condamine market and its various restaurants and stores.

The Le Condamine district is a sought-after area for real estate buyers because of its proximity to the world famous "Formula 1 Grand Prix" track. Good investments in this area would be the apartments with terraces facing the track as well as those that have a straight on view of the port, as prices will nearly always increase per year. Certain buildings in the area like the "Palais Heracles", the "Ermanno Palace" and the "Bristol" give you an exceptional view of the Monaco Grand Prix.

The Port also offers the charm of a quaint shopping district with Rue Grimaldi, with its many local stores, pedestrian area of Rue Princesse Caroline, and the quays at the port with its many bars and restaurants.

As a result, the price per square meter in this district can vary from 38,000 Euro to more than 52,000 Euro per square meter. The most prestigious building in this district is the "Porto Bello" due to its luxurious modern living standards, however, buildings that are behind the Boulevard Albert 1st are less expensive, mainly because they do not benefit from a view of the port or the Formula 1 track.

The Ruscino, located on the "Quai Antoine 1st", is a very pleasant building with an exceptional location on Port Hercules; prices in this building are much more affordable compared to that of other buildings located on the port. This building also benefits from a panoramic view that adds strength to its apartments and resale value.

Going up from the Port is the La Condamine district of Laso, where the Princess Grace Hospital is located as well as the Exotic Garden area. Beautiful buildings such as the Ligures, the Patio Palace and the Harbour Light Palace offer a panoramic view over Monaco and the sea.

This district can be one the most attractive places for the investor or family with a lower investment budget. Moreover, La Condamine offers different construction styles to suit your preferences, from the modern to the Bourgeois style.

Les Moneghetti

Les Moneghetti is located in the northern central border of Monaco; this district is close to the French town of "Beausoleil, France."

Moneghetti is perhaps the least accessible area of the Principality; however, there are interesting apartments that are located on the "Boulevard de Belgique" and "Boulevard Rainier III." For example, the "Eden Tower" which is located in 'Boulevard de Belgique' includes apartments with a very pleasant view of Port Hercules and the rock.

The price per square meter in Moneghetti is lower compared to the rest of Monaco; investors with a lower budget may be interested in this sector.

The "Les Ligures" building for example offers an excellent residence because it offers a variety of advantages for people who are willing to live a short distance away from the center of Monaco, these apartments have a nice view, offer larger size apartments, sport facilities and parking access.

Fontvieille

Fontvieille is located in the western part of Monaco and this district covers 22 hectares reclaimed from the sea in the 1970s.

In 1905, a brewery, flour-mill and a chocolate plant among other industries were located in Fontvieille. Today, Fontvieille is home to the Stade Louis II, heliport, shopping centre, main industries and a marina.

Fontvieille is a very dynamic area and known for being the industrial and commercial hub of Monaco. Furthermore, it is a residential district that provides a very high-quality standard of buildings such as the "Seaside Plaza". One significant advantage of properties in Fontvieille is the large size of apartments compared to the older building constructions in other districts around Monaco.

Inhabitants in this area are in walking distance to the Carrefour supermarket and sport facilities in the Louis II Stadium. In addition, inhabitants who own a yacht may have the opportunity to base their boat in the port of Fontvieille, providing easy access from their apartment.

In Monaco, the calculation of an apartment's area also includes the area of the outdoor terrace. Prices of apartments located in the centre of Fontvieille range from 36,000 to 48,000 Euro per square meter, and apartments located on the harbour with a sea view can easily reach 50,000 to 90,000 Euro per square meter.

Insider tip: Fontvieille is home to Monaco's only Heliport, noise caused by the frequent flights of helicopters needs to be considered when you are looking in this district. The most luxurious apartment buildings in this district is the "Terrace du Port" and "Seaside Plaza".

The new district: Anse du Portier

The upcoming new district, Anse du Portier, also known as Portier Cove, is the real estate future of Monaco and it will be finished by 2025. The aim is to accommodate up to 1,000 residents.

Monaco was always a symbol of luxury and success, and even in the great global recession and economic crisis of the year 2008, the Principality of Monaco maintained this status. Thanks to its national and international effort, Monaco's population is continuously growing as more and more residents are coming to the Principality each year.

With Monaco being the second smallest country in the world right after Vatican City and with more than 39,000 people in its 1.98 km^2 territory, it has generated a housing crisis where demand outweighed the supply.

To answer a growing need, the Princely government decided to extend the borders of the country by reclaiming 60,000 m^2 of new land (6.5 hectares) located in the waters just off the Grimaldi Forum and Avenue Princesse Grace.

This extension will increase the Principality's size by 3%, featuring 120 luxury apartments, 10 over-the-top villas, a seaside promenade extending to Monte-Carlo Beach. The new district will also have a new port inspired by the Pritzker Prize-winning architect Renzo Piano.

The first steps were taken back in 2016 with the removal of the protected marine species, which were carefully relocated into nearby natural reserves. This crucial step was taken to ensure the project did not disturb or damage the coastal ecosystem. This extremely complex project required very careful planning; however, the government and the town's representatives unanimously approved the land extension.

As it is today almost half of the 18 concrete caissons are in place. It is interesting to mention that each concrete caisson weighs 11,000 tons.

Monaco's new sustainable development will offer new high-end luxury standards to its residents, with new apartments planned for over 700 people, and when completed, Monaco's residents will be able to enjoy the new district with all its urban developments, including housing, shops, a 30-berth marina and beautiful garden areas.

This two billion Euro project with its extension out to the sea will have a major impact on the social landscape and will forever change the topography of the Principality of Monaco.

Monaco and France have always worked hand in hand throughout history, and France often provided protection for the population of this modest country. This French-Monégasque relationship was built on strategic pillars, and due to its location between the borders of Italy and France, Monaco always played an important strategic role.

However, we must emphasise that the Principality of Monaco is not a French country or a French territory. There are many differences between the two cultures even if they share some of the social backgrounds and economic aspects. The sea and the surrounding mountains are natural boundaries that protect Monaco from many external influences. Therefore, it became a natural decision to extend out towards the sea, and remain independent from France and Italy.

In addition, the famous Grimaldi Forum, home of some of the most important conferences in The new waterfront promenade will provide a spectacular view to the Rock and to Monte-Carlo.

It is luxury and business mixed together, this two billion Euro project is to be completed at no cost to Monaco, since this new district is entirely financed by the private sector.

All these efforts show that the Monégasque Government will continue to fulfil the needs of its residents and find a balanced solution for everyone.

However the Government had a good proof of concept due to its reclamation efforts in the 1970s. Prince Rainier III "the builder prince", built the industrial Fontvieille neighbourhood on nearly 10 acres that contained only Mediterranean water. Back then it was a 20% increase on the size of the Principality of Monaco, compared to the present project which adds only 3% to the current size of Monaco.

Monaco recently become home to the world's most expensive penthouse in the Tour Odeon, the price, a staggering estimated 300 million Euro, most probably the new sea-front villas may reach similar price-heights.

It is also notable to mention that the new district, the Anse du Portier is a major part of H.S.H. Prince Albert II's plan of transitioning the Principality of Monaco into a carbon-neutral country by 2050.

For example, the district will follow a pedestrian-only design, with such sustainable features as e-bike stations and rainwater recovery systems. 40% of the energy consumption will derive from photovoltaic solar energy panels and thermal pumps, which will use the temperature of the sea to control heating and cooling systems, as well as power 80% of the street lighting.

Why to work with a real estate broker

It is almost impossible to make a real estate transaction without a real estate agency in the Principality of Monaco. There are multiple reasons for this, starting from the privacy of the owners through the legal aspects. For this reason and unlike in many other countries, in Monaco one cannot save money on the agency fees. The smartest choice is to convert this to one's own advantage, since one will pay an agency fee anyway.

If you are interested to buy or rent a property in Monaco, I would definitely suggest for you to find a motivated real estate broker. A good broker represents many benefits for you and can help you to make educated choices. However, a great broker can also find you special off-market properties and they have a fiduciary responsibility to their clients.

I would also highlight that a qualified real estate broker will have unparalleled knowledge of the Monaco property market, including the buying and selling trends. This experience will make it easier to determine all the information necessary for the property sale or purchase. They have intimate knowledge about Monaco and its surrounding area, and they know exactly what to look for, what are the key factors. Without them you might identify a value of a property incorrectly.

In the past 10 years hundreds of people have approached me for recommendations of real estate companies in Monaco. I tried to work with some of the actors in Monaco, even with Monegasque owned agencies. However, I often experienced a lack of motivation and willingness to advice if the size of the deal was small. Make no mistake, everyone is excited for the 100 million Euro purchase deal, but they are not necessarily motivated by small rentals.

A typical problem in the Principality of Monaco is that there are way too many real estate agencies, over 150 actors for a tiny 1.98 km² territory. Yet, plenty of them are just waiting for the one big fish per year. If you think about it, they are entitled with a minimum of 3%

commission. In the world's most expensive real estate market, a single real estate sale - let's say in average of 10 million Euro - already brings them an incredible 25,000 Euro/month income.

Luckily enough, over the past years, I have found some really good people around me and one of them is Maya Ivdra. She is an amazingly enthusiastic real estate broker, working for Monaco-Villas.

MONACO VILLAS

REAL ESTATE

Monaco Villas

2 Avenue St Laurent
98000 Monaco

www.monaco-villas.com

What I appreciate in her and the reason why I would recommend this agency, is because even if they are specialised in villas, they always appreciate the small leads as well. They have very good people skills, and they understand that people might upgrade their properties in the future.

What also makes a real estate broker great, is that they are able to listen and identify the independent needs, since each client has his or her own demands and tastes. When I work with Maya for instance, she always pays close attention to details, maintains the confidentiality and does her best to find the best property in Monaco. These are the qualities that you should look for in a real estate broker in Monaco.

Before you underestimate the value of a real estate broker, think about this: they have a wide network, which can be handy no matter whether you are buying or selling. If you want to buy a property in Monaco, they might provide you with properties that you would otherwise not see. If you wish to sell, the network of the real estate broker can provide you with pre-qualified prospective buyers, who are already searching for similar property deals. You should never underestimate the power of connections, especially if your own financial decision depends on it.

How to rent an apartment

The demand is high, the supply is low and the competition is extremely large. This is the way how I would summarise the real-estate market of Monaco.

The Principality has over a hundred registered and active real-estate agencies in a market where usually you cannot find fifty free apartments for rent at the same time. Therefore, the real estate agencies have huge competition.

You can also observe that you can find the exact same property offers in the supply of many agencies. It is a fact that Monaco has a common real estate database, therefore many real estate agencies are extremely limited with exclusive offers.

One of the number one rules when you are aiming to rent an apartment is that you have to be quick with your decision. Since an apartment is offered for rent by multiple agencies, it is always good to make your decision on the spot. Usually, one week thinking time is enough to take the opportunity. This might not be true for purchasing a property however it definitely rules for rentals.

In the Principality, rentals are offered with a quarterly payment. This means you have to pay always three months in advance every quarter of the year. Furthermore, when you sign a rental contract you are obliged to pay three months deposit to your new landlord and another ten percent of the annual rental fee as an agency fee. So, facing the cruel reality, we can say that any rental agreement starts with an in advance rental fee of over seven months based on the following calculation:

> 3 months rental fees as deposit payment
> 3 months rental fee for the first quarter
> 1,2 months (10% of the annual fee) as agency fee

Of course, it is a much better offer than I experienced few years ago, when I met with agencies that requested two months of agency fees. Nowadays, the 10% (of the annual rent) agency fee is a common base for most of the real estate professionals.

The rental price is always a very important issue because it can change dramatically after the expiration of your lease contract. The owners can have full right to dictate the rental fees.

Always try to negotiate a fixed price for the upcoming three years, otherwise, you might have unexpected and sometimes unrealistic rental fee increases.

On the free market after the expiration of your lease contract the landlord has the free possibility to change and overrule the conditions. It is always recommended to have a minimum three years of rental agreements to protect your interest and to avoid an unexpected surprise.

If you are coming with friends to the Principality of Monaco, you have to take into consideration that based on the usual practice, you have to have one bedroom for each person in order to successfully apply for your residence permit. Another very important thing to consider is to be very careful with the shared apartments because it can happen that the residence permit will not be issued for all the tenants.

Obviously when you are relocating with your family you can share the bedroom with your wife but if you have children then you need to provide an individual bedroom for them. I know friends with a child under one year, where one bedroom apartment was accepted, but there was a black and white warning that the apartment had to be upgraded in the next year. Monaco is very sensitive regarding the living space and this is an important consideration when they issue the residency permit for you.

Before you sign any kind of rental lease be sure that you have checked the related legislations of the apartment you have chosen. The real estate market in Monaco is not always based on the rule of the common market. In many cases, there are different laws applying, which are not always flexible for the owners. This could ensure you more leverage for the negotiation of your rental conditions.

In many cases, when the apartment is regulated by law, the owner does not have the usual freedom during the rental period. Do not forget that by becoming a resident in the Principality of Monaco, you can enjoy its protective philosophy.

It can happen that the landlord is obliged to rent to you his/her apartment for up to six years, while you have the freedom of choice to terminate your lease agreement at the end of every year. Therefore, the law supports you and secures your living environment. In situations like this, the only chance for the landlord to terminate your contract after the expiration of the first lease period is if he/she can prove that the apartment is needed for living for his/her family and they have no other solutions within their other resources.

Rental contracts can be tricky...

After the expiration of your lease contract, the landlord has the free possibility to change and overrule the conditions, so it is always recommended to have a minimum three-year agreement to protect your interest and to avoid any unexpected surprises.

In addition, it is highly important to read your contract very carefully. It might happen that you need to leave your apartment during significant events, such as the Monaco Grand Prix or the Monaco Yacht Show. It is an unfortunate practice that many landlords prefer to rent out their apartment for these major events for a radically increased price. This means that even if you have an annual rental agreement, you could be forced out for a Grand Prix weekend. It is a very challenging situation where strangers could use all your furniture and personal belongings. To avoid this, you always need to re-check the mostly French contract.

Also, of important note is that some of the apartments can be used as your business address during the first two years, however, not every apartment is accepted by the Government for this purpose. The apartments allowed for business use are usually labelled as "Mixed Usage" or as "Usage Mixte".

Usage mixte

Few years ago, I aimed to find an apartment with the purpose of establishing a business office. In Monaco, you have the possibility to use the same apartment where you live for business purposes as well during the first two years. This is what they call "Usage mixte".

I asked the agency to create a clausal in the rental agreement, whereby I was able to immediately quit from the contract without any payment obligations in case the Economic deportment refused the business usage of the apartment for any reason.

The agency kindly informed me that of course it is possible to request this condition from the owner, but it is never possible to request it from the agency. In the moment that I sign the contract I am still obliged to pay their agency fee even if the real estate agency has offered me a useless apartment for my original purpose. For obvious reasons, I did not take this risk.

Since then I know that "Usage mixte" highly depends on the landlord as well, especially when you have a newly formed business. Based on regulations you are not allowed to welcome visitors if the apartment is used as a living space as well. Therefore, since you cannot welcome visitors, it is just a written acknowledgement from the landlord that you use his/her apartment for a company address as well.

How to buy/sell an apartment

Buying or selling an apartment in the Principality of Monaco often requires a guided decision. In most of the cases, it is important to work with the right real estate partner who is more client-oriented rather than transaction-oriented.

Unfortunately, in Monaco some agencies focus only on their bonuses and forget the best and long-term interests of their own clients. It happened to my friend who bought an apartment in Monaco. The transaction driven real estate agency forgot to tell him that from the next year on there would be construction next door. It brought loud noises, destroyed the view and also will decreased the future value of the property. Ouch… Yes, it was the fault of my friend because he did not do his homework properly. When you make your decision to invest into a multi-million Euro apartment, do not rely on one source only and learn from others' mistake. Convert it to your advantage.

By working with a good partner, you can easily identify and estimate the market value of your property, which is not always equal to the emotional value that you might prefer to obtain. I believe that a good real estate partner who really represents you is able to negotiate the best possible conditions for you and your budget, which will definitely respond to the demand of the current market.

The real estate agencies in Monaco usually work for an average of 3% intermediary fee from the buyer and a further 5% from the seller. When you enter into a business relationship with an agency make sure that you phrase the intermediary fee as a success fee. The wording could be important for you.

In some cases when a buyer or a seller steps back and he/she refuses to sign the final contract, the agencies will still ask for their intermediary fees. This means that it might happen that you get nothing valuable and you are still obliged to pay a serious amount without any exchange.

In any contract, it is important to see clearly when the real estate agency is entitled to a fee.

Once a friend of mine had an interesting experience from a different angle when he tried to sell his own apartment through a local real-estate agent. The agency successfully found him a person who was interested to purchase the property. They signed the contract whereby the buyer ensured a ten percent deposit payment and the buyer aimed to find a financing solution for the rest of the balance during a mutually agreed timeframe. Unfortunately, the buyer could not manage the financing, and therefore the deal was terminated. The interesting part was that even if the agency could not close the deal, or provide the right buyer for my friend, they were ready to charge the three percent fee from the total price of the property.

Therefore, whether you buy or sell real estate in the Principality, it is always good to agree on the success fee. And by definition, success fee means that the real estate agency provides a prospect and closes the deal. The importance is on the closing; do not pay for intentions or unclosed deals. A real estate deal should be considered closed when the beneficiary has received the full exchange for his/her property.

Tips for buying

Despite most of the European real estate markets, in the Principality of Monaco, real estate agents and property owners do not prefer negotiations. Since Monaco is in the unique position that its real estate prices have been continuously growing during the last decades, there is no place for negotiations. When you purchase a property in Monaco you can be almost hundred percent sure that its value will rise even in a short-medium period.

Tip: Before signing any commitment always check the city development plans because a new building or construction could affect the aesthetic and material value of your property investment. It might happen that the agency has forgotten to present you the long-term value of your specific apartment.

Once you have found your ideal property, which clearly matches all your criteria, you can start the acquisition process. Usually in Monaco, the acquisition process is a combination of four steps:

1. Purchasing offer
2. Final offer
3. Commitment
4. Notarised agreement

Step 1. Purchasing offer

When you have made your final decision and have chosen the property, it is your time to place your initial purchasing offer. It is a common real estate practice in Monaco that no negotiation process starts without a written purchasing offer from the prospective buyer.

In most of the cases, real estate agencies do not forward verbal offers or negotiations to the property owners. You might have a possibility to create a verbal negotiation, but for this the reason has to be a very special circumstance.

Once you have placed your purchasing offer, always ask for a written delivery confirmation from the real estate agency. This way you will have a legally enforceable commitment from the agency and can also gain time to revisit and reconsider the conditions.

Step 2. Final offer

Once your initial purchasing offer – with all its details and concerned goods – is interesting for the owner you will have the first opportunity for negotiation. During this period, you have to define all the purchasing terms, especially the terms related to the payment conditions such as the timing of the acquisition.

Step 3. Commitment

Once the offer is acceptable for both parties, the good faith of the buyer must be confirmed by a deposit payment. In most cases, the deposit payment does not exceed the ten percent of the final purchasing price.

The deposit down payment is used to demonstrate the serious intent of the buyer, therefore, all the deposit is collected by a Monaco-based notary.

In order to proceed further, the buyer is also obliged to pay the legal fees of the notary, which is six percent of the final purchasing price. Therefore, any purchasing intent must involve a minimum of sixteen percent of the down payment of the final purchasing price.

Usually, this is the point when the seller or buyer (it depends) also receives the invoice for the intermediary commission from the real-estate agent for its intervention. The real estate commission is usually three percent calculated on the final purchasing price. The commission is regulated in the Principality of Monaco, however, it is not declared when the deal can be considered as closed and fulfilled by the real estate agency. It depends on your initial negotiations with the real estate agency.

Furthermore, there is a 19.6 percent commission towards the Real Estate Board of Monaco.

In Monaco, the deposit payments are generally made with a single bank cheque from any bank located in the Principality of Monaco. For the remaining balance, the accepted way is a bank wire-transfer. If the buyer has no bank account in the Principality of Monaco, then the confirmed bank wire transfer is the requested way to proceed further.

The benefit of the bank cheque is that usually the notary never collects the down payment before the signed agreement. Therefore, you do not need to move and allocate your money before there is a finalised legal binding from both parties. However, right after the signed agreement the notary is obliged to collect and allocate the down payment in order to protect the best interest of the seller and to avoid any conflict by an unsecured cheque or even a fake one.

The signed offer to purchase is a very serious commitment, a document that has a legal value in the Principality of Monaco. It is highly recommended to find an advisor to accomplish every act dealing which such a purchase, particularly in view of the fact that this is a several million Euro operation.

The accepted and signed offer is a firm commitment for both parties. In case the buyer withdraws its intent from the final transaction, the seller will be entitled to its deposit cheque.

Once the commitment is signed, the only possibility for the buyer to get back the bank cheque is if the seller fails to fulfil his/her conditions on the purchasing agreement. In these rare cases, the Principality of Monaco protects the buyer, by asking the notary to force the seller to pay an extra compensation to the buyer, which is usually the same amount as the ten percent of deposit payment. Therefore, it is more convenient for the seller to go through the actual sale process instead of stepping back.

Step 4. Notarised agreement

The purchasing process usually ends with a formalised agreement notarised by a Monaco-based notary. The final agreement is usually more detailed than the previous offers and commitments.

Since the notary is a public officer of the State, his sealing gives a guarantee of authenticity for the purchase.

In this step, both parties testify when they have to express their will and liability to fulfil all the content of the final purchasing contract. Once it is signed and notarised, this document will protect the buyer by stating the date for the hand over. From this time on, the buyer becomes the new owner.

The final payment is usually performed after this notarised agreement.

Tips for sellers

Selling a property might sound easy compared to purchasing one, but still it is a much more detailed process than just hiring a real-estate agent. Selling real estate involves a kind of marketing process where many things depend on how you are able to present your property to the prospective buyers.

In most cases a prospective buyer has many decision criteria. Even if your property is located in the perfect spot in Monaco, you still have to be sure that you or the real estate agency utilises all its potential.

You need to identify the best visiting hours for the exposure with the optimum lighting. You also have to consider the timing from the point of view of the traffic and the possible disturbing noises. It is always important to let the real estate agency know about the preferred timings.

Obviously be sure that when the exposure happens, the property is in the best possible condition. By this, meaning it will be clean and freshly ventilated.

It could be considered a major selling point if your property is empty. By overwhelming an apartment with furniture, artwork and various decorations, you can limit the imagination of the prospective buyer. People love to identify their own personalities in a new living space they are aiming to purchase.

Therefore, it is not considered helpful if your apartment is still rented out and used by someone you cannot influence. Usually it is very difficult to showcase these types of apartment.

Furthermore, for a successful sale be sure you have the following documents:

- » Certificate of ownership
- » Floor plan of the apartment
- » Proof of annual charges
- » Proof of previous or future renovations

By having these basic documents, you can support the activity of the real estate agency which is your mutual interest.

But selling an apartment and finding the prospective buyer does not mean that the job is done. Unfortunately, it can happen that a buyer is not able to provide the full selling price after the agreed deadline. Therefore, your legal protection can be a very important priority.

It can happen that a buyer fails in the total payment and he/she writes to the three notaries of Monaco to block the situation pretending in bad face to be a victim of some bad misleading. Various excuses could come up in order to get back his/her down payment, and they can try all kinds of possibilities for contestation. Cases usually follow in court.

As regulated and easy it seems, the selling process does not always go in order to the expectations. In many cases there are people who purchase or deposit a property in order to quickly resell it for an increased price, and to gain some extra profit. It is a type of investment gambling. These types of speculations often lead to the failure of the final payment after the agreed period, which is usually six months, but often can go up to a year with high-value properties.

When you sign a deal, do not rely only on the real estate agency, dare to ask for legal advice from any Avocats-Défenseur in the Principality of Monaco. They can secure and care for your best interest and in case of suspicious events, they have all the legal power to block someone from selling the real estate or to make any further benefit from it.

Be aware of real estate gamblers

Whether you buy or sell a property in the Principality of Monaco, you must be very careful with the "commitments". If you do not clearly define when the real estate agency is entitled for its fee, you can face some very unpleasant surprises.

There are foreigners just like in any other city in the world doing investment gambling in Monaco. It typically happens when you list your property for sale and someone shows an interest.

For example, they are ready to place a deposit on the property (generally, this is when the real estate agencies immediately take their 3% fees on the total selling price). However, the supposed buyer may not have a great interest to buy the apartment because he or she is a real estate gambler, whereby they aim to resell the booked and deposited apartment within the allowed 6 months' timeframe, which is their legal right; there is nothing against this in the Monégasque law.

However, if a new buyer has not been engaged in the 6 months, you can be faced with the situation that they ask you for the refund of the deposit. This means you not only have lost a buyer and over 6 months of selling time, but you also paid 3% for your real estate agent for nothing.

You may also face a similar situation when the buyer is not financially able to afford the property. The buyer will aim to find a financing solution for the rest of the balance during the mutually agreed timeframe. Unfortunately, if the buyer cannot manage the financing you might have already paid your success fee to your real estate agent for the unsuccessful deal.

Real estate mortgage

Real estate mortgage is a highly important financial service in the Principality of Monaco since its lifestlye, the political and economic landscape are all attracting the high net worth (HNW) and ultra-high net worth (UHNW) individuals.

One would assume that the wealthy never takes a mortgage, but that is not so. Generally speaking most of the Monaco residents do not need a loan, however wealthy people like to increase their wealth by making smart decisions. Paying in full for a multi million euro worth property is not necessarily a smart idea. It can result in having one's money stacked there forever. Instead, most wealthy people prefer liquidity, since utilising part of their cash flow can bring them much more results.

Addressing the liquidity challenges in 2020/2021 will be also among the key factors in the real estate sector of the Principality of Monaco. Many businesses were influenced by the Coronavirus pandemic, and despite the government aids, short term liquidity problems can arise.

We often have conversations with Olivier Milliex, the owner of OMYS Consulting, a regulated mortgage provider in South of France and his wife Maya Ivdra, from Monaco Villas about the importance of real estate financing and re-financing in Monaco as well as in all close locations on the Cote d'Azur where many Monaco residents own secondary homes.

OMYS Consulting

contact@omys-consulting.com
www.omys-consulting.com

First of all mortgages in Monaco have historically low interest rates, which motivate many people to remortgage or restructure their borrowings. Basically, by converting one's mortgage to free up liquidity for personal or business commitments can assist with short-term liquidity problems, and it can immediately increase the cash flow.

There is also a great demand for and more people are looking towards second charge mortgages and bridging finances. These allow the owners to use additional collateral and equity in their properties in order to almost immediately release capital.

When I work with Olivier he has this "four steps" method he uses.

1., Identifying property type & eligibility

It is important to highlight that just as you have a special taste when you choose your home, banks and lenders are also picky on where they put their money.

In the Principality of Monaco the typically accepted properties are the standalone villas and the large apartments. However, mortgage is not limited to private homes, you can use it with mixed-use buildings and high-end retail spaces, such as boutique spaces. This can significantly help entrepreneurs to have an additional cash-flow when their business needs it.

2., Understanding client needs

As easy as it sounds, getting a loan is much more complicated. There are countless opportunities for owners, based on what they really need.

Just a few examples are the amortizing loan, interest only loan, remortgage, second charge mortgage, bridging, short-term finance, commercial lease, business loan, overdrafts and many more others.

There is always a comprehensive range of efficient financial products available.

3., Choosing the right financial instrument

Understanding one's specific needs can help to identify the right financial instruments. Also it is always important to look for the most competitive lender for the project.

A good partner can always lift the stress from one's shoulder by helping them to draft the credit and compliance memorandums, and to negotiate with the credit committee until the final decision. At the end of the day financial advisors can speak the same "language" as the lenders.

4., Structuring a turn-key solution

High-end asset optimization and finance never stops by drafting the application. Financial advisors can help to coordinate with all relevant third parties to structure the transaction and advise the client until final implementation and drawdown of funds.

At the end of the day if you decide to look for real estate financing in Monaco, I would suggest to look for someone who provides accurate, timely, high quality analysis and advice. This can be highly important because along the road you might face various challenges which they can help you address, or even better, to anticipate.

A good financial advisor can support one's needs with instant property value comparables and they can mitigate any issues, which may arise during the process.

Always be upfront and transparent with your financial advisors. Many people make the mistake that they "forget" to mention that their deal was already presented to banks and might be rejected. If your financial advisor does not know about this, then it can happen that the same request will be presented again to a bank, which can create a negative taste. By being transparent from the very beginning, you can achieve more. Just trust the skillset of your financial advisor.

You should never forget that the Principality of Monaco is a "village", a face-to-face type of world where everyone knows everyone. In this specific market a well-connected financial advisor can seal the deal for you.

Also, I consider as a key factor in every business area, that the selected partner has to be involved and able to advise through the whole process of acquisition and finance. One should never be satisfied with a partial solution. Always look for someone who is there for you all the way along, from the start until the finish line.

165

Postes
Distributeur
de billets
La Poste Monaco

CHAPTER 6

Administration

Opening a bank account

Once you have decided to relocate to the Principality of Monaco, you will have to open a local bank account. In many cases opening a bank account is the very first step that foreign people take. It can be a very obvious choice because without (an employment contract or) the proof that you have enough funds to live in the territory of Monaco, you have no chance to successfully apply for a residence permit.

Monaco's banking and financing sectors offer you an estimated forty banks and another fifty wealth managers, family offices and financial advisors. They are managing together a fund, which is almost 100 billion Euro.

Banks (institutions entitled to receive all types of deposits)	2010	2011	2012	2013	2014
Companies under Monegasque Law	18	18	18	18	18
Branches of banks with headquarters abroad	4	4	4	4	4
Special status institutions	1	1	1	1	1
Branches of French banks	13	13	13	12	12
Branches of French foreign-controlled banks	0	0	0	0	0
Total	36	36	36	35	35

What is interesting is that even if Monaco offers almost hundred banks, wealth managers and family offices, very few of them are empowered to receive all types of deposits. Therefore, if you need a specific deposit service in the future, then it is always better to make a pre-check before you choose and commit yourself to a bank.

Financial corporations	2010	2011	2012	2013	2014
Financial companies under Monegasque Law	1	1	1	1	1
Branches of French financial corporations	2	2	2	2	2
Total	3	3	3	3	3

It is also good to know that all licensed banks in the Principality of Monaco, as well as the fund and portfolio manager companies belong to the Monégasque Association of Financial Services, which is a member of the European Banking Federation. Therefore, Monaco is in the Eurozone and SEPA (Single Euro Payments Area).

All the members of the Monégasque Association of Financial Services are subject to regular supervising. These supervisions take place of course with the highest confidentiality to secure the undisturbed operation of the Monégasque banking establishments. They happen in order to protect the residents and the investors' best interest.

Monegasque mutual investment funds	2010	2011	2012	2013	2014
Number	61	59	60	62	64
Net assets (in billion euros)	5.11	4.60	4.98	5.05	4.62

For many years now the Principality of Monaco has taken serious steps and an active fight against money laundering, corruption and terrorists financing. These steps often reach international levels as well.

The Principality of Monaco has also created its own Financial Investigation Unit, called S.I.C.C.FIN (Service d'Information et de Contrôle sur les Circuits Financiers). The S.I.C.C.FIN works together on an international level with more than 130 countries around the globe. It has a role to suspend financial transactions carried out by professionals who are subject to legal matters.

This special attention and care helps Monaco to develop and modernise its banking system and its whole financial sector. It supports practices and quality standards, which are globally recognised by all European financial centres.

Is the amount really important?

No, it is not. Or let's say, there is flexibility in the system.

Most banks and wealth managers prefer the big accounts whereby they can offer more services, but you should not make your decision based on the requested opening amount. Furthermore you should never allow the wealth manager to control you because they need you much more than the other way around.

One of the most important thing to consider is how the banks can serve your best interest in the Principality. At this point, the amount is irrelevant since even if you have a small amount of funds, you can open a bank account starting at 150,000 Euro. (Despite that, The Association Monégasque Des Activités Financières or AMAF association in Monaco recommends that its members ask for a minimum deposit of 500,000 Euro)

However, if you need a custom-tailored wealth management service and/or some independent investment advisor team, perhaps you will look for a different level starting from the AMAF recommended 500,000 Euro.

I would also consider whether you need a bank, a wealth manager company or a small family office. They all can co-operate together to assist you but from your own perspective, it could be a key question which one has the power of attorney to your assets.

The most important for you is to find the right partner which is able to fulfil your needs. Do not be afraid to look around and get an impression from the possible banks. If you have a few days in Monaco, you can do a little "window shopping" to compare the possibilities and gain a first-hand impression. Believe me, you will find a great contrast between the beautiful new offices and the super small and not so fancy ones. It is worth it to have a look before you commit, because the environment you choose can have large implications.

You will also see that once you are considered by the bank as an important partner, the amount will never be important again. In many banks, you can also create good bargains by renegotiating their conditions. Do not forget that even if they will never admit it publicly that they really need you since you are the client. Additionally, I would add that they know that your savings account is probably much higher than a standard commercial account.

As a final advice and as insider knowledge, please note that most of the banks and wealth managers are obliged to publicly disclose their financial results.

For example, on MonacoWealthManagement.com the members have a chance to compare the published results of multiple Monaco-based financial actors and to see which of them has gained profit and those who continuously lose the funds of their clients.

They love you for your money (personal story)

When I arrived in Monaco, I spent my first weeks in the Hotel Monaco Port Palace, which has an amazing view of the Port Hercule. It was a very small hotel, but I loved every minute there. The hotel is basically a seaside, one just in front of the port, and you have the feeling that you can almost reach the super-yachts from your room. It is a superb feeling. Anyway, I chose the hotel because I wanted to find an apartment locally from Monaco and not from Germany via Internet without even seeing it.

On my second morning at the hotel, I asked the concierge whether he could suggest a bank for me or not. He simply replied to me without even answering my question:

- "Just be aware of the Crocodiles."

It was a little bit unusual as an answer and spooky for me so I immediately tried to understand his point.

- "Why? Is there a blacklist?"
- "Every bank is good in Monaco, but you have to be careful before you make your decision," he continued in his own mystical way.

I was not in the mood to play so I closed this conversation with him very quickly.

- "Ok. Then wish me good luck," I smiled at him.

On my way out through the main door, I started to think about how incredible it was that the only suggestion he could give me was that I will probably meet some crocodiles.

I was always aware that the Principality offers more than one hundred banks and wealth managers in a less than two km2 territory, which probably causes big competition fights among the institutions. However, I also believe that the key for a long-lasting business relationship is the ability to build it up in an ethical and trustworthy way.

So, I went to the very first bank not far from the Hotel Monaco Port Palace. After entering the building, I have to admit that I was really impressed.

I went to the front office and I told the receptionist that I was there to open a bank account. She was really nice, and even if I had no pre-arranged appointment she organised me the possibility to meet with one of their client representatives.

After a few minutes of waiting a young man came out of the door:

- "Good morning," he greeted me.
- "Good morning."
- "I heard that you are aiming to open a new bank account. How can I help you, sir?"
- "Yes, that is my aim," I confirmed back his information and meanwhile he escorted me to one of their meeting room.
- "Okay. The minimum amount is one million Euro to open a bank account in our branch," he started immediately.

His answer for me was quite to the point and surprising in the same time. Basically, he did not even introduce his bank or offer me a glass of water. However, since I was already there I was keen to know the rules so I went along with his game.

- "I understand," I replied to him.
- "Okay. So do you have any questions?"
- "Yes, maybe you could introduce me to your bank," I said to him referring that I am there as a prospective client and not a fool.

Finally, he introduced me to his bank very accurately and also highlighted many of the aspects and benefits of his branch, which were quite impressive. I also really appreciated that he highlighted an extremely important thing, which was their customer care. He mentioned that their bank has an impressive ultra-rich client base and they are thrilled to create businesses as intermediaries among their valued clients. I really liked this because I felt that they really take care of their clients' wealth. They are not just putting it on the trade market, but are supporting the business growth as well via their most precious resource, their connection base.

I started to feel very comfortable, and in the meantime my brain was continuously ticking about what the concierge said to me at the Hotel Monaco Port Palace. I could not imagine where the crocodiles were. Maybe I was just lucky to go to the right place. So everything went well so far until the client representative made a mistake.

- "So do you have one million Euro to start an account with us?," he asked me.
- "Yes, I am able to start an account with you," I replied even if I did not like the question, because I felt a little bit of prejudice from his tone.
- "Okay," he said, because if it is a problem then there are other banks that accept smaller amounts as well.

At this point I had to grab on to my chair to avoid falling down because this was an unexpected turn. I was there in their meeting room as a prospective client. Based on his continuous interrogation I confirmed many times that I could be his client and then he offered me another bank? It was a shockingly big mistake but I believe he did not even realise it, he just wanted to be helpful. However, these kinds of helpful gestures could make me question whether I am in the right place or not. So, I could not hold back to ask him further about his bank.

- "Could you tell me how your bank performed in the last years?," I started my question.
- "Yes, of course."

He started to feel that maybe he made a mistake, but he continued.

- "Well as you probably know many banks lost in 2008-2009 during the economic crisis."

It was not the best start from him but I became very curious.

- "However, we are very proud to say that our bank did not lose as much as its competitors, actually we did very impressively," he continued.
- "But you had some losses, right?"
- "Right. But we still performed better than many of our competitors."
It was enough for me to get a full picture of the bank. I was aware

that many banks lost incredible amounts during the economic crisis, but I thought it was a mistake to be proud of not losing as much. I was looking for a bank that stated that they learnt from their mistakes and were working two-hundred percent more to satisfy their clients. I did not really receive this here only the interrogation part for the one million Euro, so I went to the next bank.

At the end of the day, I started to understand what the concierge meant regarding the crocodiles. I realised that most of the client representatives are living a kind of easy going life and they are only going for the fast money, without even understanding the expectations of the prospective clients.

However, it is very important to mention that I had these experiences in 2010-2011, and since then, many years have passed by. So, maybe they have changed and developed towards a more customer oriented service.

For the record, I cannot make any bad comment about the mentioned bank itself because they were really nice, they had a very impressive appearance and without any doubt they are quite good in what they are doing. However, their client representative could not convince me and I think it was a personal mistake to continuously force the one million Euro, and in the meantime to offer me competitor banks and wealth managers. One person's mistake led the bank to lose a prospective client and probably some further mutual benefits.

Suggestion for the right choice

My best suggestion for you is to look for the differences. No matter whether you are looking for a bank, a wealth manager or a family office, you can always find valuable and individual experiences.

When I searched for and visited many banks, I had some very weird experiences such as the previously mentioned one, but I also got great and exceptional ones with good client orientation.
You can find various approaches in the Principality of Monaco from the traditional to the new, modern ones. Many client representatives will take you for fancy dinners, perhaps for clubbing or they will offer you some gifts, invitations to the Formula One, etc... But frankly, you cannot replace a fancy promise, a shiny advertisement with the real-life experience. Furthermore, if your first impression is not convincing, then why would you place your money in that bank?

It happened with a friend of mine that she was invited for a lunch by the assistant vice president of one of the major banks in the Principality. It was a real experience because while the vice president was proud about the long-term results of the bank, the assistant vice president continuously talked about the job cuts. He expressed himself as one of the lucky ones who still had his job. Weird, isn't it? It was not so promising...

Sometimes you can find great contrasts by approaching people from different levels. I always suggest to meet with these people outside of their office environments because in the office they act based on the regulations. When you are outside, you can open up easily anyone and sometimes you can get some small signs and indicators, which can guide you in your decision.

Listen to the whispers, but do not believe in gossip. My advice for you is to start to build up local human relations and look for their personal recommendations and observations. Ask them which banks they prefer and why they chose them.

It is also an interesting fact that many wealthy residents diversify their wealth by using multiple banks. Try to approach them and create a close relationship where you will be able to ask them why they chose their banks and what the individual benefits are. Using their experiences, you can have a more secure choice.

How to register your car

Even if Monaco is a small territory, having a car could be essential for you. Anyone who has a Monégasque ID card or a residence permit can register his/her vehicle in the Principality.

Interestingly, Monaco offers the possibility to register your car even if you are not living in the Principality. If you are not a resident in Monaco but you own a property under your own name, then you are eligible to request the registration of your vehicle in the Principality of Monaco on an annual basis.

The Monégasque vehicle registration plates are unusually smaller than many of the European ones and the plates are a colored blue font on a white background and are composed of four numbers and/or letters. Prior to 1979, the color of the plates was white on blue, without borders.

"Principauté de Monaco" is written at the bottom of the plate and has the Monégasque coat of arms on the left side with the year number (on the rear plate only) to attest that tax has been paid.

All plates starting with '000' belong to the Prince's family and all the rental cars have license plates only prefixed with 'V'.

The registration process is relatively easy, you need to fill out a form called "Demande d'immatriculation d'un véhicule" which is downloadable through the internet or you can personally collect it at the Driver and Vehicle Licensing Office.

By filling out this document, you can go directly to the Driver and Vehicle Licensing Office with your driving license, a valid ID card (or residence permit) and with the official papers of your car.

The process is very easy and an appointment is not necessary, you can simply hand in the file to the Driver and Vehicle Licensing Office.

In most cases, registration plates can be obtained immediately if the car is less than 4 years old or has had the technical inspection.

You can also obtain a custom license plate based on your preference. All you have to do is send a written request with a list of all your preferences. If any of them is available, it will be granted to you.

The registration certificate can be collected normally 72 hours later from the Driver and Vehicle Licensing Office.

In the case that you do not have residency in Monaco, but you own a property, you need to prove that you have a parking space for your car for the period when you are not in the Principality of Monaco. You will also be asked to provide a copy of the latest electricity bill of the property you own in the Monaco territory.

Unless there is no significant change in your living circumstances, you will be eligible to keep and use your license plate.

Insurance

Private insurance can be requested for many purposes during your stay in the Principality of Monaco. The majority of insurance companies offer international health insurance for the territory of the European Union, however, it is recommended to check whether your provider will cover the Principality of Monaco, because Monaco is a country outside of the European Union. You may be required to extend your cover to include Monaco.

For those who are aiming to change insurance, there are some minor things to consider.

The first consideration is whether to use personal insurance, business insurance or a combination of both.

Secondly, make sure you compare the benefits of having European insurance or specific Monégasque insurance; this could be interesting when international health costs apply.

In the case that you are not just relocating, but working as well in the Principality of Monaco, you can find yourself in a much better situation. Monaco offers 80-100% refunds on health care expenditure for employees and their families, since its public welfare system is funded by employers' contributions.

The Monaco Social Security Fund offers Monaco-based employees and employers the "C.S.M." app for tablets and smartphones, which allows them a clear view on their benefits. Once this app is installed on the smartphone of their spouse / children's F.S.E. card (electronic health records), they can benefit from the same services at their medical appointments.

Health Insurance Funds

The Principality of Monaco offers three different health insurance funds:

» Social Services Compensation Fund (Caisse de Compensation des Services Sociaux)

» Social Security Fund for the Self-Employed (Caisse d'Assurance Maladie, Accident et Maternité des Travailleurs Indépendants)

» State Medical Benefits Office (Service des Prestations Médicales de l'État)

Social Services Compensation Fund

The Social Services Compensation Fund known as Caisse de Compensation des Services Sociaux is financed by contributions from employers and calculated based on declared gross salaries within an upper limit.

It provides salaried workers and others covered by the scheme with health, maternity, invalidity and life insurance.

Beneficiaries such as spouses and dependent children who are not entitled to join other insurance schemes and who are residents in the Principality or in France (or in Italy for Monégasque and Italian nationals) are covered for expenses related to sickness and maternity.

The Social Services Compensation Fund provides family and social benefits such as prenatal and family allowances, housing benefit, education allowance, a special allowance for the start of the educational year, an end of year payment, holiday cheques and vouchers for crèches and after school childcare.

Social Security Fund for the Self-Employed

The Social Security Fund for the Self-Employed, known as Caisse d'Assurance Maladie, Accident et Maternité des Travailleurs Indépendants is compulsory for anyone authorized to carry out an artisanal, industrial, commercial or professional activity in the Principality.

It is financed by a flat-rate contribution for each calendar month and payable quarterly in advance.

Other eligible people can benefit from the fund on the condition that they do not qualify for another scheme and are residing in Monaco or France, as can retirees from Monégasque or French schemes for self-employed workers residing in the Principality.

State Medical Benefits Office

The State Medical Benefits Office known as Service des Prestations Médicales de l'État is both a health insurance scheme and family allowance fund for all employees working for the State or the Commune.

Those eligible to benefit from this scheme are:

» Civil servants, other Government or Commune officials, temporary staff and Monégasque students

» Spouses who do not work and dependent children/young people under the age of 21 who attend an educational establishment, are eligible for the social security scheme because of their connection with the insured person

Insurance claims

Even if you have a good insurance policy, bad things can happen in life. It is a general view that dealing with an insurance company can be a real nightmare. Let's face the truth, even if the insurance company accepts the case, the payout is usually way less than the damage itself.

I am not a big fan of insurance companies because I have had some negative experiences in the past. Such was an example when my limited 40th Anniversary Lotus was damaged in an underground garage, without a single witness around, their payout was ridiculous. The damage was very costly, so it seemed to be a more reasonable solution to sell the car.

Did I have an insurance? Yes. Did they cover the cost of reparation? No. They argued that there is no evidence that any third party has damaged my car. At that time their reasoning made me very angry. I was also disappointed because such assets as my car can lose value significantly when they are damaged.

Then life brought me together with a very interesting entrepreneur and long term resident of Monaco. Georgy Chesnokov and his son Nikita Tchesnokov, who are the solution for every insurance nightmare. I just wish that I would have met with Georgy 8 years earlier.

They are professional insurance claim advisors, however their work is based on an entirely different model than most of the companies I have ever dealt with in this sector. Their slogan is: "No Win, No Fee".

www.claimmakers.com

Understanding how stressful the unexpected can be, Claim Makers do not charge you any upfront fees. Moreover, they do not charge you at all if they cannot negotiate you better conditions than your original settlement offer. Basically, they aim to achieve the maximum settlement against your policy.

Whether it is a residential or commercial property claim, yachts, aircraft, or interruption to your business, they can handle your entire case from the beginning to the end, and see you get the fastest and best outcome possible. And the best thing of all is that since they are working on a success fee base, they will recover all possible benefits awarded by your policy. I have seen many success stories with them, even with the most unique assets such as scubas, private jets or superyachts.

They are one of those rare businesses who take over all the stress from your shoulders, in order to create a win-win situation. I wish that you will not have any insurance claim in the future, but if you do have one and you are in Monaco (or UK or USA), then do not forget to approach Georgy or Nikita at Claim Makers. Your life will be much easier. They will help to put your lives back on track without days of unnecessary confusion and anxiety.

Health, welfare and standard of living

The Principality of Monaco does not offer the typical job assistance programs available in many countries. Many people believe that they can come into the country and ask for Government support; however, this type of benefit does not exist in Monaco. Furthermore, if you lose your job and you cannot support your living conditions, your Monaco residence permit will be terminated. However, everything changes when you become a long-term resident.

The health and welfare services are getting increasingly important in the Principality since the average of the residents are in their mid-forties. As we can observe, Monaco's population is getting older, therefore, the health and welfare are coming into focus.

The standard of the health care in the Principality is excellent, the life expectancy in the Principality being one of the highest in the world.

Monaco also carries exceptionally-equipped hospitals and medication centers, and the Principality offers approximately 6 doctors for every 1,000 people.

A public welfare system is funded by employers' contributions and provides 80-100% refunds on health care expenditure for employees, registered self-employed, and their families. All other residents have to take out private health insurance.

There are three medical establishments in the Principality:

» The state-run Princess Grace Hospital (CHPG, Centre Hospitalier Princesse Grace)

» The Monaco Cardio Thoracic Center (CCM)

» The Institut Monégasque de Medecine et Chirurgie Sportive (IM2S), which specialises in sports medicine and surgery.

The Principality also offers homes for the elderly.

How to apply for a job

Looking for a salaried job in the Principality of Monaco is significantly harder than in any other country in Europe. Talent, skills and degrees are not enough to be employed in Monaco, since no foreigner may occupy a private salaried position without Government authorisation.

The Government of Monaco monitors all salaried job positions since having employment in Monaco also could constitute a green light towards the residency permit.

One of the biggest mistake that people commit is the false belief that a Monaco-based job will make you rich instantly. It is a sad fact that in many segments the salaries are not always competitive to the European average. This can be easily observed by the employees' strike at many places such as Hotel de Paris, Hotel Columbus or Carrefour in the previous years.

However, in many sectors Monaco is highly competitive and it allows you to achieve your highest ambitions. Therefore, applying for a Monaco-based job could be one of the most important topics for a foreign resident.

In many cases, it can happen that you, your wife or husband is looking for a job in the Principality to support the family household. However, in Monaco, no foreigner may occupy a private salaried position without government authorisation!

Having a fixed job in Monaco also constitute a green light towards the residency permit, therefore, all the salaried job positions are monitored by the Government of Monaco. No one can start to work unless he/she possesses a work permit.

The work permit is not granted automatically and there are serious employment priority preferences for every open job position, which are meant to protect the local labor force.

The following order of priority is observed:

» People having Monégasque nationality

» Foreigners married to a Monégasque woman and not legally separated and foreigners born to a Monégasque parent

» Foreigners living in Monaco who have already held a job there

» Foreigners domiciled in one of the neighbouring towns (Cap d'Ail, La Turbie, Beausoleil or Roquebrune-Cap-Martin) and having previously worked in Monaco

The employer who wishes to engage or re-engage an employee of foreign nationality must obtain permission in writing before the applicant starts to work. This permission may be refused if there are people in the same profession or specialisation, who have priority registered with the Employment Office on the lists of those seeking work. Therefore, finding a job in the Principality of Monaco is not only about your personal skills and education, but about your luck us well. If there are other people waiting for similar job possibilities who enjoy the priority protection, then you might never receive a work permit in Monaco.

Registering with the Employment Office:

» If you are looking for a job in Monaco you should go directly to the Employment Office in person, taking with you:

» Your ID card (or Monégasque residence card)

» Proof of address, if you live in France

» An up-to-date CV

Obviously, the Monaco-based companies also know this, since by regulation in order to allow their application, employers are required to declare any job vacancy to the Employment Office. It is also a very important thing that the Employment Office sends candidates to the employers within four days of the job post.

The process is very protective of those who are already on the priority list.

In case none of the sent candidates are acceptable to the employer, after five days of the job post, the employer has the possibility to search for new candidates and to make suggestions towards the Employment Office. However, it is almost impossible to provide new candidates if the new ones maintain the same skills as the ones provided by the Employment Office.

The employer needs to create a written explanation why it prefers the selected candidate, but the Employment Office has the power to refuse the employer's choice. In some cases, even if the employer would be open to offer you a job position its hands are tied.

Any new employee or candidate must hold one of the following:

» If he lives in the Principality, a valid Monégasque residence card

» If he lives in France, a French identity card or a valid residence document

» If he lives neither in Monaco nor in France, the applicant must conform to the rules concerning the entry and residence of foreigners

In every case, the employer must establish a work contract for a foreign worker. This contract, after approval by the Employment Office, will make it possible to obtain the residence permit required for settlement in the Principality of Monaco. The formalities for the issue of a work permit are only launched after the issue of a Monégasque residence permit.

From information supplied by the employer, the candidate will receive a pre-printed request for engagement and issue of a work permit which he/she is required to complete and return as quickly as possible to the Employment Office.

Permission to engage someone is only issued if the person concerned passes a free medical examination carried out by the Employment Medical Service.

The biggest chance to find a job position in Monaco is in the hospitality, real estate and the financial sectors. Monaco's largest employer is the Monte Carlo SBM which runs the famous Monte-Carlo Casino, many

WORKERS

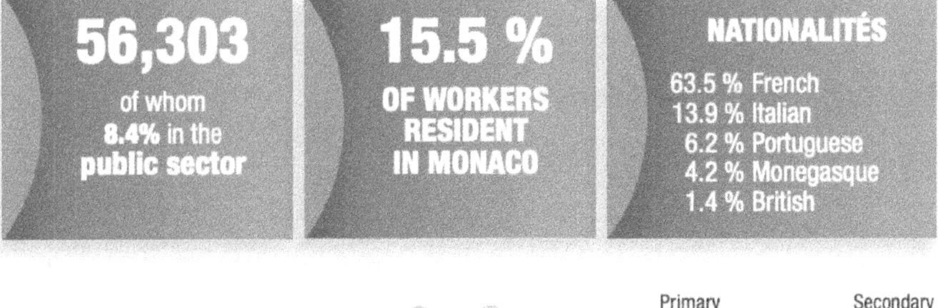

EMPLOYMENT PRIVATE SECTOR

of the luxury hotels and some of the most exclusive restaurants. Even if some of the businesses are producing debts, the income of the Casino provides a great stability for the employees.

Right after the Monte Carlo SBM, the real estate market is the second largest employer in the Principality competing with the employers from the financial sectors such as banks, wealth managers, family offices and financial advisors.

It is also very important to consider before you apply for any type of job that Monaco has approximately five thousand enterprises, however over forty percent of them are run by registered independent workers.

Marriage and Divorce

Marriage and the fascination

Even if Monaco does not have the typical wedding tourism, its location provides exclusivity for the precious moment. It also has a special feeling by having the wedding in the same territory where Charlène Lynette Wittstock became the Princess of Monaco.

And what does this royal wedding mean for people? Everything.

Let me tell you a quick example going back to my previous example with my best friend, the artist Dodo Newman, who created in 2012 a Jewelry-artwork called "The Biggest Love Story" as a commemoration for the Royal wedding and the forever bonding love of His Serene Highness Prince Albert II and his beloved wife Her Serene Highness Princess Charlène of Monaco.

Dodo also had a long-time admiration for the Princely Family in Monaco since the time of Princess Grace and Prince Rainier III. She admired them for the love and passion they shared for each other even, if they came from different and contrasting backgrounds.

Just as Princess Charlène's mother, Lynette Wittstock who is an artist, Princess Grace also had a strong dedication to supporting the arts. She always believed that cultivation and training of emerging talent is essential to ensure sustained excellence in the arts.

Understanding the South African roots of the Princess, she immediately linked it back to the Titanic project. At the time, she decided to create something special for Princess Charlène to celebrate her love with Prince Albert with the thought of Princess Grace and Prince Rainier III as well.

The marriage of Princess Charlène and Prince Albert was a great occasion for this work and in Dodo's mind she already saw that it will consist of two pieces that are actually one. For this reason, she decided to cut the 3 meter long piece of PlexiGlas in half, representing the couple who belong together bonded by love. This is how the two complementary pieces came alive.

The royal jewelry-artwork covered with diamonds is a celebration of love, birth and death with the Princess's favourite purple colours. The reflections of the water and the purple shades were also inspired by H.S.H. Princess Charlène of Monaco.

Dodo hid an original Titanic coal from the ship wreck in both sides of the jewelry-artwork. These pieces of coal in each part are there to commemorate the passengers. The 100 year old coal pieces are encircled with diamonds that are symbols of renewal, rebirth and life.

One side of the artwork is dedicated to Monaco and H.S.H. Prince Albert II. This side is also a commemoration for Monaco's forgotten hero, Roger Marie Bricoux as well. He was one of the legendary Titanic musicians, a brave cello player who never left the sinking ship. Roger Marie Bricoux played on his cello during the sinking of the Titanic.

The other part of the composition is dedicated to South Africa and H.S.H. Princess Charlène. This side is a commemoration as well for the South African passengers of the ill-fated Titanic ship.

The two pieces which complement each other, have a special wave cut in the middle of the composition, representing the endless ocean and the forever bonding love. Therefore, the two complementary pieces fold together just as the „A" and the „C" in Her Serene Highness Princess Charlène and His Serene Highness Prince Albert II's dual cypher.

A peculiarity is that when Dodo started to create the jewelry-artwork, called "The Biggest Love Story", she was four months pregnant. This was an element that added to the inner beauty and the uniqueness of the work.

I only understood later from her private mailings with the Princess how meaningful the precious moment of the wedding was for her and probably for so many other people.

"I remember when I saw the wedding with you and Prince Albert, and I saw that very special moment in the old chapel, when the tears covered your eyes. It was a very emotional moment for all of us, because it was the moment where everybody realized how deeply you were moved and how profound your Love for Albert is. And as you appeared in your amazing dress, it was like an Angel coming down to Earth. The simplicity was surrounded with a heart breaking feeling that day."

- Quote from the private mailings of Her Serene Highness Princess Charlène and Dodo Newman

Even if all the colours, the reflections of the water and the purple shades were inspired by Her Serene Highness Princess Charlène, the royal jewelry-artwork encapsulates the undoubtable message that death, roots, life and birth are all part of us, especially with a folding and forever bonding love.

Interestingly, since Dodo was 4 months pregnant during the creation of this work when she implemented the diamonds in each side of it, she wished the birth of a new life for H.S.H. Princess Charlène as well.

Only two years passed after the creation of the artwork and the news ran around the world like fire that the 36-year-old South African Princess was expecting twins to deliver in December 2014. Princess Charlène gave birth to H.S.H. Prince Jacques Honoré Rainier and H.S.H. Princess Gabriella Thérèse Marie on December 10th, 2014.

Dodo's prediction from 2012 came into reality.

I believe this example shows how strong the effect of the Princely wedding is on the people who admire the couple the same way as they do the Principality of Monaco.

Monaco delivers Europe's most beautiful fairytales

The life of an offset of a noble house was never easy. A few hundred years ago in the Royal houses, marriage was considered nothing else but a trade. The kings handled their heirs simply as goods. True love was a fairy tale which always faded away in order to maintain the state interests.

For this reason, the fate of the heirs was often decided at a very early age, mostly in their childhood giving no chance for them to discover their true feelings. Since the royal marriages were ties between different states, often the Princess or Prince was forced to live in a different country than her/his own homeland with a husband/wife whom they had never seen before.

Looking back to this era, we could easily say that it is a cruel and victimising one. However, we should never forget that in a royal family, the state or sovereign interest always came first, because as a royal heir they had the obligation towards their people.

Nowadays, the situation has changed a lot. Just thinking about the past decades, we could see many royal weddings tied between a royalty and a commoner.

In Europe, many people labelled England's royal couple Kate Middleton and Prince Williams as the "dream couple". It was a love developed from a friendship and their relationship had many ups and downs. They even separated a few years before their marriage. However, true love found its way to the light and England could celebrate a new Princess and a new role model in Kate.

And recently another commoner married into the British Royal Family, Rachel Meghan Markle. Meghan, Duchess of Sussex is an American retired actress who became a member of the British royal family upon her marriage to Prince Harry.

Interestingly, before her love with Prince Harry, she was already married to actor and producer Trevor Engelson. The couple divorced in 2013. Meghan announced her engagement to Prince Harry, grandson of Queen Elizabeth II in 2017. She became the Duchess of Sussex upon her marriage to Prince Harry in May 2018, with whom she had a son in May 2019.

In Spain, the journalist Letizia Ortiz Rocasolano, who came from a simple civilian family, married into the Spanish royal family, when the Spanish King Felipe VI. proposed to her. What made this marriage more difficult was the fact that this was not the first marriage for Letitia; but, no obstacle could overpower Felipe VI. and his true feelings towards her princess.

Talking about true love, Denmark has its own love story as well. Mary Elizabeth Donaldson was born in 1972 in a big civilian family as the youngest of four children and she probably never imagined that she would become the Crown Princess of Denmark. In the year 2000, she visited the Sydney Olympic Games where she met a handsome man called Frederik (accidentally in a pub, called Slip Inn). The couple fell in love, but Mary had no idea that Frederik was actually the Crown Prince of Denmark.

Interestingly they met in the exact same year when Prince Albert II met with Princess Charlène. Three years later Frederik, got engaged to Mary, who in 2004 finally became the Crown Princess of Denmark.

These are great examples when the charming Prince chose his future Princess from the commoners. However, sometimes even a Princess went against the sovereign rules and followed her heart just as Victoria Ingrid Alice Désirée, the Crown Princess of Sweden.

When it come to love, Princess Victoria decided to follow her heart and she chose her personal trainer Daniel Westling. With this act to follow her true love, the Princess was ready to give up her right to the throne. However, the Swedish Government rewarded true love with the final consent for a dynastic marriage.

The reason for the increasing marriages between royalties and civilian people can be found in the structural change of Europe. In many countries, the royalties have only a symbolic power and they almost have nothing more than a ceremonial role. In most countries, the royalties have no more political power, therefore the importance of marriage has shifted away from state interest to real values, such as love.

The Principality of Monaco also has its own fairytale story when a Prince or a Princess chose a civilian to marry, showing that true love can be free. The truth is that all three children of Grace Kelly married to civilians, just as their father Prince Rainer III chose the American actress as his beloved wife in 1956.

One can say that when it comes to Royal families, the state interest is the highest priority; however, Monaco has proved many times that it can combine both the state and personal interests very well.

Many people remember the wedding of American actress Grace Kelly to H.S.H. Prince Rainer III. Their marriage greatly contributed to the glamour of the Principality and she has remained a cherished memory to the world.

H.S.H. Princess Grace was not the first American commoner to marry a Monaco prince. The first American-born princess was Marie Alice Heine who wed H.S.H. Prince Albert I in 1889, becoming Her Serene Highness Princess Alice of Monaco.

Currently H.S.H. Prince Albert II of Monaco, who married His beloved H.S.H. Princess Charléne on 01 July 2011, rules the Principality of Monaco.

Before his marriage with his beloved Princess Charlène on 1 July 2011, Prince Albert II was often labelled as a Playboy. Among his lovers and trophies, you could find internationally-recognised people such as Gwyneth Paltrow, Brooke Shields, Naomi Campbell or Claudia Schiffer.

Because of his past lifestyle when the Prince was inaugurated as a Sovereign Prince in 2005, many people questioned his ability to rule the Principality of Monaco. It did not help either that back in 1992, a young girl, Jazmin Grace was born as the illegitimate daughter of the Prince from the American Tamara Rotolo. The DNA test proved the fathership.

In 2005, another woman came out to the public stating that Prince Albert II is the father of his son Alexandre Éric Stéphane Costé.

However, many people who were close to the Prince also knew that by the time of his inauguration as a Sovereign Prince, he already fell in love with Charlène Lynette Wittstock, the 20 years younger South African swimmer. Their relationship and her loving bond seemed to be a strong one.

Their relationship became officially public only in 2006, when Princess Charléne rested her head on the shoulders of H.S.H. Prince Albert II during the Winter Olympic Games in Torino (Turin, Piedmont, Italy).

Many people started to spread the gossip that the Princess is not happy and therefore she tried to escape from the marriage multiple times. Some press also stated that the Princess had tears in her eyes during the wedding because she felt the pressure.

On the one hand, Princess Charlène was in a very difficult position because of her new obligations and also because of the fathership scandals. However, I believe that anyone who watched the wedding could see clearly that her tears were ones of happiness. Personally, I truly believe that even if the Princely couple had difficult times they both loved and respected each other.

Very close sources, so called friends of Prince Albert II also suggested that actually the Prince was the one who sent away Princess Charlène because he needed to reconsider the marriage. Some bad-mouthing locals also spread the rumor that the Prince only married Princess Charlène because it was too late to cancel the wedding and the pressure was too big, especially in the light of the other wedding in England of Kate Middleton and Prince Williams.

We will probably never know the truth, but frankly, it is not really important anymore, since the Princely couple is glowing from love and care towards each other. They have a beautiful family where they both care for each other. That is the only thing that matters.

Even if the gossip is true and they had bad times and periods in their relationship, I think the past years just strengthened their respect toward each other which also made their love flower again.

Since the birth of their lovely twins, I think there is no doubt that they started to build up a lovely family, and the ex-Playboy father became the charming and caring prince of the hearts.

For those who followed the events and announcements around the twins, H.S.H. Prince Jacques Honoré Rainier, Marquis of Baux (in Provence) and H.S.H. Princess Gabriella Thérèse Marie, Countess of Carladès (in Auvergne) they can clearly see how caring Prince Albert II is.

However, Prince Albert II is not the only one in the family with an interesting past. His oldest sister Princess Caroline also married civilians, and she married not only once, but three times.

Princess Caroline's first husband was a Parisian banker Philippe Junot. The couple divorced only after two years of marriage, however, the Princess needed to wait twelve years more until the Roman Catholic Church granted her a canonical annulment in 1992.

However, this did not bother the Princess, since in the meantime she remarried with her second husband the sportsman and businessman Stefano Casiraghi in a civil ceremony in Monaco on 29 December 1983.

They formed a truly loving couple and Princess Caroline gifted her husband with three beautiful children, Andrea (1984), Charlotte (1986) and Pierre (1987).

The offshore powerboat racer Stefano decided to defend his World offshore title one more time on 3 October 1990 before he planned to retire and to live for his family. With life's cruel twist, it turned out that day during the race, that the 30 years old Stefano was killed in an offshore boat accident close to the coast of Monaco. Life made a sad end for this fairytale.

Princess Caroline's third and present husband is Prince Ernst August of Hanover. The couple married in 1999. However, by 2010 the marriage and the love was already questioned when photos emerged of her husband kissing a woman who was definitely not identified as Princess Caroline.

The marriage survived the incident and Princess Caroline lives in Monaco-Ville at the Villa Clos St Pierre with her family.

Of course, you can find the opposite as well with the youngest sister Princess Stephanie who has been a singer, swimsuit designer and fashion model as well.

Princess Stephanie was almost like the lady version of Prince Albert II when it came to international trophy lovers. She had dated Paul Belmondo, Anthony Delon, Rob Loew, Jean-Yves Le Fur, however, she gave her heart finally to her bodyguard Daniel Ducruet.

The couple had two children Louis (1992) and Pauline (1994) before they divorced in 1996.

Two years later, the Princess gave birth to Camille (1998), but she never identified the name of the father of the child. As rumours suggested, the father of the third child is Jean Raymond Gottlieb who was the head of security to the Princess.

In 2001, the Princess began a new relationship with the elephant trainer Franco Knie. The unlucky Princess divorced again already in the following year, 2002.

The Princess never gave up on finding true love, therefore, she opened her heart to the Portuguese acrobat Adans Lopez Peres who was a member of Knie's circus. The couple married in September 2003 and their marriage ended in divorce in 2004.

Since then, the Princess lives with her family just next door to her sister's home at Villa Clos Saint-Martin.

She is definitely not the lucky one in the family and from a very young age, she suffered a lot from the cruelty of the media. She was often labeled as rebel in order to intimidate her publicly.

However, the Princess tried to stand out multiple times. She released two music albums, and even had a single with Michael Jackson. She was cover girl on Vogue and Vanity Fair, launched her own swimwear collection and introduced her own perfume fragrance.

But the main reason why she was rebellious is related to her childhood trauma and a terrible gossip which overshadowed every step she made.

On 13 September 1982, the 17-year-old Princess Stephanie was returning home from Rocagel, France with her mother Grace Kelly. They suffered a car accident which caused the death of her mother Grace Kelly.

Although the official version was that Princess Grace suffered a stroke while driving, it was rumoured in Monaco that the car was actually driven by Princess Stephanie, and she was the one responsible for the terrible accident which had taken the life of her beloved mother.

The fact that Princess Stephanie missed the funeral of her mother due to recovery reasons also strengthened the guiltiness of the Princess linked to the accident of her mother.

For seven year Princess Stephanie refused to talk about the accident and to speak publicly about the death of her mother. However, in 1989 she gave an interview to Jeffrey Robinson insisting that the story was untrue.

"There was a lot of pressure on me because everyone was saying that I had been driving the car, that it was all my fault, that I'd killed my mother... It's not easy when you're 17 to live with that."

Until 2012, the Princess was not ready to speak again about this subject, while in an interview with Paris Match she repeated her earlier denial, but she discussed her feelings and the trauma she experienced back then.

"Not only did I go through the horrible trauma of losing my mother at a very young age, but I was beside her at the moment of the accident. Nobody can imagine how much I've suffered, and still suffer."

Obviously, it is the topic that people do not like to mention in Monaco, however, when someone judges the Princess's "rebel" life, I would recommend first understanding the person, the human being behind the surface. This is someone who has lost so much in her early life and who is just trying to find her way back to happiness.

Marrying in Monaco

Obviously, no wedding can be celebrated in the Throne Room of the Princely Palace, where Miss Wittstock was married to His Serene Highness Prince Albert II in a civil ceremony on July 1st, 2011, however the Principality offers many beautiful places to celebrate a wedding.

If you are aiming to get married in the Principality of Monaco, spring and summer could be ideal seasons to celebrate such a wonderful occasion. But do not forget that Monaco is a luxurious haven and is blessed with 300 days of sunshine, so there is a big variety for the perfect timing you desire.

No matter whether you plan your wedding at the Principality of Monaco or you just aim to spend an unforgettable honeymoon there, the picturesque views, romantic abundance and the tremendous beauty of Monaco's gardens make any wedding special and it will enchant every heart.

The Princess Grace Rose Garden is an area of calm and serenity where the scent of some 4,000 roses hang in the air. It is a truly romantic place.

I would also recommend the Japanese Garden with its zen feeling for a small wedding reception. This is one of my favourite spots in Monaco; it always re-energises me when I spend some time there.

Obviously, Monaco is full of other possibilities since it has many historically filled churches and special atmospheres for important occasions. Just to give you an idea, you can also consider the panoramic views like the Oceanographic museum and aquarium, the Jardin Exotique, Avenue Saint-Martin, and the Prince's Palace.

As we know a marriage, a wedding is (usually) a once-in-a-lifetime experience and everyone tries to make it their best and most memorable moment in their life. And for this, Monaco offers a perfect ground with its gastronomy delights through many of its Michelin star restaurants, historical attractions, best-in-the-world spa treatments, fashion and lifestyle.

You can also harmonise your wedding and romantic journey with some exceptional music experience to enjoy the classic ballet and opera concerts, since music and romance are synonymous to each other.

Once you have made your decision of a lifetime, the primary requirement for foreign citizens to get married in Monaco is to reside in the Principality for at least 30 days prior to the wedding.

Furthermore, every wedding must be preceded by a publication through an announcement. This announcement is posted on the door of the Town Hall for a period of 10 days, which must include two Sundays.

The following documents are to be submitted:

» Certificates of birth of the couple to be married or an attested affidavit issued by a Justice of the Peace or another magistrate at the birthplace or place of domicile

» Certificate of death of the mother and father, if necessary, where one of the couple to be married is a minor

» Certificate of death of the husband or wife in the case of a widow or widower remarrying

» Certificate of consent signed in the presence of a notary by the father or mother who will not be present in person at the wedding where one of the couple to be married is a minor

» Certificate of granting of a divorce in the case of a husband or wife whose first marriage has been dissolved

» Translation of foreign documents submitted, being countersigned by the consuls of the country or countries of which the couple to be married are subjects

» The customary certificate issued by these same consuls

» Certificate of publication of the marriage banns and of no caveat being entered if one of the couple to be married does not live in the Principality or has not resided for one month without a break on the date of publication laid down by the law, which is obligatory

» If a marriage contract has been made, the couple to be married must produce the certificate of the notary who received it (the marriage settlement used in Monaco is that under which husband and wife administer their separate properties)

Talking about a marriage contract is almost like a preference (requirement) in Monaco.

I remember when I aimed to change banks, I went to meet with the client representative, and they immediately mentioned that a marriage contract is essential for opening a bank account. When I started to wonder why, I was kindly informed that most banks like to maintain a very closed and confidential relationship with their clients. By having a divorce, the bank can be faced with the situation whereby it has to disclose financial information regarding its client. To avoid this, they prefer a marriage contract. And the process and the benefits of a divorce are extremely different in the Principality from the other countries.

SUGGESTION:

Prenuptial agreements could be useful to protect your wealth and heritage. It is also a good way to avoid any misunderstanding.

For those who are interested in an unbiased opinion I would highly recommend Mr. Donald Trump's legendary book called "Think Big: Make It Happen in Business and Life". I am not a US citizen and I have no interest in the US politics. I read his book many years before he was elected. So, no politics here just a suggestion of an old book.

In this exceptional book, the real estate icon, Trump dedicated a full chapter for marriage contracts. I always loved its title: "I love you, sign this".

Nobody plans to divorce, but Trump creates a very clean argument about prenuptial agreements since he saw people and businesses being destroyed because of not having marriage contracts.

Obviously, the marriage changes many things, because the number of people in a household is key in the calculation of the yearly living fund, and it can happen that you need to raise your original bank account opening amount to maintain your residency under the new circumstances.

Many banks calculate the basic living fund for the statement they provide to the Government based on the number of people in the household. (And also based on the yearly living costs which is often influenced by your family status.)

Divorce in Monaco

There are three times more marriage ceremonies than divorces in Monaco; however, the Principality has approximately 60-90 divorce cases each year. Due to the wealth of the residents, some of those divorces are truly high-profile cases with world-wide media attention. But it is still worth it because divorcing in Monaco offers exceptional benefits for the super-rich.

It is interesting to know that you can divorce under the legislation of the Principality of Monaco in the very first days that you have received your residence permit, however it is good to consider that Monaco does not offer the European comfort of separation since there is no legal concept of shared marital property in Monaco.

Most of us go into a marriage without even imagining the possibility that something may go wrong. In many cases, the heat is not burning anymore and we are often weak to face the fact that the love is gone. Therefore, when a divorce is coming, it can be extremely painful. Many people also do not take the responsibility because they are scared of the fight that may occur during the process. What others think is none of your business, do not even listen to their opinions. If the fire is out and you feel that your relationship is over, then do not stay in the marriage because of necessity or social opinions. Everyone deserves to live a happy life, even if there is temporary loss in it.

SUGGESTION:

Divorce can be very tricky in the Principality. Sometimes you need to check whether the local laws apply or you have to use the law of your country of origin.

The process of divorce in the Principality is often difficult because of the country of origin of the foreign residents. For example, if a Swiss man marries a German woman and they both reside in the Principality of Monaco, they need to take into consideration three different legislations (Swiss, German, Monégasque).

According to the Anglo-Saxon Laws, the judge can give a percentage of your wealth to your husband/wife. In the Monegasque system, the key word is the level of life and the duration of the marriage. For very wealthy people, this difference is fundamental, because it can have extreme financial implications for them.

In many cases, the decision depends on the judge who decides on his/her ruling based on one of the nationalities. Of course, parties also have the possibility to request the ruling based on their country of origin.

In many cases, and especially when there is no settlement between the parties the applied law can be crucial. Even if you are able to divorce under the legislation of the Principality of Monaco in the very first days that you have received your residence permit, Monaco does not offer the European comfort of separation.

In Monaco, the base of compensation for the spouse is never based on the actual wealth. Based on the law, what you brought into the marriage stays yours after the divorce. Therefore, if you had a house before the marriage you can keep the house and your spouse has no right to it. The separation is based only on the commonly-built wealth.

In case your spouse had no income during the marriage, the court is entitled to create a basic calculation of her monthly living cost, which is an indicator of maintaining the same level of lifestyle that the spouse had during the marriage.

Based on the ruling, you could be directed to ensure this living cost to your spouse for a maximum period of five years.

This is an exceptional benefit for the ultra-rich residents, since by applying the Monégasque law they can save multimillions on a divorce. For example, if you are a wealthy guy having 100 million Euro and you live with your wife with a monthly living cost of 5,000 Euro, then based on the standard law practice in Monaco, the maximum you pay to your ex-wife is 300,000 Euro, which is the monthly living cost for five years. This means you will still keep the 99.7% of your wealth.

SUGGESTION:

The question of competency is among the very first things you have to identify in a divorce case.

In a case like this, in many European countries, the wife would be entitled to at least half of the assets and wealth, especially if there are children involved.

In the Principality of Monaco, the person who built up the wealth enjoys the protection. It could be also considered a protection of true love and relationship against the gold diggers who go into a marriage because of the wealth and lifestyle. Obviously, this is the major reason why competency plays an important role in the divorce process.

Once the divorce is done, the Certificate of Transcription of Divorce applies to all divorce judgments by the Court of First Instance in Monaco. The Registry Office of the Mairie de Monaco (Town Hall) will issue the certificate immediately on presentation of your proof of identity.

Back to the competency and jurisdiction, one of my favourite examples is the divorce case of the Swiss businessman Maurice Alain Amon and Tracey Hejailan. Mr Amon had a truly unusual legal claim, arguing the question of residency which was at the Le Mirabeau building in Monaco.

His lawyer claimed that Manhattan, New York cannot be the right jurisdiction for the divorce, arguing that his socialite wife's extensive shoe collection sits in their Monte-Carlo closet and not in their Manhattan pad. He claimed that the vast shoe collection showed that the Monaco apartment was her primary residence, and thus the Principality was the proper court venue.

This move aimed to save tens of millions for Mr Amon, because there's no legal concept of shared marital property in Monaco. To be more precise, Ms Hejailan-Amon expected to get as much as $70 million in a US court, but only received $1.26 million by the Monaco court. (Mr Amon is worth a rumoured $1.4billion.)

Interestingly, not so long ago, the socialite Tracey Hejailan-Amon restarted the battle. She claimed that her $122,858 a month divorce settlement is not enough for her glamorous lifestyle. Ms Hejailan-Amon blasted the settlement as insufficient, claiming she needed four times that amount – nearly $500,000 a month – to maintain her lifestyle of year-round private plane and yacht travel.

Obviously, the question of residency did not turn out very well in the case of Dmitry Rybolovlev and his wife Elena. For many years, the dirty laundry was aired, and unwarranted attention attracted throughout six different jurisdictions.

The couple had reached an amicable deal in order to put an end to all legal procedures launched in different jurisdictions. The case was labelled as: "The most expensive divorce in history".

Mr Rybolovlev is the world's 165 wealthiest man with a net worth of $8.5 billion. Although the size of the monetary settlement was not disclosed, it is important to acknowledge that an award of four billion Swiss francs (£2.7 billion) was already granted by the Swiss court to Elena in May 2014.

Expecting a baby

Approximately one thousand mothers give birth to their child every year in the Principality of Monaco, and what is interesting is that approximately 70% of these parents are non-residents.

It is very important to know that unlike in many countries, giving birth to a child in the territory of the Principality of Monaco does not mean that the child automatically receives Monégasque nationality.

Therefore, 'birth tourism' for a Monégasque passport is not applicable in the Principality of Monaco. Monégasque nationality does not even apply for children born from parents who are residents in Monaco.

However, what the Principality does provide is the protection of the working mother, an exceptional healthcare system and a world-class hospital in which to deliver your baby.

Before birth

One of the greatest moments in every family is the news of a new life. It is always a miracle when a new soul arrives to the family, especially if you are able to look back to your infinite childhood imagination and your belief in angels and fairies. One of the best description for the relationship between belief, fairies and babies was written in the story of Peter Pan:

> *"When the first baby laughed for the first time, its laugh broke into a thousand pieces, and they all went skipping about, and that was the beginning of fairies.*
> *…*
> *When a new baby laughs for the first time, a new fairy is born, and as there are always new babies there are always new fairies."*
>
> - J. M. Barrie, Peter Pan

Monaco is very protective and well-equipped for supporting the growing families.

As soon as a pregnancy is confirmed during the first examination, the doctor completes a declaration of pregnancy which will be sent to welfare bodies. From this moment on, you can be entitled to various benefits and compensations. However, you are not obliged to inform your employer about your pregnancy. You may inform your employer of your pregnancy whenever you want.

You are legally protected during a medically-confirmed pregnancy and during maternity leave. An employer cannot use pregnancy as a reason to refuse to employ someone, terminate a contract of employment during a probationary period or transfer an employee to another post.

In Monaco, you are not obliged to reveal that you are pregnant unless you are requesting to benefit from provisions to protect pregnant women.

Once you have revealed your pregnancy, you should notify your employer, without any particular deadline, of:

» the date of the start of your maternity leave

» the date of your return to work

The cessation of work during statutory maternity leave suspends the contract of employment for the corresponding period and is not grounded for a termination of the contract.

You may request a temporary change of employment on health grounds. Your employer can also request this, following advice from an occupational doctor. There must be no decrease in remuneration if this request arises from your employer or if you have worked at the company for less than one year.

Pregnant women may leave work five minutes before the agreed time with no reduction in salary. From the date of the start of your maternity leave you are entitled to various financial compensations. Maternity leave is calculated on a daily basis.

In the case of deliveries before the expected date, there is no reduction in the total amount of maternity leave.

In the case of a medical condition that is confirmed by a medical certificate, the maternity leave can be extended by two weeks before the expected delivery date, and by four weeks afterwards.

As a pregnant woman and in cases of medically confirmed pregnancy, you can resign from your job without notice and without having to pay any penalties for resigning at short notice. However, the employer cannot terminate your contract during your pregnancy, maternity leave or up to four weeks after the end of this leave, except if:

» he or she can prove that there is serious misconduct not linked to pregnancy

» the company closes or reduces its activity

» you have a fixed term contract that has expired

In these cases, the dismissal must be notified to the Labour Inspector and will first be examined by the committee on dismissals and redundancy. A dismissal cannot take effect or be notified during the scheduled period of maternity leave, i.e. eight weeks before the expected date of delivery and eight weeks afterwards.

If you are dismissed but your employer is not aware that you are pregnant, the dismissal can be cancelled. In such cases, you should send your employer a medical certificate certifying that you are pregnant. This should be sent by registered post with confirmation of receipt within 15 days following the notice of your dismissal.

Giving a birth

One of the most common choices for the delivery of the baby is the state-run Princess Grace Hospital (CHPG, Centre Hospitalier Princesse Grace).

After giving birth to a new life, the family has four days to declare the birth at the Mairie de Monaco (Town Hall). When you declare the birth in order to apply for childbirth allowance the Mairie de Monaco gives you a standard letter. By this time, you also need to be sure about the name.

It is a very important thing to know that giving birth to a child in the territory of the Principality of Monaco does not mean that the child automatically receives the Monégasque nationality.

Based on law the following has Monégasque nationality:

» any person born in Monaco or abroad of a Monégasque father

» any person born in Monaco or abroad of a mother born Monégasque who still had this nationality at the time of the birth and of an unknown father;

» any person born in Monaco of unknown parents.

With regards to legitimate offspring, Monégasque nationality is passed on without it being necessary to fulfil any other condition; on the other hand, in the case of natural offspring, this handing-on of nationality only takes place if the child is recognized or legitimized by marriage of its parents.

Right after the birth, you are obliged to inform the authorities of the birth and the change in your circumstances. If you are not Monégasque citizen, you have to declare the birth at the Embassy of your country of origin.

After birth

After the maternity leave and the allowances, you can continue in the same work or similar work with remuneration that is at least equivalent. Your rights relating to length of service are not affected.

If you decide not to return to work, you must tell your employer through a registered letter with confirmation of receipt 15 days before the end of your maternity leave. This resignation is exempt from the usual notice period.

During the following year, you can request to return to work through a registered letter with confirmation of receipt. Your employer is obliged to re-employ you as a priority within a deadline of one year, in a post suited to your qualifications. If you are re-employed, your employer must afford you all the benefits that you were entitled to before your departure.

Recommended partners:
OMYS MONACO
Strategic Consulting
OMYS
CONSULTING

CHAPTER 7

Yacht registration and chartering

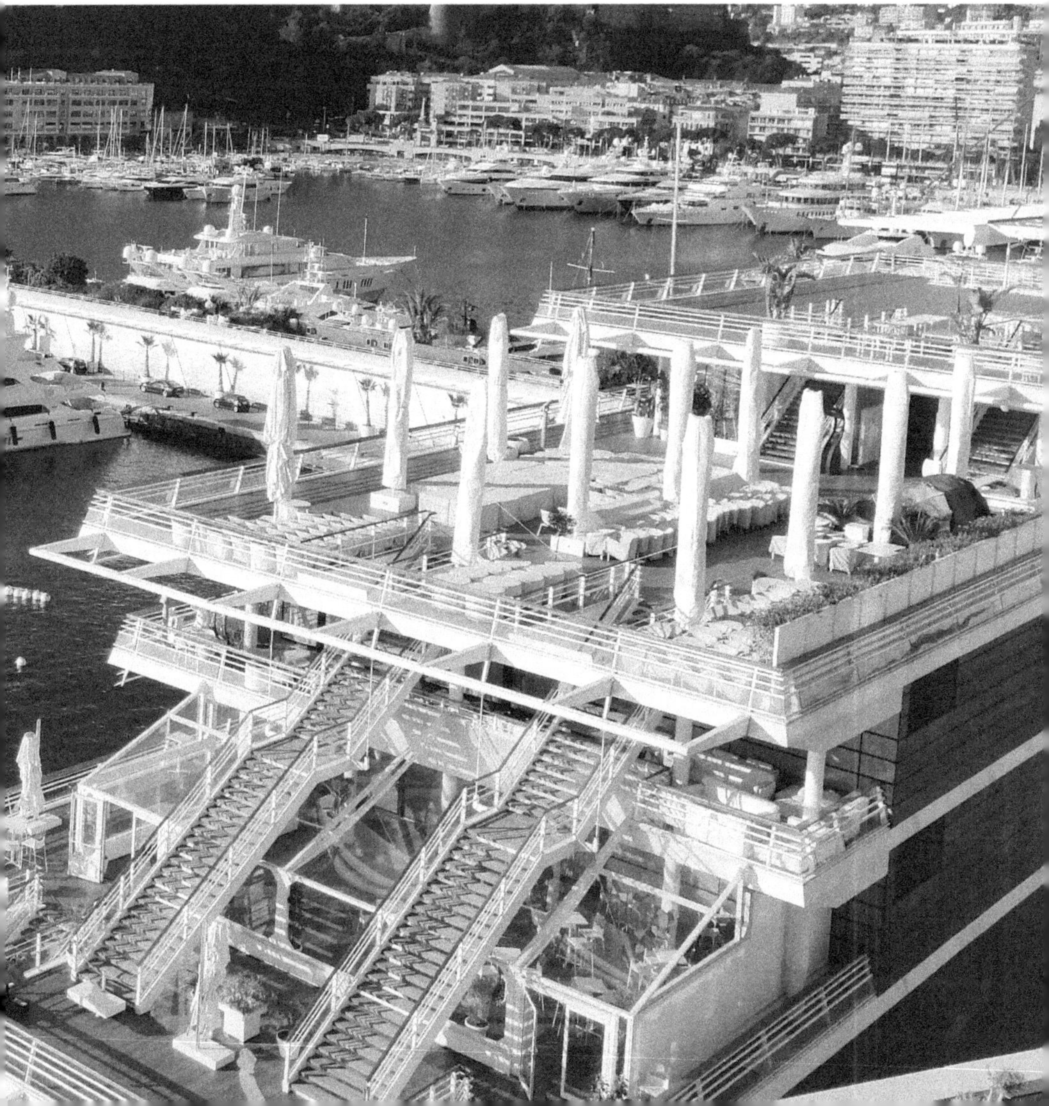

Registering your yacht under a Monaco flag

Superyacht registration under a Monaco flag is one of those things that you do because it is highly prestigious, and not because of common sense, especially when your vessel is over a certain size.

Superyacht registration in general can often be a grey area. It can be a challenging process, one could easily be confused and even industry experts can become unstuck. Even in the Principality of Monaco, there are many legal firms focusing exclusively on legislations around superyachts.

One example is the fiscal (VAT) status of a vessel, and the other the registration process. (jurisdiction and commercial or non-commercial activity of the vessel).

To avoid any confusion, the very first thing one must do is identify whether the vessel will be used for commercial purpose or for private use.

One of the major objectives for superyacht owners is the correct registration and ownership procedure of their valuable asset, especially in regards to having an efficient Tax and VAT structure. This includes, but is not limited to tax jurisdiction, domicile status, or VAT and operational use of the vessel.

The main European Union jurisdictions for registering a vessel are the UK, Malta, Madeira, France, Italy, Cyprus and of course the Principality of Monaco. However, jurisdictions such as Malta, Greece being scrutinised heavily by the European Union.

It is important to know that the flag you choose can have a direct impact on your potential liabilities, privacy and enjoyment. As mentioned before, important future considerations for example are whether you intend to use the superyacht for private or commercial use.

Each flag state has the authority to enforce varying regulations based on their specific requirements including certification, safety, inspection and pollution prevention.

Normally the superyacht owner's residence and tax status will be taken into consideration, as well as where the yacht will be located.

In general Monegasque nationals and residents can apply to register a boat under the Monegasque flag.

The Principality of Monaco has two primary requirements:

1., All vessels under the Monegasque flag must show their name and the word "MONACO" on the stern, to the exclusion of any other wording.

2., Yachts people who wish to appoint a captain and/or a crew must notify the Department of Maritime Affairs.

The vessel registration is quite simple in Monaco once you have the invoice to prove ownership, examples of this would be photos from all sides of the vessel and the necessarily certificates that accompany the vessel. The application must then be submitted to the Department of Maritime Affairs in Monaco.

An annual naturalisation fee is payable for all boats under the Monegasque flag. Payment must be made within a month from the date of the bill being sent by the Department of Maritime Affairs to obtain the annual stamp. This stamp is essential, as without it, the naturalisation is not fully valid.

It is also important to know that for vessels of over 5 meters, a proof will be requested that the radio complies with all obligations.

Furthermore, for vessels over 7.5 meters purchased within the E.U, you will need to present a confirmation that the boat complies with all tax obligations.

On the insurance side, the yacht, crew and all passengers must be properly insured in the event of accident, incident or liability issue.

One of the misconceptions with yacht registration comes in regards of the moorings. It is highly important to consider that granting permission to navigate under the Monegasque flag does not automatically include the allocation of a mooring in one of the Principality's ports.

The general rule is based on the first come first serve basis. For this reason, even for long-term residents it is impossible to get a mooring space in the Monaco ports. The waiting list is more than 10 years, and there is no place for short cuts and exceptions through corruption.

This rule is very strict, and even the moorings are not transferable to a new ship belonging to an owner who already has a mooring already in the port, or subsequently to a new owner of a ship that is already moored in Monaco.

Challenges with superyacht registration in Monaco

Due to the limited port space, only Monegasque or Monaco residents can register a vessel in the Principality. There is a saying that Monaco is for supercars and not for superyachts.

One of the most important things for superyacht registering, is that Monaco has no Monegasque commercial flag. For this reason, registering a superyacht in Monaco is not VAT free, and yachts will have to have the VAT paid, which is 20% of the purchasing price.

The 20% of VAT paid on every new yacht could be for example, a hefty 20 million Euro on the 100 Million Euro purchase price. To put this in a simple form, the Principality of Monaco is not the most cost-efficient choice, but the most prestigious one.

Other countries such as Malta and Cyprus offer much better advantages for the fraction of the VAT that would be payable in the Principality. However, it is also important to understand that the European Union has started to crack down against yacht registration in Malta and Cyprus. The European Commission has put Malta, Greece and Cyprus on notice of infringement proceedings for not levying the correct amount of Value Added Tax on the provision of yachts. The infamous Paradise Papers revealed widespread VAT evasion in the yacht sector, facilitated by national rules which do not comply with EU law.

For this reason, Cyprus does not really except anymore superyacht leases, while Malta is still in a fight with the European Union. One of the predicted outcomes of this fight is that superyacht owners may need to pay the VAT difference, and this sum can be relatively huge on large vessels. However, on the human side, most owners do not want to be involved in a tax evasion investigation which brings back their attention back to safe jurisdictions such as the Principality of Monaco.

In reality, registering a small yacht with maximum 2 crew members can be very well executed in the Principality of Monaco, while for bigger vessels the owners might consider alternative international registry options in order to avoid the numerous restrictions in the Principality.

Also worthy of note is that the crew of a Monaco based yacht must be hired through the Monaco Employment Office, and full social security is due. Furthermore, the Captain must have Monegasque or French certificates. Generally speaking, the bigger is the vessel, the more certificates and compliance it needs. This is very challenging for very large yachts, because it is difficult to have all necessary certificates, often up to 45-60 in total.

Truth to be told there are very few large vessels registered under the Monaco flag.

For example, a Cayman Island flag (which registers your vessel as a British Ship) allows the owners to hire captains in a much more flexible way, and they do not need to do it through special authorities such as the Monaco Employment Office in the Principality. This can also save owners up to 45% of Social Security Funds payable in Monaco.

You might also want to consider registering your vessel under a flag which is highly respected in the European Union. Obviously, there are huge differences between the different flags and in their prestige as well. For example, the Cayman Islands have a Red Ensigned flag, which means a high standard for the maintenance of the yacht.

By having the Red Ensigned flag, authorities know that all papers, equipment and crew related documentations are in order. It shows a high standard compared to other countries such as Madeira which is more flexible on its regulations. Choosing the right flag can also save time, energy and more importantly the hassle in the ports where your superyacht will take a visit.

Yacht owners should never forget that by owning a vessel they will need to comply with multiple jurisdictions. One is the jurisdiction where they register the yacht, and the second is the jurisdiction where the yacht will visit in the future. A poorly chosen flag can bring lot of unnecessarily port checks, technical inspections and so on.

Many port authorities do a "random" port safe control check based on the flags of the vessel. To give you an example from the car industry, say there are two BMW cars, both cars have the exact same specification, however one is registered in Germany and the other in Romania. Knowing the Germany car registration and TÜV standards, when they enter a police checkpoint, it is highly likely that the authorities will check the car from Romania as opposed to the one from Germany. Prejudice or not, your flag will immediately show a picture of your yacht profile to the port authorities.

Another good important point to consider is that your chosen flag brings with it specific consular help. Therefore, if you have any port issues it can be very handy if the country of your chosen flag has an embassy of consular office in the same country. Consular help can be very helpful when a non-EU registered ship enters an EU custom zone, or an EU registered ships leaves the European Union.

If one decided to choose the Monaco flag for yacht registration, pays the VAT and decided to accept the employment though the Monaco Employment Office, you will still be faced with certain restrictions. One of those restrictions is the distance that the superyacht can travel. Due to the agreement between Monaco and France, from 1963, no Monaco flagged vessel can go further than the France flag authorises it. It is another point where the Monegasque legislations merge together with the French one.

Summarising, for small vessels with limited crew members Monaco can be an ideal destination for yacht registration, however for large superyachts the main consideration is the status symbol of having a Monaco registered superyacht. We can conclude that registering a superyacht in Monaco is a question of prestige.

In the case you decide to register your vessel in the Principality of Monaco, it is highly recommended to seek professional advice.

Registering a vessel for chartering

When chartering a superyacht, we need to understand the difference between the owner of the superyacht, and the client who will rent out the vessel for an agreed period of time.

Most of the superyachts that are used for commercial purpose (chartering) are owned by companies, which makes complete sense due to the VAT obligations of the owners.

The Principality of Monaco has no commercial flag, therefore all the vessels registered under a Monaco flag and intended for charter are due VAT, but at a much-reduced level, making it competitive compared to superyachts being classified as private use.

Many of the banks in the Principality of Monaco are equipped to offer lease options for superyachts, which helps to reduce and possibly offset the owner's expenses. For this reason, most of the chartered superyachts are under corporate ownership.

Comparing the VAT on chartering versus buying, one can immediately see the benefits of chartering. While the superyacht owner is obliged to pay 20% VAT which is 20 million Euro on a 100 Million Euro yacht, he is only due to pay 2 Million Euro in the case the yacht is used for chartering. In this example, VAT payable was calculated based by Monaco rental on an annual 4% depreciation of the yacht over 5 years of period.

All crew members employed on a commercial yacht will be required to hold STCW 95 Basic Training certificates and provide evidence they hold the necessary Monaco approved qualifications specific to their position on board. Minimum standard clauses will be compulsory within employment agreements for crew on commercial yachts, in accordance with the Maritime Labour Convention 2006.

The crew must be hired through the Monaco Employment Office and full social security is due. Furthermore, the Captain must have the required Monegasque or French certificates. This is very challenging for very large yachts, because it is difficult to have all necessary certificates, about 45-60 in total.

Chartering from the owner's perspective

Most of the superyachts that are used for commercial purpose (chartering) are owned by companies, which makes complete sense due to the VAT obligations of the owners.

The Principality of Monaco has no commercial flag, therefore all the vessels registered under a Monaco flag and intended for charter are due VAT, but at a much-reduced level, making it competitive compared to superyachts being classified as private use.

Many of the banks in the Principality of Monaco are equipped to offer lease options for superyachts, which helps to reduce and possibly offset the owner's expenses. For this reason, most of the chartered superyachts are under corporate ownership.

Comparing the VAT on chartering versus buying, one can immediately see the benefits of chartering. While the superyacht owner is obliged to pay 20% VAT which is 20 million Euro on a 100 Million Euro yacht, he is only due to pay 2 Million Euro in the case the yacht is used for chartering. In this example, VAT payable was calculated based by Monaco rental on an annual 4% depreciation of the yacht over 5 years of period.

This is still considerably higher than flying the Malta or Cyprus flag, however it comes with the benefit of a Monaco flag. And as it was previously described, one can avoid the legal challenges and possible future VAT payments with flying the Malta and Cyprus flags.

It is also important to know from business perspective, that any chartered trip within Monaco and/or French waters, is due VAT, which is 20%. So, if a charter week starts in Monaco and finishes in St. Tropez for example, then 20% VAT is payable on the charter cost.

However, sailing out into international waters, meaning being more than 12 nautical miles away from Monaco and/or the French borders, and you decide to anchor in Italy for example, the VAT is immediately reduced to 10%.

On the insurance side of owning a superyacht, the crew and all passengers must be properly insured in the event of an accident, incident or liability issue. Often the Employer will have to take on private medical and accident cover for each crew member. Commercial yachts shall be insured for chartering activities and hold a greater third-party liability or P&I coverage. Insurance wise it is important to consider that the deductibles are high and not all risks are covered.

Among other matters, commercial yachts also must be in Class, and comply with the Commercial Yacht Code Regulations in accordance with the chosen registry.

Chartering under a Monaco flag raises the same problem with the crew. All crew members employed on a commercial yacht will be required to hold STCW 95 Basic Training certificates and provide evidence they hold the necessary Monaco approved qualifications specific to their position on board. Minimum standard clauses will be compulsory within employment agreements for crew on commercial yachts, in accordance with the Maritime Labour Convention 2006.

Finally, again the crew must be hired through the Monaco Employment Office and full social security is due. Furthermore, the Captain must have the required Monegasque or French certificates. This is very challenging for very large yachts, because it is difficult to have all necessary certificates, about 45-60 in total.

In Monaco there are multiple companies maintaining charter vessels, however very few of them have their yachts registered under the Monaco flag. Most of these yachts are leased through 3rd party companies and they typically have offshore flags such as the Cayman Islands or Isle of Man.

Chartering from the client's perspective

Monaco is and will also be the place to be for those who want to charter in the South of France.

Among the main attractiveness of a holiday cruising on a superyacht one can find the unique destinations reachable by yacht only, the incomparable luxury, world-class service, the unparalleled cuisine, the privacy and of course the unforgettable moments on board.

Due to Monaco's world-class programs and luxurious atmosphere, renting out a boat for charter is attractive for many nationalities. Even French people come to the Principality to enjoy a nice stay on a superyacht. They can find the best onshore restaurants in the area, best facilities and services.

Chartering is also there fore families. Charterers are becoming more and more educated on what the yacht charter is all about and what they can request and find on board. For example children friendly yachts for families is of absolute importance. For this reason many vessels offer various water toys, slides and other funs for all members of the family.

The charter season typically starts hand in hand with the Monaco Historic Grand Prix, which is early May. It is not far from the truth if we say that most of Monaco's chartering clients in May are petrolhead car lovers linking their private vacation or corporate events to the Historic Grand Prix and to the Formula One Grand Prix.

It is also important to realise that typically there are two types of chartering offers, the standard and the static charter. Most of the charters are static charters in May due to the fact that during the major events of the year, the yachts are not allowed to leave the port of Monaco.

However, the real chartering season with connected travellers around the French and Italian riviera start right after the Monaco Grand Prix, from early June. The season usually lasts until the final week of the Monaco Yacht Show, which is typically the last week of September.

Charter agencies in Monaco always hope in the Indian summer, meaning having an unseasonably warm, dry weather in October, which can allow them to attract more people to experience a final superyacht charter.

It is interesting to observe the trend that overall most charter clients ultimately aim for cruising holiday charter. However, during the major events of the year, such as Monaco Historic Grand Prix, Monaco Grand Prix, Cannes Film Festival, etc, 99% of the charter deals convert into static charters requested by event companies.

The typical charter booking is coming either through a personal contact or a family office. In general these people first "meet" with the charter agencies through their website and newsletter database.

For booking a charter yacht in Monaco, the earlier is better. The typical superyacht is booked at least a month in advance of the planned departure. Educated clients know and understand that forward planning is imperative to find the best suitable choices.

By planning a charter well in advance, a good charter agent can provide different solutions that would meet a client's exact requirements. It also can also give the client an opportunity to see the superyacht in person and to have a brief first meeting with the captain and crew to understand the vessel. All these small things can give you the right impression towards making a satisfying decision.

Special requests as not unknown in the industry either.

For an enjoyable trip, breaking down the language barrier is amongst the very first things to do. It often happens that for example a Russian family aims to cruise for a week on a Superyacht, however they can only communicate in Russian. In such cases the charter agents can find a crew that are multi-lingual.

Another typical example could be for instance is that a Jewish family rents out a vessel and they are requesting Kosher food to be served. In this case, it is highly important to provide them with the right chef to serve the client and to satisfy the needs and requirements of the Jewish law.

There are many varied examples of special requests, however a very common request is interestingly linked to the wine cellar on a superyacht. High-net worth clients typically have special wine preferences, so advance booking is highly important to fulfil their requests, since wine importation can take multiple days.

And then there are the prestige questions, a typical holiday cruising trip where there are multiple families coming together and they all pay an equal share of the charter. By paying equally they normally expect equal quality as well, this means that the charter agent is usually asked to provide equal sized cabins for each family.

These are just a few examples to show why is it important to ensure enough time is allocated before departure to ensure proper planning. And to be honest, charter agencies want to be prepared for the guests, since this is a direct reflection of their services.

Based on current trend, most superyacht charter bookings in the Principality are happening in March and April, for this reason people who are coming or booking later, may be faced with lack of options.

On some occasions, the first-time charterer may decide to charter a yacht up to 48 hours before their preferred departure, thus making it a very challenging time for the agencies. There is a saying that the higher the rental price, the less the time that the client allows for preparation, which is always risky, because the agency wants to ensure quality of service and meet the special the special needs of the client.

From the yacht owners' perspective one of the charter agencies most important task and main responsibility is the due intelligence and the identification of the KYC. Know Your Customer is the process of a charter agent, verifying the identity of its clients and assessing potential risks of illegal intentions for the business relationship. With all this the charter agents aims to secure that owners of the vessels who should not be facing any issues on the yachts.

Typically they also check references if they are repeat with the captain of the yachts they chartered. In general clients are all very educated and they do respect the asset. Obviously you will also have some exceptions but that is a very low percentage.

However, risk is always two sided, for example, it is a charter industry practice that no credit card is accepted in the Principality of Monaco for superyacht chartering. All payments must be done by wire transfer and always in advance.

Also worthy of note is the security rule, being all the passengers must ensure they have a copy of their passports before departure, this is important for security, liability and insurance purposes.

There are many chartering agents in Monaco who are taking client education very seriously, for example a month before departure, they normally send the client a brief information on the vessel and the itinerary of the trip, then a week before departure a pre-boarding document with all the useful information and important rules.

Superyacht financing

No matter whether it is a challenging period or not, maintaining liquidity is of key importance even for wealthy people. Superyacht loans are perfect for acquisitions, construction finance, refinancing and also for equity release.

Many superyacht owners use financing solutions with their superyachts in order to maintain their cash-flow. They see it as optimization tool, as owners can facilitate an amount up to 90% of their yacht's fair market value – meaning, depending on the client's residence, between 40% to 65% net of any financial collateral, and for a maximum period of seven years.

The equity made available makes considerably large amounts that the owners can use for other purposes, instead of locking it with the asset.

To be honest, entrepreneurs like to use their capital to re-invest in higher yield projects, especially given favourable conditions today available on the market; optimized structuring may include

(i) part bullet payment,

(ii) annual capital repayment in arrears,

(iii) rates between 2.5% and 3% amongst other.

It is widely known that in general banks accept various motor and sailing yachts, but the process is never that simple.

A friend of mine, Olivier Milliex the owner of OMYS Monaco, who is highly specialised in these deals, shared with me the most important prerequisites to be eligible to yacht financing.

There are three key important indications, namely

1., the yacht's value,

2., how she is managed,

3., and obviously the creditworthiness of the Beneficial Owner

Olivier told me that the most successful loans are those where the fair market value of the yacht exceeds the seven million euro mark, and she is operated by a recognised yacht management company.

It is also important to know that lenders typically prefer Red Ensign, Maltese, Luxembourg, French or Italian flags on the yachts.

In the Principality of Monaco the main indicative terms for a superyacht loan range between 5 million and 50 million euro, and the process take about 3 to 4 months until draw-down, depending on legal complexity.

OMYS Monaco

14 Quai Antoine 1er
98000 Monaco

contact@omysmonaco.com
www.omysmonaco.com

in cooperation with

OMYS Consulting

contact@omys-consulting.com
www.omys-consulting.com

Yacht registration and chartering

231

Yacht registration and chartering

CHAPTER 8

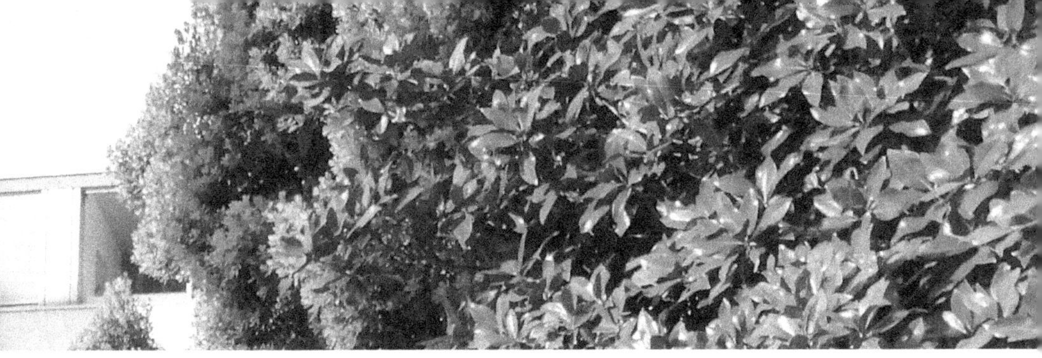

Administrative assistance

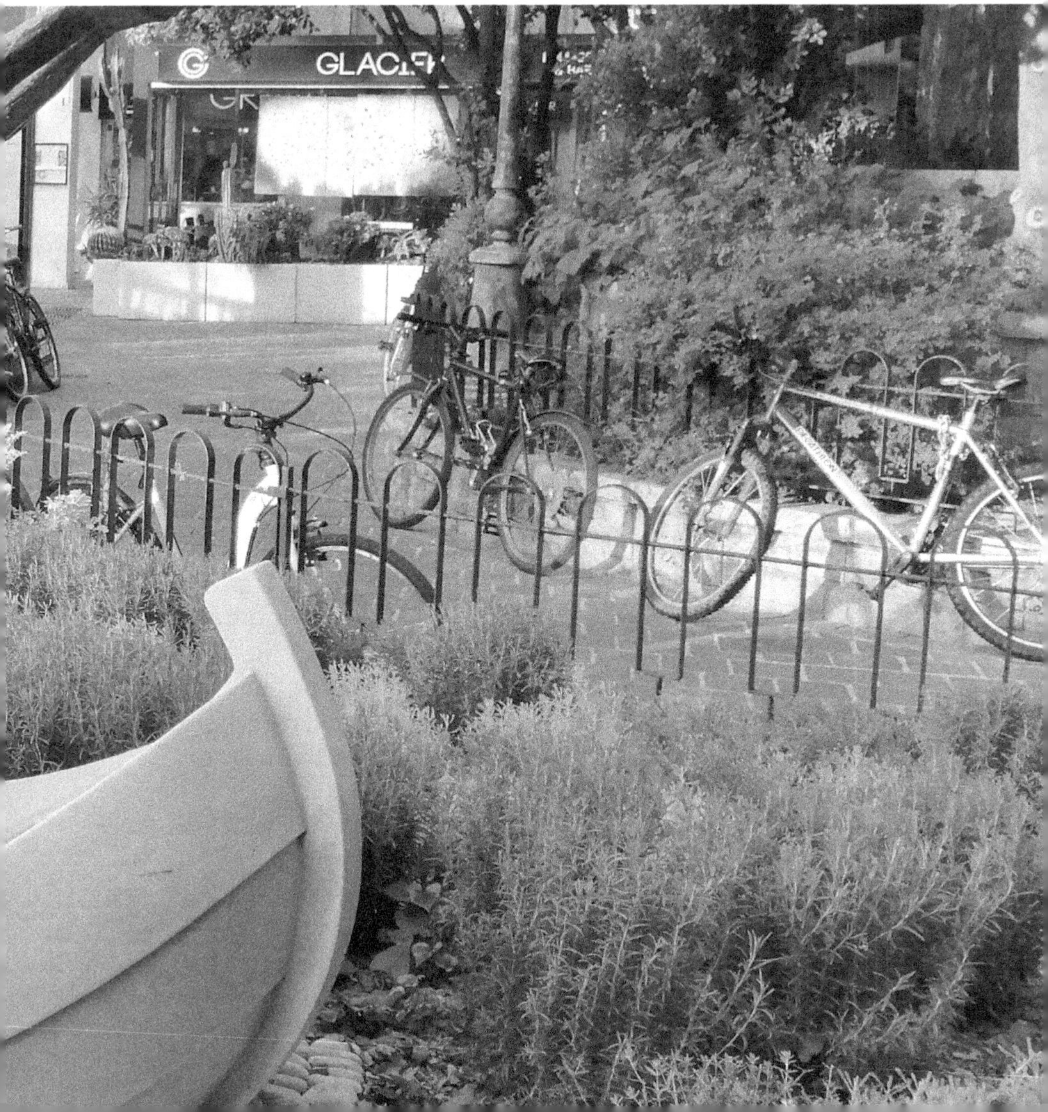

Administrative assistance

Anyone new to the Principality of Monaco might need guidance to navigate through Monaco's administrative challenges.

There are many businesses specialised in Monaco when it comes to topics such as administration assistance, personal relocation and business incorporation. The benefit to work with them is the fact they they have a full overview about every aspects of your needs. For example, if you are looking for advise on personal relocation you might need more than an address and a bank account. The above mentioned businesses can point you to the right professionals in all areas, such as estate planning, enrolling your child(ren) to school, they can help you with transportation, insurance and advice you on the best way to integrate with ease into the local community.

You will also notice that multiple businesses in the Principality involved in the residency process such as banks, wealth managers, lawyers, notaries and real estate agencies who offer advisory services, however, many have limited knowledge of the full relocation process. They often look for their own financial interest first, rather than the full overall needs of the clients. Obviously the bank is more interested in the bank account than the schooling; and the school is more focused on the enrollment than the size of your apartment etc.

For this reason, having an independent and unbiased advisor can help you to create a smooth and stress free integration.

Unfortunately, there are some unofficial advisors from the surrounding of Monaco targeting the wealthy individuals in the hope of gaining some fast profit. Therefore, in many cases it is extremely important for your own protection to double-check their licenses whether they are allowed and authorised to deal and advice in the territory of the Principality of Monaco or not.

When you are choosing an advisor, be sure it/he/she actually lives, works and maintains government approved licenses to deal in the Principality. Obviously, I do not have to write about the significant risks by accepting any advice from an advisor who is not even located or does not maintain a business license in the Principality of Monaco.

My most important advice is: do not sign anything without having yourself backed with a licensed lawyer from the Principality of Monaco. In case anything bad happens without them, it is very hard to enforce your rights, however, with them it can be smooth as silk.

Of course, in many cases, you can save time, energy and money by involving legal advisors or administration assistance service, but be sure that they have the licenses to fulfill their services under the Monégasque law.

In general, a person who is proficient in English or Italian might able to deal with the local administration without learning French. The Principality of Monaco offers various sources to protect your best interests and to help your relocation to Monaco. At the end of this book you can discover some of the selected and highly recommended sources.

I also would like to highlight again that in Monaco you can always approach the Monaco Welcome & Business Office which offers a free of charge guidance for new residents and new business owners. This can be a highly valuable service compared to the independent professionals who are charging 10,000 Euro for a company registration and further 400 Euro/hour on average for the consultancy and preparation works.

However, to have the best possible outcome and support for yourself and your family during this transition, it is highly recommended to engage an independent advisor after your first consultation with the Monaco Welcome & Business Office. Normally, they can recommend you someone who can walk you through the relocation by taking into consideration your individual requirements. This way the process of relocation can be smooth and free from any burdens.

There are companies offering their supporting guidance for you and your family regarding your relocation to the Principality. A good administration assistance partner can expedite and simplify the process because they are working closely with the right service providers to achieve your goals.

I always say that there are two benefits to using an administration assistance partner:

1., Sometimes a good administration assistance partner is able to fasten up the processes because they are working closely with the Avocats-Défenseurs and they are able to save serious administration time.

2., Furthermore you can also secure the best outcome from your perspective by using the administration assistance companies, because it is always easier to enforce the law on them for a possible underperformance. When you have an administration process related case, Avocats-Défenseurs have no responsibility whether your permit will be granted or not, meanwhile you can make the administration assistance company responsible for the successful execution of your request. This should be one of the milestones reached before the payment of their fees.

Few months ago I was contacted through LivinginMonaco.com by a guy who lives in the USA and wishes to relocate to Monaco. He told me that he already talked with his US bank, Goldman Sachs and he aims to open a Monaco based bank account with them.

I suggested him that he should have a local advisor to guide him through the process to avoid surprises. I also pointed out to him that Goldman Sachs (Monaco) S.A.M. has been closed since 2016. So whoever advised him this bank in 2020, they had a very outdated knowledge. I also sent him the reference statement from the government to prove it from a valid source.

The guy came back to me with a very angry tone, saying that he only trusts his bank and he does not trust any local advisor with his wealth.

I promote Monaco since more than ten years and I have helped hundreds of people and businesses, so I thought I send him some reasonings why to hire an unbiased advisor. I explained to him that if he opens a bank account with a foreign bank, he will still face personal income taxes. This is quite understandable, since the bank is not in Monaco. I also highlighted that administration assistance has nothing to do with handling the wealth. Banks and wealth managers will deal with his assets, not the relocation advisors.

Just to top it up, I also highlighted to him that most of the banks will prefer an investment account. Only a handful of banks offer commercial accounts in Monaco. For example many people from the UK believe that they can have a Barclays or HSBC commercial account, just as in the UK. But in reality, these branches in Monaco hardly open a bank account under a million Euro starting deposit.

What I forgot is that in some cases you can not change the preconception of people. They have to learn it in a hard way. Nevertheless, in many cases people are open to listen and to make conscious steps for their own best interest.

Relocation assistance usually costs around 3,000 Euro, which is nothing compared to the further amounts one has to pay during the process. One should not forget the risks without local guidance versus the benefits. Benefits such as experience, connection and in-depth knowledge. It is not just about money, it is guided help to develop and integrate into the community.

Working with an independent administrative assistance company, you can also create a strong base for your future plans. Some business owners plan to have their Monaco residency at a later point; and many Monaco residents might incorporate later a company for business activities. It is good to be prepared and make steps that will fit the long-term goals.

Chapter 9

Schools in Monaco

Schools in Monaco

The education system of the Principality of Monaco conforms to that of France, but differs in some of the obligatory classes. All public and private educational establishments under contract to the Principality are recognised as approved French schools abroad.

The Principality is able to offer places to approximately 6,254 school children and employs about 450 teachers. (Based on the data from the Institut Monégasque de la Statistique et des Études Économiques.)

Schooling is obligatory for children aged from six to sixteen years. In addition, children can attend nursery school from the age of three.

The school year is divided into 36 weeks, from September to July, separated by four holiday periods (Autumn half term, Christmas, February half term and the Easter holidays). Typical holidays are All Saints' Day holiday, National Day, Immaculate Conception, Christmas holidays, winter half-term-holidays, Easter Monday, Spring half-term holidays, Ascension, Whit Monday, Monaco Grand Prix, Corpus Christi and naturally the Summer holiday.

State education is free of charge for all residents, and within the state education system in Monaco, there are six nursery and primary schools.

There is a collège (secondary school) for children aged 11-15, and there is a general and technological lycée for pupils aged 15 years to 18 years, and a vocational lycée.

As your children progress through their schooling, there are options to enrol in local or private schools as well.

Lessons are taught in French, however, most schools offer a multi-language education, which can help non-French speaking pupils to better integrate into their school.

The timetables, teaching programs and diplomas correspond to those of the French national education system. For examinations, the Principality's educational establishments fall under the aegis of the Nice education authority.

The Principality of Monaco offers a high-quality standard of teaching in small and children-focused classes. Numerous options are available to pupils throughout their schooling to suit individual needs and aptitudes, and there are various international classes available.

Interestingly, English is taught from the age of three, and children can learn to swim from the age of five. Also fascinating is that children can learn the Monégasque language as well, which is taught in both primary and secondary schools.

Religious instruction is included in the curriculum, unless parents expressly refuse it. Students are taught Monégasque history and language, and great importance is attached to artistic and cultural educational activities.

When the time comes for university, the International University of Monaco offers well recognized educational and MBA programs.

Finally, the education system in Monaco places an emphasis on mastering the English language.

Having a knowledge of English is highly important for the future of your children; the environment where we live strongly influences us. The Principality offers a truly multi-cultural environment where many successful people allow you and your children to learn from them, and to get inspiration to move forward and to achieve their own ambitions.

When you make your foothold in the Principality of Monaco, you will see that Monaco deeply appreciates creative people, new ideas and out-of-the-box thinking. You can find in Monaco the combination of all the qualities and attributes of other people you may admire. You will see that your children will be able to develop habits that will help them to be competitive, successful and motivate them to achieve their deepest desires and goals.

State education

Within the state education system in Monaco, there are six nursery and primary schools, a secondary school, a general lycée (upper secondary school) and a technical and hotel school:

École des Carmes
33 bd du Larvotto
Phone: (+377) 98 98 86 68
Website: ecole-carmes.gouv.mc

École du Parc
32 bis bd de Belgique
Phone: (+377) 98 98 86 71
Website: ecole-parc.gouv.mc

École Stella
16 rue Hubert Clerissi
Website: ecole-stella.gouv.mc

École de la Condamine
4 rue Saige
Phone: (+377) 98 98 86 65
Web site: ecole-condamine.gouv.mc

École de Fontvieille
5 avenue des Guelfes
Phone: (+377) 98 98 47 65
Website: ecole-fontvieille.gouv.mc

École Saint Charles
11 avenue Saint Laurent
Phone: (+377) 98 98 86 70
Website: ecole-stcharles.gouv.mc

École des Révoires
63 ter boulevard du Jardin Exotique
Phone: (+377) 98 98 86 83
Website: ecole-revoires.gouv.mc

Collège Charles III
Avenue de l'Annonciade
Phone: (+377) 98 98 86 75
Website: college-charles3.gouv.mc

Lycée Albert 1er
2, place de la Visitation
Phone: (+377) 98 98 80 54
Website: lycee-albert1er.gouv.mc

Lycée Technique et Hôtelier de Monte-Carlo
7 Allée Lazare Sauvaigo
Phone: (+377) 98 98 86 72
Website: lycee-technique.gouv.mc

Private education under contract

With regard to private education under contract, there is one primary school and one establishment that comprises a nursery school, primary school, secondary school and lycée.

Cours Saint Maur
33 bd des Moulins
Phone: (+377) 93 50 61 51

Établissement François d'Assise Nicolas Barré
11 rue Princesse Marie de Lorraine
Phone: (+377) 97 97 10 50 Website: www.fanb.mc

Other educational establishments

There are also the following educational establishments in the Principality:

The **International School of Monaco**, a private school offering bilingual education, which falls within the competence of the International Baccalaureate Organization (IBO), whose headquarters are in Geneva.
10-12 quai Antoine Premier
Phone: (+377) 93 25 68 20
Website: www.ismonaco.org

The **Princess Grace Dance Academy** provides an artistic education; it offers training in dance combined with secondary-level teaching.
5 avenue de la Costa
Phone: (+377) 93 30 70 40
Website: www.balletsdemontecarlo.com/en/academy

The **Le Petite Ecole Monaco**, a bilingual (English-French) Montessori pre-school in the Principality of Monaco.
4 quai Antoine 1er
Phone: (+33) 06 40 61 77 17
Website: www.la-petite-ecole-monaco.com

Unfortunately, due to the small size of Monaco, students who want to continue into higher education usually leave the Principality to study elsewhere.

About 28% of the residents have obtained the baccalaureate or similar diploma, and a further 35% have continued their education beyond that. Employment opportunities within Monaco can be limited, but could include art at the Pavillon Bosio, or business at the International University of Monaco.

Pavillon Bosio
1 avenue des Pins
Phone: (+377) 93 30 18 39
Website: www.pavillonbosio.com

International University of Monaco
14 Rue Hubert Cleriss
"Le Stella"
98000 Monaco
Phone: (+377) 97 98 69 86
Website: www.monaco.edu

How to enrol your children into nursery school

Nursery schools (écoles maternelles) accept children who are too young for compulsory education. Children of three years of age and over, or children who have reached this age during the first quarter of the school year, and children aged four to five, can attend nursery school.

Nursery school is not compulsory. State education is free, while private education is fee-paying.

All Monégasque children, or children with at least one Monégasque parent, can be enrolled in a state nursery school on request. Non-Monégasque children whose parents live in the Principality will be admitted if places are available.

In general, the school enrolment periods are from the middle of January until the middle of February. Registrations are always taken in the secretarial offices of the selected schools during official enrolment periods and by appointment only.

You must enrol your child or children during the time periods stipulated by the Department of Education Youth and Sport, unless you have moved to the Principality during the school year.

In the state sector, the school in which your child will attend, depends on the geographical area in which you live. If you want your child to attend a school in a different area, you should send a letter to the Department of Education, Youth and Sport before the 15th of June requesting an area exemption.

State education

École des Carmes
33 bd du Larvotto
Phone: (+377) 98 98 86 68
Website: ecole-carmes.gouv.mc

École du Parc
32 bis bd de Belgique
Phone: (+377) 98 98 86 71
Website: ecole-parc.gouv.mc

École Saint Charles
(it has nursery classes for children aged 4 and 5 only)
11 avenue Saint Laurent
Phone: (+377) 98 98 86 70
Website: ecole-stcharles.gouv.mc

Education under contract

Établissement François d'Assise Nicolas Barré
(school caters for children from nursery age to year 13)
11 rue Princesse Marie de Lorraine
Phone: (+377) 97 97 10 50
Website: www.fanb.mc

Other educational establishment

The Le Petite Ecole Monaco
(bilingual (English-French) Montessori pre-school in the
Principality of Monaco)
4 quai Antoine 1er
Phone: (+33) 06 40 61 77 17
Website: www.la-petite-ecole-monaco.com

How to enrol your children into primary and secondary school

Education is compulsory for all children aged six to sixteen who are Monégasque nationals or living in Monaco. Education in the state sector is free while the private sector is fee-paying.

In general, the school enrolment periods are from the middle of January until the middle of February. Registrations are taken in the secretarial offices of the selected schools during the official enrolment periods or by appointment only. Outside these periods, you should contact the Department of Education, Youth and Sport.

Starting children into school can be challenging for parents, since they will be faced with some serious decisions to consider, and these selection possibilities could form and define the life of their child.

What is also important, is that in primary school, secondary school and lycéé, a test will be carried out to assess your child's level if:

» his or her mother tongue is a language other than French

» your child was previously enrolled in a private school that was not under contract

In both cases, the Department of Education, Youth and Sport will send you the contact details of the head of the school; you can then arrange the date of the test with him or her.

After passing all the tests and initial requirements, the very first question you must ask yourself is the following: Do you want a public or a private school?

In the public sector, you can find options for international education, which means learning the English language as well. Being in these kinds of schools can be very tough for your child since they usually spend less time with the general topics because of the English ones. The public schools in the Principality of Monaco maintain a very high standard of education and many people believe that the new smart generation will come from the public sector.

Obviously, this is a very debatable statement, and many of the private schools will defend their education that maintains similar high levels; however, the decision should not be purely based on the level of education, but the way you aim to educate and form your own child.

Private education under contract, (subsidised by the Monégasque State and separate from state schools) has to fulfil the same requirements with regard to timetables, teaching programs, examinations taken and teacher recruitment.

The International School of Monaco is an exception, since it is not under a contract subsidised by the Monégasque State. This establishment offers bilingual teaching in French and English.

The Principality of Monaco is an ultra-wealthy and extremely luxurious living environment, which you can see in the early ages of children. Young babies are dressed in Dior and Gucci, super-rich teenagers are running around in Louis Vuitton, and young boys and girls spending over a thousand euro each night for clubbing multiple times a week.

By choosing between public and private school, one of the main questions that parents should ask themselves is about the influence their child will receive. This question is highly important, because once you have enrolled your child, it is your obligation as a parent to help her/him to fit into the chosen society.

An environment not chosen wisely could alienate your child, and by that, you can damage her/his self-confidence and development.

Primary school

Primary education starts at age 6, although there are nursery schools for even younger children. Secondary education is from age 11 or 12 and lasts for 4 years, after which students take a further 3 years to obtain the baccalaureate.

In addition, and with regards to private education under contract, there is one primary school and one establishment that comprises a nursery school, primary school, secondary school and lycée.

Education is compulsory for all children aged six to sixteen who are Monégasque nationals or living in Monaco. Education in the state sector is free, the private sector is fee-paying.

Children must be enrolled in primary school at the beginning of the calendar year in which they reach the age of six, prior to starting school in September.

You must enrol your child or children during the time-periods stipulated by the Department of Education, Youth and Sport, unless you have moved to the Principality during the school year.
You can choose between:

» State education

» Private education under contract

» Private education

You can also educate your child at home, subject to the terms and checks set out in Article 5 of Act no. 1.334 of 12 July 2007 concerning education.

In the state sector, the school your child will attend depends on the geographical area in which you live. If you wish your child to attend a school in a different area, you should send a letter to the Department of Education, Youth and Sport before the 15th of June, requesting an area exemption, while awaiting a reply, you should enrol your child in the school in your area.

State education

École de la Condamine
(it offers an adapted timetable to accommodate a music option)
4 rue Saige
Phone: (+377) 98 98 86 65
Website: ecole-condamine.gouv.mc

École de Fontvieille
5 avenue des Guelfes
Phone: (+377) 98 98 47 65
Website: ecole-fontvieille.gouv.mc

École Saint Charles
(the school offers special education classes, as well as a section where
French is taught as a foreign language)
11 avenue Saint Laurent
Phone: (+377) 98 98 86 70
Website: ecole-stcharles.gouv.mc

École des Révoires
63 ter boulevard du Jardin Exotique
Phone: (+377) 98 98 86 83
Website: ecole-revoires.gouv.mc

Education under contract

Cours Saint Maur
(it is a Catholic primary school under contract)
33 bd des Moulins
Phone: (+377) 93 50 61 51

Établissement François d'Assise Nicolas Barré
(school caters for children from nursery age to year 13)
11 rue Princesse Marie de Lorraine
Phone: (+377) 97 97 10 50
Website: www.fanb.mc

Private school

The **International School of Mona** is a private school offering bilingual education, which falls within the competence of the International Baccalaureate Organization (IBO), whose headquarters are in Geneva. The ISM caters for children from nursery age to Year 13.

10-12 quai Antoine Premier
Phone: (+377) 93 25 68 20
Website: www.ismonaco.org

Secondary school

The "collège" is a secondary school for the first phase of secondary education.

Education is compulsory for all children aged six to sixteen who are Monégasque nationals or living in Monaco. Education in the State sector is free; the private sector is fee-paying.

You must enrol your child or children during the time-periods stipulated by the Department of Education, Youth and Sport, unless you have moved to the Principality during the school year.

If your child will be joining the 6e (Year 7), 5e (Year 8), 4e (Year 9) or 3e (Year 10) you can choose between:

» State education

» Private education under contract

» Private education

At the collège level, all students receive the same general education, and may also take some additional options. The core curriculum includes the following subjects: French, Mathematics, Foreign Language, History, Geography, Civics, Sciences, Technology, Art, Music and Physical Education (EPS). Support and supervision of individual work are also available to students.

In addition to the usual curriculum, the school offers four special sections: English plus / European section, International option, Music, Sport.

Support is available at all levels as is a self-service canteen, a swimming pool and gymnasium, and an information and documentation centre.

State education

Collège Charles III
Avenue de l'Annonciade
Phone: (+377) 98 98 86 75
Website: college-charles3.gouv.mc

Lycée Albert 1er
2, place de la Visitation
Phone: (+377) 98 98 80 54
Website: lycee-albert1er.gouv.mc

Lycée Technique et Hôtelier de Monte-Carlo
7 Allée Lazare Sauvaigo
Phone: (+377) 98 98 86 72
Website: lycee-technique.gouv.mc

Lycée

The "lycée" is a secondary school for the second phase of secondary education.

The various options for secondary education at a lycée are:

» The general education prepares students for General Baccalaureate, in Economics and Social Sciences (Baccalaureate ES category), in Literature (L category), in Science (S category)

» The technology option, which leads to specific baccalaureates in the service, industry or hotel and catering sectors

» The professional option, which opens up to three sectors: hotel and catering, industry and services

General education

This option prepares students for the General Baccalaureate and for higher education at a University or a foundation course for the Grandes Ecoles (prestigious higher education institutions that are not universities).

It offers three categories:

» ES category: General Baccalaureate in Economics and Social Sciences

» S category: General Baccalaureate in Science

» L category: General Baccalaureate in Literature

Technological education

Technological education prepares students for short graduate courses.

There are 3 sections available:

» STG category: Technological Secondary Education Diploma in Science and the Technology of Management

» STI2D category: Technological Secondary Education Diploma in the Education Science and Technology of Industry and Sustainable Development, Energy and Environment option

» Hotels and Catering category: Technological Secondary Education Diploma in Hotels and Catering

Vocational training

This channel is available to students at the end of Secondary School (Classe de 3eme – Year 10) in three areas of specialisation: Hotels and Catering, Service Sector and Industrial Sector.

The courses last 3 years and lead to one of the following eight professional diplomas:

» Hotels and Catering Category

» Vocational Secondary Education Diploma in Cookery

» Vocational Secondary Education Diploma in Marketing and Catering Services

» Service Sector Category

» Vocational Secondary Education Diploma in Secretarial

» Vocational Secondary Education Diploma in Accounting

» Vocational Secondary Education Diploma in ARCU Reception and Customer and User Services

» Vocational Secondary Education Diploma in Commerce – Industrial Sector Category

» Vocational Secondary Education Diploma in Maintenance of Industrial Equipment

» Vocational Secondary Education Diploma in Electrical Engineering, Energy, Equipment and Electronic Communications Devices

Once students receive a vocational diploma, they can continue their studies at the graduate level.

International University of Monaco

The International University of Monaco is the only university which provides a business education fully taught in English on the Cote D'Azur. With 60 nationalities represented in the student body and faculty, it is the premier institution for higher education in the Principality of Monaco.

The mission of the International University of Monaco is to deliver an excellent business education in an unparalleled multicultural context where diversity in personal and professional backgrounds, cultures and languages is imperative.

The International University of Monaco offers various education programs such as summer programs, bachelor programs, Master of Science, MBA programs and doctoral programs.

The International University of Monaco prides itself on its small class size where students receive individual attention in their academic endeavours. There is a high level of interactivity between professors and students and creative thinking is encouraged.

They encourage students at the International University of Monaco to go beyond the theories and data taught in the lecture hall by using the skills learnt in real world situations. This allows them to develop strong analytical and cognitive skills that provide them with the foundation for their development as successful business people.

Students learn in a multi-cultural environment that brings together people from all over the world to share ideas, change lives and create opportunities on a global scale. The International University of Monaco students take with them a sense of who they are in the world of commerce and pride in themselves as confident business people and the entrepreneurs of tomorrow.

Monaco is one of the top centres for business in Europe and renowned for providing a safe business environment. The International University of Monaco students graduate with the business skills, practical experience and personal development that will serve them for life. Its mission is to inspire the global generation.

International University of Monaco
14 Rue Hubert Cleriss
"Le Stella"
98000 Monaco
Phone: (+377) 97 98 69 86
Website: www.monaco.edu

CHAPTER 10

Taxation

Taxation

The main attribute of Monaco's fiscal policies is the total absence of direct taxation for Monégasque residents, as there is no income tax, capital gains tax or wealth tax (except for French nationals).

However, despite all the common beliefs, the Principality of Monaco is not an offshore jurisdiction. It may offer zero percent personal tax for its residents, but many other taxes may apply.

The Principality's main source of income is the value added tax (VAT) and is paid on goods and services in the usual way.

The main direct tax levied in the Principality of Monaco is corporation tax on industrial and commercial activities.

Companies earning more than 25% of their turnover outside of Monaco, and firms whose activities consist of earning revenues from patents or artistic property rights, must pay a tax on profits.

The tax on profit was 33% until 2018 and it will be progressively decreased to 25% in the few years:

» 31% as of 1 January, 2019;
» 28% as of 1 January, 2020;
» 26,5% as of 1 January, 2021;
» 25% as of 1 January, 2022.

Therefore, basically the Principality of Monaco will offer the exact same corporate tax regime as France.

French Nationals who are unable to prove that they have resided in the Principality for five years before October 31, 1962, are not allowed to enjoy the taxation benefits of the Principality of Monaco.

A highly important note: If you are investing in Monaco, but are not maintaining a residency in the Principality, you will be obliged to pay tax based on your actual residency.

The absence of personal income tax only applies if the person lives more than six months in the territory of the Principality of Monaco, and his/her activities do not infringe on any rules imposed by other countries.

The good news is that even if you are not living in the Principality for more than six months, you will find banks that are open to help you in taxation issues without disclosing your actual wealth held in the Principality to your country of origin. The name of this solution is Taxation of Saving Income.

The Taxation of Saving Income is a European directive, which introduced a withholding scheme as an alternative to the exchange information. This withholding tax has been applied in Monaco since July 1st, 2005 in accordance with a convention between the Principality of Monaco and the European Community. The revenue from this withholding tax is paid every year.

The best way to imagine this directive is to think about a common pot. The local banks collect all the taxation percentages from people who are non-residents in the Principality in a country-specific common pot. The taxation percentage is lower than in the country of original residency, and the banks provide proof that tax is paid.

The benefit of this system on the first hand is that you pay a considerably smaller amount of your tax, and secondly the bank only states that you have paid your duties and it keeps your actual wealth confidential. In addition, since they place the taxation amount into one pot, it is very hard to find out the actual individuals' wealth indicators. For many individuals, the Taxation of Saving Income is a very useful concept.

Business can be tax free

In the Principality, almost one third of the business formations are sole traders or small companies effectively run by one single person.

Forming a business has its potential since it can be completely tax free during the first two years. Also during this first two-year period, it can be operated from your home apartment without maintaining any physical office.

In many cases, business entities are also useful to diversify or reallocate assets.

Anonymous taxation

If you are investing in Monaco and you are not maintaining a residency there, since you are not staying for more than six months a year, you are probably obliged to pay tax based on your actual residency.

In Monaco, you will find banks that are ready to help you in the taxation issues without disclosing your actual wealth held in the Principality to your country of origin. The name of the solution is Taxation of Saving Income.

The Taxation of Saving Income is a European directive, which introduced a withholding scheme as an alternative to the exchange information. This withholding tax has been applied in Monaco since July 1st, 2005, in accordance with a convention between the Principality of Monaco and the European Community. The revenue from this withholding tax is paid every year.

First, I met with this solution in 2010 when my client manager mentioned to me that they have a so called common pot. I came to Monaco from Germany, so in this example, this means that the bank has a common pot to collect all the taxation percentages from people from Germany who are non-residents in the Principality. The taxation percentage obviously is lower than in Germany and they also provide proof that I paid my taxes.

The benefit of this system on the first hand is that you pay a considerably small amount of taxes, and secondly, the bank only states that you have paid your duties and keeps your actual wealth confidential. Also, since they send the taxation amount in one pot, it is very hard to find out the individual wealth indicators.

Obviously, it can be different with each country. I have only experienced taxation issues related to Germany, but without any doubt, the Taxation of Saving Income is a very useful concept.

Inheritance tax

As you can always read from various media sources, the Principality of Monaco offers zero percent of inheritance tax, which is not quite true. The zero percent tax is only valid in direct line of descendants. The taxation level highly depends on the family relationship level; therefore, tax rate varies from 0% to 16%.

If you create a comparison purely based on the inheritance taxation, the result could be surprising. Just to give you an example, Monaco's neighbour country Italy also offers zero percent of the inheritance tax, and in Italy it is applies on indirect lines as well.

Monégasque law makes no provision for inheritance tax and claims, no tax on direct donations or on donations between husband and wife.

The tax due in other cases of donations is attractively low:

» Direct line of descent: 0%

» Brothers and sisters: 8%

» Uncles, aunts, nieces and nephews: 10%

» Collateral other than sisters, brothers, uncles, aunts, nieces and nephews: 13%

» Non-related persons: 16%

Transfer dues according to Monégasque law, only apply to assets legally owned by the deceased or donator and located in the Principality of Monaco or with situs in Monaco at the date of death or donation, whatever the place of residence and nationality of the deceased or donator.

In the Principality of Monaco, the inheritance percentage is not as important. Monaco's legislation is much more attractive since it protects your children. In the Principality, the widow who survives does not have the classical protection of La Reserve (Last will). Furthermore, the widow has no right to the assets.

In case you have three children, the widow has a freedom of choice to decide:

» to accept one quarter of the total asset

or

» to get the right to use the assets until her death

By choosing the right to use the assets, the widow accepts that after her death, all the assets will belongs to the children. During her lifetime, the widow may rent out the assets but she cannot sell them.

The complete system protects the children and their future, and this could be a very positive reason, a more beneficial one than the pure percentage of taxation on the heritage itself.

Property value added tax

Value Added Tax (VAT) is applicable on operations contributing to the production and commissioning of real estate.

The property VAT applies to the sales of buildings, land and buildings occurring within five years of their completion by taxpayers for that purpose.

Completed properties are taxed on the total price and calculated based on:

» The sales price, the amount of compensation or the value of the social rights corresponding to the gain, plus the additional charges

» Or the real, actual market value of the property, if this real market value is higher than the price, the amount of the expenses or the value of the social dues, increased by the charges.

VAT is generated by the act which defines the transaction, or if no such act exists, the transfer of ownership.

The VAT rate is applicable on property transactions of 20%. The tax is always due by the vendor.

However, VAT is not applicable to operations involving buildings or parts of buildings of over five years of age or, which, during the five years following completion have already been sold to a person other than an estate or property agent.

Such operations are normally subject to transfer dues. In addition, VAT does not apply to sales of land upon which building is not permitted.

It is good to note that sales of such properties by taxpayers may be the subject of optional taxation.

The following are taxed on the margin if their purchase by a taxpayer did not give rise to any deduction entitlement:

» Sales of building land

» Sales of buildings completed more than five years ago where optional taxation rights have been exercised

Transactions not subject to VAT are normally subject to inheritance/ transfer tax.

Chapter 11

Typical administrative challenges

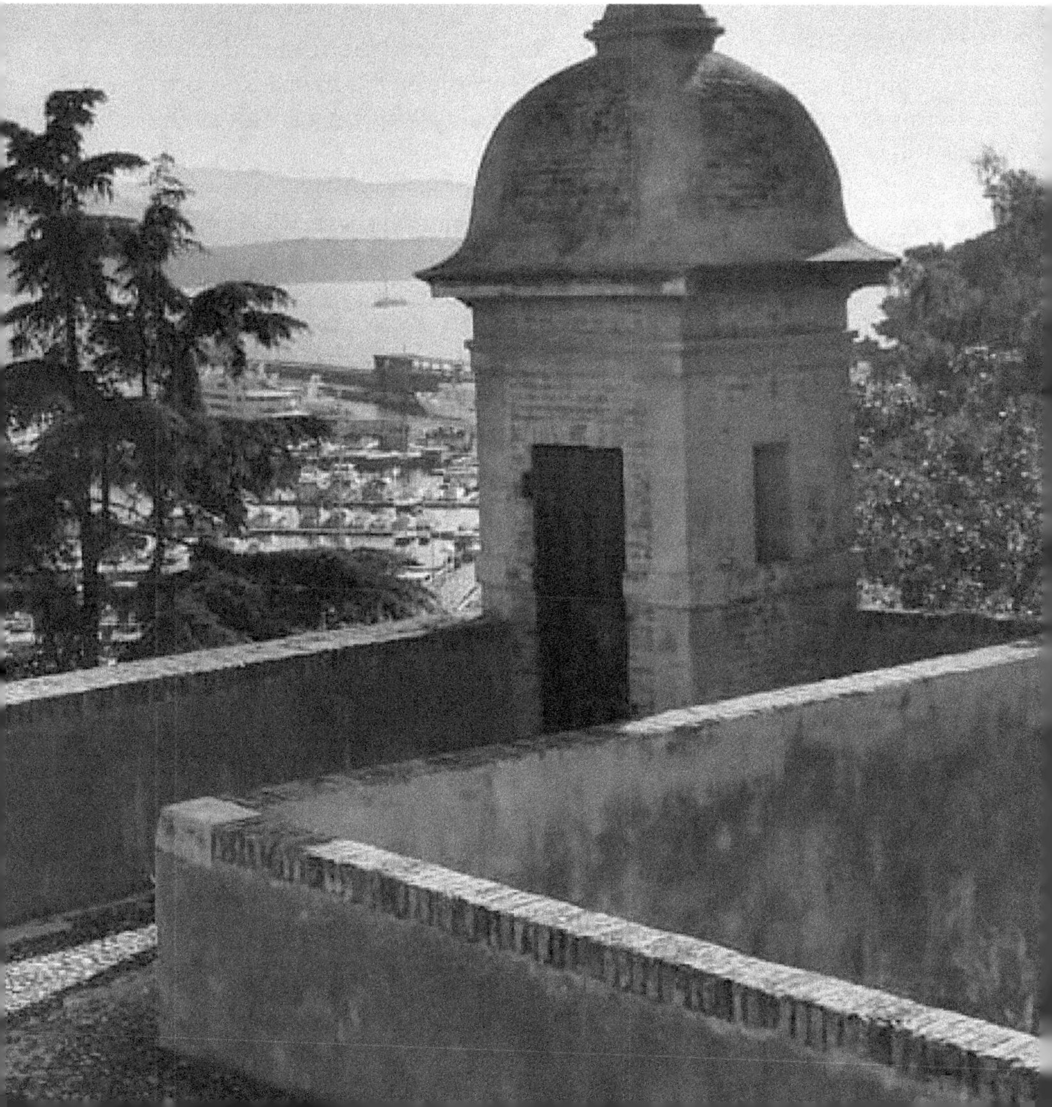

Typical administrative challenges

Let's summarise the most important administrative challenges and differences you might face when you aim to relocate to the Principality of Monaco.

As with any relocation to a new country, there are always challenges to overcome, whether it be cultural or in-country processes, etc. With all relocations, there are support services available to help guide you through this process, via government support or support from private companies.

Obtaining the right information from the right people and places is one of the most important things to consider, otherwise the process of transitioning your life to the Principality of Monaco can be full of obstacles.

– Firstly, the Principality of Monaco has a highly regulated relocation process, and truth be told, Monaco is one of the most regulated countries in the world, which can be good or bad depending on your view. A common challenge can be how to fit into the system.

– Secondly, Monaco and France have many similarities, which can create confusion, so understanding the intricacies and differences is of paramount importance.

– Thirdly, where there is a concentration of wealth, there can be frauds as well, so by educating yourself on the processes that you have learned throughout this guide and by taking the time to select the right partner to help you in Monaco, you can decrease the risk substantially.

As we mentioned before, it is extremely difficult to receive a residence permit if you are in a middle-of-divorce settlement, and it is most likely that many banks and wealth managers will not support you with the necessary paperwork.

What you need to understand is that the process to get a residence permit in the Principality of Monaco takes up to three months and it involves a serious amount of work, such as police interviews, double checks on international criminal records and financial proof that you have the required funds with which to live in Monaco.

Of course, you can obtain an address in Monaco immediately when you sign your apartment rental lease, however, it will only authorise you to stay a maximum period of 3 months in a year, and many people underestimate the serious implications of the resident permit application if it is not approved.

This is the reason why you should always work with trusted advisors, because there are many people targeting potential residents with 'more economical offers'; however, an uneducated advisor will be able to get the job done.

In addition, by using an established trusted advisor, they can personally introduce you to the established authorised Monaco-based businesses.

Banks

Once you have decided to relocate to the Principality of Monaco, one of your very first steps will be to open a local bank account.

It is an obvious step because without an (employment contract) or confirmation from the bank that you have the sufficient financial means to live in the territory of the Principality of Monaco, you simply have no chance to successfully apply for a residence permit.

Monaco's banking and financial sectors offer you an estimated 40 banks and 50 wealth management companies, family offices and financial advisors from which to choose, and together they are managing funds of almost 100 billion Euro.

The amount required to open a bank account for residency is a prerequisite for the government. It has never been regulated; however, the Association Monégasque Des Activités Financières or AMAF recommends a minimum of 500,000 Euro as deposit.

The government only requests your chosen bank to provide a letter stating you have sufficient means with which to live in Monaco. For this reason, the volume of your deposit is only important for you and your chosen bank or wealth manager.

Monaco offers a good selection of banks, wealth managers and family offices, yet very few of them are empowered to receive all types of deposits. Therefore, if you need a specific service in the future then it is always better to pre-check before you select and commit to a bank or wealth manager.

Also, try to decide whether you need a bank, wealth management company or even a family office. If you are moving to Monaco because of employment, there are many options to open a bank account with a small deposit, however on the other scale, if you need a custom-tailored wealth management service and/or some independent investment advice, there are many options in Monaco.

The most important for you is to find the right partner who can fulfil your needs and speak your language.

It is also good to know that all licensed banks in the Principality of Monaco, as well as the fund and portfolio management companies all belong to the Monégasque Association of Financial Activities, which is a member of the European Banking Federation; also note that Monaco is in the Eurozone and the SEPA (Single Euro Payments Area).

All members of the Monégasque Association of Financial Activities are subject to regular supervising, and these supervisions take place with the highest level of confidentiality to ensure the undisturbed operation of the Monégasque banking establishments. They are there to protect the residents and the investor's best interests.

For many years now, the Principality of Monaco has taken serious steps and an active fight against money laundering, corruption and terrorist financing. These steps often reach international levels as well.

The Principality of Monaco has created its own Financial Investigation Unit, called S.I.C.C.FIN (Service d'Information et de Contrôle sur les Circuits Financiers). The S.I.C.C.FIN works together on an international level with more than 130 countries all around the globe. It has a role to suspend financial transactions carried out by professionals who are subject to legal matters.

For example, S.I.C.C.FIN recently signed a reciprocal memorandum of understanding designed to facilitate cooperation between S.I.C.C.FIN in Monaco and the Swiss Financial Market Supervisory Authority (FINMA), in their respective efforts to combat money laundering and terrorist financing. The signature of this memorandum by the Swiss and Monegasque supervisory authorities represents a new stage under the recommendations issued by the Financial Action Task Force (FATF) and the provisions of the EU's 4th and 5th Anti-Money Laundering Directives.

The dedicated care and attention helped Monaco to develop and modernise its banking system and its financial sector. It supports practices and quality standards that are globally recognised by all

European financial institutions.

When you look for a bank or wealth manager, you can find various offices in the Principality of Monaco, from the traditional to the new. Many wealthy residents diversify their wealth by using multiple banks.

Finally, try to avoid the moral hazard. In the wealth management industry (in general all around the world), many brokers and fund managers are highly bonus-oriented, based on the transactions they make. This compensation is not always based on getting results, but on the number of charged transactions on the client, and the result can become secondary.

In Monaco, it is standard practice that many client representatives take you out for fancy dinners, perhaps for clubbing or offer you some nice gifts like invitations to the Formula 1, etc... However, frankly, you cannot replace a fancy promise or a shiny advertisement with real-life experience.

Start to build up local relationships in Monaco, and ask for their personal recommendations and observations, why they chose them and what the benefits of their chosen partner are.

Business acquisition

Unlike most countries in the world, the Principality of Monaco does not allow you to invest into to a local business. Owning any type of local business in Monaco requires government authorisation. The transfer of shares is only allowed freely if it is happening to a Monégasque national.

The transfer of shares to a third party is subject to authorisation from the Minister of State - if the transferee is foreign nationality - or requires a declaration made to the Minister of State. Buying an existing business in the Principality of Monaco is very similar to applying for a business permit.

The only exception is the company formation of Société Anonyme Monégasque (SAM), where the shareholders (exception made for the founders) are anonymous. This is the only form of company allowing an acquisition of the shares without an application process. However, business permit will be required if the acquirer wishes to become a managing director.

With regards to all other legal forms, to protect Monaco's trusted business community, the Monégasque government will pre-check the potential new business owners before it authorises the business transaction.

For this reason, new shareholders will undergo a strict legal background check, very similar to that of new resident permit applicants. Therefore, family status, police record, current residency and many other factors are considered before the deal receives the green light.

The statutory period for review of the application is three months from notification of its eligibility.

This Monaco-specific process can often cause difficulties in business expansions and fundraising, because investors typically do not like the fact that they need to wait three months for a third-party decision.

It may be common around the world that investors purchase existing companies utilising their infrastructures and want a quick turnaround; however, this is not the case in Monaco.

In the case that you purchase a company without prior government authorisation, the business license of that company may be subject to termination.

If you are interested in investing into a Monaco-based business, do not forget that in any investment decision, your due diligence is one of the most important tasks that you simply cannot overlook. It is very important to get firsthand information regarding the investment offers and the people involved in the investment process. Do not allow the legal process to get ahead of the due diligence, especially not the payment of shares before the government authorisation.

Finally, you have to consider the purpose of your acquisition and the future goals for the business. The corporate purpose, referred to as "objet social" in French, defines the activity that a company is allowed to perform.

The Monegasque Government is very cautious with the authorisations to be delivered, and they tend to allow companies with a narrow company purpose. The only exceptions you can see are companies established in the previous century, having a broad range of services or activities, but this is very rare.

Once the acquirer has gone through successfully the background check for the business authorisation, the acquirer needs to assess the compatibility between their project and the company's purpose. In some cases this might require an amendment and further authorisations. Please note that the acquirer cannot change much the purpose of a Société Anonyme Monégasque legal form.

The reason for this is that the company's purpose allows the company to be part of a certain sector, and the sector of activity is a key element for any business authorisations. The Monegasque Government makes enormous efforts to avoid "overcrowding" in some sectors, in order to guarantee the safety and the stability of the local economy.

Since purchasing a company implies a business authorisation process, when it comes to these oversupplied areas, the purchase may well be rejected by the Government.

There are also several areas where it is nearly impossible to obtain a business permit anymore, such as real estate, legal advisory and transportation. Nevertheless, in these same oversupplied areas, the purchase can be accepted and the business authorisation granted if the company to be bought is more than 10 years old.

6 months in a year

The Principality of Monaco is not part of the European Union, however due to its close relationship with France; the Principality is part of the Schengen zone. For this reason, there is no border between France and Monaco and people can move freely between the two countries.

However, if you are considering Monaco residency for taxation reasons, you will need to prove without doubt that you live at least 6 months in a year inside the borders of the Principality; otherwise, you will lose your tax benefits.

Since the Principality of Monaco offers zero personal income tax for its residents, the government does not really check this during the first ten years, however, in most residential cases, the countries of origin will come after you. If you are leaving your country of origin for taxation reasons, you can expect regular checks on the days you spend in the Principality.

It is important to know that due to the Schengen zone, in most cases, the authorities request a proof of your electricity and water usage to ensure you are living daily in your home.

When advisors overstep their limits

As you spend more time in Monaco, you can discover some very interesting human behaviours among some of the employees in the Principality. For many people working in the Principality of Monaco, it is more than having a job; it is a lifestyle.

By watching the reactions of people, you can see that many of the employees believe that they are some kind of mover or shaker of Monaco because they work there.

The most common place where you can feel this effect is in the business arena. When you meet a company representative and start communication with them on a managerial level, you will notice that almost everyone is a decision maker; it really is amazing. However, the very the minute you are ready to move forward with a proposal, they will tell you that they need to run it through a higher level, or they need to talk it over with their team. At that point, you will immediately understand that you have spent valuable time with the wrong person. So, choose carefully whom you take advice from and ensure they have the right authority to engage and sign off on the deals.

Prenuptial, marriage and divorce

A marriage contract is almost a preference (requirement) when you open a bank account in Monaco.

The Principality highly respects your privacy, and the last thing the bank wants to do is to be in the middle of an international financial settlement fight, where they might be legally forced to disclose the assets of their respected clients.

Understanding some people might want to hide their assets under the Monégasque legislation, most banks are taking precautionary steps and most of them prefer prenuptial agreements.

It is reasonable, since prenuptial agreements can be useful to protect your wealth and heritage, and waive the banks responsibility to disclose your financial indicators.

The number of people in a household is a key component in the calculation of the yearly living fund, and it can happen that you need to raise your original bank account opening amount to maintain your residency under these (new) circumstances if you are or become married.

Many banks calculate the basic living fund for the statement they provide to the government based on the number of people in the household. Therefore, banks need transparency on your family status.

This is also the reason why it is very difficult to get a residence permit for those who are in a middle of a divorce settlement. Most banks do not want to engage in these kinds of sensitive situations.

Inheritance and donations

It is exceptional how the Principality handles the question about heritage, and the focus placed on your children. For each family, the question of inheritance is highly important; therefore, it is important to have a good understanding on this topic.

Many people believe that since the Principality of Monaco offers zero personal income tax, it also offers zero percent inheritance tax. Unfortunately, this is not exactly true.

The zero percent inheritance tax in Monaco is only valid in the direct line of descendants.

Regarding inheritance tax, and purely based on inheritance taxation, many other countries offer much better conditions. For example, Monaco's neighbour Italy also offers a zero percent inheritance tax, and more importantly, it applies on indirect decent lines as well.

It might be a surprising fact, that the Principality of Monaco protects the primary family member and not the relatives; therefore, Monaco supports the direct line of descendants.

Monégasque law makes no provision for inheritance tax and claims, no tax on direct donations or on donations between husband and wife. The taxation level highly depends on the family relationship level; therefore, tax rates vary from 0% to 16%.

The tax due in other cases of donations is attractively low:

» Direct line of descent: 0%

» Brothers and sisters: 8%

» Uncles, aunts, nieces and nephews: 10%

» Collateral other than sisters, brothers, uncles, aunts, nieces and nephews: 13%

» Non-related persons: 16%

Transfer dues according to internal Monégasque law only apply to real estate located in the Principality of Monaco or with situs in Monaco at the date of death or donation, whatever the place of residence and nationality of the deceased or donator.

Also, it is good to know that in the Principality, the surviving widow does not have the classical protection of La Reserve (Last will), and furthermore, the widow has no right on the assets.

In many ways, Monaco's legislation is much more attractive since it protects your children.

However, it is important to note that Monaco is not unfavourable with the indirect descendant, such as a widow. For example, in the case you have three children, the widow has the choice:

»   to accept one quarter of the total asset

or

»   to get the right to use the assets until her death

By choosing the right to use the assets, the widow accepts that after her death, all the assets will belong to the children. During her lifetime, the widow may rent out the assets, but she cannot sell them.

We can state that in the Principality, the children are the biggest beneficiaries of all your wealth and assets, not your spouse.

The complete Monégasque system protects the children and their future, and this could be a very positive reason and a more beneficial one than the pure percentage of taxation on the heritage itself.

By relocating to the Principality of Monaco, one can secure the future of his/her children, protecting them from the endless legal battles over the assets. All the legal systems within the Principality are there to protect your family and to serve in the best interests of your children in every aspect.

Legal protection

Strong legal system

The Principality of Monaco has always maintained a strong legal system to protect its Monégasque people as well as its residents. There used to be a saying that the Principality of Monaco is one of the most regulated countries in the world.

The accession of the Principality of Monaco as a member of the Council of Europe happened in 2004. It marked Monaco's wish to ensure that the Monégasque law is compliant with the international standards of human rights and individual freedom. However, at the same time Monaco successfully maintained the special characteristics of its own community.

Foreign peoples' biggest mistake

Human nature has a big problem related to confidence. It is very hard to admit to ourselves when we do not understand something. We are in a society where everybody is "forced" to know everything, to be involved in various activities, and to be an expert in their field.

In my business field as a revenue specialist, during the first meetings, almost 99% of my clients state that they understand their field of business, the need of their customers, as well as their market. However, the truth is that even if you know your business field exceptionally, the market is in continuous change. Just imagine how the economy was in 2005, in 2015, and how it is now. To give you an example I share with you my own experience in the Principality of Monaco which served as my own learning cycle.

In 2010 when I arrived in Monaco, I decided to improve what the local market was offering, and I was ready to create something great to support the local businesses. Obviously, I hoped that by doing this, I would be able to gain some trust for myself and the services I provide. So, I created a news and information aggregator portal called MonacoWealthManagement.com, which targeted my potential clients by offering them valuable information (the site was working in this form until January 2020).

I pushed this business aggregator service, but somehow it did not really perform as I imagined. I also received a letter in 2012 from Mr. Michel Roger, the Minister of State of Monaco, that my activity did not seem professional. One year later, after finally realising my mistake which was never disclosed in details, I have to admit he was right.

Frankly this is another great thing in the Principality of Monaco, which is a very rare thing in the world, specifically that a Minister of State writes you a personal letter after reviewing your contribution to his country. I really respect Mr. Roger for this – he is a great man. Because of him, I was able to understand my mistake and to learn from it.

During those times, I was really sad because I believed that my service was excellent and I was ensuring the highest quality for the local needs. In my mind, my business model was perfect. The number one reason for my temporary failure was my ego.

If you are not open to understanding your market, you have a strong chance of failing. By that time, I had sixteen years of business experience with Fortune 500 companies in various countries. I got the National Quality Prize and was the Entrepreneur of the Year, therefore, I already decided what Monaco needed. Looking back at those years, I have to confess that I was so wrong. My ego overtook my capability for objective observations.

Every market is different and every business sector and country has its own specialities. This is a learning cycle where we can build up things based on our experience and knowledge. However we cannot leave out the local market specific views from the execution of our visions.

In order to give you a short and little example, the MonacoWealthManagement.com portal had a section specifically dedicated for lawyers. I collected and listed all the lawyers and financial advisors I found. You can find them under the section titled "Lawyers and Legal advisors".

I relocated to the Mediterranean seaside from Berlin, Germany, and in Germany, every lawyer is called a lawyer. Honestly, I did not understand what the problem was with the service I offered to the lawyers.

In the Principality, I saw and knew that there are some different titles such as "Avocat-Défenseur" or "Avocat", but I was sure that Avocat-Défenseur stands for defence lawyer, while Avocat is a general lawyer. Again, I made the mistake to decide what those words stand for, instead of researching them.

As we all know, in many cases, success relies only on one tiny thing. For me, this was the meaning of the words.

In 2013, I got a message from Régis Bergonzi, who's law firm, the Régis Bergonzi Law Firm has been awarded as the "Law firm of the year – Monaco" at the Citywealth IFC Awards 2020.

Instead of just ignoring my offer, Mr. Bergonzi took the energy to sit down with me, and he property explained to me how the Monegasque system works. He did this free of charge, because he knew that my aim was to bring value to the Principality of Monaco, and he perfectly understood how to put me back on to the right track.

In Monaco, there is a huge difference between these words. When you finish law school, you start as Avocats-Stragiaire for three years. After that, for the next five years you are an Avocat. So basically, you will be a full powered lawyer, called Avocat-Défenseur only after eight years.

So it is no wonder that the Avocat-Défenseurs did not want to be put in the same box as the Avocats-Stragiaires. Naturally the difference is significant and not just because of the years of practice, but also because of all the experience coming with it. The professional experience really counts in Monaco.

The legal hierarchy is extremely important in Monaco:

» **Avocats-Stragiaire (first 3 years)**

» **Avocat (next 5 years)**

» **Avocats-Défenseur (minimum 8 years of experience)**

Therefore, when I listed the "juniors" with the "masters", they were not happy and they refused all co-operation. Not to mention that many of them criticised that the Legal advisors are not even approved by the Monaco BAR.

The realisation of this "little" misunderstanding with the words took me almost three years. It delivered a big struggle for me before I finally found out the reason; however, the solution was very easy. Since then, I have created different sections and now everybody is happy; the business prospers.

What I would like to share with my example is that understanding your market is considered among the number one priorities in any business. One little misunderstanding, one tiny detail, one wrong approach can destroy your business. If you are patient enough to take the energy to understand your market, then you can capitalise on all of its potential. Therefore, you are ready to be in charge of your future and make significant steps to achieve your aims.

What you need to understand is that in Monaco every business is measured by their professional licenses, and the same rule applies for the lawyers as well. Therefore, it is always better to look for a lawyer experienced enough for your business or personal needs.

Also, be aware that a legal advisor or a foreign lawyer has no power of attorney to represent any client in front of the Court of Monaco. You can find countless legal advisors in Monaco, but before you commit, it is always good to know about their capability under the regulations of the Principality of Monaco.

If you are uncertain of anyone, do not hesitate to reach out to the Monaco Legal Bar and they will guide you.

Not every "lawyer" is an authorised lawyer

Another learning cycle for me was to realise that the majority of the legal advisors in the Principality of Monaco are not authorised. This is a biggie, considering the fact how many private people and corporate entities are looking for legal advice when they aim to move to Monaco, or when they aim to start a business activity related to the Principality.

It is highly important to know that based on the Monegasque law, only Monegasque lawyers can practice in front of the court. The list of the authorised Monegasque lawyers is published on the website of the Monegasque Bar Association, both in English and French (https://www.avocats.mc/index.php/en/lawyers-directory).

So why is Monaco filled with legal advisors who are not members of the Monaco Bar at all? One can say that it is because most people who are coming to Monaco do not know this, offering an easy target for quick money. I made my learning curve to understand this and it took years to realise it.

I asked Mr. Bergonzi about this and he explained me that there are two kinds of legal professionals in the Principality of Monaco. We can roughly define them as attorneys-at-law (avocats) and legal advisors (conseillers juridiques).

The first ones, attorneys-at-law (avocats) need to hold the Monaco nationality and they have to pass the Bar Exam. This basically means that only Monegasque nationals are allowed to plead before Courts in Monaco.

On the other hand, legal advisors (conseillers juridiques) who are mainly foreigners, may have another Bar exam (usually from an EU country) or not, and are not allowed to plead before Courts of the Principality of Monaco.

For me the most interesting thing is that the two professions are authorized to practice in Monaco, but under very different rules.

When I asked Mr. Bergonzi the main difference, he simply said to me that for instance, the "avocats" need to comply with ethical rules and have to pay an insurance, which is not the case for legal advisors.

This was the point when I saw red flags in front of me. So there is a profession, called legal advisor, which can basically freely target clients without complying with the same rules as I would expect in an other foreign country such as in Germany.

On the other hand, we have to be fair because most of the time, "avocats" and legal advisors do not compete on the same market as they do not attract the same kind of clients. Still, some legal advisors tend to create confusion in order to nurture upsetting competition.

Hopefully in the future there will be a plan to create further differentiations or restrictions to protect the members of the Monaco Bar, as well as all the people who are unaware about these differences.

My recommendation is to alway check who is authorised and who is not.

How to find a great lawyer in Monaco

If you need a good attorneys-at-law (avocats) for any reason it might be hard to decide who is the best lawyer for your case.

When I decided to add this chapter I quickly reached out and asked Mr. Bergonzi about his suggestions on how to seek legal assistance in Monaco, and what the first step is to find a great lawyer. He gave me an unexpected answer, but it was all very reasonable.

He advised to try to ask somebody who works at the Courthouse such as judges, court clerks, etc. Basically people who work in legal or related fields and professionals, such as certified public accountants for instance, who are in the best position to recommend the best lawyers.

This showed me again the humble character of my friend. Mr. Bergonzi could have easily said to me that look Zsolt, we are the Law firm of the year in Monaco. Instead of this, he advised from his heart. He also explained to me that not every lawyer has the same experience in various types of legal cases. Some lawyers are specialised in the routine cases such as a company formation, and they can be in real trouble when they have to face with an experienced avocat, who is challenging the case during a court hearing. As a great example Mr. Bergonzi even challenged the police custody law in Monaco back in 2010. Sometimes lawyers have to think out of the box and maintain some creativity to find solutions.

For instance, if someone is looking for a lawyer for a criminal matter, he suggested to me to ask police officers too, as they are particularly aware of the quality of lawyers in this area. More broadly, any person who works in the legal sphere can advise.

We also talked about the budget, because that can be a great differentiating factor as well, since some lawyers are more expensive than others. Although it does not mean that a more expensive lawyer is better than a cheaper one.

It is important to determine one's budget first, which will help to find the most appropriate lawyer. But equally important it is to check whether the chosen lawyer is authorised in Monaco, and whether he/she holds the necessary professional experience to represent one's best interest.

Why do you need a lawyer?

I believe there could be many reasons in life why you have to work with a good lawyer. In this book, I have written a chapter called "Traps and Fraud alerts", which I believe also offers you many great examples.

Even if you are not faced with a crook, maybe you will have questions relating to your business or to family-related topics such as heritage, divorce, etc… Or it can happen that you will face the cruel reality of greediness and power plays, which can seriously damage your interests.

A year ago, I saw an interview with Paulo Coelho, and something really caught my attention. I am not sure it was phrased exactly like this, but the message is the same:

"In the cycle of nature, there is no such thing as victory or defeat, there is only movement.
Defeat is for warriors…
Failure is when you don't have any more interest in fighting.
Defeat ends when we launch into another battle. Meanwhile failure has no end, because it is a lifetime choice."

- Paulo Coelho

In any business, but especially in your personal life, you have to protect yourself. Expressions such as "that's life!" should not be considered. You have to protect and know your own rights.

To give you a typical example from the past years, I can tell you that many of my friends lost ten of millions of euros through their wealth managers (NOT just in Monaco, but all around the world).

A loss on a portfolio and/or a fund that a wealth manager handles is only acceptable when he/she is fighting for the result and the correction of the balance. The fact is that you can create results even in an economic crisis. But when your wealth manager is incompetent or less experienced you can be faced with temporary loss.

A real wealth manager handles every loss as a defeat, but not as an end, because he/she is a warrior for his/her client. But what happens when he/she is not?

When I started the MonacoWealthManagement.com website, this question was really interesting to me, especially from a legal perspective. I know that you sign multiple predefined papers when you open a bank account; you even authorise your fund manager with the power of attorney, but I was curious about the legal security for my own.

I was always educated that in life you can find only four types of exchanges:

1.   Perfect: when you get more value for your investment
2.   Equal: when you receive the same value
3.   Bad: when you get less value
4.   Criminal: when you get nothing at all

In the wealth management industry, many brokers and fund managers are highly bonus-oriented, based on the transaction they make. This compensation is not always based on result, but on the number of charged transactions on the client. And the result become secondary.

If there is one thing I really hate, it is moral hazard. When someone takes your money, your hardly earned funds, and he/she is losing it and blaming outside factors, that is what I call moral hazard. It is like playing or gambling with others' money without having any responsibility on their shoulder. This attitude is really questionable, and this is why it is called moral hazard.

My German friend lost a serious amount of money in 2009, and the only explanation he received was that the economy was bad. The economic crisis became a great tool for many banks to cover their losses with a highly published excuse. Shortly thereafter, we found out that the wealth manager received a one million Euro bonus for handling my friend's account. I knew immediately that something was not right, because why would someone receive a one million Euro bonus for losing the complete fund of the client? It is because he got the bonus based on the number of the transactions he booked and not on the result he brought back to the client.

If I gave 50 million Euro to my girlfriend who is losing it, well I will still have some visible results in terms of some sexy clothes and quality time… I know it is a rude example but I always think about the exchanges. This is a bad exchange, not a criminal one.

Because of this experience, I remember I started to create a topic on LinkedIn searching for a possible solution for my friend. The question I raised was simple, something like: do you have the right to take out an extra bonus on clients, if you lose the funds?

The question was like a time-bomb. Hundreds of so called fund managers told me that of course they have the right. Why? Because they worked hard. I saw a magic mirror which only showed their egos.

For me, the person who takes away your money with a promise of return can be considered a wealth manager. But a person who loses 90% of your funds and he/she takes out the rest of it as his/her bonus for the "hard" work is a crook.

After many months my original question was still unanswered, as I expected, so I asked it again: As a client, what do you have as an exchange if a crook, sorry, a so-called individual wealth advisor, loses all your money?

I got no answers, just angry attacks. If LinkedIn would offer voice mail I would have listened to shoutings of anger all day long. They started to say that I do not understand the business, and if I promise results, then I am the crook. It became a childish game and I had no energy to fight gossips, blogs, attacks, etc.

I know that crooks will do anything to overshadow me and to push their fairy-tales, as they label me as the evil of the century, simply because I raised a simple question. I knew that I had already received my answer from the reactions. It was a great confirmation, and a perfect reason to continue my unbiased wealth guide.

I know a guy who is an amazing business lecturer. After 5 years of hardship, his company went bankrupt, and he decided to teach people regarding his lessons from his own business mistakes. He wants everyone to do better. Of course, the critics always say that he cannot teach, because he went bankrupt. I always say he went through a learning cycle and is noble enough to not let us make the same mistakes! Sharing our experiences is part of giving back to our society.

By having a good lawyer, you can avoid these and many other problems or reduce their risks. A good and experienced lawyer has seen many diversified cases, and Monaco Avocats-Défenseurs have fantastic palettes to protect your best interests.

I believe it is always an individual decision whether you are ready to fight for your right and for the things you deserve, but having good legal support can open brand new doors in front of you, even doors you thought were locked forever.

The real lawyer

In 2012, I decided to open a company in the Principality, therefore, I personally contacted the Monaco Welcome & Business Office. I knew that there are various companies that are able to do this for you, and they have enough skin on their face to charge even 40,000 Euro for the "preparation", which they call an "all-in package". However, this informal service is free of charge and the Monaco Welcome & Business Office is capable of speaking perfect English too. So, I decided to take the time to send over my inquiry via email.

After a few days, my request was dedicated to a manager (they call them Administrateur) and we started to clear every single requirements for the planned activity. I have to tell you, I asked a lot, really a lot, from them and the dedicated person from the Monaco Welcome & Business Office was very helpful and extremely patient. He was very kind to send me detailed explanations and he also showed me the ways that I could double-check some related resources.

However, he always said that the best way is to use a local lawyer or a financial advisor, although he never forced me to do that. It was just a recommendation from the part of the Monaco Welcome & Business Office. I kindly acknowledged, however, I wanted to do the preparation work myself.

Many months went by because I was extremely busy during that time and my business partner was expecting a baby, so from the starting date in spring, we went to the end of summer. The truth is that the summer period is the worse period for any kind of administration in the Principality of Monaco. The offices and Administrateurs are usually fully overloaded with inquires. However, I was so motivated that I did not really care about this delay.

For the summer, we organized all the requested documents in originals with a certified translation into French. The package included the clean police records, birth certificates, bank references, personal introductions, professional references, etc.

We also agreed on the corporate purpose ("Objet social"), which I considered as one of the most critical pieces. The corporate purpose is the part which will determine the requested permits and laws in the Principality of Monaco.

That was it; we were ready. The only thing missing was the "Statuts", as they call in Monaco, which basically includes the Articles of Association and the Shareholding agreement. This was the document where I needed a lawyer.

So I started to contact some of the lawyers I found on the internet. I realized that I could find four types of them:

1. The busy one, who was ready to create the Statuts for us, but since it was summer, asked for two-three months. Obviously, they were not my target because I wanted a faster solution.

2. Then I found the crooks, who said that they could do anything, even in a 24-hour timeframe. I just needed to transfer them a payment in advance. This was quite understandable, but when I asked for a personal appointment, they said that we could not meet before the transfer. It was weird, but probably the reason was simple, they had no office in the Principality.

3. Then there were the "package deal guys", as I called them. They said that they could do the Statuts for me. In order to do so, I only had to sign a contract for one of their packages. The minimum was 40,000 Euro at the time, but many of them asked for more than a hundred thousand. When I mentioned that I only need the Statuts, they tried to convince me how hard the preparation process is. So, I sent them the letter from the Direction Expansion Economique, which stated that all other documents are ready, so I and just need to send over the Statuts. Usually this was the point when they had no more interest in working with me, because they were unable to charge me the full package.

4. But life always helps and if you are persistent enough, usually life guides you in the right direction. So finally, I find the fourth type of lawyer. I had a chance to keep in contact with a very kind guy in the Boulevard d'Italie, who was ready to make us the Statuts in a very short timeframe. It was not easy to convince him, because he was

very busy too, but luckily he understood that if he helped me, then I would probably be his client for a long time. This was the first time that I felt customer care, and in his office, I was the real client.

He charged me everything in advance in a much more realistic price, kept his word, and prepared everything well. Furthermore, he was kind enough to offer his services to bring all the Statuts documents to the Tax Office to get the official stamps on it. And he did this as an added value, which felt more than great.

He managed everything with utmost professionalism, from the preparation to the stamped papers within a week. His professional service was worth every cent.

I am the kind of person who likes to be involved in the preparation processes, because I like to know the options and possibilities. I do not like it when people say I have only one way. It is always good to see the options because they give you a variety of choices. However, there is always a point when you need to ask for professional help.

I believe that to find a good lawyer who is not busy and overloaded with VIP clients, it is almost impossible in the Principality. However, if you are persistent enough, they will be ready to work with you and they will fasten up all your processes with the highest possible level of legal security.

CHAPTER 13

Top business reasons to relocate

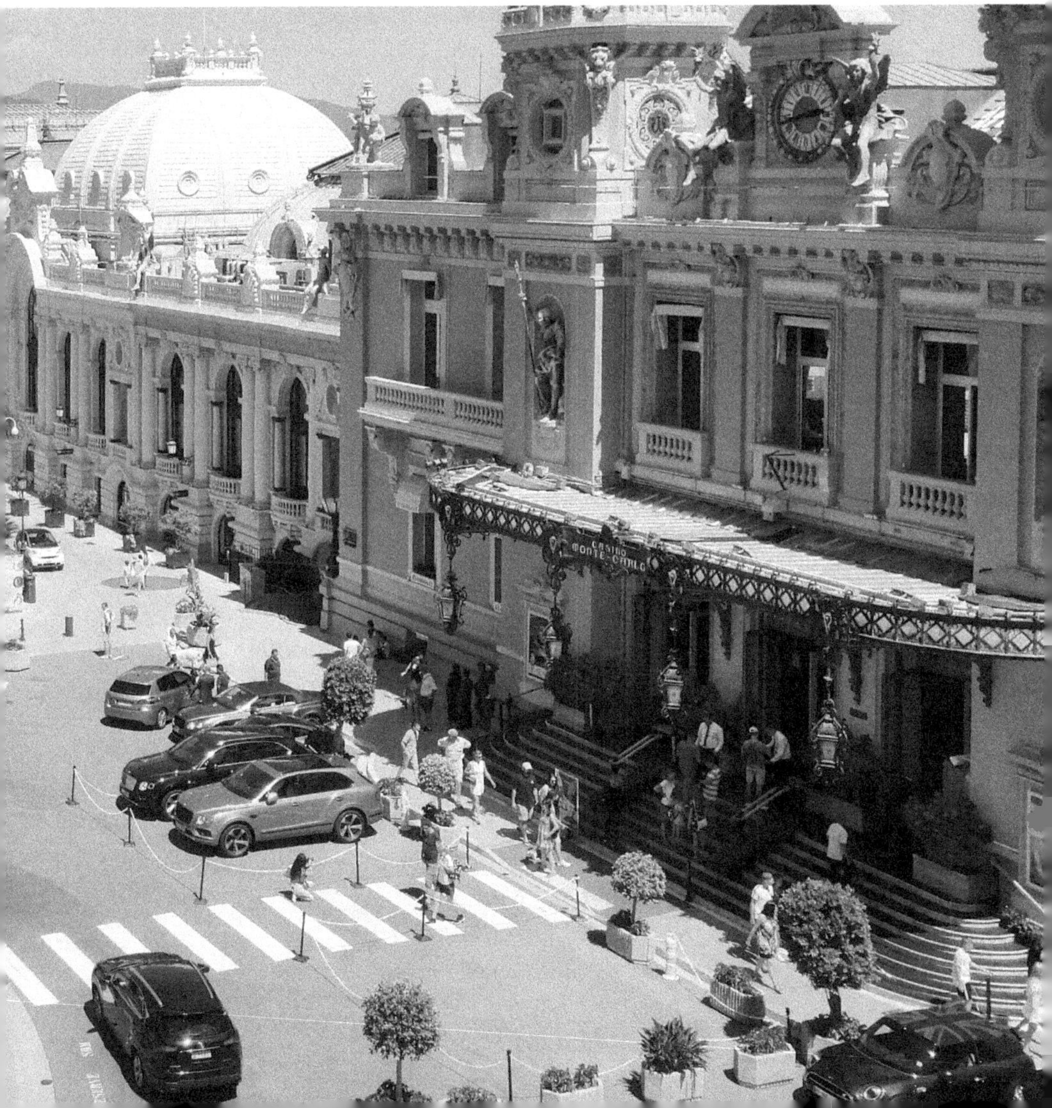

Top business reasons to relocate

The majority of the residents of the Principality of Monaco are successful celebrities, entrepreneurs, business owners and/or high-level leaders. Most of them own and operate their businesses or family offices in the Principality of Monaco.

The Principality of Monaco offers a diversified and dynamic economy and residents are continuously enjoying the fruits of their activities. Just to give you one example, the business taxation is measured on profit alone. Therefore, if you have a one-person company, called sole trader, and at the end of the year you balance the numbers well, then you can be tax-free.

Despite the obvious financial benefits, it is also beneficial to be part of such an environment since all of Monaco's efforts are focusing on maintaining the momentum of its economic growth. In the Principality of Monaco one of the priorities and main objectives is to promote new business activities by which Monaco can also attract new residents as well.

When you relocate with your family to Monaco it can be also essential for you to operate your business from the Principality. Many residents establish a family office to handle the family related wealth and assets. It is essential, because once you achieve financial stability and well-being, you deserve to spend more time with your family, instead of the exhausting and long international flights to a foreign country.

Not to mention that every day more than 139 nationalities bring together their experiences and knowledge from all over the world to the small territory of Monaco. It is a unique business society with high profile people, where entrepreneurs focus on results and profits.

The Principality makes this all easy for you thanks to its Monaco Welcome Office, which is an authority to ensure you free advice and guidance for your relocation. It is especially true when you bring a new business to the Principality of Monaco.

Many years ago, I had a great chance to deal with the Monaco Welcome Office, and they very extremely patient with all my "stupid" questions. It was a real client oriented service where I truly felt that they are actually caring about me and my business concept. And unlike any legal advisors or banks, the Monaco Welcome Office offers its help for free of charge.

To this point, if you have a business, it is worth it to consider opening an administration office in the Principality. Just approach the Monaco Welcome Office and they will help you find the most beneficial option for you. It is something that you can highly capitalise on at the end.

The truth is that operating a business in the Principality of Monaco always involved extraordinary benefits and clear reasons/motivations. As I see it, the top three reasons are flexibility, added values and, of course, taxation.

Each one of them are key reasons to relocate your business to Monaco. Utilising these individual benefits can easily improve your business, and you can focus on further developments as well.

It is also very interesting to see how much change has been implemented in the last decade in Monaco, ensuring more and more benefits for those well-established people who are combining the joy of the luxurious quality lifestyle with the business potential that the Principality of Monaco offers.

However, it is important to understand that since 2012, the words "Monaco" and "Monte-Carlo" are trademarked by the "Brands of the State of Monaco". Therefore, it is not easy to use the word "Monaco" or "Monte-Carlo" in your company, brand or in your product name anymore.

Flexibility

The Principality offers multiple business formation possibilities from a one person sole-trader to a multi-million Euro company. You can easily find a solution for every size of business, and the Monaco Welcome Office will gladly advise you for free regarding the possibilities and the involved benefits they offer.

People typically like formations such as "sole trader". These businesses are typically run by a single person. Due to the importance of the privacy in the Principality, owners have the chance to choose a trading name instead of publishing their own name. For example, if Mr. James Bond registers a one-person company, he can advertise it as Global Spy Agency Monaco. It is a relatively efficient way to utilise the Monaco address.

A little over ten years ago, the Principality granted the possibility to create limited liability companies, which Monaco calls S.A.R.L. (Société à Responsabilité Limitée). It is very interesting to see the economic boost effect of this change. A SARL is formed between two or more people with limited liability to the amount of their capital investment. There is a fixed minimum capital investment of 15,000 euros, which must be released to a bank account at a Monaco-based bank, opened for this purpose.

This was an important strategic step, because before the Société à Responsabilité Limitée existed, you could only form corporate entities with full legal liability. Now days the S.A.R.L. represents one of the greatest benefit for new businesses.

The Principality also offers administrative offices and branches for foreign companies. Administrative offices are established by companies whose registered office is not in Monaco. Usually the sole purpose of this kind of set-up is for management, coordination, or supervision activity. They are perfect solutions for those residents who are not ready, or physically cannot relocate their businesses. These administrative office entities specifically help wealthy foreign business owners and residents.

It is also considered a great benefit that during the first two years, you have the possibility to operate your business venture from your home apartment, if your landlord accepts it. Usually these properties are labelled as Mixed Usage (Usage Mixte), which basically means that the landlord agrees and acknowledges that a company will be performing in the apartment. It is flexible and it ensures you the necessary timeframe to adjust your business to the local needs before you would invest into a new office. Therefore, many family-owned companies prefer this type of solution.

Added values

Monaco itself provides you with many added values, which you can easily capitalise on, since there are fundamental differences between Monaco and most of the countries in the European Monetary zone.

Zero debt country

In the greater public, Monaco was always known as a zero-debt country, which makes and highlights the Principality of Monaco as an outstanding place in the European Monetary Zone (as well as all around the world).

The truth is that there is a little "trick" in it, as the Principality has a double budget.

The Monégasque government has an autonomous accounting body with its own assets and enjoys a special status. The Government has its annual budget as well as the Constitutional Reserve Fund (FRC / Fonds de Réserve Constitutionnel), which is considered as a strong guarantee.

However, combined with specialties in the economic model of the Principality, this Constitutional Reserve Fund helped to achieve Monaco's independence. This is also a guarantee for the Principality of Monaco to maintain its attractiveness all around the world.

From your perspective, having your business in a zero-debt country also strengthens your positive image and PR value. People will automatically associate the exceptional wealth of the Principality with the image of your company. It is a great tool for positioning your company in the eye of your target group.

This is also the reason why many foreign companies choose Monaco as their destination for various events, conferences, and product launches.

Green environment

Monaco is committed to supporting the green environment; it is also a highly sustainable country. In order to provide a great example, in June 2006 H.S.H. Prince Albert II established his foundation (Foundation Prince Albert II de Monaco) with the purpose of protecting the environment and encouraging sustainable development.

Seeing the remarkable efforts of the Prince, many Monaco-based companies are committed to following in the footsteps of this initiation.

One of the great green technology examples is the Monaco based and award-winning car manufacturer Venturi Automobiles. The company was formed by a Monaco-born billionaire, Gildo Pallanca Pastor who is a pioneering visionary in sustainable mobility and energy efficiency.

Mr. Pastor is a very interesting person and his automotive achievements make him a truly authentic person in this Formula E world. For example, in 1995, he set a new world ice speed record of 296.34 km/h with his Bugatti EB110 Supersport, and in 2015 the FIA EV World land speed record was reached by his company Venturi Automobiles.

He is not just a "petrol head"; In fact, he is not even a fan of petrol. Venturi Automobile creates fully electric automobiles. Mr. Pastor's company launched the world's first sports car powered solely by electricity. And this was back in 2004 many years before TESLA. Mr Pastor told me once that "I always believed that in some way that Venturi Automobiles is larger than its products. We are proving that we are are developing things that are innovative and amazing".

In December 2013, Venturi announced the creation of the Venturi Grand Prix Team. Back then, the team was co-founded with actor Leonardo DiCaprio. Since 2013, the team has shown tremendous foresight in their decisions to create an environmentally friendly racing team. Venturi maintained its role model leadership in sustainable car developments. However, only a few people know that the Sovereign Prince, H.S.H. Prince Albert II of Monaco, was a great influence and contributor in the realisation of the Formula E series.

As Mr. Pastor shared with me once in person: "It is not a secret the Prince (Prince Albert II) has contributed to the emergence of this new electric race series. We mutually respect each other. We talked about the possibilities in Formula E and the rest is history".

I believe everyone who lives in the Principality of Monaco knows the "Pastor" name and the Venturi brand, but not many people might not know the passionate person behind those brands. I am among the very few who had a chance to spend a day with Gildo Pallanca Pastor.

One can say that he is a business man, but in reality, he is much more than that. He is an author, a philanthropist (one of the donors of the Prince Albert II Foundation) and a passionate "petrol head" man who brings alive innovative developments. And as I mentioned before Monaco loves innovative people.

People have the misconception that billionaires are living a loud and eager-for-attention type of life, however, I saw a very humble and down to earth person in Mr. Pastor. A man who is able to transform his passion and visions to reality and who safeguards his human side the entire way.

During the Berlin Formula E-Prix in Germany, we spent two days together because I was his guest in the Venturi team garage. I arrived in the early morning to the race track, but the Venturi Team was already busy with the preparations. Mr. Pastor toured around school children in the Venturi box and summoned a magical smile on their faces.

The future generation has always been an important part in the philosophy of Venturi, no matter if it is about a sustainable product development or the education of the next generation. Venturi has even recently launched the first academy for electric motorsport drivers, the VENTURI NEXT GEN with the ultimate aim to take budding young drivers to the very top of electric motorsport.

That day was very interesting for me because Mr. Pastor only granted one interview for an Italian magazine due to the fact that they announced Felipe Massa, a former Formula One driver as VENTURI's new pilot, but no-one else was allowed to talk with him.

Trackside with Mr Gildo Pallanca Pastor in May 2018

That morning, we decided to be much more casual and sat down at the trackside where we talked about life, health, success, cars, and all the topics that mattered for us. It was a great two days during the E-Prix when it was proven that even abroad the Monaco community still sticks together.

Now back to business advantages Monaco is inspiring and the benefits of a sustainable country for anyone.

For many years now the Government has supported – with financial benefits – those who are ready to drive eco-friendly cars. This is a great ambition from Monaco to improve the living quality and the public health by offering quality air in its surrounding. The encouragement to buy clean vehicles, to create solar energies, and to realise water waste treatments all represent key aspects of a sustainable city. No to mention that Monaco's green environment and its efforts are attracting millions of people at the global level.

Competition ready

I love it. Yes, really. The whole economy is built up in order to provide excellence. Obviously, you can find some lazy-bones and gold diggers, but the important and influential mass is there to create better economic results for the Principality. This effort is also supported by the taxation, which is purely revenue oriented. Therefore, the businesses and the government are going hand in hand for mutually-beneficial results.

The competitive mind is both a tradition and a passion in Monaco. Competition is also in the air; it is enough just to observe the events at the Principality such as Tennis, Formula One, Boxing, Polo, Swimming, etc... Monaco is the home of the biggest sport personnels in the World.

I have to also mention here that His Serene Highness Prince Albert II is a great example for competition, for he has been a member of the International Olympics Committee since 1985 and is the president of the Monegasque Olympic Committee. This is not surprising given that the H.S.H. Prince had an exceptional past as a bobsledder. H.S.H. Prince Albert II participated in five Olympic Games, from Calgary in 1988 to Salt Lake City in 2002, as a member of the national bobsleigh team.

Furthermore, both His Serene Highness Prince Albert II and his beloved wife, Her Serene Highness Princess Charlène of Monaco have a serious and respected past in the world of sports.

High profile people

Since the Principality attracts the wealthy and influential people in a very small and concentrated place, you have higher chances to find valuable contacts for your own business. There are partners who might not only push you further, but can also be your role model in your future development strategy.

What makes Monaco really unique from a business perspective is the fact that almost 80% of the residents are high-profile decision makers and company owners with a well-established business and financial background.

1 in 3 people in Monaco are millionaires, however, most of them are established ultra-high net worth (UHNW) individuals, which means they have a minimum of 30 million euros in assets.

Since Monaco is full of key players it is always easier to get the right contacts. The magic usually happens when you meet with these people in multiple events, because they will start to recognise you and they will see that you are not just a seasonal tourist, but one of their community.

Already well positioned

The names "Monaco" and "Monte-Carlo" are already well-positioned marketing tools for those who are ready to capitalise on their potentials.

In many cases, the sole reason why people open a business in Monaco is to utilise the brand. Having a company in the Principality of Monaco can be also considered as a door opener label, since most people immediately think about wealth and stability when they hear about a Monaco-based company.

I will share with you more thoughts about the "Monaco" and "Monte-Carlo" brands later because they are protected trademark.

Taxation

Despite the common belief, Monaco is not an offshore jurisdiction. Having a business in the Principality involves various taxation obligations as well. Luckily Monaco's tax regime is built on some extremely supportive pillars.

As a new business owner, you have the possibility to start and build up your business without interfering with any taxation issues. During the first two years of business operation, your company is tax free, which can support the establishment and improvement of your business.

After three years, you will be due to pay tax, but not based on your income. In the Principality of Monaco, the corporate taxation is mainly based on revenue. Therefore, you only pay tax if you are able to gain profit from your business activity (and if you have not transferred your revenue to yourself as an annual bonus, because in that case, no revenue stays in the company and there is nothing to pay for tax).

Without any doubt, Monaco's taxation is very attractive for businesses comparing its profit-based taxation method to most of the income-based taxations offered by other countries.

Talking about taxation, Monaco also maintains its strong reputation when it comes to confidentiality. Just to compare Monaco to Switzerland, forty-one Swiss banks recently signed an agreement with the US Government that they will disclose how they helped the US citizens to avoid their taxation obligations. And if it is not enough, they will even disclose the name of the involved bankers and financial advisors.

Disclosing confidential information was unimaginable in Switzerland before; now, it has become a reality and very real threat to the millionaires (which luckily drives more attention to the Principality of Monaco).

Of course, this dramatic wealth management and banking situation in Switzerland started already in 2009, when one of the biggest bank in Switzerland, UBS was accused by the US government. The case ended with a settlement payment of 780 million USD, but it was just the start, since the USA accused fourteen more banks in Switzerland.

After putting strong pressure on the Swiss banking system, the USA took a very new approach. They offered a clean start without any examinations of all the banks who are ready to reveal their best practices for avoiding taxes. Although the offer had a very tricky part as well, since the reduced penalty depended on the fact of how many clients these banks were ready to disclose, including their bank account details, as well as all the financial advisors and bankers who were involved with those clients and accounts.

This is something unimaginable in the Principality of Monaco. All government experts know that if they were to disclose the assets of their clients, they would lose trust, and the Principality would risk a heavy financial crisis. Monaco puts its residents first and this will hopefully never change.

Monaco's taxation system is smart and built on strong pillars.

The dark side or challenge

Even if the Principality of Monaco sounds really attractive for you and your business, it has its own dark sides. This reflects also in the fact that most of the new residents are leaving Monaco in the first three years.

But to be fair, whether it is a dark side or not, at the end of the day it all depends on your mindset and your attitude.

My advice for anyone is simple: Do not come here to lose, come here to WIN!

And to be a winner as a foreign "outsider", you have to be prepared for some major differences in the daily business methods and recognise that if something is different, it does not mean it is worse.

One of the most common problems for foreign people is that the communications and the business decisions are very slow. I would say extremely slow… In most cases you can wait for two-three weeks for a call back, and this is considered to be normal. Sometimes you will get a reply to your e-mail only after two months. There is no such thing in Monaco as time sensitivity (especially with digital communications), and I believe there is a reason for this.

There is a law in Monaco called Article 6., which basically says that as a business owner you cannot fire your own employee. If you, you will have to pay a serious penalty. This influence and controlling power of the government protects the employees and the residents of the Principality, but I truly believe that in many cases, it may slow down the business and the economic development.

During the last four years, I have experienced many times that some employees become very comfortable in their positions; I would almost say lazy. This lack of motivation can really destroy ambitions, since it is very hard to implement any kind of changes. In many cases, it creates a lack of efficiency from the side of the employees.

One of my worst experiences, which repeats itself from time to time, is related to my own ambition to get things done, which is sometimes mixed up with "pushing" things. Asking people after two weeks to answer to business conversations can cause in Monaco a resistance in the prospects. In most countries, you would consider it a form of disrespect if someone you have met does not answer your emails after a long time. Here in Monaco, it is a part of doing business as usual. Obviously, you can always find motivated partners as well and I would really suggest sticking with them.

Based on my own professional experience, one of the biggest disadvantages of a company or business organisation is when its reaction is too slow to the market needs. This can be especially true when your company is aiming to enter a foreign market without adopting its business behaviour.

Therefore, if you want to get rich in three months, Monaco is definitely not your country. When you relocate your business, you have to be prepared for much longer business decision-making. You will be faced with this from day one, because a typical business formation takes 6 months in Monaco, unlike in many countries, where you can form a company through an online government portal. This flexibility does not exist in Monaco. As I always say in my business lessons and writings, any kind of improvement comes from fully understanding the specific area.

Yes, many people will say that they received immediate answers, but I would ask them to make a bold difference between whether they are spending money or asking for it. When you want to pay for a service you will be handled in a very exceptional way. However, when you are looking for a deal for a Monaco-based company to pay, that can be a different type of game.

The biggest problem when you are trying to implement your business into this protective and very closed environment is coming from the fact that change is one of the most feared things after death. And as much as the Principality likes innovators, creative people, and sport personnels, Monaco does not like rapid changes in business developments.

The reason why it is frustrating sometimes is because I like to be in charge. When I am passionate about something, I like to grab the opportunity and to go for it. However, slow decisions can demotivate people.

One of my favourite life and business example comes from China. They teach the freedom of choice, and therefore, in China the word "crisis" is written with two symbols.

The first symbol is called "Wei" and it means "crucial" or "danger". Therefore, Wei is often referred to as "a time of danger".

The second symbol is called "Gee", which means "opportunity" or "a time of opportunity".

So, in China the word crisis contains the "crucial" and the "opportunity" symbols as well. This is exactly the right philosophy of being a tiger or a rabbit in our life.

The decision is always yours!

Yes, it can be nerve-wracking sometimes, but it is also great because nerves can give you an adrenaline push making you capable of achieving things you never imagined before. Nerves are not equal with fear. Fear is coming from your decision, and fear can crush you. Meanwhile, nerves are a reaction to a situation, and in most cases, it brings you more power to accomplish things.

From my personal point of view, the one thing that I really hate in business is non-performance. Many people are lazy to do their homework or are simply just not ready to look around and challenge their situations. However, I have to admit that more than twenty-five years ago, I was the same too. I started to gain knowledge from books, but when something happened which was not written in books, I started to panic.

After many years, I crossed paths with Dodo Newman, the artist, and she taught me one very important thing, which was to not give up my beliefs and a positive solution. She taught me to keep up the hard work and to continuously believe in my aims.

I organised for her a speaking possibility at the Monaco Residents' Club (Club des Résidents Etrangers de Monaco) back in 2012, where among many other things she said the following:

"Passion cannot be learned, cannot be faked or copied. It is something that burns like fire, and if not kept alive, it soon can burn out.

When I first meet people, often their first impression of me is that my philosophy and the way of thinking is far away from the standards and sometimes they seem almost impossible.

"I believe that impossible means = i m possible."

- Dodo Newman

Most of us are ready to give up the fight without even realising that maybe we are already at the finish line. Thanks to Dodo, I realised that I can always challenge the existing because we are capable of improving things and innovating.

Since then, it has become my philosophy that if you try something new, you never lose, however, you immediately lose, when you give it up. And in Monaco you need to have persistence.

You can do the same old methods hoping to survive or you can take the opportunity and challenge the market. It is never easy as it seems, but it is easier to wait and do nothing. The truth is that there is always a way.

The other dark side is that I often hear in Monaco that success is dangerous. Since the Principality is very concentrated, the more you are in the spotlight, the more people are monitoring your steps. Those who are not ready to change or improve, to stand out from the rest, is almost like waiting for your own failure. If one fails, it immediately spreads across Monaco as small-town gossip.

So is success really dangerous here? I would not say it is, but I have to admit that you can find many power plays and greediness. However, at the end of the day, it all comes down to your inner peace and mindset.

One of the most basic and important business rules is that you are responsible for all your own decisions, success, or failures. Only you! When you know that you did everything right with the tools and assets you had, you will be always happy in front of the face looking back in the mirror.

There is always a way if you are ready for competition. However hard it is, you cannot blame the external factors. We are in the same business jungle and the rules are the same for all of us. No exceptions. It is on you, if you will survive or not. It is all upon you if you will be a rabbit or if you will become a tiger.

Nowadays, business is your jungle, your playground. If you do not want to be a rabbit, then change it. You are the master of your destiny. Do not blame others – that is the game of losers and cowards.

Never blame outside factors, never say what could be if... You need to focus solely on what you can do now with all your available assets. You need to bring out the best as much as possible from your current, existing knowledge.

Economy, politics, weather, your neighbour, etc... it is easy to blame these factors for your failure, but believe it or not, these factors influence your competition, not only you.

You cannot change these factors, just as you cannot change the politics. You need to accept them, acknowledge the rules, and go forward towards your aims. Sitting and waiting for the changes equals suicide, because you will lose control over things. And even in a small community such as Monaco, there is always a way to proceed.

>"Excuse = The easy way.
>An excuse is worse than a mistake because it effects everything around us and drains down all possible solutions. There is always a way, a wrong way ahead is much better than a no way at all anywhere..."
>
>- Dodo Newman

Sometimes we are all in a symbolical maze and our survival depends on our decisions, determination, and the influence of the people around us.

People like the balance and the regularity in their lives, therefore changes are often considered something negative. However, changes are never bad because by changing and challenging the existing we have a very good position to improve our skills and our business.

I would like to highlight that you cannot achieve anything without contrast and fear. However, in the business society of the Principality you will definitely need persistence as well.

Unseen treasures for investors

For many decades, Monaco and its registered businesses lived from the legacy of the Principality itself. It was easy because the name Monaco and/or Monte-Carlo already attracted people without making any serious efforts. The labels worked as great magnets to collect prospective clients.

It is not a secret that in Monaco most of the companies are related in some way to the banking, wealth management, family office, and financial industry (or hospitality). The Principality is not really the place for commercial banking and only very few banks offer these solutions among their services. Most of them are specialised in asset management and wealth management. They altogether provide a significant part of the economic power in the Principality of Monaco.

Suddenly in 2008-2009, just as every country on the globe, Monaco also felt the effect of the economic crisis. Unfortunately, some of the numbers dropped down and for a short period of time the Principality lost many residents. However, in the land of glamour and wealth, people (let's be correct, at least some people) realised the wind of change and they grabbed this opportunity.

To understand the way of capitalisation of a market gap, such as the economic crisis was, you need to start from the thesis that the value has always been a relative concept, which is based on the personal judgement of the customer. A real product has never had an absolute value, a product is worth as much as the buyer is willing to pay for it in exchange. Therefore, it was great that the financial advisors started to really focus on the personal needs as well by implementing many custom-tailored solutions.

Monaco is a strong player in the wealth management industry and its local companies are one of the greatest competitors when it comes to credibility.

For an experienced HNWI investor, trust is a very key issue, especially with high level investments. Many people tend to make the mistake of judging projects based on the promised profit and income and other so-called material factors behind them. However, the real value is not the promise, the real value at the end of the day is the result.

The past years of the economic crisis clearly showed us that the numbers and indicators are not enough anymore for the HNWI investors to invest. The HNWI investors are becoming more educated and informed because of their loss during the economic crisis, and the personal trust in the wealth managers has become first priority. They increasingly shy away from big institutions because of their negative experiences with their sales-driven representatives and their bonus-oriented account officers. That is why they are looking for fair and sometimes independent partners who are in place for a lifetime, who strive to achieve the client's "peace of mind" feeling, the nearly perfect match of personality and portfolio.

I consider this as one of the reasons why so many new family offices have opened since 2009 – they have realised a market gap. At some point of the business development, we need to open to new markets as well. There is one point in the life cycle of all business, where by focusing on local businesses, there are no further possibilities.

I believe that after experiencing the economic crisis, most of the HNWI investors are looking for long-term partners. Only those companies perform in the long term, which are not hunting for fast profit but gaining results with secured investments to show their client base their competency. Luckily, many companies in the Principality started to realise this.

The HNWI investors are keen to find partners who they trust, trust which is not entirely based on pure numbers. HNWI investors are continuously looking for result-oriented, sharp-minded wealth managers and investment advisors.

In 2012 when I talked with one of my investor friends, he provided me with a summary of the needs. HNWI investors are not looking for high return, they simply do not want to lose. They are also satisfied with small growth, but they hate to lose. The focus of the HNWI investors has changed.

In the past ten years, the local financial players started to build up value for their wealth services. This converts a potentially valuable wealth management solution into a really valuable one.

When we know that a client really wants something, then price does not really matter anymore. Because price is easy, everybody knows that the 7% interest rate is less than the 12% interest rate. However, after 2008, trust has become the number one priority. Everybody sees the promises, but wealth advisors in Monaco had to show the HNWI investors their values as well.

Let's see everything with the eye of an investor. Let's say that we have two trees, which are representing two wealth management companies. Both trees have the similar size of crown but their trunks are different in size. Because of the difference of the trunk size, they have different types of roots as well. In the picture, the HNWI investor is standing between two trees.

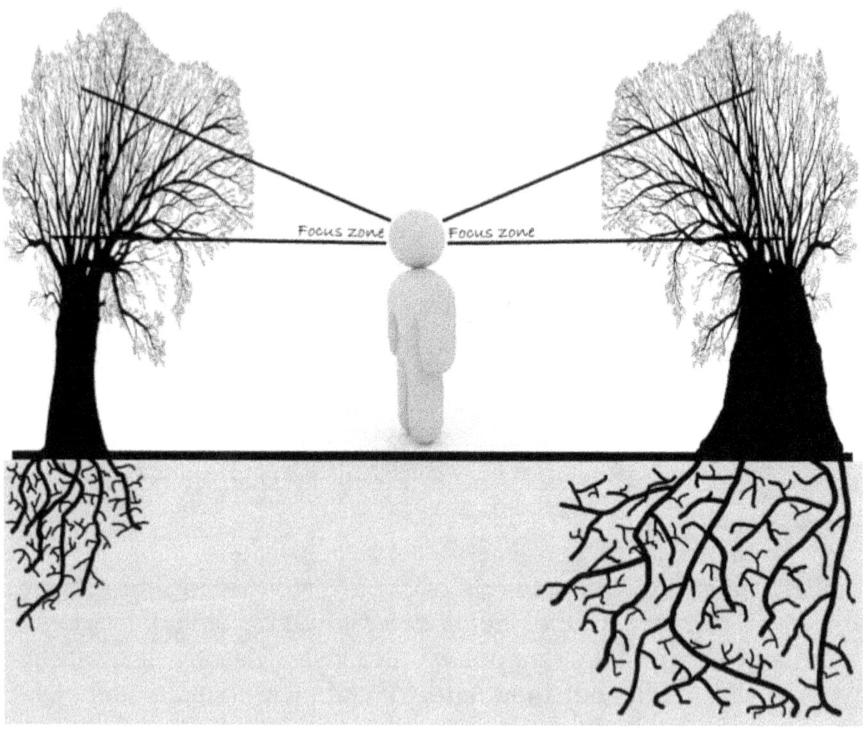

In a calm economic situation and without being educated, this is how clients see the companies. The trees are the companies and usually everybody is looking at the tree crown, which is the biggest visible surface. Let us say it is the packaging of the tree, therefore all marketing, PR, and sales experts are aiming to present it in the most delicate and fancy way.

When you are focusing only on the profit then you can easily be misled by the illusion of the crown. This is among the major reasons why so many investors have lost their funds all around the world. We have to accept that many banks around the Globe focus on the brand message instead of the intense growth of new clients. Maybe this was the biggest lesson to learn during the economic crisis. So, let us change the focus of the HNWI investor from the tree crown to the roots of the tree.

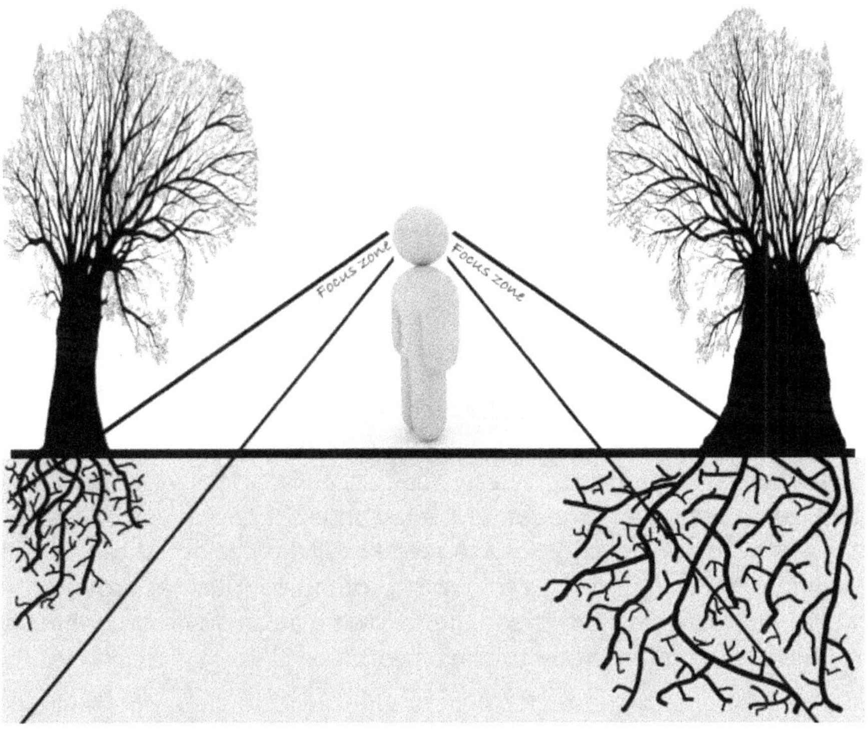

The values are usually hidden, just as you cannot see the roots of the trees. As I mentioned before, in difficult economic situations people are looking for stability. When people are looking for stability their focuses are changing. They are not looking anymore at the fancy tree-bush, not even at the tree trunk, but at the roots. HNWI investors will try to make their decisions based on the roots of the tree.

Every wealth manager knows that if their company is not able to generate profit, then it will not survive for a long time. But fewer wealth managers understand that if they cannot create value for their clients, they have no future at all.

So, closing this example, the key to prosper is to focus on the values, to present our knowledge, heritage, and uniqueness to our prospective and current clients. And frankly the Principality of Monaco holds countless great values. Its location, economy, traditions, and heritage are all marvellous.

Monaco was forced to change and to quickly adopt the economic changes.Most of their businesses understood that when the clients understand the values and can relate to them as well, then the business will prosper in the long term.

As it is today, the Principality of Monaco offers exceptional possibilities for investors and wealthy individuals. If you are wise enough, you can find experts who are able to offer you diversified solutions to protect and increase your wealth, or at least maintain its level without losing any of your funds.

But there is a saying in Las Vegas, in the city of gambling, which I would really consider in Monaco as well. When you go to Las Vegas with big ambitions to win millions at the poker table, or to spin your number at the roulette, you are full of positive energy and high expectations. However, to be fair, in most cases, you will leave the city with some major loss. As we know the casino system is not built on charity, it is among the most profitable industries around the world. Taxi drivers used to say the following as an advanced warning on the way from the hotel to the airport:

> "You are not here to become a millionaire,
> but to enjoy your stay."

Therefore, when you come to Monaco you have to be able to see under the surface, and you need to take your time to really understand its business methods, results, and reality. Without any doubt, you can find many great investment potentials, but to avoid any bad experiences I dedicated a chapter in this book for you, called "Traps and Fraud Alerts". I would highly recommend reading it beside all the legal topics to secure the best outcome for your investments.

But as scary it seems, I would like to highlight that for persistent people, Monaco offers exceptional values.

Just think about it – having 139 different nationalities among its residents, the Principality of Monaco offers colourful investment possibilities, no matter whether you invest in a traditional way, into tangible assets, to impact investments, or as an angel investor you will definitely find multiple interesting offers for your needs. Sometimes you can find really exotic or out-of-the-box types of investments as well.

You can also get good starting points from the various events organised by local financial advisors, fund raisers, or specified associations.

If you do not let the colours of the rainbow control you, and if you are ready to properly be informed about the possibilities and their backgrounds, then you will have a great chance to realise any return you deserve.

Because at the end of the day there is no better place on earth than in the Principality of Monaco to learn from the influential business elite. Maybe you can find more leaders in New York or London, but there they are the "slave" of their daily routines in an absolutely goal-oriented mindset.

In the Principality of Monaco, people are enjoying the quality of life that Monaco provides. It is more about relaxing, networking, and socialising. If you are smart enough you can meet and network with well-established people who will be ready to advise you and share with you their personal experiences and opinions. You can learn from the biggest industry players here through a very personal level of connection.

And regarding any investments, if you are not confident where to invest, you can always follow them or even make investments in a syndicate way with people you trust or admire. Investing in a syndicate in venture capital investments, often only with small amounts such as 15,000 euros per person is becoming very popular in Monaco. This way, investors share the risk, while maintaining a diversified investment portfolio.

I cannot highlight enough how protective Monaco is with its residents. However, you can also enjoy this protective mentality when you are willing to invest in Monaco.

One of the reasons why Monaco is so secured for investment purposes is that its legal system works and reacts so quickly. Not to mention that thepolice has its own right to immediately interfere when the situation requires it.

I have to admit that when a case is related to money, sometimes the court is even faster than you would expect , giving almost no chance to escape from the obligations.

Monaco has different set of values, and thanks to its legal system, if the case seems clear and obvious, you can even force out a first-level court decision against the defendant without his/her presence. In these cases, the defendant has no right at all before the judgement since he/she is not even noticed, or let us say politely, he/she is not obliged to appear.

Monaco has a very supportive police if you need any kind of help, and you should never forget that they are there to protect and even interfere. I believe this is a great advantage for all the investors to create and maintain investment portfolios, and also for business owners in the Principality of Monaco. It is a good and fair "co-operation" with Monaco built on trust.

Recommended partners:
THE OFFICE
BUSINESS CENTER
vk*p
business advisors

Chapter 14

Business formation and operation

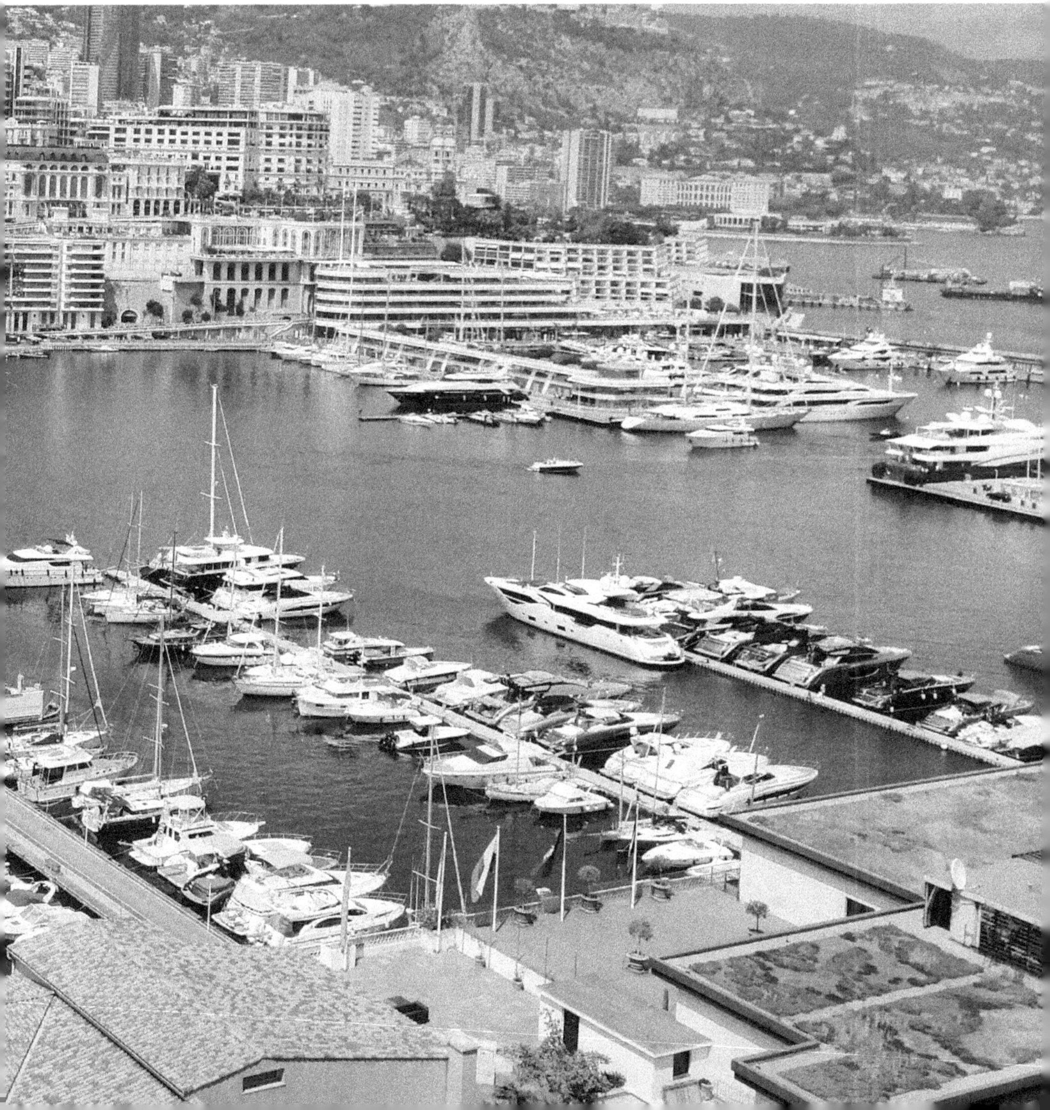

How to start a business

A Government authorisation is required for any kind of business activity in the territory of the Principality of Monaco. The approval process takes usually between three to six months, but it can be very lengthy, complex, and time consuming. The most common legal structure is a sole trader (personne physique or société en nom personnel), which involves a bit easier process compared to the other possibilities.

	2014	2015	2016	2017	2018
Personne Physique	1 915	2 010	2 081	2 222	2 313
Société Anonyme Monégasque	1 210	1 252	1 241	1 246	1 259
Société à Responsabilité Limitée	1 653	1 878	2 052	2 247	2 434
Société en Commandite Simple	150	136	120	102	96
Société Étrangère	195	107	144	154	155
Société en Nom Collectif	20	20	18	16	17
Total	**5 143**	**5 403**	**5 656**	**5 987**	**6 274**

Sources : Direction de l'Expansion Économique, IMSEE

Under Law no. 1144 of July 26, 1991, any economic activity pursued in the Principality of Monaco, regardless of its nature (i.e., whether commercial, industrial, crafts, or services, professional and non-professional alike) must have prior Government authorisation.

Business and economic activity in Monaco is promoted by the Chamber of Economic Development (CDE), which can help start-ups with advice, contacts and administrative procedures. Its website is in both French and English, and it can supply English language guides on request.

The other way for start-ups is to contact the Direction Expansion Economique (Economic Expansion Department) directly, which is also called the Monaco Welcome & Business Office (MWBO).

The Direction Expansion Economique is normally the administrative agency that examines applications for permission to establish an economic activity in the Principality.

The Monaco Welcome & Business Office is the entry point to the privileged circle of Monégasque residents and businesses. With dedicated and attractive premises, the office welcomes and assists individuals and entrepreneurs wishing to relocate to the Principality. It is a single contact point, providing support with administrative affairs and introductions to the key players in Monaco, whether public or private, to facilitate the relocation of individuals, their families and/or their businesses.

Any future resident and/or entrepreneur wishing to relocate to the Principality will find a range of tools, key contacts and useful information at the Monaco Welcome & Business Office to plan their new initiative within times that are compatible with the economic realities of our era.

If a business operational permit is granted, the authorisation is usually very detailed about what is authorised, and the duration of the authorisation – usually for several years – is normally renewable for similar periods. Renewal is not automatic and must be sought.

For many years, the business permit renewal requirement was one of the biggest fear factors for investors and companies. The process raised a big question. What if you bring your assets and relocate your business venture in the Principality of Monaco and after a few years the Government does not renew your business operation permit?

The introduced risk is still real, however, typically if you have a good conduct and a flowering business, you will successfully apply for the renewal of your permits.

Typically, the authorisation sets out the limits of the activities that may be performed. The authorisation also specifies the premises where those activities may take place as well as any special conditions applicable to the performance of those activities.

The authorisation is personal and non-transferable, except for the "leasing" of an entire business described below. Any material change in the authorised activities, the nature of holder of the authorisation, or address or premises where the activity is conducted must be approved in advance. Any authorisation may be suspended or revoked for misconduct as well as for the failure to maintain appropriate premises for conducting the activity, the absence of real activity, activities not in conformity with the authorisation, etc.

Foreign companies that wish to set up an administrative office or branch in Monaco also require authorisation.

The Monaco Government website provides information in English on the different company structures.

The main principle

Setting up a business or taking over an existing firm is challenging and requires careful preparation and support from competent advisors. Obviously, you can contact many independent advisors who will be ready to help you during the process, but take into consideration that their services are not free.

Once you contact the Monaco Welcome & Business Office, you are entitled to get free advice and guidance from the exact same place where your application will be decided. Therefore, it is always recommended to contact the Monaco Welcome & Business Office first to avoid unnecessary circles and high advisement fees.

Monaco Welcome & Business Office

9, Rue du Gabian (1er étage)
Fontvieille, 98000 Monaco

(+377) 98 98 98 98

The business section of the Prince's Government's Public Service offers assistance and advice to those setting up or taking over businesses to help them achieve success. Entrepreneurs need to be made aware of the conditions for entering and remaining in Monaco, how to set up a business, taxation, social security legislation and any state aid available.

SUGGESTION:

The Principality offers you the possibility to operate your business from your home during the first two years. In some cases, it is worth considering.

You also need to understand the official procedures to be followed during the course of the business' existence, as well as their obligations. Key agreements related to goodwill are also discussed. First and foremost, entrepreneurs must be aware of the fundamental rule governing business relocation to Monaco – the fact that a licence must be obtained before initiating business activities.

Business permit

In order to run a business in Monaco, whether in trade, industry, crafts or as a freelancer, as a sole trader or as a company, those without Monégasque nationality must acquire a business permit issued by the Minister of State.

SUGGESTION:

One of the most important pre-conditions to be granted by the administration is good morality and a clean criminal record.

The permit is issued according to the following criteria:

» Professional reputation: The professional reputation is assessed according to any criminal or judicial record on the part of the entrepreneur and following an official inquiry.

» Professional qualifications: Professional qualifications must be held in the entrepreneur's own name. Some activities are subject to specific entry conditions (certificates, nationality, guarantees, etc.)

» The creation of a stable business activity: Authorisation is only granted if the operational structure is appropriate to the nature and size of the business.

The conditions for issue of the permit, processing of the application and retaining the license are laid down by Law n. 1.144 du 26/07/1991, except where a specific law governs the profession.

Persons of Monégasque nationality must send the Minister of State a declaration of business activities unless the activities envisaged are subject to entry conditions defined by a specific regulation or where they are creating a société anonyme monegasque (SAM) or a société en commandite par actions (SCA).

Setting up a société anonyme or a société en commandite par actions is subject to specific conditions (authorisation to set up the business, approval of the Memorandum and Articles of Association, share capital of 150,000 €, etc.) (Ordonnance du 05/03/1895 sur les sociétés anonymes et en commandite par actions and Code de Commerce).

Also be aware that the Monegasque Government makes enormous efforts to avoid "overcrowding" in some sectors, in order to guarantee the safety and the stability of the local economy. There are several areas in which it is nearly impossible to obtain a business permit anymore, such as in real estate, legal advisory and transportation.

Comparison of legal forms

	SARL	SAM	SNC	SCS	Sole trader
Name	Company name: > Preceded or followed by the initials "SARL" > May include the name(s) of one or more shareholders	Company name: > Preceded or followed by the words "société anonyme anonyme monégasque" or the initials "SAM" and a statement of the share capital > May include the name(s) of one or more shareholders	Company name: > Shareholders' names only	Company name: > Name(s) of one or more active shareholders	> Trading name only
Shareholders	> Minimum of 2, no maximum > Natural or legal persons > Managing Director: must be a natural person, may or may not be a shareholder > Neither shareholders or directors are considered as traders.	> Minimum of 2 shareholders, no maximum > No person may be a Member of the Board of more than 8 commercial firms having their registered office in Monaco	>Minimum of 2 shareholders, no maximum > Natural or legal persons > All considered as traders	> 2 types: active partners, considered as traders, and limited partners > Minimum of 2, 1 active partner and one limited partner, no maximum > Natural or legal persons	> A natural person
Activities	Commercial	Commercial or non-trading	Commercial	Commercial or non-trading	Commercial or non-trading

	SARL	SAM	SNC	SCS	Sole trader
Contributions	> Contributions in cash and in kind, contributions in skills or services not permitted > Contributions in kind must be fully paid up when the company is formed > Cash contributions must be paid up when the company is formed and at least equal to the minimum capital > The share capital must be fully paid up within 3 years	> All shareholders must make a contribution > Only the contributions in cash and in kind are taken into account in the share capital > Contributions in skills and services	> All shareholders must make a contribution > Only the contributions in cash and in kind are taken into account in the share capital > Contributions in skills and services	> All shareholders must make a contribution > Only the contributions in cash and in kind are taken into account in the share capital > Contributions in skills and services (only for active partners)	N/A
Share capital	> EUR 15,000 minimum > Contributions in cash are paid into an account opened for this purpose with a credit institution established in the Principality, proof of which must be given when applying to be listed on the Trade and Industry Registry	> EUR 150,000 minimum, fully paid up > Subscription and payment of capital is recorded in a notarised deed	No minimum capital	No minimum capital	N/A

	SARL	SAM	SNC	SCS	Sole trader
Liability	Shareholders only bear losses up to the amount of their contributions	> Directors: only liable for the performance of the mandate that they have received. They do not contract, as a result of their management, to any personal or joint and several obligation in respect of the company's undertakings > Shareholders' liability is limited to the amount of their contributions	> All shareholders are indefinitely jointly and severally liable for company debts in respect of all their assets	> Active partners: indefinitely jointly and severally liable for company debts > Limited partners: liable up to the amount of their contributions	>Held liable in respect of all their assets
Company formed by	> Privately-signed or official deed > A transcript of the Memorandum and Articles of Association is published in the Journal de Monaco	> Official deed drawn up by a Monegasque notary >The Memorandum and Articles of Association are published in the Journal de Monaco >The Memorandum and Articles of Association approved by Ministerial Order are returned to the offices of the drafting notary. The authorization granted only produces its effects once the Memorandum and Articles of Association have been deposited in the official records of the drafting notary	> Privately-signed or official deed > A transcript of the Memorandum and Articles of Association is published in the Journal de Monaco	> Privately-signed or official deed > A transcript of the Memorandum and Articles of Association is published in the Journal de Monaco	N/A

	SARL	SAM	SNC	SCS	Sole trader
Set-up costs	> Registration tax > Publication fees	> Registration tax > Publication fees > Notary's fees	> Registration tax > Publication fees	> Registration tax > Publication fees	N/A
Misc.		In practice, the SAM is managed by a Board, but there are no rules as to its functioning	The Memorandum and Articles of Association may appoint one or more shareholders authorized to sign under the company name. In this case, the latter's signatures alone bind the company	The limited partner may not carry out any act of management, even by virtue of a power of attorney. If he/she does so, they may be subject to the same liability as the active partner	Sales representatives and craftsperson applying for an authorisation to work as a sole trader.

Types of legal entities

Sole trader

This legal form concerns natural persons wishing to carry out commercial, professional or craft-based activities without creating a company. In short: a one-person company.

Basically, the fastest and easiest way to establish a business in Monaco is as a sole trader. Any individual, must normally be a resident of Monaco to pursue activity as a sole proprietor. Anyone can register to carry out professional work, retailing, contracting or manufacturing as a sole trader with unlimited liability.

As a sole trader, you can start your business quickly and easily, without the constraints of forming a company (drafting Articles of Association, publication formalities) and without having to set aside a minimum amount of capital.

The Monegasque Government also allows the possibility to choose a trading name. A trading name is basically a fictitious business name used by sole traders, who do not want to operate under their registered legal name. For example, you can register for the sole trader license as "James Bond", however you will be allowed to publicly promote your business as "MI 6 Agency". This will partly protect your privacy.

Management as a sole trader is not subject to the same formalities as companies (having to deposit accounting documents with the Trade and Industry Registry and even having to appoint auditors under certain conditions).

The individual's real and personal property is then subject to the claims of the creditors of the business to the extent specified in articles 1928 and 1929 of the Civil Code on Obligations. Personal status is important, since according to the matrimonial system and the activity of the spouse, the spouse's property may also be affected by the sole proprietor's business commitments. Therefore, married sole traders should be aware that if the business fails, the spouse's personal assets might be at risk.

Persons prohibited from carrying out commercial activities following a judgment declaring personal bankruptcy cannot set up as sole traders (art. 587 of the Code de Commerce).

Anyone who regularly and customarily engages in commercial activities are normally considered merchants.

For commercial activities, the business must be run from commercial premises (commercial lease, short-term lease or temporary tenancy agreement).

For non-trading activities (the licensed professionals for example), the business should be domiciled at office premises.

The sole trader may work from their home if no legislative, regulatory or contractual provision is opposed thereto, if their business activities do not require clients to be received, if storage is not necessary and if no staff are recruited.

It is possible, under certain conditions, to domicile the firm either with a domiciliation company for a period limited to one year (may be renewed once) or on premises occupied by another firm.

Société Anonyme Monégasque (SAM) /
Partnership limited by shares (SCA)

A Société Anonyme Monégasque (SAM) is a joint stock company and the company objects may be commercial or non-trading. The professions may thus be incorporated in the form of a non-trading SAM.

Public limited companies and partnerships limited by shares must have notarised articles of association that are published in the Journal de Monaco and filed with the court registrar.

There must be at least two shareholders, and the Board of Directors must also contain at least two shareholders. There is no maximum number of shareholders and they may be natural or legal persons.

The good thing is with the Société Anonyme Monégasque (SAM) that since commercial capacity is not required, minors, even those not yet able to vote, and adults under judicial protection, guardianship or curatorship may be shareholders.

However, share capital divided into shares of equal value must be fully subscribed and each shareholder must pay at least one quarter of the nominal value of their shares for the incorporation to be valid. (Art. 3 de l'Ordonnance du 5 mars 1895)

Contributions must be in cash or in kind and at least 150,000 Euro (Sovereign Ordinance n° 13.845 of 06/01/1999). For certain activities such as finance, the share capital laid down by the law is of a higher amount.

As a side note, I would remark that in some cases, contributions in skills or services may also be made, but are not taken into account when calculating the share capital.

In principle, the registered office of a SAM must be established on commercial premises (commercial lease, short-term lease or temporary tenancy agreement). However, it is possible to domicile the firm at the "private" offices of a domiciliation company.

A Société Anonyme Monégasque (SAM) is managed by Directors chosen from among shareholders owning a number of shares defined by the Articles of Association. The first shareholders' meeting must be held within three months of the license being granted. The company's auditors must be based in Monaco.

The first Directors (at least two) are appointed either by the Articles of Association for a period of three years if it is stipulated that their appointment is not subject to approval by the General Meeting, or by the initial Shareholders' Meeting for a duration of six years.

Directors are only held liable in respect of the mandate that they have received. They do not incur personal, joint and several liability in respect of the company's undertakings. (art. 39 du Code de Commerce). Their liability, as for all shareholders, is limited to the amount of their contributions.

For shareholders, they have a right of oversight regarding the management of the company insofar as they actively participate in corporate life by voting on resolutions pertaining to the functioning of the company.

The Articles of Association determine how many shares are required in order to be admitted to the General Meeting, either as an owner or as a proxy, and the number of votes allocated to each shareholder with regard to the number of shares they hold.

Shareholders may group together in order to reach the number of shares required by the Articles of Association, and appoint one among them to represent them at the General Meeting (Art.11 of the Ordinance of 5 March 1895).

If the Articles of Association make no specific requirement, any shareholder is entitled to participate at meetings and to vote.

Every shareholder of the Société Anonyme Monégasque (SAM) has a twofold right to information.

Before any meeting is held, documents enabling shareholders to vote in full knowledge of the facts must be sent to them. For the Ordinary General Meeting, a list of shareholders, the balance sheet, the profit and loss account, the management report, and the auditors' report must be made available to them.

And at any time during the year, any shareholder may examine, at the registered office, either in person or through a proxy, the minutes of all General Meetings held during the last three years as well as all documents submitted to such meetings.

Société à Responsabilité Limitée (S.A.R.L.)

The Société à Responsabilité Limitée (S.A.R.L.) is one of the most common legal forms in the Principality of Monaco next to the Sole Trader. It limits the shareholders' liability to the amount of their contributions.

It gives a family touch to the firm. It enables a firm to be set up with less capital. It can be managed by a third party.

However, it is important to note that the Société à Responsabilité Limitée (S.A.R.L.) must carry out commercial activities. The professions and non-trading activities cannot be performed by an Société à Responsabilité Limitée (S.A.R.L.).

Also, some other activities cannot be performed by an Société à Responsabilité Limitée (S.A.R.L.), such as finance and insurance, with the exception of insurance brokerage.

A Société à Responsabilité Limitée (S.A.R.L.) is formed between two or more people with liability limited to the amount of their capital investment. Since commercial capacity is not required, minors, even those who are not emancipated, and adults under judicial protection, guardianship or curatorship can be shareholders.

There is a fixed minimum capital investment 15,000 Euro, (contributions in skills or services are not authorised) which must be released to an account at a Monaco-based bank, opened for this purpose.

The minimum share capital may be composed of cash contributions (money) and/or contributions in kind (equipment, patent, etc.).

When the share capital is formed, in whole or in part, of property assets subject to land registration at the Mortgage Registry Office, the notarized deed must be used. As a general rule, contributions are made by transferring ownership of the asset to the company.

Proof of this is required when applying for registration with the Trade and Industry Register (Registre du Commerce et de l'Industrie, RCI).

In principle, the registered office of a Société à Responsabilité Limitée (S.A.R.L.) is established on commercial premises (commercial lease, short-term lease or temporary tenancy agreement).

However, it is possible to domicile the firm at the Managing Director's personal address in Monaco for a duration of one year, that may be renewed once, as from publication in the Journal de Monaco of the transcript of the Memorandum of Association. For this, the Managing Director needs to have a Monaco-based apartment allowed for Mixed Usage (Usage Mixte).

The Managing Director must hold two kinds of meeting: Ordinary General Meetings (OGMs) and Extraordinary General Meetings (EGMs). If there is a meeting, the Managing Director must invite the shareholders and send them all documents enabling them to vote in full knowledge of the facts.

The Managing Director may carry out any and all acts that are required or appropriate in fulfilling the company objects, subject to powers bestowed by law or the Articles of Association upon the shareholders.

If the Articles of Association have not limited his/her powers, the Managing Director may thus carry out any and all acts of management insofar as the latter are related to the activities of the Société à Responsabilité Limitée (S.A.R.L.) and are in line with the firm's interests.

In this regard the Managing Director may, in the name of the firm and in line with the company objects, sign contracts and agreements, hire staff, take legal action, etc.

Since the company objects enable the extent of the Managing Director's powers to be defined, this clause of the Articles of Association should therefore be drafted with particular care.

The shareholders have a right of oversight concerning the management of the firm insofar as they participate actively in company life by voting in resolutions pertaining to the operation of the company.

The Managing Director is responsible to the company and to third parties for negligence that they might commit in carrying out their duties. In this regard, the Managing Director incurs their civil and/or criminal liability.

General partnership (SNC)

General partnerships (Société en Nom Collectif, of SNC in short) are established by two or more people operating under a company name. One of the owners should be a resident of Monaco and the Société en Nom Collectif (SNC) must carry out commercial activities.

What is really interesting here is that the law Monegasque does not lay down a minimum amount for the share capital of an SNC. It can therefore be defined freely by the shareholders in the Articles of Association. The law makes no provision concerning payment of the share capital.

However, the company must include the name(s) of the shareholders.

The Articles of Association of the company must be registered with the Tax Department and an excerpt of the incorporation certificate must be published in the Journal de Monaco (government gazette).

The SNC is a company in which the shareholders are all considered traders and are indefinitely, jointly and severally liable for all company debts. Therefore, the general partners are jointly responsible for all partnership liabilities.

The partnership agreement may limit the authority of certain partners to commit the partnership; otherwise, any single partner may commit the partnership.

In principle, the registered office of an SNC is established on commercial premises (commercial lease, short-term lease or temporary tenancy agreement).

However, it is possible to domicile the firm at the Managing Director's personal address in Monaco for a period of one year, that may be renewed once, as from publication in the Journal de Monaco of the transcript of the Memorandum of Association. For this the Managing Director needs to have a Monaco-based apartment allowed for Mixed Usage (Usage Mixte).

In a société en nom collectif, all shareholders are Managing Directors except where stipulated to the contrary in the Articles of Association. The law allows shareholders to provide, in the Articles of Association, that one or more of them may sign under the company name. The signature of any of the shareholders binds the firm in that case (article 29 of the Code de Commerce).
This means that all shareholders are indefinitely, jointly and severally liable in respect of all their personal assets for all company debts.

With regard to the tax administration and social security administration, they may incur their personal liability if it is proved that, through fraudulent manoeuvres or through serious and repeated non-compliance with their tax and/or social security obligations, they have made the recovery of sums due by the company to said administrations impossible.

Limited partnership (SCS)

Limited partnerships (Société en Commandite Simple, or in short SCS) are established between one or more managing partners, and one or more financial backers. An SCS may have objects that are not of a commercial nature, unlike an SARL or an SNC.

The Société en Commandite Simple (SCS) is a company with two categories of shareholder: 'commandités' (active partners) and 'commanditaires' (limited partners). No maximum number of partners (shareholders) has been laid down by the law.

Active partners have the status of shareholding partners; they are considered as traders and are jointly and severally liable for all of the companies' debts.

Limited partners are only responsible for company debts up to the amount of their contributions; they are not considered traders.

The company name must include one or more active partners. And it is important to know that only the active partner names can be mentioned. The name of a limited partner cannot form part of the company name.

Managing partners have unlimited liability, whereas financial partners' liability is limited to the amount invested. Financial partners may not play any role in managing the partnership, even by proxy.
The law does not lay down a minimum amount for the share capital of an SCS. It can therefore be defined freely by the shareholders in the Articles of Association. The law makes no provision concerning payment of the share capital.

The articles of association of the company must be registered with the Tax Department and an excerpt of the incorporation certificate published in the Journal de Monaco.

In principle, the registered office of an SCS is established on commercial premises (commercial lease, short-term lease or temporary tenancy agreement).

However, it is possible to domicile the firm at the domicile of an active partner for a period of one year, that may be renewed once, as from publication in the Journal de Monaco of the transcript of the Articles of Association. For this, the Managing Director needs to have a Monaco-based apartment allowed for Mixed Usage (Usage Mixte).

It is also possible, under certain conditions, to domicile the firm either with a domiciliation company for a duration limited to one year (may be renewed once) or on premises occupied by another firm.

Limited partners and active partners have a right of oversight concerning the management of the firm insofar as they participate actively in the life of the firm by voting in resolutions pertaining to the operation of the company.

The Managing Director must hold two kinds of meeting: Ordinary General Meetings (OGMs) and Extraordinary General Meetings (EGMs). If there is a meeting, the Managing Director must invite the shareholders and send them all documents enabling them to vote in full knowledge of the facts.

The Managing Director is responsible to the company and to third parties for negligence that the Managing Director might commit in carrying out his/her duties. In this regard, he/she incurs his/her civil and/or criminal liability.

In the event of collective proceedings, a Managing Director may be ordered to cover all or part of the insufficient assets from their personal assets, if they have committed mismanagement, on the basis of article 560 of the Code de Commerce.

The Managing Director may incur their liability if they commit the criminal offences laid down in loi n°1144 du 26 juillet 1991, such as, for example, carrying out activities outside the limitations of the company objects.

Alternative ways to operate as a business

Administrative offices and branches of foreign companies

Administrative offices are established by companies whose registered office is not in the Principality of Monaco. Their sole purpose is for management, coordination or supervision where oversight is carried out on an actual and regular basis.

Licenses are granted for a limited period and must be renewed. No commercial activities may be performed by an administrative office.

The firm appoints a management agent for this administrative office, known as "agent responsable", who generally has the status of a salaried worker.

The opening of an administrative office is subject to being granted official permit.

Branches of foreign companies must obtain a license and register with the Trade and Industry Register (Registre du Commerce et de l'Industrie, RCI).

SUGGESTION:

> I consider it a great advantage if you have the power to decide what budget you will give to your company, therefore, you will have a choice between taxation on annual profit or based on percentage of the income.

Commercial agency

A commercial agency is a branch office of a firm whose registered office is located abroad, which has the aim of developing commercial activities in Monaco.

It must first obtain a business permit issued by the Minister of State and appoint a director for the Monegasque branch.

The application for authorisation must be made by the legal representative of the parent company.

The sales office must be entered on the Trade and Industry Registry.

It is subject to corporate income tax if it generates more than 25% of its turnover outside the Principality of Monaco.

Commercial agent

A commercial agent is a proxy who, as a self-employed worker on a regular basis, negotiates and may conclude purchases, sales, rentals or provide services, in the name and on behalf of producers, industrial clients or traders.

The commercial agent is usually a natural person; however, this profession may be exercised by a company. Any foreign national who wishes to operate as a commercial agent either under their own name or through a company must apply for a permit.

The commercial agent is not a subordinate of their principal(s). This distinguishes the commercial agent from a salaried representative.

The commercial agent is free to organise their own business and they may recruit their own staff without having to obtain authorisation. They also have the initiative in developing the marketing of the products for which they are responsible. They do not have to comply with instructions from the principal.
The commercial agent is free to choose their activities – they may act on behalf of several principals subject to compliance with a non-compete obligation. They may perform other professional activities on their own behalf, in particular those of a commercial nature, insofar as they do not compete with their principals' activities.

However, since the commercial agent must perform such activities on a regular basis, the Monegasque Government excludes seasonal workers and those exhibiting at trade fairs.

The benefit is that the commercial agent has a "legal status" that has been put in place to protect them.

The law thus states that the undertakings binding commercial agents and their principals are entered into the parties' joint interests. This concept of joint interests is twofold – the continuous nature and duration of the collaboration inter-parties and the forming of a joint clientele. Since the mandate has a twofold interest, it may only be revoked by mutual consent or for legitimate reasons.

If the mandate is terminated by the principal without the latter being able to provide justification of misconduct on the part of their proxy, the agent is entitled to pecuniary compensation for the prejudice suffered.

Lease management

Lease management is a way of operating a business based on a lease agreement granted by the owner of the business to a natural or legal person. The lease management agreement is governed by the Act no. 546 of 26 June 1951 aimed at regulating lease management, as amended.

There are no conditions for the duration of operations in regards to the owner of the business. Therefore, a person inheriting a business, and who cannot operate it, may immediately grant a lease management agreement.

There are no conditions regarding the duration of the business. A newly created business can be placed under lease management. The lessee must have commercial capacity.

A lease management agreement must be drawn up either as an official deed by a Monegasque notary, or as a privately-signed deed registered with the Department of Tax Services of the Principality.

A lease management agreement is a fixed-term contract – it cannot be renewed automatically.

When business authorisation is notified or when the certificate of deposit of a new business declaration has been issued, notice of lease management of the business must be published in the Journal de Monaco.

Publication of notice of lease management is a prerequisite for the entry of the lessee-manager on the Trade and Industry Registry and the amendment of the business owner's registration.

The lessee-manager's obligations is to post a notice on the premises in a clearly visible manner, to the effect that the business is operated under lease management. Such notice must also appear on commercial correspondence.

The lessee-manager may not in any way change the purpose of the business, except by express written authorisation from the lessor. They cannot sublet or pass on lease management to any third party.

The lessor must provide the lessee with peaceful enjoyment of the premises and may not require any payments provided for under the agreement to be made prior to expiry of the period allowed for opposition to be expressed.

When lease management begins, any lessee-manager that makes the payments provided for in the agreement before expiry of the period allowed for opposition to be expressed or notwithstanding said opposition shall not be released from their obligations with regard to third parties.

Notice of lease management coming to an end is required in support of the application for the lessee-manager to be removed from the Trade & Industry Registry and the application to amend or cancel the business owner's registration.

Upon expiry of lease management, a lessee-manager or lessor making payments to their co-contracting party prior to expiry of the period allowed for opposition or notwithstanding said opposition shall not be released from their obligations with regard to third parties. The lessor must publish notice of said expiry in the Journal de Monaco within 15 days.

Licensed professionals

The term "Licensed professionals" encompasses all the professions that are undertaken by one person, individually, on their own personal responsibility. Professions classified as Licensed professionals offer intellectual and conceptual services to the public.

Insurance, accounting, legal and financial activities

» Insurance brokers & general insurance agents

» Lawyers

» Banks, financial and credit institutions

» Chartered & authorised accountant

» The management of securities or futures portfolios

» The management of undertakings for collective investment, receipt and transmission of orders on financial markets

» Process servers & bailiffs

» Multi Family Office

» Notaries

Property

» Architects

» Estate agents

» Administrators of jointly owned property

Media

» Production, distribution, imports and exports of films, etc.

» Setting up and using private radio-relay stations

Construction activity

» Construction and public works

Personal domestic services

» Protection - caretaking - private security

Health sector

» Medical auxiliaries
» Dental surgeons
» Medecine
» Osteopathy
» Pharmacy
» Psychology
» Healthcare transport (on land)
» Healthcare transport (by air)

Food sector

» Production, manufacturing, processing, packaging, storage, and transport of food products or animal feed
» Retail sales of food products or animal feed, such as, for example, caterers, restaurants, snack-bars, supermarkets, pet shops

Cosmetics

» Opening and running an establishment for the manufacturing, packaging, wholesale distribution, import or export of cosmetic products

Transport

» Taxis - vehicle rental with driver
» Driving school instructor
» Air transport
» Road transport of passengers or goods and services incidental to transport
» Maritime transport of a commercial nature
» Shipbrokers

Other business activities

- » Weapons and ammunition - manufacture and sale of firearms or ammunition - intermediaries or advertising agents for a manufacturer or retailer of firearms and ammunition
- » Motor vehicle testing and inspection of hygiene, safety and environmental protection
- » Opening a garage
- » Service stations

Activities for which the conditions of business are regulated

- » Antiques dealers
- » Importing, marketing or rendering operational medical devices
- » Manufacturing, placing on the market, distribution, import or export of medical devices for in vitro diagnosis
- » Tattooing, permanent make-up and piercing
- » Sale of and making available to the public certain items of sun-tanning equipment using ultraviolet radiation

Activities to which access is not regulated but that are subject to obtaining authorization

- » Legal advice
- » Teaching - opening a private teaching establishment - home schooling
- » Hotel-keeping - landlords of furnished property
- » Precious metals - Assay commissionner
- » Pawnbroking

Professional Independent Artist (API)

The Principality of Monaco loves creative people and supports its cultural place in the world of art. In order to enrich its cultural heritage, the Principality of Monaco is paying the social charges (CAMTI/CARTI) and/or part of the business rent (in the case of an artist's studio) for a period of 2 years renewable for 1 year for the selected artists.

Act no. 1.360 of 04 July 2009 concerning support and social protection for professional self-employed artists states that performers and people that fall within the scope of Act no. 491 of 24 November 1948 concerning the protection of literature and works of art, who practice their activity in a continuous, habitual manner for profit with no relation to legal subordination are considered Professional Independent Artists (APIs).

In order to be recognised, as a Professional Independent Artist (API), you need to contact the Department of Cultural Affairs. A printed form is available from the Department of Cultural Affairs.

Applications are processed by the support commission for professional independent artists (Commission de soutien aux API).

Since artists do not necessarily have a large income, the state has set up a support initiative for first-time applicants for API status.

If your application is accepted, you will receive a letter explaining the steps to take in order to obtain an official declaration of this status.

The grant for setting up as a professional independent artist is given to Monegasque citizens, their spouses or people who have lived in the Principality for at least ten years and who are setting up a professional artistic activity in the Principality for the first time.

When I started Niche Media

Registering a business in Monaco is not as easy as it seems. Even if you comply with all the previously mentioned criteria, the authorisation is not an automatic process. The Government decision will take a long time, the estimated company registration period is usually between three to six months. It can be even longer based on the complexity of the activity, related regulation and restrictions. For example, some activities are strictly limited to Monegasque nationals, such as legal and dentistry.

Previously I mentioned the benefits of getting free advice from the Monaco Welcome & Business Office, yet with Niche Media I took a very different way in order to secure the success of my business application.

Instead of the free opportunity by going to the Monaco Welcome & Business Office, I decided to entrust my friend Aymeric Pazzaglia and his company vk*p business advisors to guide me through the company registration process.

Make no mistake I am fully aware of the process, I wrote about it many times in my book, but I was also aware that implementing a theoretical knowledge into reality often ends in a bumpy road.

Very few people realise when they apply for a business permit in the Principality that if the Monegasque Government rejects your application, you can't just re-apply again. The only chance you have is to start a legal case and argue the rejected business authorisation at court. Meaning, you literally have to sue the Government of Monaco which is not a good start of any professional relationship.

This can take an enormous amount of money because by law only Monegasque lawyers can appear in front of the Monegasque court and everything has to be submitted in French. The whole process can be very pricey. Even if you have a chance to successfully overturn the rejection of your business authorisation, you can expect a significant delay of your business goals in Monaco.

When I decided to apply with Niche Media I knew something that gave me confidence. Aymeric was actually employed by the Monaco Welcome & Business Office for eight years, managing thousands of business applications. He has an unparalleled knowledge and more importantly a real-life experience in the business administration processes.

Also, if you have read the acknowledgement section, you might have realised that every year since its very first edition published in 2013, I have dedicated the "Living in Monaco" book to Aymeric. The reason for this is because when I first arrived in Monaco he offered me an enormous help with all private and business related questions. Without him present book would be less valuable.

So for me it was a no brainer to go with an experienced expert. Just like at the Monaco Welcome & Business Office, Aymeric is delivering information free of charge to entrepreneurs. However, the big difference is that vk*p business advisors (or generally the government authorised business advisors) can carry out a complete range of services and process, such as application, head office arrangement, registration, banking, etc.

They can also advise the entrepreneurs on a wide range of topics related to their businesses. For me everything was compensated at the end when my business application was finally approved and the process was carried out in the smoothest way possible.

I am the type of person who is always looking for the result and not at the price. I firmly believe that everything that brings you the desired results can not be considered expensive. The only thing that you can call expensive are the things that do not bring you the expected results.

When I decided to go with Aymeric and vk*p business advisors, I was simply looking for a result oriented solution instead of a cheap one. This choice was very fruitful because business registration does not stop with the authorisation. There are multiple other steps to implement before you can be operational including the office address in the Principality of Monaco, the trade registry number (RCI), VAT number, Monaco statistic number, business bank account, health insurance (CAMTI/CARTI), etc.

Business address

It is possible to set up a business or a company head office in a business center for varying lengths of time, under certain conditions. The Principality of Monaco also highly supports start-up businesses, therefore, you can find multiple business centers to start your company in the size you desire.

In general, for SAMs a minimum space of 25m² is required, which must be increased depending on the number of employees.

For all other legal entities: a minimum space of 9m² is required, which must be increased depending on the number of employees.

Typically, the Monaco-based business centers are working with various formulas. If you have a small business as a sole trader, you can rent out a shared office with a less than a day in a week physical availability, or there is a "campus" option for SARLs. All these options are convertible to exclusive office possibilities as soon as you are confident in the development of your business or if you wish to have your own space.

Running a business from your home address

For commercial activities carried out by SNCs, SCSs, or SARLs, the registered office may only be established at the managing director's home. Domiciling commercial business activities at the entrepreneur's home in the Principality Monaco is possible if the legal form of the company allows it and if:

» No legislative, regulatory or contractual provision is opposed thereto

» The firm's activities do not involve reception of clients or the storage or display of goods

» The firm employs no staff

A home address can be used under the conditions described above, upon start-up and for a limited period of one year (may be renewed once). Ordinance no. 993 of 16 February 2007 implementing Act no. 1331 of 8 January 2007 pertaining to companies.

The managing director must be the leaseholder, the leaseholder's spouse, or be residing with the leaseholder. In state-owned properties, if the managing director is residing with the leaseholder, they must be of Monegasque nationality. If they are the leaseholder's spouse, they are not required to be of Monegasque nationality. In state-owned properties, a single company may establish their registered office at the managing director's home. However, running a business from your home address is slightly different if you are a sole trader. Basically, no restrictions are laid down by the regulations regarding the juncture or duration of domiciliation. The duration of domiciliation in the private sector corresponds to the duration of the lease.

The firm may be established at the sole trader's domicile upon start-up or during the course of business activities. The sole trader must be the leaseholder, the leaseholder's spouse, or be residing with the leaseholder.

A maximum of three firms may be domiciled per household in state-owned property. There is no maximum in the private sector.

Why did I choose a business center?

For many people using a home address for a business setup is the most reasonable choice. So why was I even thinking about a business center instead of a private apartment?

One of the most important, yet often overlooked reason is the scaleability. Why would you burn money in the first period, when you can also use that capital to make your business recognised in the Principality? In every business the first few months are the grow-or-fail period. Therefore from the very beginning my goal was to increase my revenue and not my expenses.

Another good reason to choose a business center is the cost. For startups, choosing a business center is even cheaper and offers much more flexibility. For example, you don't have to sign a two years long contract such as you are forced to do when you rent out a private apartment. The minimum contract with business centers usually start from 3 months and you can always extend it.

Start-up formula starts from 400 Euro/month (excluding 20% VAT) which is ridiculously cheap compared to the rental prices. 6 months of start-up formula also offers you enough time to understand the market reaction and the appreciation of your business in Monaco's extremely closed market. Based on your business performance during this period you can easily decide whether it is the right choice to scale your business into a larger office space.

From my perspective, owning the Monaco Residents' Magazine and also being the author of this "Living in Monaco" book I decided to give a chance to capitalise these assets. I decided to approach few business centers in Monaco to see whether we can work out some sort of co-operation.

One of the three owners of the The Office business center in Fontvieille, Olivier Blanchy decided to invite me for a first talk. Olivier wanted to get to know each other even before he went into any offer. It was clear to me that for him a good relationship was more important than the financials.

When we met he took his time to listen to my business goals and he gave me valuable inputs on how to proceed. I truly appreciated that he invested his time to build up a relationship because he made the process literally stress-free for me.

One of the greatest advice Olivier gave me was the information on the "Accord de Principe".

In the Principality of Monaco every business activity has to have a physical address. Without a Monaco-based address the Government will not authorise your activity. This was very clear from the beginning for me. Also this is why most new businesses sign a long-term real-estate lease even before the application, risking two years of rent.

I knew before that there is a possibility to request the Government approval on your business concept without having an address yet. In Monaco they call this "Accord de Principe", meaning that the Government pre-approves your profile and the scope of your activities.

However, since previously I always talked with real-estate agents they always tried to convinced me that without the local address the applications are usually rejected. Obviously, this is a great sales tool for them to push the real-estate deals. But the reality was far away from this.

Olivier, who worked for the Government (as the head of the company creation division) before he co-established The Office business center, took his time to walk me through the process in the safest way for my goals and budget. On the other hand, others just tried to rush me into sign a rental contract.

The difference between applying for a business authorisation with or without an address in place is technical only. If you already have the address and the government approves your activity, then you can already start with the next steps.

If you don't have an address by the time of the approval, then you will receive the pre-approval ("Accord de Principe") with a maximum three months of time to find a Monaco based address for your business. The final business authorisation will be rolled out only after you have presented the signed lease documents to the government. However, you are not forced to engage into a contract before the authorisation which is a great relief.

I realised in business life that when you help people to find solutions for their small problems, they will hire you for their big ones too. This is especially true in crowded markets such as business centers in Monaco. As you might know, the Principality has 16 business centers and over 130 real-estate agencies for its less than 2km² territory. If you don't want to engage into a price fight, the value comes handle, and (added) value can be many things. In my example, Olivier focused on my doubts and gave me value by properly explaining an area of misunderstanding.

One of the important rules in business is to never tell your prospects that something is not working because of their fault. Nobody wants to hear that they are not good or that they made a mistake. The good approach in my case with the business address was: "Zsolt, it is a very common misunderstanding that you are obliged to sign a two-years of rental agreement even before your business authorisation. It is not your fault, you just met the wrong people, using the wrong systematic approach." This way my fear was justified, Olivier confirmed my suspicions and he helped me to beat the "enemy".

As you might have seen on the cover of the book I decided to choose The Office. I chose it not just because of the kind gesture of Olivier at the beginning of the process, but also because they have a great atmosphere for work in a good location.

Furthermore, I like the fact that they have co-working spaces and also private offices which is a great combination, especially if you add the best coffee in town. I might start to sound a bit biased, but the truth is that for me it really worked out well. The team, the location, the catering, everything is right for my needs.

I always appreciate those who are looking for a long-term business relationship instead of quick money. Exchanges are highly important in life and not just in business. Generally I believe in three types of exchanges: criminal, fair and beneficial.

Criminal exchanges are when you receive much less value for your money/service than you have expected.

Fair exchanges are when both parties are receiving the value they have originally expected.

And finally, beneficial exchanges are when someone receives more value than it was originally expected.

For me the meeting with Olivier provided this beneficial exchange, because at the end of the day I received more than I ever expected. Few months later when I received my government authorisation, it was a no brainer for me to sign with the The Office business center. I used to say that a happy client equals happy life. In this case, this was definitely true for me.

Closing these thoughts, I decided to choose a business center over a private apartment because of smaller initial costs, privacy between home and business, possibility to meet with new people and more importantly because of the scalability.

I love to meet with new people. I love great personal stories, this is also the reason why I wrote this book and I am involved in other human related projects. It was truly surprising for me to meet even with Monegasque entrepreneurs at The Office. One would simply assume that Monegasque people don't do small business, but it is pretty interesting to see that opportunity comes in multiple sizes.

The various options available in business centers

These options do not apply to regulated activities.

"Start Up MC" option

Shared office which can accommodate a maximum of ten businesses. Exclusively for sole traders, Professional activity (PR), Craftsperson (AR) and Commercial Agent (AC).

Conditions:

- » For nationals and spouses who are in receipt of a grant to set up a business
- » Available only during set-up
- » Businesses may not hire staff, receive customers or store stock on the premises

Duration: Six months, renewable once (maximum of one year).

"Start Up" option

Shared office which can accommodate a maximum of ten businesses. Exclusively for sole traders, Professional activity (PR), Craftsperson (AR) and Commercial Agent (AC).

Conditions:

- » Available only during set-up
- » Businesses may not hire staff, receive customers or store stock on the premises

Duration:

- » For non-Monegasques: three months, renewable once (maximum of six months)
- » For Monegasques: Six months, renewable once (maximum of one year)

"Primo" option

Open space with dedicated office which can accommodate a maximum of five businesses, for a minimum of one fixed day per week, specified in the contract. Exclusively for sole traders, Professional activity (PR), Craftsperson (AR) and Commercial Agent (AC).

Conditions:

» During set-up, following the use of the "Start Up" option or once the business is up and running

» Businesses may not hire staff, receive customers or store stock on the premises

Duration: Maximum of three years.

"Primo +" option

Open space with dedicated office which can accommodate a maximum of five businesses, for a minimum of one fixed day per week, specified in the contract.
Exclusively for sole traders, Professional activity (PR), Craftsperson (AR) and Commercial Agent (AC).

Conditions:

» This option offers an extension of the "Primo" option on condition that the business has already been resident in the same business centre

» Renewable once with the agreement of the Business Development Agency

Duration: Maximum of two years.

"Primo R" option

Open space with dedicated office which can accommodate a maximum of five businesses, for a minimum of one fixed day per week, specified in the contract. This is exclusively for sole traders, Professional activity (PR), Craftsperson (AR) and Commercial Agent (AC).

Conditions:

» During set-up, following the use of the "Start Up" option or once the business is up and running

» Businesses may not hire staff, receive customers or store stock on the premises

Duration: Unlimited (certain conditions apply).

"Administrative accommodation" option

This is an open space with dedicated office which can accommodate a maximum of five businesses, for five days per week: this will be specified in the contract. This option is for individuals only.

Conditions:

» During set-up, following the use of the "Start Up" option or a "primo" option or once the business is up and running

» Requests will be assessed on a case-by-case basis and depending on the business, in consultation with the Business Development Agency

» Businesses may not hire staff, receive customers or store stock on the premises

Duration: Three years, renewable for three-year periods, subject to certain conditions.

"Campus" option

This is an open space with dedicated office which can accommodate a maximum of one business, for five days per week: this will be specified in the contract. This is available only to the following types of business: SNC, SARL and SCS. Not available to SAMs.

Conditions: Business may not hire staff, receive customers or store stock on the premises.

Duration: Maximum of three years, non-renewable, from the date of publication of the notice of the company's establishment in the Journal de Monaco.

"Campus +" option

This is an open space with dedicated office which can accommodate a maximum of one business, for five days per week: this will be specified in the contract. This is available only to the following types of business: SNC, SARL and SCS. Not available to SAMs.

Conditions: This option offers an extension of the "Campus" option on condition that the business has already been resident in the same business centre for a year.

Duration: Maximum of two years.

"Exclusive office" option

This option is available to all legal entities with the exception of those operating as a Company Services Provider (CSP).

Conditions: During set-up or once the business is up and running; business may hire staff.

Duration: Unlimited

Few things that I learned about business formulas

When you choose the basic Start-Up formula, as well as when you are a sole trader (self-employed), you are not allowed to hire an additional employee inside the co-working area. Most of the co-working spaces are limited by this. The solution is to rent out a private office inside the business center which will allow you to include employees.

On the positive side, the prices are exactly the same in all the business centers around Monaco. Unlike with the private apartments, with business centers the base prices are government regulated.

One should argue that the private apartment can be used for Monaco residency as well. This is partly true, especially if you are already a resident of the Principality of Monaco. However, the pre-conditions for residency were changed in 2019. Before that many people simply formed a company, employed themselves in it and it was the easiest (but not the quickest) way towards having a Monaco residency. Since 2019, if you aim to have a Monaco residency by owning a local business, you need to prove that your annual salary is at least four times that of your rental fee. For this reason, you always have to prove your income before the government approves your residence permit. This can be complicated at the beginning, while after few months of business activity you have better chances to change for a private address and apply for a residence permit.

Top reasons to consider to incorporate your business with a business center

Previously I mentioned scalability and cost which is often priority number one. However, there are many other reasons to consider for a business center.

For instance, working from a business center often makes you more productive. You don't have the typical distraction. When you are working from home it is very easy to get distracted by other activities, such as cooking, cleaning, and various works around the house. Also, in your private office you might run out of paper or ink and these things can set you back. These are hours of work you are loosing.

In an office center you don't have to take care of the supplies. Even if they are not working for you, they are working with you, offering a productive environment where you can focus on your business without distraction.

Furthermore, it goes without saying that it is always easier to meet with new people in a business center. Especially for those who are not well-connected in Monaco. In a co-working space usually you can easily meet 30-100 entrepreneurs. It is very easy to engage into casual conversations over a coffee in the bar, or during your lunch break without the feeling that you are prospecting them. Unlike cold calls, being in the same business center already lifts the "pressure" and opens the doors for networking.

I also found it amazing that co-working people are more helpful because you are in the same "boat". They are much more open to listen to your activity and even if they are not necessarily your potential clients, they will remember you. I got many referral leads from co-working entrepreneurs.

List of business centres

3ACS
9, rue des Oliviers
98000 Monaco
Mrs Corinne JUNOD
Phone: (+377) 97 98 10 19 - (+33) 6 32 38 49 53
Email: info@3acs.com
Website: www.3acs.com

A Business Center
5-7, rue du Castelleretto
98000 Monaco
Phone : (+377) 99 99 63 20
Email: info@abusinesscenter.mc
Mrs Mélanie ESPAGNOL

Bellevue Business Centre
1, rue Bellevue
Bellevue Palace
98000 MONACO
Phone : (+377) 99 99 77 20
Courriel : accueil@bbc.mc

Cats Business Center
28, Boulevard Princesse Charlotte
98000 Monaco
Mrs Sophie GUILLOU
Phone: (+377) 93 10 54 54
Email: info@cats.mc
Website: www.cats.mc

D.C.S Business Center
13, Boulevard Princesse Charlotte
98000 Monaco
Mrs Elena D'ISCHIA
Phone: (+377) 93 30 30 45
Email: info@dcs.mc

Hades Business Center

Villa Léopold – 33, rue Grimaldi
98000 Monaco
Mr Michel MONFORT
Phone: (+337) 99 99 70 00
Email: info@hadesbusinesscenter.com
Website: www.hadesbusinesscenter.com

International Business Center

2, rue du Gabian
98000 Monaco
Mr Alexander SIBONY
Phone: (+337) 97 77 27 00
Email: contact@ibcmonaco.com
Website: www.ibcmonaco.com

MBC 2

Le Thalès
1, rue du Gabian
98000 Monaco
Mrs Manuela VARON
Phone: (+377) 97 98 29 29
Fax: (+377) 97 98 29 30
Email: info@mbc2.mc
Website: www.mbc2.mc

Monaco Business Center

20, Avenue de Fontvieille
98000 Monaco
Mrs Florence GERAY
Phone: (+377) 92 05 58 18
Email: info@mbc.mc
Website: www.monacobusinesscenter.net

Prime Office Center

Le Bettina
14 bis, rue Honoré Labande
98000 Monaco
Mr Steve SASPORTAS
Phone: (+377) 97 70 84 48
Website: www.primeofficecenter.com

Regus Monaco
74, Boulevard d'Italie
98000 Monaco
Phone: +377 99 99 45 45
Email: monaco.montecarlo@regus.com
Website: www.regus.com

Sun Office
74, Boulevard d'Italie
98000 Monaco
Mrs Anna BOERI
Phone: (+377) 99 99 77 77
Email: annaboeri@sunoffice.mc
Website: www.sunoffice.mc

Talaria Business Center
7, rue de l'Industrie
98000 Monaco
Mr Clément PETIT
Phone: (+377) 99 99 47 47
Email: contact@talaria.mc
Website: www.talaria.mc

The Office
L'Albu
17, avenue Albert II
98000 Monaco
Mr Olivier BLANCHY
Phone: (+377) 97 77 62 22
Email: contact@theoffice.mc
Website: www.theoffice.mc

Further steps after the Government authorisation

Registering a business in Monaco is a complex process. All business owners have to be prepared for the fact that once they have the authorisation, it is going to take another while until they can start to fully operate with their business.

To put it simply, the Monegasque Government authorisation itself does not give the right to invoice. Without the possibility to create invoices the business cannot have an income.

Once you have the principal agreement, called "Accord de Principe" and the physical address then you will still need to take additional steps.

You have to register your company for a Trade and Industry Register (RCI) number. The RCI number references all natural or legal persons, deemed as trading by law, and carrying out their commercial activities on the Principality's territory.

The RCI number is very similar to a company's house identifier.

If you don't find a business name in the publicly available RCI database (https://www.rci.gouv.mc/rc/), then you can be sure that it is not authorised to operate in the Principality of Monaco.

Your business will also need a Statistical Identification Number (NIS). The Statistical Identification Number (NIS) is a unique identifier allocated by the Monegasque Institute of Statistics and Economic Studies (Monaco Statistics) when a business is established.

The NIS is the new appellation of the DSEE number or VAT code which was allocated by the Statistics Department of the Business Development Agency.

The NIS is composed of two parts: an NAF code (French Classification of Activities, Revision 2, 2008) , and a unique sequential number. The NAF code is an alphanumeric code assigned by Monaco Statistics to each economic entity: natural person, company or association to indicate its main business activity.

You must proceed to your statistical registration (NIS) when you start a business in the Principality.

You will be also obliged to declare your business to the Department of Tax Services. This will ensure you the TVA number (VAT number).

As soon as the authorisation to carry out a business activity has been granted or a receipt of declaration has been received, any company established in Monaco must be declared to the Department of Tax Services. Declaration of the existence of a company is an obligatory formality stipulated in article 66 of the Turnover Tax Code.

There is no charge for this formality. The declaration is made directly to the Department of Tax Services, at the Tax Division counter.

With all these identifiers mentioned above you will be able to open a Monaco based business bank account. However, Monaco based banks are quite selective based on the profile and the income projection of your business. It is important to know that a bank account is not an automatic process. You might be rejected a few times before you find a bank who accepts you as their client.

You will be also obliged to register for social services, known as CAMTI/CARTI.

Any individual who is authorised to run a business in Monaco (including commercial, industrial and craft activities, and the professions), with a few exceptions, is required to register with the Independent Pensions Fund for the Self-Employed (CARTI) and the Sickness, Accident and Maternity Insurance for the Self-Employed (CAMTI) schemes.

Non-employee directors of Sociétés Anonymes Monégasques are not required to register.

For businesses which require administrative authorisation and Managing Partners of SARLs, registration forms are automatically sent to the relevant individuals. They can also be collected from the reception desk at the Social Security Contributions Collection Office.

For SARL Managing Partners, CAMTI and CARTI registration takes effect from the date of registration of the SARL in the Trade and Industry Register. The application for registration must be submitted within one month of this date.

For self-employed individuals who operate as a Sole Trader, SCS or SNC, registration with CAMTI and CARTI takes effect from the date on which the business begins to operate, based on the supporting documentation, even if it has not yet generated any turnover.

The application for registration must be submitted within one month of the start of activity, or from the point at which activity began again, if it was previously suspended.

Generally speaking these are the minimum steps before you will be able to create your fist invoice. As you can imagine these administrative processes will take time.

Also, it is important to know that for some other activities there are further steps to be taken, such as export-import custom duties.

It is easy to see why it is worthwhile to entrust an advisor to guide you through the administrative tasks.

Monaco business bank account is not automatic

It is a strange thing in Monaco that opening a business and getting the official Government authorisation, does not necessarily qualify one to be able to open a bank account in Monaco.

As I have briefly mentioned, the Principality does not draw any line on how much funds you need to relocate and to live in Monaco. Despite all the expectations, it has never been regulated. Opening a business bank account is a very similar situation.

The minimum share capital is regulated, zero for sole trader, 15,000 Euro for SARL and 150,000 Euro for SAM. Yet, the majority of the banks are so selective with their future clients, that they actually reject most of the small accounts.

I know someone in Monaco, who has an authorised sole trader activity since almost 8 months, yet no bank is ready to open a bank account for her. She is a European Union citizen, she has no criminal record, the Monegasque Government approved her, and still the banks are not ready to open for her a small account. The sad reality is that the banks have all the rights to do this, since there is no binding law for them to open a bank account for local business owners.

Since many years this is a serious topic in the Principality, but no related regulations or even a suggestion from the Association Monégasque Des Activités Financières (AMAF) have been bought up so far.

.mc domain name

.mc domain names are reserved exclusively for the Monegasque companies listed on the Register of Commerce and Industry of Monaco. Therefore, only authorised business can own a .mc domain name. Applications for persons or informal groups are not accepted.

NIC MONACO (Network Internet Center) is the entity within the Department of Electronic Communications which registers first-level Internet domains within the ".mc" country code.

It runs and maintains the technical infrastructure for managing domain names within the ".mc" zone. The organisation is also responsible for developing the regulatory framework surrounding the naming system and drawing up registration agreements defining the contractual relationship between NIC MONACO and the domain name registrars.

The process of registration and activation of a domain name typically takes 5-10 business days.

The Direction des Communications Electroniques accepts only applications for Monegasque domain names from legal commercial entities or public or private organizations. The application must imperatively contain an extract from the Register of Trade and Industry less than 3 months old.

In order to create, amend or delete a .mc domain name, go to NIC website: https://www.nic.mc/

Direction des Communications Electroniques de Monaco
NIC MONACO
Stade Louis II - Entrée C
19, Avenue des Castelans
98000 MONACO
Phone: +377 98 98 88 00 - Fax : +377 97 98 56 57
E-mail: nic@gouv.mc

When making an application to register a domain name, it is the responsibility of the applicant to check that the name requested does not violate prior rights under the intellectual property code or trademark law.

As an interesting fact, all the .mc domain names are publicly listed in Monaco at the NIC website: https://www.nic.mc/

GDPR in Monaco

As I mentioned at the very beginning of the book General Data Protection Regulation, known as GDPR does not apply for Monaco. Nevertheless, a significant number of the clients of the Monaco businesses are coming from outside the Principality, therefore those businesses have to comply with both Monaco data protection laws and GDPR.

GDPR is now in force in the European Union. However, even if Monaco has entered into specific treaties with the EU - in particular on financial matters - the Principality is not a member of the European Union. It is good to know that GDPR is out of the scope of such treaties.

However, things can change if a Monaco based business deals with clients from outside the territory of the Principality of Monaco.

My friend Régis Bergonzi, the President of the Monaco Bar is in the opinion that Monaco should harmonize its legislation with GDPR, but no bill on GDPR has been voted yet.

A new law in Monaco, amending the current data protection legislation is soon expected. This change in legislation is also required to obtain the long-awaited "adequate level" of protection for the Principality of Monaco, which will facilitate data transfers from an EU controller.

How-to operate a business

Trade and Industry Registry

Among the very first things you need to do once your business permit request is accepted, is to register your newly formed company at the RCI, which is the short version of the Trade and Industry Registry. Registration must be completed within two months following the commencement of activity.

Natural persons carrying out commercial activity and businesses (except partnerships and economic interest groupings) are registered on the Trade and Industry Registry. However, people who carry out manufacturing activities or are self-employed are not recorded on the RCI.
The Trade Registry Service ensures that the legal publication formalities have been fulfilled. Registration is subject to provision of evidence showing the license to exercise the activity or, for Monégasque nationals who do not exercise a regulated activity, the provision of a receipt of notification of exercise.

Registration of SAMs takes place after the following publication formalities:

» Publication, in the Journal de Monaco, of the ministerial decree which authorises and approves the memorandum and articles of association of the public limited company

» Publication of the entire memorandum and articles of association in the Journal de Monaco

» Publication, in the Journal de Monaco, of the date that a certified copy of the memorandum and articles of association, the statement of subscription, the statement of the payment of capital made by the founder and the minutes of the founding general meeting were filed with the General Court Registry

Registration of other businesses (SARL, SCS and SNC) takes place after submission of a copy of the articles of association to the General Court Registry and their publication in the Journal de Monaco. This is at the expense of the company by intermediary of the Business Development Agency.

The Trade and Industry Register is also useful to prove that you have an authorised business in the Principality of Monaco.

An extract from the Trade and Industry Register can be used to prove that your company is legally established. It can be requested by any of your business partners such as banks, suppliers, potential future partners, to ensure that your company has been registered, and find out about its legal situation.

Employment

As I previously gave you a glimpse regarding the process of the recruitment in the chapter "Relocation and what it takes...", any employer in the Principality who wishes to recruit must go to the Employment Office to create an employer's file and to affiliate itself to the necessary social bodies.

Any job offer must be reported to the Employment Office which will then forward the suitable candidates who have priority status in terms of employment in Monaco.

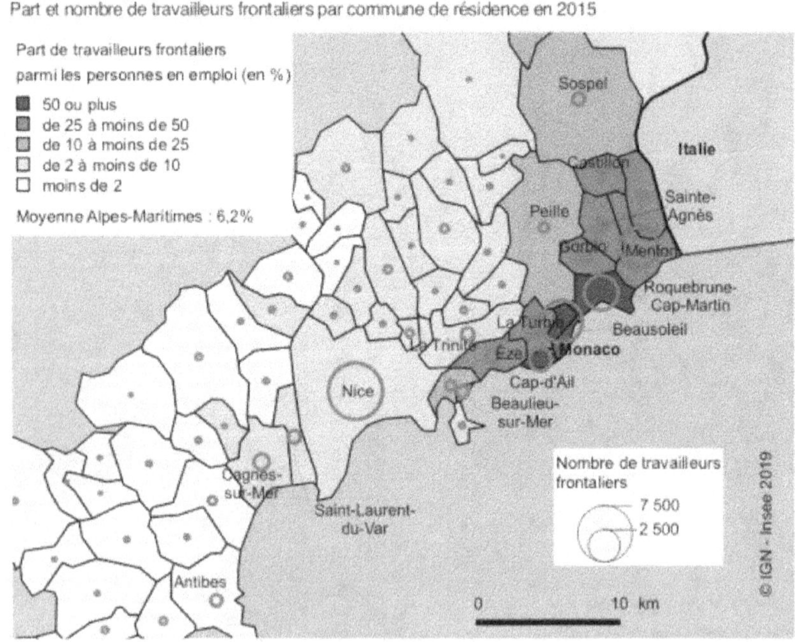

Lecture : 5,8 % des actifs occupés qui résident à Nice travaillent à Monaco. Cela représente 7 500 personnes.
Source : Insee, recensement de la population 2015

Without the written approval of the Employment Office, you are not allowed to employ any new person in your company. Employing someone without the approval of the Employment Office would immediately terminate your business permit in the Principality.

Candidates benefiting from employment priority status are:

1. Individuals of Monaco nationality
2. Children or spouses of Monegasque
3. Residents of the Principality of Monaco
4. Residents of the surrounding communes (Cap d'Ail, La Turbie, Beausoleil, Roquebrune-Cap-Martin) who have already been employed in Monaco

The job offer submission is quite flexible, you can also submit it online. In all cases you will receive an acknowledgement of receipt by email within twenty-four hours of posting your job offer.

The Employment Office will provide you with the suitable candidates within four days of the deposit of the job offer who has priority status in terms of employment in Monaco. If during these four days no candidate has contacted you or no candidate is selected, you can submit a candidate of your choice.

SUGGESTION:

If you have a specific person in mind to employ, it can be useful to create an incredibly detailed job description, which absolutely fits your candidate. It can strengthen your chances, however, there is no guarantee at all that the Employment Office will grant the work permit to your candidate.

Once you have chosen a candidate, complete the acknowledgment of receipt including the selected candidate's details and return the document to the Employment Office.

Following the return of the acknowledgement of receipt, and if the candidate you are putting forward is validated by the Employment Office, you will receive a pre-printed form called "Demande d'autorisation d'embauchage et de permis de travail" that will have to be completed with the employee.

In order to submit the employment request and the work permit you will need to return the form "Demande d'autorisation d'embauchage et de permis de travail" to the Employment Office, duly completed and including five Euro of stamp duty of which three Euro are borne by you.

Once the employee receives a work permit and a registration number for the social security contribution fund and independent pension contribution fund, he/she will be able to start working for your company.

Working hours

Monaco takes the working hours very seriously. While in many European countries, the usual working hours are 40 hours per week, in the Principality, the statutory number of working hours is set at 39 hours of actual work per week. This 39 house includes the time during which the employee is carrying out his or her duties (which, in principle, excludes time taken for dressing, snacks, etc.)

In certain occupations, because of the nature of some of the activities, systems of equivalence have been introduced. An attendance period of more than 39 hours is therefore considered equivalent to 39 hours of actual work. However, the actual daily working hours must not exceed ten, except with the authorisation of the Labour Inspector. And the rest period between two consecutive days of work must not be less than ten hours.

Interestingly, at the request of the employer, an employee can work more hours than the legal limit. These working hours are counted as overtime. Subject to a minimum increase in wages, an employer can extend the working hours to 47 hours per week.

Unless a special exemption has been granted, the hours of overtime worked must not exceed the maximum amount of hours stipulated by law, which is up to 60 hours per week in some companies in exceptional circumstances and for short periods with the agreement of the Labour Inspector. Employees who have several jobs must conform with these limits, considering all the jobs as a whole.

But talking about a very interesting side of the employment in the Principality of Monaco, there is a difference between the regulation for working hours for women and men.

Women's daily work may be interrupted by one or several rest breaks, the total duration of which must not be less than one hour. During these rest periods, the employer cannot ask employees to undertake any work.

Women cannot be employed for night work in factories or workshops unless they are part of the management or occupy a position of responsibility. As a general rule, any work undertaken between 10 pm and 5 am is considered night work.

80% of Monaco's employees do not live in the Principality

A fascinating study in 2019, conducted by INSEE Provence-Alpes-Côte d'Azur, has revealed that more than 80% of Monaco's employees do not live in the Principality.

Évolution entre 1990 et 2015 du nombre de personnes en emploi, selon leur lieu de travail (base 100 en 1990)

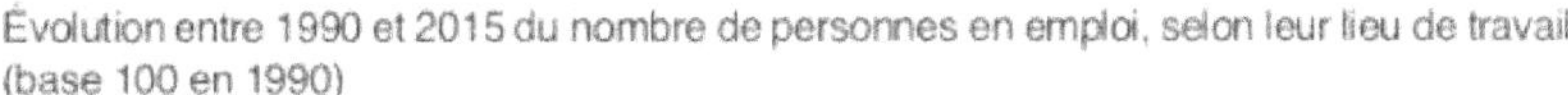
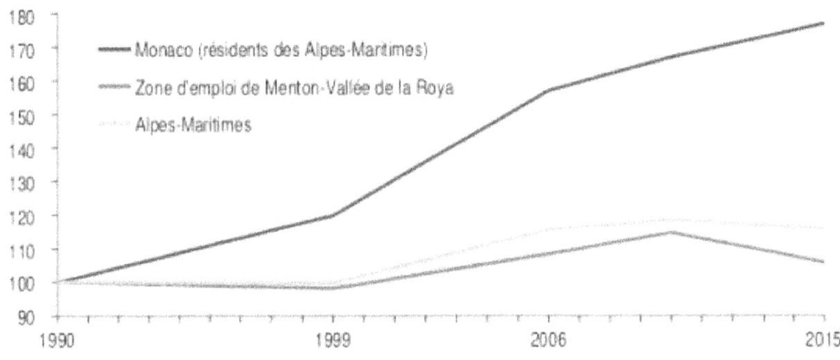

Source : Insee. recensements de la population

It is a huge number showing how difficult it is to relocate to the Principality of Monaco without sufficient financial means.

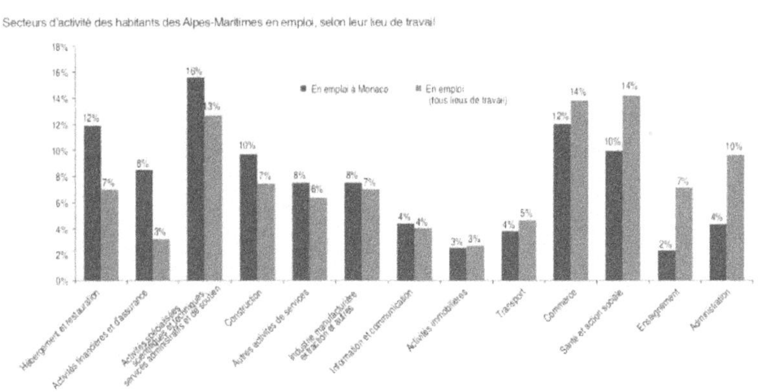

Lecture : le secteur de l'hébergement et restauration est surreprésenté chez les frontaliers : 12 % d'entre eux y travaillent contre 7 % de l'ensemble des habitants du département ayant un emploi.
À l'inverse, l'administration est sous représentée : 4 % des frontaliers y travaillent contre 10 % des personnes en emploi dans les Alpes-Maritimes.
Source : Insee. recensement de la population 2015, exploitation complémentaire

This study on cross-border workers was conducted in partnership with Monegasque Institute of Statistics and Economic Studies (IMSEE). The impact of Monaco's labour market on the Alpes-Maritimes, the modes of transport and the activities of cross-border workers were studied in this analysis.

Nombres d'actifs en emploi résidant en France selon leur catégorie professionnelle et le pays où ils travaillent

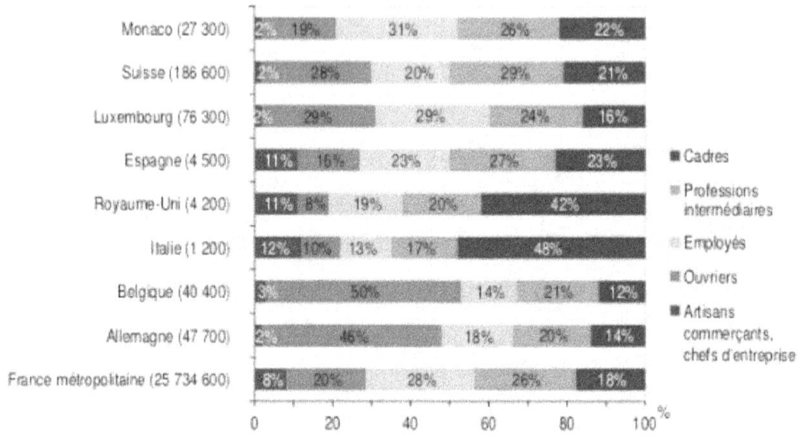

Source : Insee, recensement de la population 2015, exploitation complémentaire

According to the study, 26,700 people travel into Monaco every day from the Alpes Maritimes department. In contrast, 600 Monegasques cross the border into France for work.

To get to their place of employment, 45% of cross-border workers prefer taking the car, while 26% use public transport, 22% use two-wheelers, and 21% choose to walk, most likely from Beausoleil or Menton.

Professional networks

Once you have decided to relocate to the Principality of Monaco, networking either for personal or professional purposes will be a very important thing for you to do.

Interestingly the tiny Principality offers hundreds of member clubs, associations, various business clubs and societies. The Principality of Monaco is proud of its colorful and international base of residents, and many nations have their own clubs holding great networking events.

From a professional perspective, being a member of these clubs and associations could be a very interesting way for you to easily understand how you and your business could succeed in Monaco. It is also beneficial to create mutual co-operations and agreements with companies and vendors who are already well established in Monaco.

However, networking clubs are also available for the entire family, since many clubs such as the Monaco Residents' (Magazine) Club are targeting non-entrepreneurs as well, not to mention various ladies and children's clubs.

For business purpose I would invite everyone to discover the UHNW Business Club in Monaco which bring together Monaco residents and leaders in the international HNW and UHNW industry. Basically the UHNW Business Club conducts exclusive bespoke networking events designed to connect, educate and expand global business relationships between Monaco and the world.

Intellectual property

Since 2012 Monaco also protects its name as a brand, therefore it is not easy to use the word "Monaco" or "Monte-Carlo" in your company, brand or in your product name anymore. However, in many countries, especially in the European Union, you might still have the right to use the word "Monaco" or "Monte-Carlo". Here, let me explain..

Everything started back in 2010 when the World Intellectual Property Organisation (WIPO) granted the government of the Principality of Monaco the word trademark "Monaco".

On 6 April 2012, a Monaco-based limited company was created protecting the "Brands of the State of Monaco"; it is called Monaco Brands. It is safeguarding, promoting and defending the entire portfolio of brands they own or license.

However, the legal challenge started when in 2013 the Office for Harmonisation in the Internal Market (OHIM) refused the protection of the trademark in the European Union in some cases.

Generally speaking, you can refer to Monaco as a location or as a country since the trademark Act at Section 3(1) (c) prohibits the registration of marks designating geographical origin. However, once you use Monaco as a company or commercial name, or as a product name, you breach international trademark rights.

The two most important brands you might aim to use in your company is "Monaco" and "Monte-Carlo". Since 6 April 2012, they are both trademarked and protected, and the chief function of Monaco Brand's activity is the general protection and promotion of any element of intellectual property.

It is obvious that Monaco and Monte-Carlo are names which have been a magnet for prestigious and luxury brands, therefore, the Monaco Brands offers partnership and licence agreements for the usage of these labels.

Trademarks are important elements of any business and they can identify the brand with the product or services. Having trademarks are also great tools to stand out from the crowd of competitors. Therefore, it may be interesting for your business as well to register a trademark and patents related to your business.

Once registered, a trademark offers protection to its owner for ten years. The ten years is continuously renewable. Many companies prefer trademarks because it offers a monopoly for the holder of the trademark. The holder has full power to forbid any of its competitors to use or refer to the trademark which can be a serious benefit in the market.

The intellectual property right is called a patent. A patent offers its holder the exclusive right to authorise or oppose rights at the national or international level.

Patents are usually granted for a maximum period of twenty years. By owning the patent, you can control all the rights related to your intellectually property or invention, rights such as distribution, usage, sale, reproduction, etc… However, it is important to know that an idea itself cannot be protected by a patent.

A patent filed in Monaco will be granted without a guarantee by the government, therefore, a patentability or anteriority search is highly advised before you approach the Intellectual Property Division.

Finally, on 15 January 2015, the General Court in Case T-197/13 Monaco v OHIM stated that the OHIM was also correct in 2013 to find that the word "Monaco" could be used in trade, to designate origin, geographical destination or the place of supply of services, so that the trademark has, in respect of the goods and services concerned, a descriptive character.

Therefore, the word "Monaco" can be used in goods and services applied for magnetic data carriers, paper and cardboard goods not included in other classes, printed matter, photographs, transport, travel arrangement, entertainment, sporting activities and temporary accommodation.

Corporate taxation

Summarising the biggest taxation benefit, for the first two years, the income and profit of your business activity can be completely tax free in the Principality of Monaco. However, it does not mean that the activities are free from Value Added Tax (VAT).

In Monaco, you have to make a difference between Value Added Tax and Business Profit Tax.

The Value Added Tax is levied on the same basis and at the same rate as in France. The intra-community tax regime has been applicable since 1 January 1993.

Any business carrying out an industrial or commercial activity and generating more than 25% of their turnover outside Monaco is subject to Business Profit Tax from the third year of its operation. This is also true for firms whose activities consist of earning revenues from patents or artistic property rights.

The legal form of the company is irrelevant with regard to the application of the tax. The nature of the activities and location of transactions determines liability for tax.

In addition, income received from patents and copyright gives rise to liability for corporate income tax if the income in question is received by the company, but remains outside the scope of the tax if it is received by natural persons.

Taxable profit is established after deducting all expenditures, in particular the remuneration of the entrepreneur, directors or executives performing actual activities within the firm. A scale setting out levels of deduction for remuneration has been established for firms whose turnover does not exceed 3.5 million Euro for services and 7 million Euro for other firms.

For other companies, the level of remuneration is determined with reference to recognized international practices, in particular those used in the European Union.

- » 33.33% for financial years commencing before 1 January 2019
- » 31% for financial years commencing on or after 1 January 2019
- » 28% for financial years commencing on or after 1 January 2020
- » 26.5% for financial years commencing on or after 1 January 2021
- » 25% for financial years commencing on or after 1 January 2022

The taxation based on business profit is a great model, which truly motivates the businesses to gain revenue. In case your company is not profitable, you have no obligation to pay tax.

There is also a special tax relief offer in the Principality:

Firms created in the Principality and falling within the scope of corporate income tax that carry on a genuinely new business are exempt from said tax for a period of two years and subsequently benefit from a favourable regime for the three following years, namely:

- » 1st & 2nd year: no corporate income tax
- » 3rd year: the tax is calculated on 25% of profit
- » 4th year: the tax is calculated on 50% of profit
- » 5th year: the tax is calculated on 75% of profit
- » 6th year: the tax is calculated on 100% of profit.

Interestingly, it is a small gap for some privately-owned companies, because many owners take out the profit as an annual bonus, compensation or benefit and leave the company with a very small line of profit before taxation. Probably, this is also the answer to the question why Monaco has so many sole trader companies. It is a question of morality, but frankly the legislation allows this possibility, and it is part of the local business life.

Lessons to consider

I did not have to stay long in Monaco to face the ugly truth that not everything that is shining is gold.

The first thing one notices is that everybody wants to be part of the unique world and community of Monaco. Therefore, you meet many people who say "I live in Monaco" or "I have a business in Monaco", however, you will experience soon that 90% of these people have no residence permit, no license to operate any type of business in the Principality of Monaco, and most of them are actually not even living there, only in the surroundings. I call many of them seasonal people who are usually coming and staying in the surroundings of Monaco from April to September, trying to fish in the golden pot of the Principality.

Can you trust these people in Monaco? Yes, of course. But you have to be extremely careful and pay attention to the little signs. Let me share with you my very first experience.

I had been staying in Monaco for only a month when I decided to co-operate with a company that was asking for a very high initial joining fee. They seemed to be experts, and based on all the materials I received such as flyers, brochures and websites, I found their quality to be very high.

During the previous years, I learnt not to invest a dime until I have not met in person with the other party. Perhaps it sounds a little bit old fashioned, but it was not a hundred Euro internet Pay-pal transaction; investments in Monaco usually involve very serious amounts.

I wanted to be careful, therefore, I went to their office located in Fontvieille. The first impression was a little bit weird because their office was located in a private building in an apartment. However, if you get to know Monaco, you get to understand that many start-up companies are operating in private apartments – these types of apartments are called "Usage Mixte". So, I met with the company members and they seemed to be very nice people. I actually sat down with five of them because the CEO immediately introduced her most valuable employees to ensure me that my initial joining fee would be in good hands.

The address was real, the CEO and her team was very persuasive and I saw that they had a company formation S.A.R.L., which stands for the Limited Liability company form in the Principality of Monaco. All in all, they made a very good impression and they seemed trustable for me, therefore, I decided to sign the contract with them.

Afterwards, I received the bank details of the company for the fulfilment of the initial joining fee. When I opened the letter with the bank details, I started to feel a bit weird in my stomach. Everything was fine except for the location of the bank account. The company had a bank account in Nice, France, and this was very strange for me, especially because Monaco is tax-free in the first two years of a company.

I immediately went to the office of the company, and luckily, they were there, so I highlighted my concerns to the CEO. She looked really well prepared, and she explained to me that they still have the French bank account because the transformation of the company wealth takes more months in Monaco, therefore, they collect all the income into one account to ensure a smoother change of bank account with their new, future bank in the Principality.

She was pretty convincing, and I felt at this point, there was no way back because I had already legally committed myself by signing the contract. My only hope was to try to trust that lovely woman and her team. So, I asked my bank to release the transfer. That day was the last time I saw my money, and it was too late to discover for me that the company was not in Monaco anymore, especially since I did not suspect anything because we were in a continuous e-mail communication. When I checked the company, I realized that they were never registered in Monaco, they were a French company.

This was the point when I started my non-profit, internet-based business portal, the MonacoWealthManagement.com, to collect the most reliable banks, wealth managers, family offices, lawyers, notaries and financial consultants in Monaco, that are able to give me and all investors a clear background regarding real and unreal business transactions. I never felt sorry for my money loss but I knew that I would not allow this to happen to me again.

The conclusion was very simple for me: Monaco is one of the safest places on earth, however, it also attracts the fake so-called "I live in Monaco" blood-sucking leeches, whose only aim is to gain access to your wealth. But honestly, what should we expect? Can you imagine Las Vegas without poker tricksters and other cheaters? I do not think this could be possible, and this is the way it is. However, I raise my hat in front of the Government of Monaco because they try to do as much as they can against such people.

As I previously mentioned, one of the greatest advantages in the Principality of Monaco is that the police can act extremely quickly, and the police force is also allowed to step into a case which requires intervention.

Obviously, Monaco learnt and experienced a lot and probably still learns from the fortune hunters. One of the great examples which truly amazed me during the last years is a story I found out through a friend of mine.

A few years ago, a limousine was ordered to the Nice Airport to transfer a passenger to Monte-Carlo. When the limousine arrived, the driver welcomed a beautiful and elegant lady. Because of legal considerations, let's call her Ursula. She introduced herself to the driver as an ultra-rich lady from Albania, stating she just arrived with her private jet.

During the forty-minute drive to Monaco from the airport, she told the driver various stories about the wealth of her family and the heritage she just inherited. When the driver asked the nature of her trip to the Principality, she said that she was aiming to relocate and to enjoy the French Riviera. She said Albania cannot ensure the luxury, elegance and the glamour she deserves. She also told the driver that she does not want to go back to Albania at all, and she decided to transfer all her wealth and asset to the Principality of Monaco.

Ursula was a very wise woman and she knew that the easiest way to accomplish her aims was through word-of-mouth type of recommendations. She was also confident that the limousine drivers give away information and possible leads to hotels and banks in

Monaco. So, the first forty minutes of the drive were perfect to create a strong base for her plans.

Late in the evening, the big black limousine arrived in front of one of the luxury hotels in Monaco. The concierge and the valet immediately noticed that someone very important had arrived.

While Ursula went into the hall, the driver immediately started his work just as Ursula expected and the driver started to share what he had already heard during the drive. He was so enthusiastic that he convinced the concierge that Ursula was undoubtedly an ultra-rich client.

So, without saying anything, Ursula was immediately surprised with a free upgrade to the luxury suit and her request to pay her suite later after her settlement instead of at check-in was immediately granted. She told the hotel that she was looking for a bank and she asked for their kind recommendation. Since, by now, the hotel team already knew her inheritance and relocation story, they decided to ensure a royal VIP guest treat for Ursula.

The hotel also knew that they would receive an introductory fee from the wealth management company as well, therefore, everybody was satisfied and happy.

The next morning, Ursula was escorted to the bank where the high-profile client managers welcomed her. Of course, by this time, everyone had exchanged quick information about this wealthy lady.

During a two-hour conversation regarding why she is in Monaco, Ursula talked about her amazing richness, lifestyle, wealth and her membership in the ultra-luxury society to the client managers.

Everyone was sure that the golden fish had arrived in Monaco, and the crocodiles were hungry. Therefore, the bank was ready to open a bank account for Ursula without any initial payment. Understanding her inheritance situation and the sensitivity of her position, the bank also ensured her a temporary bank cheque book to cover her expenses until the wealth arrived.

In the next months, Ursula was not afraid to use the cheque book and she lived the life of the ultra-rich, buying the most exclusive fashion, and spending a fortune on elegant services and gastronomic pleasures.

After six months, when the bank realised that nothing was coming towards their bank account, it was already too late. Ursula had spent enormous amounts on her lifestyle, and she had even purchased a ten million Euro super yacht for herself.

Obviously, after the bank realised this, the alarm bells began to ring and the police acted swiftly. Ursula was arrested for committing fraud. Probably, she stayed too long, forgetting that one day, someone would realise the truth.

We all learn from experiences and this is just one story about how cheaters and fortune hunters are trying to stretch the boundaries. In any other country, the prosecution would be far too long and cheaters could slip away leaving serious damages behind them, but not in the Principality of Monaco.

CHAPTER 15

The local investment scene

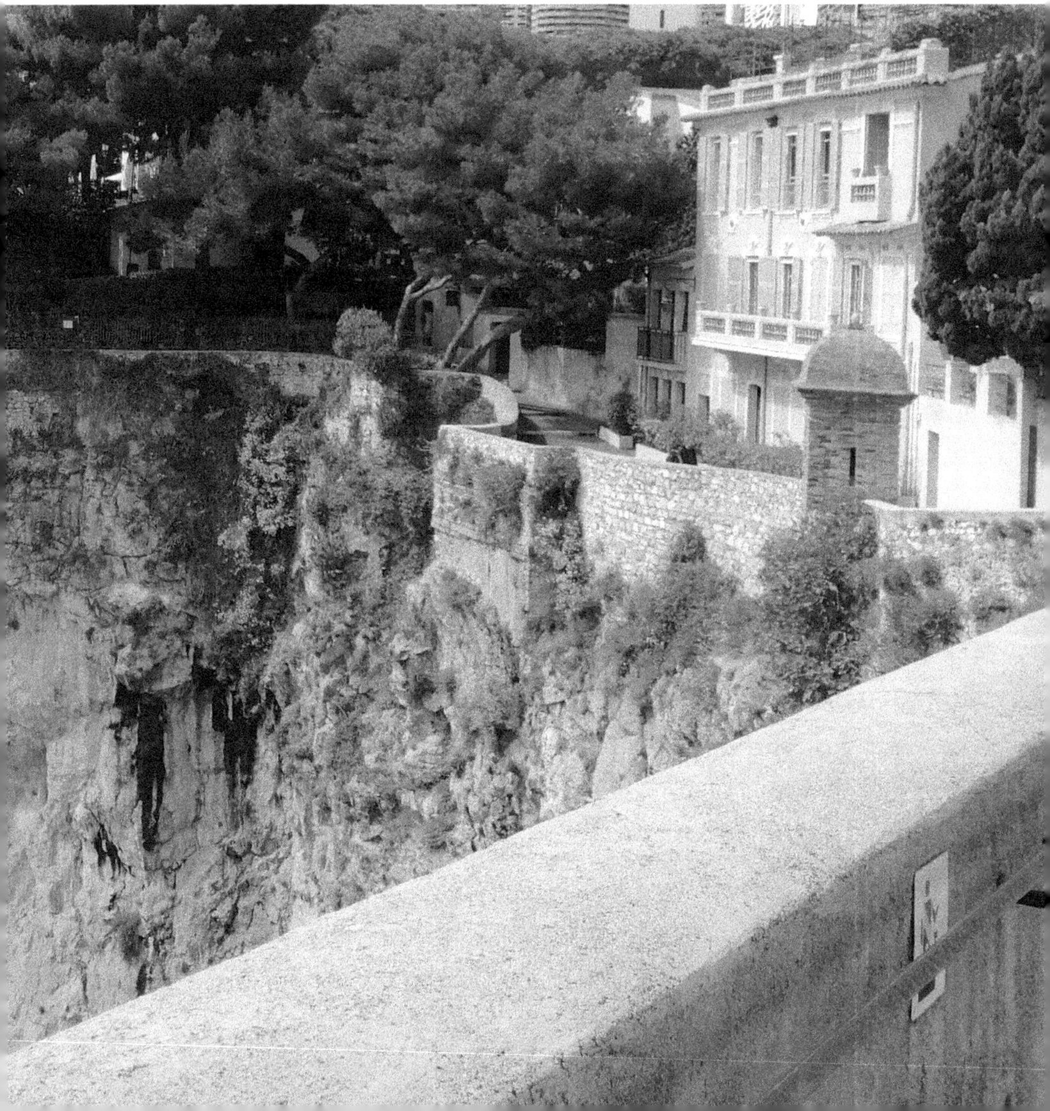

Investing in Monaco

The Principality of Monaco is an exclusive and unique place with many advantages for investors through its location, taxation, security, stability and also its high-profile business community which provides exceptional reasons to invest in Monaco.

> **When a company is authorised to advise on various topics such as funding approach, valuation, break-even point, and the clarity of proposition, then you can be confident that investment offers are in a fit state to raise funds from private investors.**

Monaco is a strong player in the wealth and asset management industry, and its local companies are some of the greatest competitors when it comes to credibility. However, Monaco also offers great associations as well when you are aiming to invest. Through them, you can reach an incredibly wide range of portfolios combining traditional investments with new breeds of investments.

Typical investments in the Principality of Monaco are:

» Venture Capital and Business Angel investments

» Art investment

» Gold investment

» Diamond investment

» Diamond and Jewellery

» Real Estate investment

» Non-traditional investments

» Supercar and Hypercar investment

» Whiskey and wine investment

» Investment into Blockchain

However, before you engage in any type of investment, it is always advised to have a basic understanding about the portfolio. In this chapter, I aimed to collect some of the most basic things I have learnt in the past.

Venture Capital and Business Angel investments

We can see a very flowering type of investment in the Principality of Monaco, called Business Angel investment. However, the Business Angels in Monaco are slightly different from the traditional Angel investors. Their portfolio is a mixture of Venture Capital and Business Angel investments.

Probably, it is coming from the fact that many successful entrepreneurs, who reside in Monaco have business experiences as well, not just the liquidity to invest.

We refer to "Business Angels" as private investors who are investing small amounts of capital into early-stage or start-up companies. Usually, the average equity investment is between 10,000 Euro and 500,000 Euro.

In many cases, Business Angels are investing into the idea, the concept and the persons behind it.

Business Angels invest either individually or as part of a syndicate in high growth businesses.

What makes this type of investment very interesting is the excitement factor. Business Angels are usually looking for attractive financial returns, high growth potential and clear exit paths. To achieve their investment aims, they are often ready to take higher risks as well.

In these type of investments, the pitch is everything. It is a compelling story which is the most important element to attract the attention of an investor. However, since it is a kind of storytelling, it often falls into broad or fictional categories.

Comparing the past years' statistics, we can see that only one out of ten investments are able to bring a tenfold return on capital invested. Meanwhile, almost sixty percent of the investments fail to return the capital.

The risk is high, but the expectations are clear. Business Angels are usually looking for a tenfold return on their investment capital over a three-year period.

The most popular start-up venture types are those which stand out from the competition and which, with their product, are able to change the landscape of their industries. It is even better if their product is a patented innovation.

However, the most successful fundraisers are those that solve a truly massive human problem. Or, at least they liberate people from automating tasks, freeing up valuable time. In these cases, the story focuses on what the world will look like when the problem will be completely eradicated.

One of the most important things for you as an investor is to look beyond the product and to try to discover its advantages and potentials. You can always change the surface of a product or the way you market it. Personally, I am a partner in a watch company which created a new label and a new chemistry patent. Many investors I approach stopped at the look of the watch, which is always an individual feeling. However, they forget that an industry patent can be a big game changer. An investment is supposed to focus on the possible returns without allowing play for emotions.

When you spend time in the Principality of Monaco and you are interested in the field of investment, you notice that every month there are various events dedicated to Business Angels. Many start-ups that are looking for additional funds, travel to Monaco to make an often eight-minute long presentation to catch the attention of the Business Angels.

They know that the Business Angels are willing to invest in early stage and these equity investments can dramatically increase the business potential of these companies.

Based on my experience, many investments will require further capital injection. The follow-up funding is usually a further 50% in the upcoming years.

When an idea is exciting and the concept is clean, Business Angels are willing to take the risk in the hope that the concept and great execution will bring the desired success.

As you can see, in other investment areas such as Venture Capital, in many cases, Business Angels go in syndicate to reduce and diversify the initial risk. This way, they also have the potential to invest in various projects securing a higher success rate on the return.

Usually, a person behind the start-up company or the idea and his/her capability for success is considered a main factor. Therefore, one of the most important pre-investment considerations is the due intelligence of the people involved. In many cases, Business Angels trust people more than the idea itself.

Business experience is not requested, but obviously it could bring a huge advantage to the table. When a funding project involves experienced business people, who understand their obligations towards the Business Angels and how to commercialise their ideas, it can deliver a very positive impact during the fundraising process.

Investors are not aiming to fund someone's lifestyle. Many people make the mistake that they are seeking funds for relocating in Monaco, to purchase a house or a car from the funds. An investor invests into the development of the company and not into the personal lifestyle of someone.

> **Keep director salaries under control. It is always better to offer them higher compensation with corporate shares related to business results, instead of exceptionally high, fixed monthly salaries.**

The whole fundraising process can be fastened up by the people involved. To develop and gain results and quality in any business sector, the most important thing is to create simple and well-connected business processes that business investors relate to in a clear way. This gives a transparent overview to all the involved parties and a much better understanding.

When people fully understand the corporate processes, they are ready to come up with innovative ideas.

This is especially important since investing as a Business Angel always requires that "first instinct". To reach this, we have to agree that any kind of improvement comes from fully understanding the specific area, and by making it as transparent and clear as possible to the people working within it.

When we can reach the full understanding of the business model or idea, we can be in a very good situation. Despite other investments, Business Angels do not spend that much time on the legal process and they never allow the legal steps to overtake the importance of the due intelligence.

Forex/Trade/Stock market

Investment into Forex/Trade is considered among the most traditional types of investments. Many investors who are afraid to take risks consider this type of investment portfolio a priority.

It is also the favourite of banks world-wide, since they can add transaction and profit-based services as well. Transaction-based services are also one of the major sources of income in the financial industry.

In many cases, the banks and wealth managers are asking you to sign a clausal that they have the power of attorney to use and invest your funds in Forex/Trade portfolios in the hope of securing a significant return.

It is a very traditional way to invest with relatively low risk, and also with low return. Some traditional residents are only looking for a positive result and they do not care about its volume. It can be as low as 0,01% of growth, but the original wealth must be maintained.

Be careful because many wealth managers love the transaction-driven accounts. They even move the investment funds without any specific reason just to charge for the transactions. It may happen that your trade account is unnecessarily changed and re-invested every 2 days just to charge more.

On an important note, and according to the Kondratieff theory, the "Kondratieff winter" is coming. It is especially true for Europe. The standard investment forms will change to tangible assets, such as gold, art, etc.

The doomed Russian economist, Nikolai Kondratiev created a theory of cycles that has accurately accounted for economic developments over the past two centuries. He published his book, "The Major Economic Cycles," in 1925.

Averaging fifty and ranging from approximately forty to sixty years in length, the cycles consist of alternating periods between high sectoral growth and periods of relatively slow growth.

In 1939, the Austrian-born economist Joseph Schumpeter named waves describing cycles Kondratiev Waves. It describes alternating long-term, high-growth and low-growth economic periods. They are also known as K-Waves.

The K-Waves have stood up over time. They have correctly identified various periods of important economic activity within the past 200 years. Very few cycles in history are as accurate as the Kondratiev waves.

The Kondratieff winter is often labelled as a "depression". This is a period of correcting the excesses of the past and preparing the foundation for future growth. Prices fall, profits decline and stock markets correct to the downside. However, this period also refines the technologies of the past with innovation, making it cheaper and more available for the masses.

Based on the Kondratieff economic theory we are in a contractive cycle, where for the next 10 years wealth will be made mostly from tangible assets, including art.

Art investment

In the Principality of Monaco, the policy of supporting culture and creativity has been pursued both nationally and internationally. Art has always represented a point of interest in the Principality.

For example, the excellences of the contemporary art are honoured every year by the Foundation Prince Pierre. Furthermore, the Principality of Monaco offers financial and working studio support to its local artists.

With more than 400,000 art collectors world-wide with an estimated art asset of 1.5 trillion USD, a great demand was created for innovation around art. Since 2007, art has been identified as one of the best performing asset in the long term, and thanks to environmental changes, wealth and asset managers started to see and consider art as a reliable tangible asset.

Dr. Mei Moses at the Stern Business School found art to be a fantastic investment with minimal correlation to other asset classes, with a long-term average return of 10.47% alike SP500 of 10.95%. In the past 10 years, contemporary art has outperformed equities, bonds, property, hedge funds, and private equity.

> **The art market is in a great position, but only those who see this, will be able to profit from it.**

Many countries have also noticed the value of art, therefore, more and more free ports are opening and helping the tax-free art transactions in favour of diversified tangible asset portfolios. These free ports are also considered the most effective tools in art collection management.

Nowadays, art is considered a new type of asset class for over 40% of the asset managers. Furthermore, in 2012, almost 10% of the total net worth of the wealth was held in treasure assets. These facts have increased the confidence of the wealth and asset managers, and the economic uncertainty has increased the demand for art as a tangible investment.

Meanwhile, the main motivation to invest in art is still the emotional value. Art market professionals are now seeing the financial aspects to invest and hold art assets. During recent years, financial motivations have become more and more important in the art market, which trigged the need for new services from the wealth and asset managers. It seems art has become a great tool for them to win new businesses.

An impressive art collection strengthens your corporate image, improves the client's first impression of you and makes a bold statement of your company's identity. Some of the motivations to invest in art are: social status, philanthropy, taxation benefits, diversification, economic slowdown, capital appreciation, speculation, extended boom period, corporate identity and brand management.

The potential for growth in this area is awesome, as the economic evidence for contributing to culture and creating an inspiring work environment is mounting.

Many banks are also offering art secured lending as their complementary services for HNWI, therefore they are becoming ideal partners for the collectors. Banks are offering a new experience to them by giving transparent pricing, quick decision timeframes and personal services.

Without any doubt, the art market is going through a great expansion where more and more money and players are involved in art. Art is becoming a niche of wealth and asset management services, which will continue its revolution.

I love art as an investment and an asset class, but I truly appreciate the human nature of art. I always stand for creative people who are talented and brave enough to inspire us and the future generation with their visions and inspirations. I believe art is all around us and the aesthetic inspiration is our footprint to the next generation.

Art is not just a piece of canvas, but a passion and message from our century, something from us to our grandchildren. They are telling us their stories and sharing their emotions. Find the moment to understand them, allow them to communicate to you and tell you their individual messages. When you find this harmony, you can also combine the passion with the profitable long-term investment.

Art is not for understanding

"Art is not for understanding
it is for feeling it, and loving it."
- Pablo Picasso

Many people love art and are passionate about the feelings that artistic masterpieces communicate to them. Falling in love with a work of art almost equals love, since you can share your journey with it during your life, and it will always remind you of the moment when you first saw it. Real pieces of art are energies on canvases which are able to evoke feelings in us. Therefore, art is a passion.

However, art is more than that; it can be a form of investment as well. It can be an investment for the short term or even the long term to secure something for the future generation.

When we are talking about art collectors, we are usually making a difference between three types of collectors. The art collectors, the art investors, and finally, the art lovers. They are all looking for different exchanges from the art market and in the meantime, they are complementing each other.

When we are aiming to invest in art and to purchase a piece of art, we can make a difference between "primary market" and "secondary market". In both cases, we can deal with the same players of the art market, however, there is an incredible difference between the two markets.

The "primary market" is all about the excitement, the passion and the aim to find the never-seen-before rare diamonds in the artistic ocean. Meanwhile, the "secondary market" represents the liability and stability to make a savvy investment.

Art collectors mainly deal with the old masters and in rare cases with perfectly established artists. They purchase from auction houses and only on the "secondary market".

Meanwhile, art investors consider art as an asset in their diversified investment portfolio. Therefore, art investors are using both the "primary" and the "secondary market". This means that they are open to buying from the emerging contemporary artists, and they accept risks since they are looking for a higher return on the artworks. They are the ones who can really secure the successful rise of an emerging artist.

Many of the investors and art lovers are fascinated by and find the "primary market" exciting since the artworks are usually coming straight from the artist's studio; they have never been seen before in public and they are able to pump up the adrenaline level in all the passion-oriented people. In these kinds of art investments, the key factor is the artist and the market demand for his/her artworks.

One of the main attractive powers of the "primary market" is the price of the artworks since they are usually less than those obtained at an auction on the "secondary market". This is a great tool for galleries and art representatives who are working directly with the artists to sell their artworks quickly at any time of the year. In many cases, collectors are ready to invest in advance into an upcoming artwork, and they are ready to be on the year-long waiting list.

The current economic instability highlights an increased need to consider investments, which are able to show healthy return over the long term. Many smart investors realized that art is not just about the past, it is about the present as well. As you can find remarkable art pieces from the past, you can also discover new diamonds of the present, specifically pieces from emerging artists, directly from the "primary market".

> **The life path of a contemporary artist is one of the greatest helps to an investor. You can monitor the improvement of the artist, the social appearance, the artistic development of his/her technique and the fact whether he/she is consistently maintaining the artistic path.**

Finding original thoughts and concepts on the art market has strengthened the self-confidence of the investors, and art has become a problem solver for diversified investment portfolios. By using social networking and media, many art representatives are able to improve their artists' working liability, which stimulates productivity. During the last years, the "primary market" has given economic confidence to its investors.

In the "primary market", collectors make quick decisions before another buyer gets there first. Meanwhile, in the "secondary market", it is all about savvy decisions.

Usually, when an artist performs well on the "primary market", their artworks will cost more on the "secondary market". However, the players of the "secondary market" usually do not take risks and do not deal directly with the artists. They only deal with brokers, galleries, art advisors and auction houses. In these circles, the key issue is information, instead of the excitement factor of the "never-seen-before" artworks.

Art asset managers and pure investors are usually looking for proven track records, therefore, the "secondary market" is designed for them. In the "secondary market", you can find artworks, which were previously auctioned and sold, therefore, you can measure their auction performance and market tendency. Many of the professionals are specialized in purchase and resale, therefore, the "secondary market" is the major playground of the auction houses as well.

And we should not forget about the art lovers either, because they are also taking a serious part in the art market. They are the ones, who are purchasing for smaller amounts, mainly for their passion. They are the guardians of the emerging artists. The art lovers are buying what they like, since most likely they are actually living with these artworks.

You can always increase the price of your artwork if you offer it for public exhibitions. Many museums and institutions are welcoming artwork for public exhibition purposes.

Personally, I always invest in art because it moves my imagination. Once an artwork is able to impact me, I know that it will hold great value for many other people as well. However, you can also find other great indicators to secure your art investment.

Evaluation and art indices

After a dramatic drop during the last quarter of 2011, in the first half of 2012, the art market experienced a very significant climb. In the second quarter of 2012, while Standard & Poor's 500 started to fall, the art market indicators continuously climbed. Savvy investors realized that art is a good way to diversify their investment portfolios, since art will always have value. It will never go down to zero, like many forex/trade options.

The Sotheby's Mei Moses Index: 1950-2018

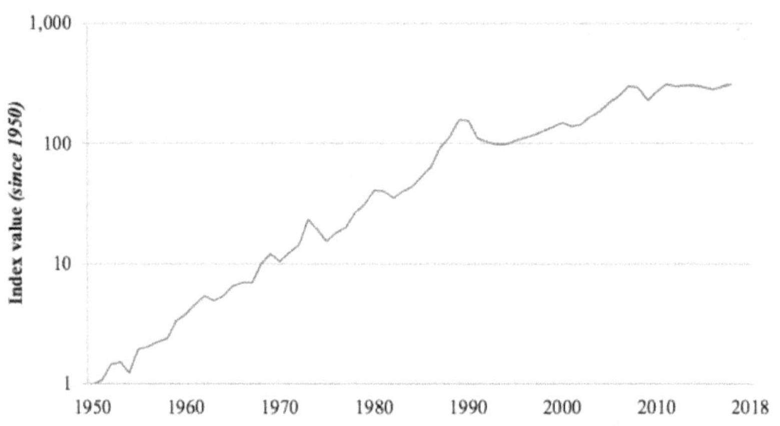

To understand the current art investment trends, I often review the latest Sotheby's Mei Moses Indices. It is always a good reference to start with since it is widely recognized to be the preeminent measure of the state of the art market. Not to mention that leveraging over 60,000 repeat auction sales for the same object over time, Sotheby's is able to produce objective art market analysis to complement the world-class expertise of its specialists.

In 2018, over $12 billion of art was sold by the top global auction houses – take a closer look with Sotheby's Mei Mei Moses as we explore the trends behind those numbers (Differing levels of quality, size, color, maker, and aesthetics of a work of art by analyzing repeat sales).

For example, this graph below shows the Sotheby's Mei Moses Index for the broader art market from 1950 to 2018. The index benchmarks at 1 in 1950 and shows the trajectory in demand for the overall market, a compound annual growth rate of 8.8%.

Monaco Freeport

Many countries have also noticed the value of art, therefore more and more freeports are opening and helping the tax free art transactions in favour of diversified tangible asset portfolios. These freeports are also considered as the most effective tools in art collection management.

In its dynamic cultural context, the Government of the Principality of Monaco has also decided in 2013 to create a free port in Monaco with the aim of promoting and developing the art market in the Principality. The new facility was entitled as "Monaco Freeport".

In many cases collecting art is about money and not about the appreciation of the artwork itself. Freeports are the secrecy jurisdictions of the art world, where art collectors and art dealers can park their speculative art purchases in complete anonymity, while being invisible to tax authorities and foreign governments. Nowdays art is considered as a new type of asset class for over 40% of the asset managers. Furthermore, almost 10% of the total net worth of the wealth are held in treasure assets.

One could assume that in general, art collectors are enjoying their beloved collections, seeing them on the walls of their homes or yachts. The truth is that a major part of art collectors are buying artworks only as part of their investment portfolios.

When art is purchased for investment, one automatically creates an art speculation, where the aim is to keep costs and tax duties low.

The purpose of a freeport warehouse is to make it possible to store works of art, items from collections, antiques and jewellery without incurring duties and taxes. In short, a freeport is a storage facility that exists formally outside of the territorial jurisdiction of any country.

In general, we can say that in their dynamic cultural contexts, countries offering freeports aim to promote and develop their art market. The freeport warehouse makes it possible to store or sell works of arts without incurring duties and taxes. Most of the freeports are located in a strategical place, close to important international airports, helping the transportation of the assets between the other freeports.

The Monaco Freeport makes it possible to store in Monaco works of art, items from collections, antiques and jewellery from countries outside the European Union, without incurring duties and taxes.

What makes a freeport truly exceptional and attractive to the art collectors is the fact that the contents of freeports are invisible to tax authorities and foreign governments. Complete anonymity is guaranteed and art collections in freeports cannot be traced to the original owners, and no government can tax these assets.

Art secured lending

Art collecting can be also very beneficial for you, since art can be your long-term collateral to secure further investments. Many banks have realised this and art is now seen not only as an object of pleasure, but also as a new alternative asset class with interesting business opportunities.

Furthermore, art secured lending is able to unlock your liquidity for investment or personal finance purposes. While you enjoy your art collection on your wall at home, you can also use it to inject money into your business.

Art secured lending is not a new business, it was first pioneered in the 1970s. It is a niche-credit service targeted to (U)HNW individuals, who wish to unlock liquidity out of their collection or art assets for investment or personal finance purposes.

Almost all of the major financial players will lend against up to 50% of the appraised fair market value of the artwork. Typically, the loans are in the 1 million to 20 million euro range, but some banks are willing to lend up to 150 million euro on a case by case basis.

The loan is usually offered up to three years (two years with the possibility to extend) against artworks which have proven track records on the secondary market.

People who know me, also know that I am a huge art lover. I also often publish articles in the Secrets of Art magazine. Speaking about my art passion, I am connected with some collectors in the Principality of Monaco. Thanks to my friend Olivier from OMYS Monaco, we have made some deals related to both old masters and contemporary artworks.

OMYS Monaco

14 Quai Antoine 1er
98000 Monaco

contact@omysmonaco.com
www.omysmonaco.com

in cooperation with

OMYS Consulting

contact@omys-consulting.com
www.omys-consulting.com

Actually I met with Olivier's wife Maya first through a real estate project and Maya mentioned that Olivier's company advises on structuring solutions for art financing. So the relationship started by accident, but quickly developed into a great partnership. I learnt a lot from him about this area.

For example, not many people know that you can also be eligible for art secured lending even if your artwork has never been presented at the secondary market, but it has a acceptable fair market valuation. Ownership tracing and estimation process might be more complex. Yet there are solutions out of the "high street" banks, such as with private art funds that are interested to look at such transactions. They are able to offer quick assessment and closing process and are often good short terms solutions for art dealers or private sellers.

Olivier also told me that based on his experiences, banks prefers artworks with a minimum fair market value of 3 million euro. This is quite interesting if you consider that in 2019, the average price of a work of fine art sold at auction was only $42,439. And even with this relatively low price, the global sell-through rate for fine art was only 65.7%.

Art against loan is not an easy process. First of all, owners need to invest in advance to apply for a loan. The process starts with the appraisal, which has to be done by an independent bank's expert at the expense of the borrower.

If the appraisal is acceptable by the lender, then the artwork has to be transported and stored in a bonded warehouse, selected by the lender. All the related costs such as the transportation, insurance and storage fees have to be borne by the borrower. Authentication and trusted valuation is a key source of concern for private bankers when it comes to art-secured lending.

How big of a market is this?

According to artnet, the total amount of money spent on postwar and contemporary art at auction in 2019 was $4.2 billion and the total amount of money spent on fine art, design, and decorative art at auction last year was $17.8 billion.

Compared to this and according to a report published by Deloitte back in Autumn 2019, the global total of loans outstanding against art was estimated between $21 billion and $24 billion.

Art-secured lending ranked among the most popular art and wealth management services in 2019. Based on a survey conducted by Deloitte, 60% of the art collectors say that art secured lending was one of the most relevant wealth management services for them. Also 69% of collectors said they would be interested in using their art collection (or parts of it) as collateral.

What I found fascinating as well is that despite significant demand for art-secured lending services, only one in three banks are willing to offer this service in Europe. In contrast to this, 80% of US private banks are open to provide art-secured lending. On the contrary, Europe has not yet reached its art secured lending, and I strongly believe - seeing the trends in Monaco - that more and more art collectors will prefer this way to overcome temporary liquidity problems.

Who are the most bankable artists?

Based on artnet's Spring 2020 Art Intelligence Report, these are the ten best-selling artists in each categories.

European Old Masters

		Artist	Life	Lots Sold	Lots Offered	Sell-Through Rate	Total Sales
1		Peter Paul Rubens	1577–1640	13	14	93%	$13,911,762
2		J. M. W. Turner	1775–1851	14	14	100%	$12,747,705
3	NEW	Joachim Anthonisz Wtewael	1566–1638	2	2	100%	$11,917,863
4	NEW	Giovanni di Paolo	1399–1482	2	2	100%	$11,604,473
5	NEW	Élisabeth Louise Vigée Le Brun	1755–1842	10	13	77%	$11,102,012
6	NEW	Thomas Gainsborough	1727–88	9	14	64%	$10,606,995
7	NEW	Jan Sanders (Jan van) Hemessen	1500–66	4	4	100%	$10,539,424
8	NEW	Jusepe de Ribera	1591–1652	16	28	57%	$9,473,362
9		Rembrandt van Rijn	1606–69	651	775	84%	$7,889,889
10	NEW	David Teniers the Younger	1610–90	15	27	56%	$7,429,679

Impressionist & Modern

		Artist	Life	Lots Sold	Lots Offered	Sell-Through Rate	Total Sales
1		Pablo Picasso	1881–1973	3,035	3,665	83%	$368,421,219
2		Claude Monet	1840–1926	36	39	92%	$298,511,422
3	NEW	René Magritte	1898–1967	89	135	66%	$127,718,117
4		Francis Bacon	1909–92	97	118	82%	$115,288,424
5	NEW	Sanyu	1901–66	83	104	80%	$109,775,923
6	NEW	Mark Rothko	1903–70	8	11	73%	$106,441,445
7	NEW	Paul Cézanne	1839–1906	24	31	77%	$100,892,898
8		Amedeo Modigliani	1884–1920	30	40	75%	$91,804,928
9	NEW	Jean Dubuffet	1901–85	206	260	79%	$89,864,367
10	NEW	Marc Chagall	1887–1985	863	1,246	69%	$88,340,194

Postwar

		Artist	Life	Lots Sold	Lots Offered	Sell-Through Rate	Total Sales
1	⌃	Andy Warhol	1928–87	1,388	1,743	80%	$231,049,586
2	⌄	Zao Wou-Ki	1920–2013	382	458	83%	$225,462,140
3	⌃	Gerhard Richter	b. 1932	284	360	79%	$130,767,997
4	⌄	David Hockney	b. 1937	445	489	91%	$130,697,377
5	NEW	Ed Ruscha	b. 1937	244	282	87%	$117,429,663
6	⌃	Roy Lichtenstein	1923–97	478	567	84%	$102,382,592
7	NEW	Robert Rauschenberg	1925–2008	219	297	74%	$97,286,817
8	⌄	Yayoi Kusama	b. 1929	679	779	87%	$92,686,867
9	NEW	François-Xavier Lalanne	1927–2008	215	239	90%	$86,002,124
10	⌄	Joan Mitchell	1925–92	54	60	90%	$62,605,222

Contemporary

		Artist	Life	Lots Sold	Lots Offered	Sell-Through Rate	Total Sales
1	=	Jean-Michel Basquiat	1960–88	78	103	76%	$128,744,319
2	⌃	Jeff Koons	b. 1955	208	298	70%	$111,444,056
3	NEW	KAWS	b. 1974	1,185	1,349	88%	$110,918,985
4	⌃	Yoshitomo Nara	b. 1959	358	429	83%	$101,478,285
5	⌄	Christopher Wool	b. 1955	49	70	70%	$54,950,102
6	NEW	Liu Ye	b. 1964	59	60	98%	$53,191,695
7	NEW	Keith Haring	1958–90	382	521	73%	$41,936,973
8	⌄	George Condo	b. 1957	112	138	81%	$36,460,535
9	⌄	Kerry James Marshall	b. 1955	23	25	92%	$35,958,962
10	NEW	Albert Oehlen	b. 1954	20	27	74%	$31,505,636

Ultra-Contemporary

		Artist	Life	Lots Sold	Lots Offered	Sell-Through Rate	Total Sales
1	=	Jonas Wood	b. 1977	93	124	75%	$22,602,971
2	=	Adrian Ghenie	b. 1977	21	24	88%	$17,327,436
3	⌃	Dana Schutz	b. 1976	21	22	95%	$9,889,672
4	NEW	Eddie Martinez	b. 1977	30	33	91%	$8,574,731
5	NEW	Nicolas Party	b. 1980	32	33	97%	$5,100,175
6	=	Ayako Rokkaku	b. 1982	88	92	96%	$4,873,740
7	NEW	Harold Ancart	b. 1980	24	27	89%	$4,845,090
8	NEW	Rashid Johnson	b. 1977	20	20	100%	$4,096,395
9	NEW	Jia Aili	b. 1979	5	7	71%	$3,800,115
10	⌄	Ren Zhong	b. 1976	32	46	70%	$3,206,820

Gold investment

With the current economic situation, gold can be used as a hedge against inflation and currency value. An investor may include physical gold or gold coins to diversify his/her assets and reduce his/her portfolio risk.

You can also notice that in the previous years there has been a sharp increase in gold prices while prices of other raw materials have decreased. Gold is indeed considered a safe currency-haven in times of crisis. It is tradable worldwide because gold is durable and rare. For centuries, gold investment has been an enduring proof of long-term wealth protection.

Purchasing gold can be quite complicated and intimidating when you do not know the market in depth but it is learnable and it can lead you to a straightforward sales process. One may think that purchasing gold is daunting and confusing, but you can make gold purchases and sales very simple.

Remember throughout history, gold has been convertible globally into local currency. It is therefore the world's highest regarded and oldest currency. Investors should have some gold in good times and more in bad times.

Originally, countries exchanged goods and services in exchange for gold because new supplies of gold could not be easily found. Even the founding fathers of the USA believed that having the nation's debts backed by gold would prevent future governments spending beyond their means, or worse, having its assets forcibly seized or held ransom by foreign and potentially hostile creditors.

The gold standard is a monetary system in which the standard economic unit of account is a fixed weight of gold. The participating countries fixed their domestic currencies in terms of a certain amount of gold.

The purpose of the gold standard was to prevent expansion of inflation and to stabilize the price in the long-run. Under the gold standard, high levels of inflation are rare as the money supply can only grow at the rate that the gold supply increases (gold supply for monetary use is limited by the available gold that can be minted into coin.)

The gold standard restricts the power of governments to inflate prices through excessive issuance of paper currency. It gives fixed international exchange rates between those countries that have adopted it, and eventually reduces uncertainty in international trade.

Gold is more than just a commodity since it is a store of value, a medium of exchange and a unit of account. As gold is considered to be an alternative investment option, it is important to understand its price trends and investigate about its specificities, secure shipping and storage.

Gold prices increased by almost 200 percent in five years (from year 2005 to 2010). Despite its price drop in 2013-2014, it is projected that in 10 years, gold prices will increase by almost 300 percent. Therefore, investors tend to turn to gold at times of financial turmoil.

How to buy physical gold

In order to create your future gold portfolio, you must know the different gold bar and gold coin choices.

Gold bullion coin sizes usually come in 1 oz, 1/2 oz, 1/4 oz, 1/10 and 1/20 oz. Bullion coins are priced according to their weight that includes a premium above the gold spot price. Most countries have one design that remains constant while other countries have a different design each year such as the Chinese Panda and Australian Kangaroo coins.

Gold bars are available in various sizes. London Good Delivery bars are approximately 400 troy ounces which is around 12.5 kg. 1 kg bars are also popular which equates to 32.15072 troy ounces.

Gold bars for sale include the following: 1 oz gold bars; 10 oz gold bars; 100 gram gold bars; kilo gold bars. All these gold bars are 99.99 percent pure (.9999).

In order to ensure that your gold purchase is tradable, one must consider buying gold that is manufactured by an accredited refiner.

You must remember that the gold's specification is mainly characterized by the combination of its weight and purity, but also by the type of gold bar and/or coin and refiner.

Before buying any gold bars or gold coins, one must know his/her minimum acceptable criteria. You can consult various gold specialists/sellers to acquire information and eventually identify your gold investment plan. Your gold investment plan will illustrate your diversified gold portfolio.

Gold coins have several key advantages over gold bars for gold investors. Gold coins are immediately recognised and acceptable anywhere. Gold bars are harder to sell because you have to make sure that it is legitimate and the gold content is correct. In contrary, you can easily sell any fraction of your gold coins. Moreover, gold coins are exceedingly easier to transport and store than gold bars.

Exit strategy with gold

Gold is a solid long-term investment and a good means for investment diversification. As we are faced with economic uncertainties after 2008, we look for secure solid assets and consider gold to be an ultimate alternative investment option next to art investments. Investing in gold is safe and advantageous as it has been recession proof for many years. In addition, gold is a medium of exchange and a unit of account.

Moreover, gold coins are extremely liquid and therefore can be easily converted into cash. Therefore, buying gold coins is a low risk investment. For this reason, gold is not just a simple commodity as it has also some form of monetary function.

To conclude, purchasing gold means that you have invested in a tangible asset. You are exposed to low risks since the price of gold has remained consistent and on the rise for several years.

Apart from gold being transportable and accepted anywhere, the ultimate reason why you should include gold in your portfolio is its liquidity as you can easily sell your gold should the need arise. Truly, gold investment is a great way to preserve one's wealth and purchasing power in difficult economic times.

Diamond and Jewellery

The percentage of diamond investment is currently small but as we are faced with economic uncertainties, investors now seek a flight to quality. By including diamonds in your portfolio, you will have more diversified assets to reduce your portfolio risk. It is a unique and also very interesting opportunity in which to invest, since diamonds are a solid asset class like other traditional precious metals.

Diamonds present similarities to gold as an alternative investment given that it is both used for jewellery and both possess special value. Both are extremely rare, but nothing matches the impeccable rarity of diamonds.

Luckily, diamonds are tangible, transportable as well as liquid investments and many of the primary benefits gold provides as an investment are applicable to diamonds as well.

Moreover, its value is independent of any government decree, and for this reason, it maintains its value even during recessions.

Purchasing diamonds

Diamonds are usually considered a solid long-term investment and a good means for investment diversification.

The price of diamonds is controlled by few major players in the diamond industry by having a supply-controlled business model. Despite continuous price increases, these few major players have been highly successful in increasing consumer demand for diamonds.

If you cannot provide the source of origin of your diamonds, you can easily loose almost the half of its possible value.

However, the diamond market can be relatively complex and intimidating. Purchasing diamonds requires very high care, much higher professional involvement than gold.

You may believe that only professionals can purchase diamonds or one should undergo years of training to acquire the secrets of the diamond trading. The days of inaccessible diamond trading are gone as you can now buy and sell diamonds like so called professional traders.

Many years ago, I visited the BaselWorld watch and jewellery fair in Switzerland, where I had the chance to purchase diamonds directly from first-hand dealers and diamond mines. It is a really interesting way to make a deal because you spend more time in selecting the quality ones rather than in agreeing on price. If you have ever considered investing in diamonds or jewellery, I would highly recommend visiting a trade fair such as BaselWorld.

By spending some time to understand the basics, you can easily learn all the essential steps to build profitable diamond investments. While intermediate channels try to give you too many irrelevant concepts and information that play no part in your effective diamond investment process, if you know how straightforward it is to purchase high quality diamonds, you will not pay a large amount of money for the very simple services that retailers are providing.

Strategy in investing in polished diamonds

The initial step is to determine "how much are you willing to invest?" Once you have identified your investment budget, one must then know where to obtain essential information about diamonds. You can gather vital information through various specialised organizations, such as the International Diamond Exchange Website (IDEX), the Rapaport Diamond Report and the Gemological Institute of America. In order to have a better understanding of the diamond industry and its price trend, one can subscribe to the Rapaport Magazine.

In verifying the quality of a diamond, one must evaluate the so called "4 C's," which include:

»   cut,

»   colour,

»   clarity, and

»   carat weight.

These "4 C's" are considered the starting point before purchasing any diamond. The following paragraphs will explain the important factors to consider in each "4 C's".

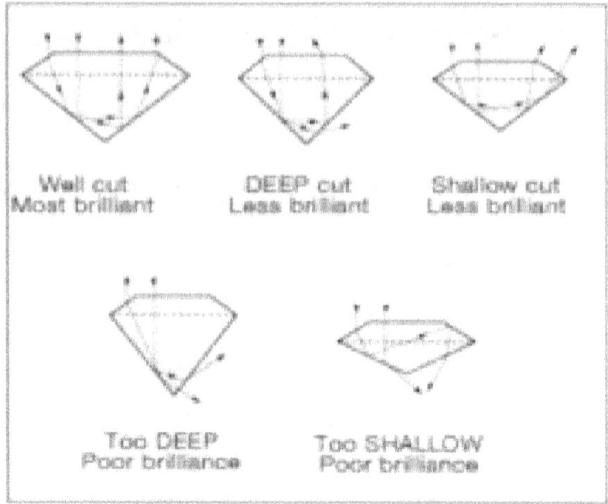

Regarding the cut, you must ask "what type of cut am I willing to invest in?" While having this question in mind, you can consider that the brilliance/light depends on the cut of a diamond.

The beauty of a diamond's sparkle is the result of how well it has been cut. The aspects of cut that contribute most to a diamond's beauty are proportion, symmetry and polish. Although nature determines the characteristics of a piece of rough diamond, the hands of the master cutter release its fire and brilliance.

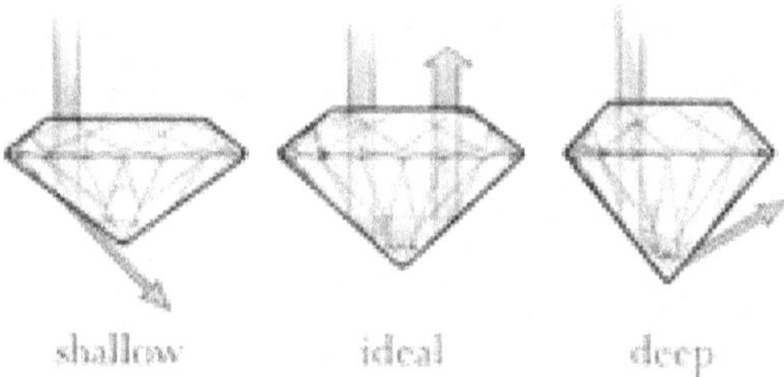

When a diamond is cut to exacting proportions – neither too deep nor too shallow – light will reflect inside the stone from one mirror-like facet to another and reappear to the eye in a flash of spectral colours.

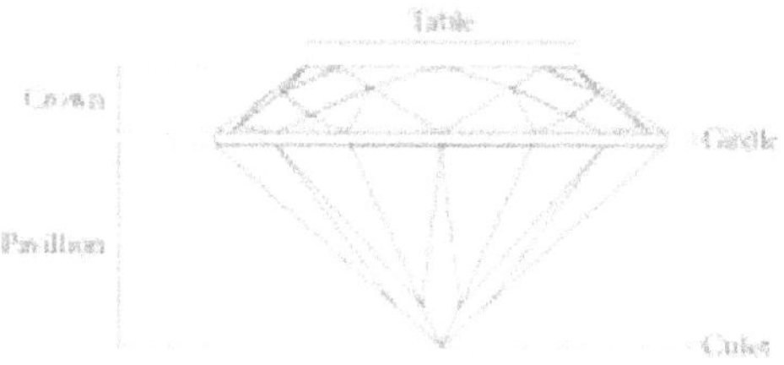

Secondly, for the colour, you must ask "what colour scale am I willing to invest in?" The more transparent the diamond is, the more expensive and the rarer it is. The following figure shown below illustrates how diamonds are graded on a colour scale.

Though diamonds are transparent, almost all diamonds display some slight hint of colour. A diamond's colour is assessed against a scale from D through Z based on a standardized colour grading system that has been internationally accepted since the 1950s.

High quality engagement rings are usually selected only from the top three grades (D, E, and F). These diamonds are deemed colourless and are therefore the rarest and most valuable.

In gemology, fluorescence refers to the property some diamonds have of glowing when exposed to ultraviolet light. When such diamonds are observed under incandescent or natural light, they can often have a milky appearance – even when they have good clarity. Try to accept only diamonds with zero to faint fluorescence, and carry no diamonds whose appearance in daylight is compromised by this unique property.

Almost all diamonds have slight internal and surface characteristics, most of them too small to be seen by the unaided eye. When viewed using magnification, they can take various forms such as tiny crystals, clouds or feathers. To determine a diamond's clarity grade, a gemologist will consider their size, location, quantity and nature.

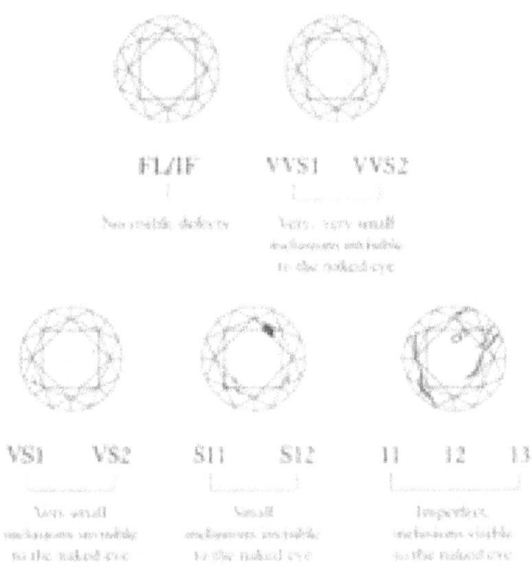

Diamonds possessing no such characteristics are categorized as Flawless (FL) or Internally Flawless (IF). In general, the greater the imperfections are in number and size, the lower the clarity grade. Therefore, you must look at a gemologist's clarity grade before purchasing a diamond and eventually ask "what clarity standard am I willing to invest in?"

The last but not least "C" is the carat weight. Each diamond size is calculated through its carat weight. Therefore, you must ask "what carat weight of diamond am I willing to invest in?"

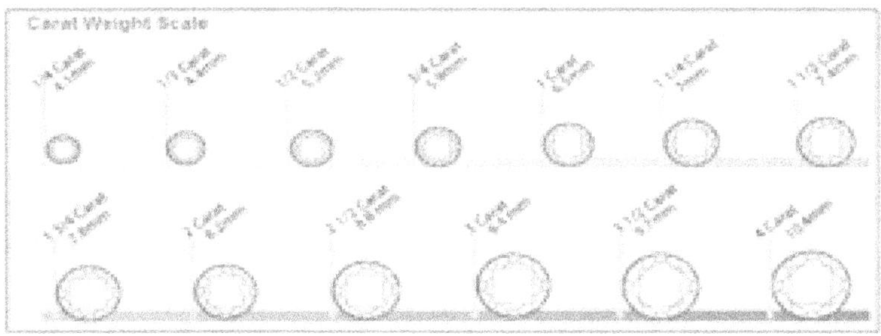

A diamond's size is measured by weight, expressed in carats divided into points. A carat equals 100 points or 1/5 of a gram. Diamonds of higher carat weight are generally more valuable because they are found less frequently in nature. But diamonds of equal carat weight may vary greatly in value because they differ in the quality of their cut, colour and clarity. Therefore, weight alone is a poor guide for evaluating a diamond, since it is an intricate combination of factors that determines a diamond's beauty and quality.

In order to verify the diamond's quality, it is important to verify its issued certificate as it confirms the diamond's authenticity and its quality ("4 C's). After learning and mastering the "4 C's", it will help you identify your "acceptable quality grade" for your diamond investment plan.

Once you have identified your acceptable quality standard of diamond, you should consider calling various diamond dealers to collect information about diamond prices, so you can set a benchmark and/or a price range. Retailers will convince you that you are paying at the right and correct price but in fact you might be paying a very expensive price.

When you are purchasing diamonds at a higher value, you should consider consulting and contacting various gemological institutions in order to acquire vital knowledge about diamond registration or certificate. By doing so, you will be able to see which laboratory has the best price for diamond grading and laser inscription.

Real Estate

It is fascinating to see that most of the non-European ultra-high net worth individuals are investing in the Principality of Monaco. It is also very interesting to compare with Dubai, where the real estate prices are often ten times cheaper. However, in the world's most expensive residential property market, price is not necessarily the major factor for the super-rich.

An investor wishing to allocate funds in a low-risk asset could eventually include a Monégasque property in his or her international portfolio. The Principality of Monaco also offers a special fund available exclusively for some of the major banks in Monaco to invest into real estate and new developments. Even if it is not the standard form of liquid fund, still, this way the banks have additional opportunities to diversify their portfolios with Monaco-based properties.

The real estate market in the Principality of Monaco has always been considered a very specific market, which offers a number of advantages for its investors in a less than two km² territory.

Mean price per square metre of a real estate resale

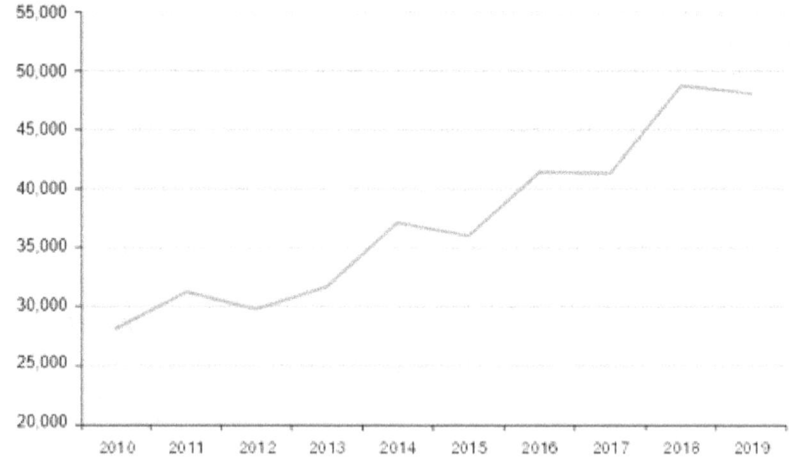

Unit: euro
Sources: Department of Tax Services, IMSEE

The political and the economic stability plays a major part in the safety of the real estate assets, which makes the Principality of Monaco the ideal destination for property investments.

To conclude, investing in Monaco can be financially rewarding as there is no income tax or capital gains tax on individuals residing in the Principality. In addition, there is no Monégasque estate duty on assets situated outside the Principality.

In Monaco, real estate professionals believe the value of Monégasque properties will not drastically decrease like in other countries. Most purchases are made without bank loan, therefore, an increase in interest rates would not considerably affect the market.

As my friend Maya Ivdra from Monaco Villas says, each client has his own demands and tastes, and, by paying close attention to detail, they can support properly all inquiries to find the best property in Monaco.

For example in early 2020, 3-4 rooms with a sea view and close location to Carree d'Or were more demanded.

MONACO VILLAS

REAL ESTATE

Monaco Villas

2 Avenue St Laurent
98000 Monaco

www.monaco-villas.com

Overall, the previous years were good years for real estate in Monaco, and with the new developments in and around the country, the trend looks to continue.

Monaco Real Estate Market Figures in 2019

» The value of transactions rose by 4.4% to almost 3 billion euros.

» Fewer apartments sold in 2019, but higher prices with a value exceeded 10 million euros.

» A total of 15 villas, which mostly were bought for real estate developments, were sold in 2019 – what is the record number since 2010. Also number of resales rose.

» After a marked increase in 2018 with 18,1%, the price per square metre fell slightly but remains above 48,000 per square metre. It has risen by almost 71% in last ten years.

» In 2019 the price per square metre exceeded 50,000 euros in three districts: Monte-Carlo, Fontvieille and La Condamine.

» The lowest price is in Jardin Exotique 35,000 euros per m.

» The highest price in Monte-Carlo, Golden Square is around 53,000 euros per m^2.

Aggregate value of real estate transactions

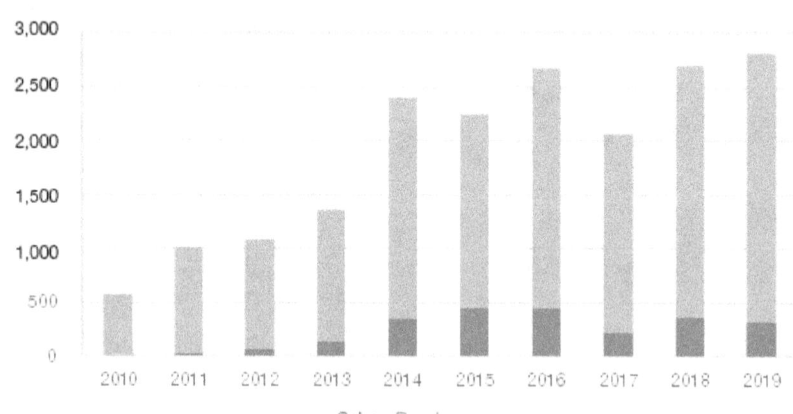

Unit: millions of euros
Sources: Department of Tax Services, IMSEE

Many new projects are planned for future, including eco-district of Anse du Portier project of urbanization at sea with the construction of a peninsula of about 6 hectares, comprising 150 upscale apartments, an underground car park, a coastal promenade, a green park, public facilities, an extension of the Grimaldi Forum and an animation port. A first delivery of the buildings should begin from 2022 then all the work should be completed in 2025.

How to gain higher profit

Investing in real estate in the Principality of Monaco and considering its medium-long term return is one thing, but capitalising its potential right away from the very first days of purchase is another one.

Instead of renting out their apartments for a long-term period, many investors consider them short-term rentals.

Smart investors are continuously searching and investing into apartments, which face directly onto the legendary Formula 1 track. Many of these apartments with their amazing views and terraces are rented out each year for the events leading up to and during the Monaco Grand Prix. Many companies are ready to pay this price due to the exclusivity and prestige they can provide to their clients.

An investor may charge ticket fees based on the number of people allowed onto the terrace. It is important to know that in the Principality of Monaco, the government regulates how many people can stand on each terrace of a property. However, an average terrace can allocate up to 15 people and based on a 2,000 Euro per person fee, including catering, one can earn up to 30,000 Euro in a single day. This amount is incredibly high, compared to a possible monthly long-term rental fee. For this reason, many investors use their properties only during this major event.

Depending on the type of the events running in Monaco, these apartments can easily gain up to 100,000 Euro per week; therefore, the return on investment can be made within a few years. After that, the owner can enjoy the property, which at this point he/she is freehold.

In addition, interesting investment opportunities can include a large space facility, which can be converted into a business center attracting start-up companies that are relocating their businesses to the Principality of Monaco.

To reap its benefits, one could easily see that for a one-day-a-week shared office, people are paying up to a thousand Euro per month per hot desk, therefore, having an office space of 50 places and renting them out for one day per week use, could easily bring you a quarter million Euro yearly income.

There are countless possibilities and benefits to what the Principality of Monaco offers to its investors.

Non-traditional investments

I used to say, this is only for the open-minded ones. I believe in the power of an innovative idea or a unique possibility, which comes in a specific time. To capitalise on these precious moments when life ensures you unique opportunities, you have to release all of the chains in your mind.

> **"Most self-limiting beliefs are really excuses for a lack of willingness to change a behavior that inhibits your success."**
>
> - Dodo Newman

These investments are not the traditional ones with promises, but rather out-of-the-box ones. Thinking and especially investing in an out-of-the-box way does not mean that one has to move away from the existing values and traditions.

To think outside the box is trying not to think of the obvious things, but to try thinking beyond them, in order to create something new, something unique. However, you need to move away from your comfort zone to create something different.

Being in an exceptional circle of well-established people in the Principality of Monaco, the ideas are countless, and by being open minded, you can discover interesting investment opportunities with high returns.

These types of investments perform exceptionally well when the product is limited, rare and collectable.

Supercars

Investment into supercars is one of the greatest way to gain quick profit turn on your investment. When a product is rare or in limited supply, if its prestige is highly accepted in the public, you can be sure that its value will increase in time.

Here is an example to prove the great return of these investments. A few years ago, Ferrari announced the LaFerrari car, a limited edition of supercar produced in 499 pieces. But even if you had the requested one million Euro to purchase them, you could not even buy one of them without fulfilling some of the main requirements. The very first requirement was to already own at least five Ferraris in the past.

At this point, many people immediately lost the opportunity to successfully acquire this piece of art, in the form of a car. However, this is the market gap that a smart investor immediately realises.

When you are a client of Ferrari you can book your car with a small deposit. In 2008, I booked a Ferrari California with a symbolic 5,000 Euro down payment. So, if you are able to fulfil the pre-selection requirements or at least you know someone who applies, you could book a LaFerrari for a symbolic 10% down payment (usually less).

When your order has been confirmed by the Ferrari factory, you can easily put the car back on the market even before its production, giving the freedom of choice to the new owner regarding the customisation such as exterior and interior colour and the technical extras.

As you can see, many LaFerrari cars are offered now for almost two million Euro in the market, which means smart investors invested 100,000 Euro and gained a million Euro profit.

This scheme is also true for various limited supplies. All you need to do is realise the potential and capitalise on the fact that you have the advantage in your hand.

Whiskey & Wine investment

As with any collectible items such as art, supercars, rare bottles of wine, the principles are the same with the whiskey as well. With time, the prices usually go up allowing the owner to gain significant returns.

Regarding whiskey investments, the commemorative, single cask, discontinued lines, limited release or small batch bottling attracts the main interest of the investors. However, you have to understand the value and the rarity of each bottle before you purchase them. It is not always true that every collectable distillery release will be profitable in the future. It is always good to see the release number of the bottles as well. Collectors usually collect special releases under 250 bottles.

Only invest if you really know what you are doing or you know someone you can trust with experience in dealing in fine wine or whiskeys. Always do your homework, if you do decide to invest.

It is very important to note that investing in whiskey and wine is always a long-term investment. The minimum timeframe, which is good to consider, is twenty years. Therefore, most of these investors are also very passionate about this topic.

From the asset perfective, you can also note that whiskey and wine is liquid, but not a liquid asset. It can take time to sell your assets, unlike stocks and shares or bank deposits which can be sold very quickly.

Investment into Blockchain

A blockchain is a decentralized, distributed and public digital ledger that is used to record transactions across many computers. Its main benefit is that any involved record cannot be altered retroactively, without the alteration of all subsequent blocks. This allows the participants to verify and audit transactions independently and relatively inexpensively.

Blockchain is typically linked using cryptography. It is a simple yet ingenious way of passing information from A to B in a fully automated and safe manner.

Many people believe that the data driven blockchain is the new oil. Blockchain solutions are showing up in the fields of utilities, healthcare, payments, supply-chain management, government, agriculture, and more. In recent years, many companies and private individuals have started investing in various blockchain-based projects and platforms.

For instance, on 21 December 2017, the draft legislation Bill 237 was approved in Monaco. With this step, the Principality of Monaco decided to promote the activity of blockchains.

The bill starts with a three-year experiment period. During this period, the state will not impose additional constraints on technical regulations.

To accompany this experimentation and to participate in the promotion of Monaco as an essential actor in blockchains, the bill's text creates the Monégasque Authority of Blockchains (AMB) composed of experts and professionals involved in the digital field.

However, Monaco is not just among the pioneer companies with this legislation, it also hosts countless blockchain-related conferences and fundraising events.

CHAPTER 16

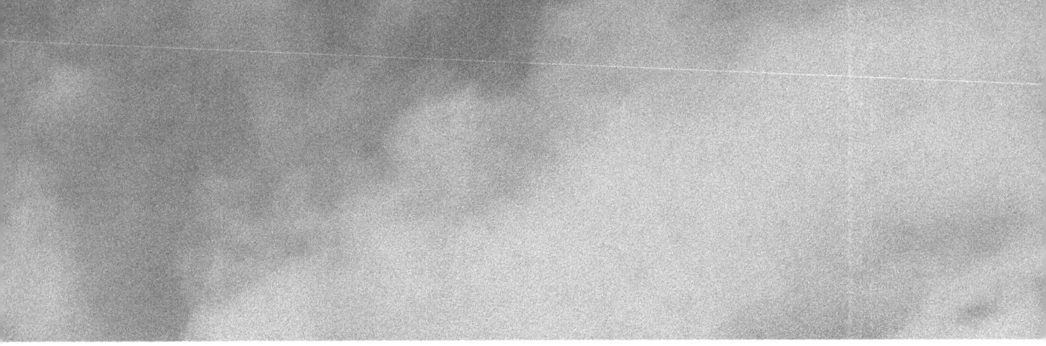

Due diligence / Who to trust?

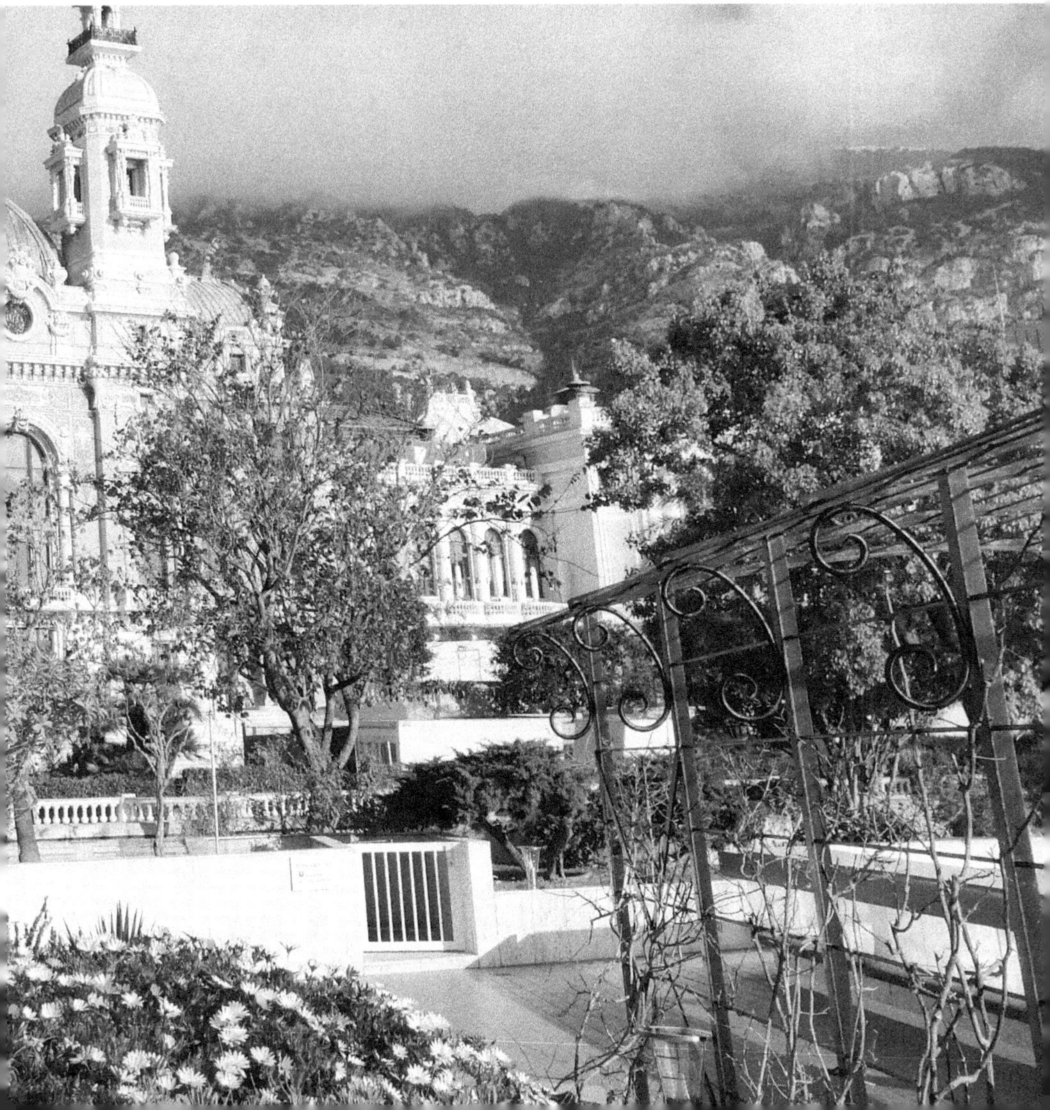

Who to trust

The Principality of Monaco often feels like a pond full of crocodiles. The majority of the foreign people are coming to Monaco for fundraising and cutting business deals. This often creates the feeling that people love you only because of your money.

This is also the main reason why it is hard to socialise with long-term residents; they simply do not like to mix with the new ones. They are cautious, and they have every reason to be.

However, in some cases, Monaco residents are open to investing; therefore, I have collected the most basic considerations, before you open your wallet.

Due diligence

In any investment decision, due diligence is one of the most important tasks that you simply cannot outsource. It is very important to get first-hand information regarding the investment offers and the people involved in the investment process.

Do not allow the legal process to get ahead of due diligence.

However, it is also very important not to "worry" too much. The key is to get first-hand information from reliable sources and to be continuously in charge of the decision you make, without any pressure or influencing factors.

Remember, do not be a worrier, be a warrior.

The thing is that people who are unable to decide often fall into the trap of analysis paralysis.

In 2005, author Malcolm Gladwell published a book called "Blink: The Power of Thinking Without Thinking". It presents research from psychology and behavioural economics on the adaptive unconscious – mental processes that work rapidly and automatically from relatively little information. It considers both the strengths of the adaptive unconscious, for example, in expert judgment, and its pitfalls such as stereotypes.

The author describes the main subject of his book as "thin-slicing": our ability to gauge what is really important from a very narrow period of experience. In other words, this is an idea that spontaneous decisions are often as good as — or even better than — carefully planned and considered ones. Gladwell draws on examples from science, advertising, sales, medicine, and popular music to reinforce his ideas. Gladwell also uses many examples of regular people's experiences with "thin-slicing".

Gladwell explains how an expert's ability to "thin slice" can be corrupted by their likes and dislikes, prejudices, and stereotypes (even unconscious ones), and how they can be overloaded by too much information.

We do that by "thin-slicing," using limited information to come to our conclusion. In what Gladwell contends is an age of information overload, he finds that experts often make better decisions with snap judgments than they do with volumes of analysis.

Gladwell gives a wide range of examples of thin-slicing. Gladwell also mentions that sometimes having too much information can interfere with the accuracy of a judgment, or a doctor's diagnosis.

> "Analysis paralysis: sometimes having too much information can interfere with the accuracy of a judgment."
>
> - Malcolm Gladwell

This is commonly called "Analysis paralysis". The challenge is to sift through and focus on only the most critical information to make a decision. The other information may be irrelevant and confusing to the decision maker. Collecting more and more information, in most cases, just reinforces our judgment, but does not help to make it more accurate.

The collection of information is commonly interpreted as confirming a person's initial belief or bias. Gladwell explains that better judgments can be executed from simplicity and frugality of information, rather than the more common belief that greater information about a patient is proportional to an improved diagnosis. If the big picture is clear enough to decide, then decide from the big picture without using a magnifying glass. However, you should never forget that even the big picture has to clarify the most important facts and legal indicators.

The people

When you are investing in a business or an item which is related to specific people, you have to make your "bet on the jockey and not the horse". Therefore, the rank and trust in the involved people would be one of the most critical decision you make.

The good thing is that unlike some countries in the European Union, The Principality of Monaco offers you the possibility for a penal check on the people you intend on dealing with.

In many cases, be aware of the pitch-like presentations and be sure that all the presented companies and persons are really involved in the business. In this book, I write about the "unexperienced experts" as an example, where you can see that these so-called experts only push fancy names without having any type of expertise. The presented names probably do not even have knowledge about the investment offer.

You always have to identify the right ambitions and attitude, which can be challenging. With an older person, you can easily see this from the results he/she has already achieved during his/her life path. By understanding his/her ambitions you can also be sure whether he/she understand the obligations of involving an investor.

It sounds obviously, but beware of fraudsters.

Just to give you an example, I started Monaco Wealth Management in 2010. My aim was to build up a bridge between the residents and the trusted businesses. A few years ago, I noticed that someone registered "Monaco Wealth" in the UK and started to do investment fundraising. Generally, it would not have been a problem because they are two different legal entities, however the owner linked himself to my company and his business profile pointed to Monaco Wealth Management. It goes without saying, I never met him and he had no ownership or any kind of decision right over my business. Still, people are try to outsmart the investors by misleading tactics and colourful presentations. Therefore, one of the first questions is whether the suggested directors really on board or not? Do they really have the power to raise funds in the name of the company? Etc.

It is also important to know that the directors understand the basic business principles as well as the commercial bases. You have to make the directors responsible for the financial forecasts, and you have to let them know that you might have the right to dismiss them in case the targeted numbers are not reached. Perhaps it seems a bit draconian, but investment is a business not a charity to maintain someone's lifestyle.

Be sure that the directors are motivated by the profit, and they do not earn more than in their previous job. The key for a mutual benefit should always be a high percentage on the profit.

I also experienced this when I met with a Swiss watchmaker. He was extremely good in pitching his ideas and vision to any investor. He always got the funds, and I also was fooled by the shining surface he presented to me. After many years, I saw that almost every third year, he opened a new business because of the underperformance of the previous ones. He was able to pitch the concept to the investor, but he was unable to sell his product to the target group. It can be interesting for you whether they recognise their skill gaps and how they can fill them.

Therefore, it is very important to see some significant personal investment from the visionary to deter them from walking away at the first sign of trouble. It is always an interesting question why they cannot put their own money into the business and/or why they cannot find people within their own contact base who could invest a small start-up fund into the business.

Obviously, it can happen that the visionary has a perfect and marketable, profitable idea, but he/she is not resourceful enough to find the right contact, or he/she starts the fundraising too late. Do not have prejudice, and try to understand the real reasons before you decide. In case a visionary has no assets as a guarantee, you can still ask for a personal warranty. This could be a legal statement, which provides the basis for legal recourse if information is misleading or has been deliberately withheld.

Out of the box people

Unique people move the world forward, therefore do not be surprised if something does not exist in the books. Many advisors and experts have learnt their knowledge from different types of books, case studies, and publications. Universities focus mainly on the written knowledge.

But sometimes great things happen and are realised from inspirations, and inventions come from "nothing". Some people have the ability to create something new from "nothing" and to re-define the existing rules by breaking down the walls.

> "Every out of the box innovation starts with our imagination, with a dream. Unfortunately to have a dream has become more negative than positive because it is associated with something that is never achieved. To be a dreamer is a person who is considered to never get things done and who lives above the clouds."
>
> - Dodo Newman

These new inventions are not in the books, not in the education systems. They are not history, they are happening right now in the present and individuals who are creating them usually seem to be crazy, odd, or strange, people who think outside of the box.

The box is created to categorise people; the rules are created to define the categories, but the inventors are born to redefine all of them. They do not break the law, but they break and change the rules.

You as an investor have an obligation to realise whether someone is a wannabe entrepreneur, a potentially successful entrepreneur, or a real visionary. Heading to the advice of the "realists" cannot serve as the foundation for your decisions, because they are standard bearers of the status quo.

Some well-known people stood outside the box all their lives. They lived (or still live) in a very untraditional way and they all seem to be very "odd" to the average person. But the common thing in all of them is that they live for their aims without accepting the word impossible.

"impossible = i m possible"

- Dodo Newman

I have two business idols from the past whom I consider great and out-of-the-box people: Edison and Hughes.

Thomas Alva Edison is one of America's most famous inventors. Edison saw huge change take place in his lifetime. He was responsible for making many of those changes occur. His inventions created and contributed to modern night lights, movies, telephones, records, and CDs. Even if Edison overstepped a few people in his life, he was truly a genius.

"Results? Why, man, I have gotten lots of results! If I find 10,000 ways something won't work, I haven't failed. I am not discouraged, because every wrong attempt discarded is often a step forward..."

- Thomas Alva Edison

Edison is most famous for his development of the first electric light bulb. When Edison was born, electricity had not been developed. By the time he died, entire cities were lit by electricity. Much of the credit for electricity goes to Edison.

Edison created the world's first "invention factory". He and his partners invented, built, and shipped the product – all in the same complex. This was a new way to do business. Today, many businesses have copied Edison's invention factory design.

My other "hero" is Howard Hughes who was a complex man. He was a pioneer aviator, engineer, industrialist, film producer, and playboy. Howard Robard Hughes was a very inventive and attention-grabbing man. He was an outspoken entrepreneur who was best known for his hard work and dedication in motion pictures and the aviation industry. He became one of the world's wealthiest men, a billionaire.

"I know what you're going to tell me. You're going to tell me, probably, that you know someone who has cancer or someone who just got married or just had a baby, and that you can't do that to those people... a corporation has no soul. I can't know about those things and be a corporation."

- Howard Hughes

Hughes also built the world's first communications satellite. His dream was that anyone on or above the earth could communicate with someone else. Howard Hughes was a man of great ideas. He had many contributions to society. He will always be remembered as a very unique man.

Obviously, I have modern day heroes as well, and I am glad to highlight my close friend Dodo Newman. I remember when she had a speaking engagement at Club des Résidents Etrangers de Monaco about out-of-the-box thinking. The founder of the Monaco Business Society, Mr. Ivor Alex closed the event by stating that *"Dodo Newman is the woman version of Sir Richard Branson"*. I agree with him.

In addition to Dodo Newman, there is another lady in Monaco, Jessica Sbaraglia, who is just as amazing. She is the founder of Terra de Monaco.

I believe they are both absolutely out of the box, not even close to the box.

What is common in all the visionaries is that none of their innovation came from a predictable path or an idea that was immediately "realistic". Sadly, we are living in a culture which is driven by rules, work plans, spreadsheets, and tasks, which do not leave enough space for the courage and heart driven by out-of-the-box people.

It is difficult to identify truly out-of-the-box people, but life can guide your decision.

An ambitious woman who changed Monaco

It sounds like a utopian dream to bring back something which has not existed for 200 years in Monaco. However, thanks to an ambitious dreamer, the Monaco resident, Jessica Sbaraglia, the Principality is changing both mentally and physically.

I had known Jessica for many years before she arrived in the Principality of Monaco. I remember our first meeting in Basel, Switzerland, when I saw a young and ambitious woman filled with dreams and energy. She is a tall blonde girl who aimed to have a career as a model. Later on, she started to be involved in the designer world. However, none of these were true to her path.

In the past years, I followed up her activities and the way she started to change Monaco both physically and mentally. When I asked her what motivated her, she told me that she asked herself existential questions like: What purpose do I serve? What do I want to leave? Why do I exist?

A few years ago, she relocated to the Principality of Monaco, where she found her true calling. It was her dream project called Terre de Monaco, which took her back to her childhood family memories. She remembered that in her childhood, Jessica's parents had a vegetable garden of 500m2 for fun, and this gave her a real taste for fruits and vegetables. But agriculture in the Principality of Monaco?

The concept is exceptional since those who know Monaco also understand that the Principality is one of the smallest country in the world, lying on the coast of the Mediterranean Sea. So, it is definitely not an ideal place for huge agricultural projects seeing that there are not many free lands in Monaco. And if you agree with this, then you are wrong.

Jessica's company, Terre de Monaco, has set itself the task of integrating urban agriculture, especially green gardens, fruits, and vegetables, on rooftops, balconies and surrounding buildings of the Principality of Monaco. However, it had a rough start, because agriculture no longer exists in Monaco. (It exists again now!)

So, when Jessica wanted to create her company, Terre de Monaco, it did not make common sense, and for this reason it was difficult to start it. They took her for a blonde who wished to plant 3 tomatoes and make few salads. Her project seemed completely utopian.

Although it was challenging, Jessica's genius vision was the concept of initiating an urban and micro-farming project, by using the rooftops and balconies of the existing buildings, places that might not have been fully utilised.

When she did not find an investor, she did not quit, she just decided to change her tactic. In spring 2016, Jessica used a "crowdfunding" platform to finance her project.

Terre de Monaco's mission was "regional products are harvested and destined for local consumption". The concept was rewarded by the local residents and in two short months, she collected more than the 25,000 Euro she needed to fund her start-up.

Local restaurants are also teamed up with Terre de Monaco, because of its strong and sustainable platform, specifically limiting the transport of food and product packaging.

Terre de Monaco offers a personalised collaboration with each kitchen chef in order to respond to their needs. It also promotes good taste and a healthy living style, which is a signature of these fine dining places.

Terre de Monaco also does a lot to fulfil and support this change in the Principality in multiple ways. The residents like the concept, because there is a real change in mentality.

Basically, any individual with a terrace or private balcony who wishes to build a vegetable garden can contact Jessica and her professional team. At your request, Terre de Monaco is committed to designing a custom-made garden and offers maintenance as well as courses throughout the year for a standard flat fee.

Terre de Monaco has a good relationship with H.S.H. Prince Albert II and they supply the Prince's Palace of Monaco too. And that's an amazing result from "a blonde who wished to plant three tomatoes and make a few salads".

Time has proven her and her out-of-the-box dream, and the change can already be seen in Monaco. It was an unimaginable development in Monaco which was accomplished thanks to the persistence of a strong woman.

In 2020, in order to prove how important it is to educate the next generation, Jessica and her Terre de Monaco team are decided to set up three new vegetable gardens with lessons for children at the Ecole de la Condamine, the Ecole de Saint-Charles and the Technical School and Monaco hotelier.

Truth be told, many years ago, when we had sushi in Basel talking about her modelling dreams I could have never imagined that one day she would find her true calling by bringing major change to the lives of so many, to motivate and to inspire as all with a seemingly easy, but genius concept. But as she told me, life took her to the point when she needed to dig deep in her soul in order to find her true self and the meaning of her existence.

It takes courage to stand up during our darkest moments and to enter the light. As Albert Einstein once said: *"Try not to become a man of success, but rather to become a man of value."* and this is exactly what Jessica Sbaraglia accomplished. Terre de Monaco has become a company of value for Monaco and its residents, something that can bring long lasting results for the Principality of Monaco and its next generations. And it is a great example of a smart investment.

Business concept or Investment offer

One of the very first things I always consider in any business is its possibility to create significant revenue. It is always necessary to look for scalable businesses with the potential for explosive growth.

If it is an existing business, do not rely on the owners and directors, but ask for possibilities to speak directly with the customers. During private talks with customers without any of the owners present, you can get first-hand impression which could serve as a valuable base for you to determine the business development potential. A lot can be learnt from independent customer referencing.

Walk away if the directors cannot provide clear answers to tough questions on the market or the finances.

Check the financial plans as well to see the reality behind the ambitions. Usually a financial prediction is way more positive than it should be; therefore, it is good to consider that sales cycles can be much longer than anticipated, especially with early stage technology ventures.

Ensure there is enough "headroom" in the financials. If they are under-capitalised from the start, they could get into the vicious circle of requiring further funds when targets are not achieved, and then being distracted from the sales process to raise further funds, which gets them into deeper trouble.

When you invest into an existing business, always handle desperate cases sensitively. Some companies get into financial difficulties and appear to require funds immediately to avoid closure. These can be interesting opportunities, in spite of the fact that the company's funds may have been mismanaged. For most investors, it is essential to have board representation in order to protect minority shareholders. Also, let them have some say as to how the business and their investment fund is being managed.

Many entrepreneurs are blind to the risks associated with their ventures and insist that the risks are minimal. The earlier the stage, the higher the risk, but the more you should get for your money. Striking a balance between your perceived risk and the directors' believed certainty is difficult in an area where there are no hard-and-fast rules on valuation.

In many cases, it can be beneficial to look for business interruption insurance.

Also, be sure that all the intellectual properties belong to the company and the business is secured on all legal platforms. If not, you can still create a pre-condition before you invest.

Check the exit. Is there a realistic and credible exit plan as well as a genuine desire to exit? Too many investors have their funds tied up in investments they cannot realise.

If someone invests after you at a lower valuation, an investor can provide an option to protect himself by getting extra shares to compensate for this. This would need to be detailed up front in the Shareholder Agreement or the Articles.

Early stage business or Business in its early stage?

Have you also noticed that many people have started to refer to startup businesses as early stage businesses?

During the past year, the word "startup" might have lost its shine, and smart people have redesigned the concept. But they are wrong and it often misleads the market.

In general, when we talk about business growth, we identify multiple stages in the life cycle of a business. This is a great thing because by categorising the different growth patterns, we can offer a useful tool for the potential investors as well. However, these indicators might be more important to the company leaders and owners, offering them a full understanding on the current challenges that their businesses are facing.

Let me summarise the differences of the first business development stages in a nutshell, which are important to understand if you ever plan to invest into a business.

Stage I.: Grow-or-Fail

The first phase in every business is grow-or-fail. It effects every new business, (and it can come back later if the management is not competent enough to handle market changes).

At this stage, the main problem is to educate the market about the new products/services, and to obtain more and more clients. In this period, business owners have two main "enemies" called time and cash flow.

We also refer to this stage as the "survival period", where our existence is essential, and to overcome the obstacles is strongly time sensitive for long-term prosperity.

The keyword here is "existence".

Make no mistake, working with a startup business can also be exceptional, because it is exciting whether you can prove the concept and break down the obstacles. This is a phase when you invest your time, energy, knowledge, and money into passion and because you believe in the person behind the company.

When an idea is exciting and the concept is clean, business angels are willing to take the risk in the hope that the concept and great execution will bring the desired success.

These are the businesses that are usually looking for crowdfunding to survive, which is not a problem if they can do this parallel to survival mode.

The mistake that many startups make is that they are not focusing enough on obtaining costumers and delivering products, because they are convinced that all they need is an investor. However, in reality, an investor seeks some kind of visible achievement to decide whether the idea and concept is viable or not.

In this stage, one of the most important tasks for startups is to expand from their tiny key customer base to a much broader, possibly international sales base. This is the period when the owners do much more on their own (sometimes everything on their own).

The strategy: simply to remain alive.

To overcome any survival period, creating business value and utilising social networks are of key importance.

Stage II.: Early stage

Businesses that have obtained enough costumers to become true businesses thanks to their hard-working entrepreneurs, but whose income is still just hardly enough to exist are the early-stage businesses. These are the ventures where we can already observe some sort of proof of concept, however, they still need to make

significant efforts to stabilise their existence.
The keyword here is "survival".

By reaching this stage, the early-stage businesses have already demonstrated that they have a market need. This is usually backed with enough, and more importantly, satisfied customers; therefore, they are a workable business entity. However, their key struggle is shifting their focus from the question of existence to productivity and potential revenue.

(A few years ago, I wrote a book called "NO EXCUSE! in business" which is highly recommended to all business owners.)

Usually this is the stage when pilot products and ideas have already moved (or are ready to move) into quality production. This is why investors are willing to invest into early stage businesses; they have objective marketing results to evaluate.

In this stage, businesses are usually maintaining a simple organisation, supervised by the owners. Still, they have managed to break even with their initial cash investments. They also generate just enough cash-flow to stay in business, and might be able to finance their own growth in the future. Early stage businesses are close to earning an economic return on their work.

For the abovementioned reasons, Early stage businesses are usually targeted by venture capitalists because of their growth potential. A venture capitalist is usually seeking 10x a return on their investments in a three to five-year period.

Since an early stage business has a proof of concept, investing early into these entities is often very attractive for the venture capitalists and private investors.

Obviously, the risk is still there, since after a strong start, the business may fail completely. However, with proper partnership, specifically when the investor is not just "loaning" the funds, but mentoring and helping the business through his/her connections, the early stage business has a higher likelihood of survival than a startup.

Stage III.: Small business

We usually refer to small business as those businesses which cannot reach the 10 million Euro annual income with activities such as manufacturers/service providers and the 20 million Euro as wholesales. The difference between an early stage business and a small business is that a small business has usually already overcome "existing" problems and is prospering.

The keyword here is "success".

Small business owners usually face the dilemma of keeping their company small and stable or trying to expand for a bigger purpose. This bigger good is not always a financial motivation. Some owners aim to "retire" from their businesses, to leave the daily hassle over to their trusted employees.

Proper delegation of the daily operational tasks can ensure the owners a partial disengagement from their company. This gives them more time with their family, hobbies (such as sailing or playing golf) or simply a new and exciting business venture.

When a company has attained its true economic health, the organisational rules are set, performance indicators are defined, and the management is trusted. At this point, the owners have great potential for a successful disengagement.

These companies focus more and more on the business, marketing, and growth planning. The owners become board members, who monitor the strategy, rather than being active daily executers. Their number one task is to make sure that the basic business stays profitable in the hands of the new management without their daily presence.

Stage IV: Take off

Most likely, no explanation is needed here. In this phase, the company has a strong base for developments because their marketing plan is fully developed from extensive research and market experience. In this stage, usually, new types of challenges will appear, such as delegations, organisation behaviour, creation of sophisticated information, control systems, and well-developed, standardised operating procedures.

All of these serve as the international brand identification and the base of a stronger, revenue-steady business foundation.

To summarise it

To summarise it, Grow-or-Fail is the business period that I would define as a startup business. An early stage business is much more than a startup venture, since it already has proved that the market is open for its product/service.

The confusion is coming from the fact that a startup business is in its early stage of business life. However, it is not an early stage business. Startup businesses are also looking for funds to secure their existence, however, they want to reduce the normal timeframe without proving their concept or idea first.

Any business with proof of concept can be called an early stage business, but none of the businesses should be labelled as early stage if they do not have solid information regarding the market reaction of their target groups. Those are startup businesses waiting to verify the potential of their dream and visions.

Key importance before any type of investment

What it takes to be an Investor

Before you would even consider any type of investment field, you have to be sure that you are eligible to invest based on the requirements.

It is always good to look for advice from similar investment networks to gain first-hand information regarding experiences, benefits, and things you need to check before you commit yourself to any kind of action.

As a first-time investor, perhaps you could also seek syndicate investments to reduce the initial capital you invest and to share the risk. This could bring you great experience, specifically to see how your selected field of investment works.

Syndicate investments in Monaco usually start around 25,000 Euro; it makes the investment fun. It is easier to commit yourself to an idea with a small investment rather than a multi-million Euro one. Also, it allows you to experience and learn.

I know people who have over fifty syndicate style investments, which gives them a very diverse portfolio considering their investments stand on multiple pillars.

Legal consideration

Any investment involves risks. Depending on the field of investment, it can involve low or extremely high level of risk. The general rule is that high-level risk can be highly rewarding at the end of the investment period.

In every single investment, and before entering an agreement you have to be sure that the legal framework is in place to maximise your protection. In many countries, you have special legal rights as a private investor.

When you invest in a business ,it is not limited to an investment agreement. Be sure that you have at least the following in your hand before you make such a commitment:

» Term sheet
» Shareholders' Agreement
» Articles of Association
» Investment Agreement

Before entering into the legals, often a term sheet is written and signed by the parties. While it is not a strong legal binding, it projects the base conditions of the future investment contract.

One of the other benefit of the term sheet is that later it will save the expense of explaining the deal to accountants and lawyers who draw up any subsequent formal documentation.

A shareholders' agreement also has key importance since it sets the relationship between the shareholders following the investment. This also covers areas such as who the directors should be, non-compete undertakings, and any other matters which the shareholders wish to keep private.

The articles of association deal with the company's internal regulations board meetings as well as incorporating shareholder rights, specifically voting and minority protection. You should ensure you are satisfied with matters such as transfers of shares, dividends, voting rights, and pre-emption rights. The purpose of pre-emption rights is to ensure that shareholders have an opportunity to prevent their stake being diluted by the issuing of new shares. Usually articles are publicly available at the Monaco Government Portal.

And finally, the investment agreement sets the terms of the share subscription, including pre-conditions for the investment, such as the transfer of all intellectual property and goodwill to the company, confirmation of bank finance, warranties about the existing business, and any options or bonuses to be awarded to the managers.

Taxation benefits

Before investing into any kind of business venture, the taxation can be a very interesting consideration, often a key decision factor. Many countries offer some extremely beneficial tax reliefs for private investors investing directly into companies. Others offer tax deduction when you invest in artwork.

There are many types of taxation benefits which are good to consider. It is not related to Monaco, but for example, if you invest in a foreign venture, for example with head office in the UK, then you could have benefits such as Enterprise Investment Scheme (EIS), Capital Gain Tax (CGT), Seed Enterprise Investment Scheme (SEIS), etc., which can provide you up to a 50% tax relief.

Many of the taxation benefits are available in small investments as well, no matter whether you invest in a startup company or in an asset class such as art.

In the investment world, investors often request the founders to register an administration office in the jurisdiction which benefits the investor's best interest. It is a way to maximise the taxation benefits.

Realisation of the deal

When you realise a deal, you have to be sure about your own expectations regarding the return and your exit strategy. Most of the investors are aiming to see a significant return in three to five years.

Part of the deal is to realise the exit strategy in the very first moment, which should be crystal clean for all the involved partners and directors. Do not forget that getting your money out from an investment is always considered one of the biggest challenges you can face.

Do not let your investment be tied up further than you desire. In every valuable investment, there is a genuine desire and ability to exit within a set timeframe.

When we are speaking about a business investment, personally, I always prefer to put down multiple exit routes such as:

» The directors buying your equity

» The company itself buying your equity

» Another company buying your equity

» Going onto stock market

To have a well-built legal back up, I would highly recommend completing the final paperwork with professional lawyers. This way, it is easier to ensure your rights.

CHAPTER 17

Traps and fraud alerts

Monaco, magnet for crooks

Having the right information from the right people and places is one of the most important pieces of advice I can offer to you in the Principality of Monaco.

Beside the amazing quality of life that Monaco offers you and your family, we should not forget to mention that the Principality of Monaco is one of the greatest places in Europe to secure your wealth and investments. However, just as any place handling wealth and big money, it attracts crooks, frauds and cheaters as well.

Unfortunately, I have had some negative experiences as well in the very beginning, but it has nothing to do with the Principality, only with our good belief in people. To avoid these types of experiences, it is always great to have a professional advisor at our side.

It is not the fault of Monaco; it has more to do with the fact that the Principality is so tiny, and as a result, you can feel all the influences, both positive and negative much stronger. To understand the reason why you need to be careful, you have to dig deeper in the history of Monaco.

Centuries ago, sailors embarked on long journeys to discover new worlds and new hope. There were also pirates who hunted the endless ocean for hidden and wonderful treasures. As you come from the sea, you can consider the land of the Principality of Monaco a land of treasure, encompassed by France and Italy. Monaco is the rare pearl of Europe, the modern Eldorado, that attracts fortune hunters like a magnet who go there in the belief of becoming immediately rich.

Without any doubt, one of Monaco's main powers has always been gambling, and this is where its shining started; however, Monaco is built up on trust as well.

Monaco has gone through an incredible change since 1846 when the first plans of the Casino were mooted. During those times and under the reign of Florestan I, the House of Grimaldi was in dire need to generate cash, however, a dignitary such as the Prince of Monaco was not allowed to operate any kind of gambling house.

The Casino, which was relocated several times started to operate under the regime of Charles III. who assumed the throne in 1856.

During those times, the area where the Casino is currently located was known as "Les Spelegures" (Den of Thieves), which was not really a promising name for a Casino; even more, it was quite depressing. Therefore, Charles III. renamed the area "Mount Charles" (Monte Carlo), which cleared out the shadow from the place and allowed it to be opened as the Le Grand Casino de Monte Carlo in 1858.

During the next years, Monaco successfully recovered from its economic difficulties and it started to attract other businesses as well. The strategic combination of the Casino and the railroads gave a green light for the Principality of Monaco.

Thanks to the continuous developments such as the Oceanographic Museum, the Monte Carlo Opera House and the incredible number of Hotels, Monaco was on the right track.

The Casino was making so much income and profit that in 1869 the Principality of Monaco could afford not to collect tax anymore from its citizens, the Monégasques. After this announcement, this became one of the major powers of the Principality to attract more and more affluent residents.

But unfortunately, where there is a concentration of money, there are usually frauds as well.

My most honest advice is: do not be a worrier, be a warrior instead. This means that you have to be in charge, and once you have the confidence and the control in the business processes, then it is highly unlikely that someone will defraud you.

Fake people and fake companies

During the past 10 years I have observed that everyone is talking the big game in Monaco. Of course everyone is living here, every business is authorised, everyone is the best friend of the Prince and many other statements are circulating, which are rarely true. Luckily, there are some useful ways to find out the truth.

Once you are interested in Monaco, you will find many hucksters out there who will offer you access to billionaires, investors and various short cuts to become financially independent, and so on. The fact that one third of the Principality of Monaco consists of millionaires, does not mean that they will "let" their wealth over to you. For this reason, working with credible people and companies is highly important. Also because Monaco is like a small village and mistakes can stick with one for a very long time.

The hucksters who are fishing for "the one" big deal, do not really care, because once they "milked you", they immediately leave Monaco. Actually this is very disappointing, because most business owners leaving Monaco with a bad taste, do so exactly because of these unauthorised people. So let's see some tips how to unveil them.

When a company contacts you saying that they are a business from the Principality of Monaco, then you can simply check them out in a free of charge tool, provided by the Monegasque Government. Go to the rci.gouv.mc website, type in either the name of the business or the name of the CEO and you will immediately see whether that business really exists or not.

Business registry / Authorisations

https://rci.gouv.mc

In case you want to find more detailed information, you can also use the online platform of the Monaco Journal, which is also free of charge. Type in journaldemonaco.gouv.mc and use the search. This will even offer you a historic data of related businesses or previous employments.

Monaco Journal

http://journaldemonaco.gouv.mc

If none of these sites offer you search results, then the business is definitely not authorised in Monaco. All S.A.R.L. and S.A.M. legal entities are obliged to publish their details in the Monaco Journal. Sole traders are not necessarily in the Monaco Journal, but they are definitely listed in the government one.

At this point I would like to highlight that residents are only published in these portals if they have or had a business activity. If they are not conducting any business in Monaco, just enjoying a quiet private life, then their name will not show up.

If someone tries to play the "we have a different trading name" card, then just ask them for their "RCI number", which is basically the trade authorisation number, a unique identification to all authorised business actors.

Another noteworthy element is that the phone number with the prefix of +33 stands for France and not for Monaco. The country code for the Principality of Monaco is +377. This can be tricky though, since Monaco phone numbers can be reached by both the +33 and the +377 country codes, due to the fact that Monaco Telecom uses the French network. The quickest validation is to dial the number with the +377 country code. If it rings, then the person calling you has a Monaco number.

Yet, a Monaco phone number does not qualify someone to be in Monaco. If one is living in the 06xxx zip code area in France, and has a standard French bank account, then one can still create a contract with Monaco Telecom. This allows people even in Nice to have "Monaco" numbers and act as Monaco residents or Monaco businesses.

The easiest way to be sure that you are dealing with an authorised, Monaco based business is to check them in either the government website or the Monaco Journal.

"Illegal" events in Monaco

The Principality of Monaco is a fabulous destination to visit and live in, but also to conduct business, to hold or be part of an event. It is often the first step for companies wishing to create awareness about their brands.

However, Monaco is also a heavily regulated country; it has many regulations in place to protect its residents and companies from unscrupulous activities. What may be perfectly normal or legal in other countries, may be illegal in Monaco without an authorisation. The Monegasque Government and the residents take great pride in their country, and they try to protect its market.

On a daily basis, there are many great events being held in Monaco, and there are always events catering for the financial industry, fundraising, investor events, etc.

However if you decide to hold a financial event in Monaco, it is your responsibility to check that the event complies with the Monaco legislation.

The financial activities are strictly regulated in Monaco, including investment advice on securities or financial futures (law 1.338) that cannot be exercised without the approval of the Commission de Contrôle des Activités Financières (Financial Activities Supervisory Commission) (CCAF).

Commission de Contrôle des Activités Financières
4 rue des Iris, BP 540
98015 Monaco Cedex

Phone : +377 98 98 43 59
Fax : +377 9898 43 76

Email : ccaf@gouv.mc
http://www.ccaf.mc

As a business organiser you can expose yourself to criminal prosecution, and closure of your event by the Monaco Police. This can also negatively effect all the presenters and participants of the event.

You should never forget that what may seem normal in London, Berlin, Hong Kong or the USA, may be heavily regulated in Monaco.

If you engage into any event related to investment advice or financial futures, it is always advisable to engage local advisors who understand this unique market, so you do not make either legal or financial mistakes in the process. They can navigate you through the process to ensure you comply with the regulations that may be applicable in Monaco.

Remember, privacy, security and protecting the Monaco brand is of high importance in the Principality of Monaco. Meet these requirements and you have a successful event in the making.

Are you sure that you are dealing with a Monaco based company?

When you see a Monaco based business with a local address, a +377 phone number and with an RCI number, you might be sure that it is a legit and authorised business in the Principality of Monaco. However, identifying whether it is a big corporation or a simple one-person company can be important for you.

For sole traders, one-person companies the Monegasque Government allows the possibility to choose a trading name. A trading name is basically a fictitious business name, used by sole traders, who do not want to operate under their registered legal name. For example, you can register for the sole trader license as "James Bond", however you will be allowed to publicly promote your business as "MI 6 Agency". This will partly protect your privacy as a business owner.

This also means that one can be connected with numerous companies in Monaco, which are actually just one-person businesses.

Dealing with a one-person business is perfectly fine in some sectors such as real estate brokerage, wedding planning, marketing advising, etc. One should never forget that sole traders have unlimited liability towards their clients, which can be handy when it comes to legal and liability matters.

From my perspective I often prefer to work with small businesses, because many times they are more motivated. However in some areas such as in investing or basically any activities related to financial matters, I would definitely consider to choose a large company.

The good thing is that one can always use the Government site (www.rci.gouv.mc) to check out business structures. Let me show you how easy it is.

Business registry / Authorisations

https://rci.gouv.mc

For example, there is a local wine club in Monaco, called Club Vivanova. Searching for the company name will not bring us results in the registry.

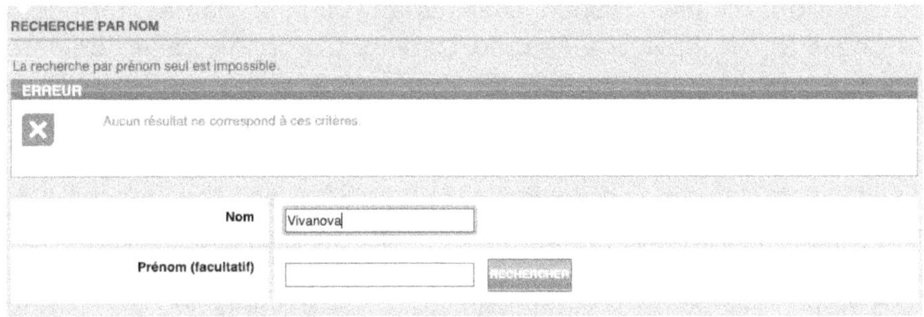

But it does not mean that Club Vivanova is not authorised. When we check the name of the ower, Bradley Mitton we will immediately have our positive result.

NUMÉRO RCI	NOM PRÉNOM	NOM DE JEUNE FILLE	STRUCTURE	RAISON	ENSEIGNE/SIGLE	ÉTAT
16P09135	MITTON BRADLEY		PERSONNE PHYSIQUE		CLUB VIVANOVA	

You will have the confirmation that Club Vivanova is a legitimate business and it is operated by Bradley Mitton. However, the Government site also reveals that it is a legal form of "Personne Physique", meaning a one-person business. The RCI number is also a good indicator with the letter "P" in it.

A one-person business in this example is perfectly fine. You do not need to have a large company to organise events. What you need is a local authorisation and your personal drive to provide quality services in your field.

The best way to decide whether you are dealing with the right partner is to always check them at the Government site.

The trap of S.A.R.L.

Since Monaco and France share many similar names for legal business forms, having a Limited Liability Company, called Société à Responsabilité Limitée (S.A.R.L.) in French is the easiest tool to create the illusion of a Monaco-based business venture.

The biggest difference between a Monaco SARL and the French SARL is the process, focusing on safety. In the Principality of Monaco, the approval process for any legal permit can be very lengthy, complex and time consuming. Under Law no. 1144 of July 26, 1991, any economic activity pursued in the Principality of Monaco, regardless of its nature (i.e., whether commercial, industrial, crafts, or services, professional and non-professional alike) must have prior government authorization.

Just to give you an example of how controlled it is typically, the authorization sets out the limits of the activities that may be performed. The authorization also specifies the premises where those activities may take place as well as any special conditions applicable to the performance of those activities.

So basically, contracting with a Monaco-based company with all the approved business permits immediately can be considered a safe decision, because the government of Monaco has already spent at least six months monitoring and setting the rules and limits of the company.

Nonetheless, many of the French companies try to take advantage of this, since there is no control in France regarding forming a business.

Always check the public RCI number (Registre du Commerce et de l'Industrie / Trade and Industry Register) **of a company. None of the businesses can exist without it, and once they have ensured you an RCI number the Monaco government offers a special tool to double check it at its internet portal: http://www. rci.gouv.mc**

The similarities with the French system are extremely dangerous. By simply having a rental in Monaco, which ensures the address and having a French company, crooks are able to make the bold illusion of having a Monaco-based business venture. With this trick, they are able to convince anyone to be involved with their funds. If one is not careful enough, legally, they can find themselves immediately in the middle of committing fraud.

The thing is, to get a residence permit in Monaco, it takes up to three months and involves a serious amount of work, such as police interviews, double checks on international criminal records, bank account, proof of the requested fund to live in Monaco, etc.

Of course, you can obtain an address in Monaco immediately when you sign your apartment rental lease. If you do not take care, then you can risk losing your apartment by failing the residence permit process, usually with the part related to the "necessary funds to live in Monaco". But this is what crooks never care about during the residence permit process. They get the address by signing the rental lease, they bring their French registered S.A.R.L. and they try to grab the most golden fish they can from the magical pond of Monte-Carlo. Following their three months of seasonal period usually they just move back to the country of their origin.

> If you feel cheated, you can always approach the police. In the Principality of Monaco, the police has full power to immediately intervene and protect you from further damages.

I always suggest to my partners and friends to double check the business licenses before spending any amount on a company, especially a S.A.R.L.

LLC and LTD

If you find someone stating that he or she is operating a business in the Principality of Monaco in the form of an LLC or and LTD, then you have a 99.9% chance that legally he or she has nothing to do with Monaco. Maybe they are there as tourists, but probably he or she has never been near any of the Monaco business permit-related institutions.

One of the most common things you will see is a UK-based company. To understand this act, there is a special regulation in the UK for companies, which are owned by overseas owners. Based on their activities, they can be considered offshore companies with their capital of 1 (one) GBP. It is similar to the Seychelles and other offshore directions as well, but having a European address is always a nicer form of approach, so London seems perfect for this.

Business forms such as LLC and LTD do not exist in the Principality of Monaco. It is like trying to explain to the Americans that the official language of the U.S.A. is Chinese. It is just a poor way to mislead people.

> **In the Principality of Monaco, one cannot operate a business without a physical address. Ask for a meeting in their office…**

I am always approached by companies that state that they are London and Monaco-based companies. It always makes me smile to see how hard they try to prove that they are there in Monaco. They might be in Monaco, but without any legal permit to operate their ventures.

In the Principality of Monaco, one cannot operate a business without a physical address.

You cannot even open a post office box, since the term PO box does not exist in Monaco. If someone does not want to disclose his/her/its address, then he/she/it can rent another apartment for the letters or he/she/it can use a shared office address.

If you want to check the existence of a company, ask for a meeting in their office, because this is the number one way to determine its existence. Many crooks or fortune hunters come to Monaco from its surrounding, therefore, they will never offer you a meeting in their office. "A lunch would be more pleasant…" or "Let's have an office free coffee." They will always find a better option rather than the meeting in the office.

Do not let yourself be fooled!

As a pre-check, you can also check their websites, which can be a good indicator. If the company has a .MC domain next to its .COM domain then you can be sure that they have an address in Monaco. Without a residence or business permit you are not allowed to register a .MC domain name. It is limited and regulated.

Obviously, you can say that the .COM is more common, therefore, they do not need it, but in many cases a simple .MC domain could be a good first indicator for you.

I am from Monaco...

It seems everybody lives in Monaco. It is amazing to see how Monaco attracts the desire of people. The glamour, the extraordinary lifestyle, the wealth and all the related benefits evoke certain emotions in people. Everyone wants to be part of the luxurious world offered by the Principality of Monaco.

Nonetheless, living in the Principality of Monaco is extremely expensive. To attain the residence permit, you have to prove that you already have a significant amount to live well in Monaco.

Everyone knows the benefits of the residence permit, the label which stands for "I am rich and wealthy enough to be part of the most elite community in the world".

But Monaco is small and its territory is limited, therefore many people have realized that living in the surrounding is not a bad choice either. I know many people who live in Beausoleil, which is just on the other side of the street of Monaco.

Frankly, I also live in Beausoleil, but I had to realize that I still live in France, not Monaco. The thing is that the monthly cost difference can be huge, however, what you really pay for in Monaco is the label and benefits you enjoy by living there. This is what makes the yearly quarter million Euro difference worth it.

I would like to highlight here that most of the people working in Monaco live in the surrounding areas. The most popular locations for the employees are Beausoleil, Nice, and Menton. In the "business formation/operation" chapter, you can find more about this.

One thing that I really do not like is when people state that "I am from Monaco" or "I live in Monaco", and in the meantime, they actually live in France.

For many people, it is the perfect illusion to catch the attention of new residents and people who are interested in Monaco. This makes sense since everybody wants to be part of the unique community of the Principality of Monaco, and it may seem to you that everybody lives in Monaco.

However, when someone comes to me with the "I live in Monaco" statement, I am nearly 100% positive that he or she is not living in Monaco. Most of the residents in the Principality of Monaco are living a quiet life.

Many of us who live in Beausoleil used to say that we live in the Monaco area. This is the technically correct term. As a matter of fact, locals often call Beausoleil Upper Monaco.

Of course, you can encounter the extreme when someone states that he/she lives in the Principality of Monaco. They will offer a business service, and in the meantime, try to convince you why Monaco is a bad choice for you.

One time, a financial advisor tried to explain to me why it is better to bring my funds to the Isle of Man instead of Monaco. It happened that he was from Italy, and had no idea about the real benefits of the Principality. He was just a fortune hunter fishing in the waters of Monaco for his golden fish.

The thing is, when someone keeps stating that he/she lives in the Principality and is continuously repeating it, I always ask the same:

- "Could you show me your residence permit?"
- "I left it at home." (this is the most common answer)
- "Ok, then you can show it to me next time before we go further with your business offer..."

At this point, usually the other party starts to sweat and feel very uncomfortable. Most often, this is the last time we speak because we both know that he/she started with the wrong approach.

The thing is that the Carte de Residence contains only basic data, so there is nothing to hide on it. There are no income, wealth or security numbers, just the simple proof that one has fulfilled all the requirements (financial and legal) and they have been accepted to live in the Principality by the government and police.

Business is about trust and this is the first step where crooks can fail in Monaco. Try it and you will be amazed by the result.

Most of the residents of Monaco like to negotiate with people who are honest and who are living in the area. There is nothing wrong with living in France; the bad thing is when someone pretends that he/she is an actual resident.

Seasonal folks

In the Principality of Monaco, the real touristic season starts in May usually with the Formula One Grand Prix and it ends in September with the Monaco Yacht Show. I always call May the Grand Opening of Monte-Carlo.

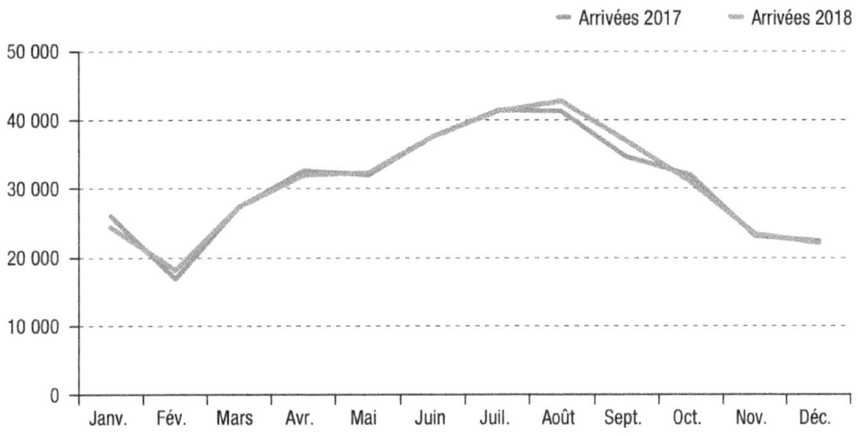

Unité : arrivée personne

Sources : Hôtels, Direction du Tourisme et des Congrès, IMSEE

April and May are two very interesting months in the Principality because the so-called seasonal advisors start to appear. Many fortune hunters come to Monaco during these months to advise on events, locations, investments, and all other money-related topics. We call them seasonal advisors because they leave Monaco after a few months.

Many seasonal advisors are in Monaco with the hope of earning fast money. They work for extra high fees, sometimes charging even ten times higher than any local business. Since these seasonal folks are pushing their messages in an extremely aggressive way in all kinds of social platforms, they are able to catch some small fish.

"Living in Monaco" illustration by Dodo Newman

The illustration symbolise the "fishpond" of Monaco where wealth managers targeting their clients.

I believe there is nothing wrong if someone tries to benefit from opportunities. I also believe that it is not their fault if someone is not careful enough and gives them their money instead of pursuing the same service for a more relaxed price. But I do think that it raises an ethical question when it comes to unauthorised business offers "against" the legally operating businesses in Monaco.

Seasonal folks have no business permits to pursue any type of activity in the Principality, therefore, most of them do not care about the liabilities either.

Illusions

The illusion of luxury

The Principality of Monaco is full of illusions. The very first illusion starts with Monaco's flag. Have you ever seen the flag of Indonesia? The flag of Monaco is identical to the flag of Indonesia. Of course, the combination of red-white can be also found in the flag of Poland or Singapore. What is really interesting is that the Indonesian flag is identical. I did some research and found out that Monaco's flag has existed in the current form since 1881 while Indonesia adopted an identical design for its national flag only in 1945.

My other favourite example in Monaco is the illusions of flowers. There are endless numbers of artificial flowers in the flower stores. But obviously, these topics are not as serious as the investment-related ones.

One of the biggest traps for investors in Monaco is the usage of the illusion of luxury. The Principality of Monaco is an eye-catching, beautiful land of magic; it is really heaven on earth. When you arrive in the Principality, the first three days are a wonderful, once in a lifetime experience. However, this experience is among the main tools for some crooks, using this euphoric state of mind to influence others.

When seasonal folks invite you to Monaco, they will guide you through the best places and the most illustrious restaurants. Since they are there every week, the service knows them and recognizes them. This way they create the illusion that they are well-known and well connected in the Principality. This feeling could be very convincing for many people from outside Monaco, and this could be a really strong reason to trust these crooks. Why not? They seem to know everybody and everything.

The thing is that being a VIP guest in a club or a frequent and returning guest in a restaurant means nothing in the world of Monaco. You can go to the best places, but that is not enough to guarantee that you will have the power of influence in the Principality to get things done.

As an example, you can spend a weekend in Disneyland, which you will really enjoy, but that does not mean that you will know Walt Disney or his team. It's the same in Monaco; you can spend years in Monaco without even getting noticed by the circle of the elite.

When you fall in love with what you see, do not listen to your heart. The real challenge is to push away your emotions and go forward with your brain. When you decide to invest, go to government licensed professionals, or at least contact one of the lawyers recommended in this book to get a review and an unbiased third opinion.

You can make the best investment in the Principality, but rule number one: do not rush into something that is shining. Be very attentive and do not be afraid to ask for third opinions.

And a very important thing is that sometimes rich people are not dressing fancily. It can happen that you find a millionaire entrepreneur in Monaco walking in jeans or in shorts. One of my friends is a multi-millionaire IT venture capitalist, and he is always walking in shorts and a t-shirt.

Do not let yourself be misled by the illusion of luxury.

Catchy wordings

Most of us believe only in things that we can see, in things that are on the surface in front of our eyes; sometimes, we are afraid to see behind the curtains. Looking behind the curtains and getting more background information about things in most cases could be extremely useful. Personally, I always like to conduct some research on things to avoid false illusions. The truth can be found under the surface as I always say.

One of the words I dislike most is "expecting". However, it is a commonly used word in the Cote D'Azur. To understand the power of the word "expecting", we have to understand the intention behind it, the reason why so many people, mainly non-resident event organizers use this magical word.

It has always been rewarding and beneficial to organize events in the Principality of Monaco. The glamour, the sparkle, the illustrious guests, the breathtaking places can really move people.

Many of the event organizers rent out ultra-luxury yachts for an event or a high-end gourmet restaurant with its terrace overlooking the Port Hercule or the Circuit of the Grand Prix. This could be a normal and acceptable way to start the organizing process, however, many of the organizers and especially some of the seasonal ones play for the big gains; therefore, they use very catchy and misleading wordings in the hope of their main aim: the big money.

These crooks and fortune hunters play on people's emotional triggers with the help of some catchy wordings because they are fully aware that our brain will do the rest of the job. Because what is the brain like? It is selective. Sometimes we only hear what we want to hear. Sometimes we only see what we want to see. But our brain is able to do much more than this, our brain is able to immediately recoup the missing information as it is the most understandable for us.

"We are expecting the presence of XY celebrity..." or "We have invited and we are expecting H.S.H. Prince Albert II...".

These statements sound amazing and catchy, however, most people misunderstand the meaning of the word "expecting". Many people believe that expecting means that the guest will definitely be there. It is not something which is guaranteed, it is just the most effective version of the "we hope" or "we wish" phrases. But the organizer is never liable, because he or she never states that the guest will actually be present.

As you can see, many events have seemingly illustrious guest lists. They always present well in advance who they are expecting during the events, however, sometimes they are not even inviting those people because they have no connection to them at all. Of course, once you are at the event, it becomes unimportant for them because you have already paid your involvement fee in advance.

The experienced people in Monaco know that there are big differences between certains events. One of the most important thing is to get to know the genuineness of the event, which can be easily checked with the help of the Monaco Office de Tourism.

Of course, sometimes you can find events organized by private and so-called local companies. It is always good to check whether they really exist or not in the Principality of Monaco. For this you can use sources such as the Chambre de Développement Économique de Monaco (www.cde.mc) or the Direction Expansion Economique (www.gouv.mc).

Monaco is a wonderful environment, which is already the base of high quality and glamour. Therefore, I always suggest a little bit of background checking to avoid a boring or "expensive" evening. I believe that anything that does not yield the expected result is expensive and damaging for the positive image and illusion.

Under the high patronage of...

It has always been rewarding to organize events in the Principality of Monaco. The glamour, the illustrious guests and the breathtaking places can really move people.

Another common phrase that you will hear and see is "under the high patronage of H.S.H. Prince Albert II.". The reason is very understandable, since one of the biggest credibilities for the quality of an event is when it is placed under the High Patronage of H.S.H. Prince Albert II. However, this is not a gift from The H.S.H. Prince; it is something to be earned.

Many new events that use this label could be misleading, as it is very rare that His Serene Highness Prince Albert II supports a first-year event, especially if it is organized by a non-resident company.

Obviously, in rare cases, you can find first year events patronized by The H.S.H. Prince of Monaco, but mostly, these are events organized by local competitors and not by foreign companies.

Before you commit yourself to a new event in the Principality of Monaco, it is always good to get a background check beforehand. If an event is placed under the High Patronage of H.S.H. Prince Albert

II, it will have an official Princely letter attached to it regarding the patronage. If the patronage is true and exists, then the organizers should have this public letter in their hands, otherwise, they are not entitled to use the name of The H.S.H. Prince of Monaco.

Everyone knows the Prince…

It is important to be a little cautious because in Monaco "everyone knows the Prince" and one of the most used sentence is "the Prince is my best friend". Obviously…

Sadly, I even know people who are really close to Prince Albert II and they still try to sell his name for money.

One of the most extreme situations I ever experienced was a woman who tried to request a monthly fee for a year just to ensure me that the Prince would not cancel his appearance. Obviously, it was not a donation to the Prince Albert II of Monaco Foundation but a direct money request to cover her lifestyle and expenses.

My suggestion to you is that you should never mistake a photo with the Prince for a true friendship. Once you spend significant time in Monaco, you will meet the Princely family on several occasions, and to have a picture of them is not a big deal at all. You will even see how friendly they are with the residents, and once they see you at many events, you can have the chance to engage in conversations with them. But does it mean that they are your best friends? Does it mean that they fully support you? I do not think so… And once someone starts to sell this friendship, be very careful.

As a resident, you will have multiple possibilities to meet with the Princely family yourself as well.

H.S.H. Prince Albert II makes countless appearances at local events not just promoting the Principality, but supporting local businesses as well.

Furthermore, there are public royal events, palace visits and public picnics where the locals are welcome to spend valuable time with many of the members of Monaco's Princely Family. The real core of Monaco is a big family.

True story: Unexperienced experts

Since I started the Monaco Wealth Management, to collect all the reliable wealth, investment and residency-related Monaco-based companies, I have been continuously receiving various requests to be an intermediary for different fundraising activities.

However, my favourite stories are when companies come to me with their big plans, stating that they already have an existence in Monaco, when in reality they have no clue about how things work there. I call them the unexperienced experts.

In 2012, I had a very interesting experience with an unexperienced expert who probably made his biggest mistake. A Zurich, Switzerland-based wealth management company contacted me via LinkedIn because they thought that I had possible investors through my business portal MonacoWealthManagement.com.

The wealth company was founded in 2005 and they already handled approximately 1,500 million CHF by 2012. They also employed over 60 people to create custom tailored services for their wealthy entrepreneurs, sports and media professionals as they stated. It was also an impressive fact that they also dealt with family offices and banks on an institutional level, not to mention their three core service divisions: Equity asset management, family office and private equity.

So, in May 2012, one of the management board members of this wealth management company approached me offering an involvement in a new brand (for legal reasons I will call it a fashion label), which was supposed to be Her Serene Highness Princess Charlène of Monaco's new fashion label.

I found this an interesting approach however I had some doubts regarding the fashion ambitions of the Princess. It seemed very unreal for me. However, you never know, so we started a very in-depth conversation with the wealth management company and they confirmed this to me many times.

After several e-mails, I received the answer that the founder of the fashion label was a well-established fashion designer, who had lived in the Principality for more than 8 years under the address of Avenue Princess Grace. I was also ensured that the fashion label project was under the full support of Prince Albert, and they had already raised 5 million Euro before May 2012.

The request towards me and my business and investor channels was to help to publish their new concept, supported by the Prince and to raise through this publicity more investment funds. To keep my interest up, they continuously sent me new information regarding the status of the project.

After many requests, finally, I received some more information regarding the investment. That was the moment when I was 99% confident that this investment deal could not be real. However, when I received the official documents about the project, the information memorandum and the executive summary, I noticed that both documents used past tense. Since the wealth management company pushed me further, I decided to conduct another round of research on this topic.

During the last years, I got to know a very kind and helpful gentleman at the Direction Expansion Economique of Monaco so I decided to use this connection to double check. He confirmed what I expected, and I realized that nobody knew about this venture there.

Based on the law in Monaco, starting a venture under the Patronage of the Prince without a physical office is almost unrealistic. This was the point when I created a concern document to clear everything. I wanted to believe that something extraordinary was happening in the Principality because the wealth management company kept pushing me further. Eventually, it was time for a face-to-face meeting.

On 16 July 2012, I flew to Zurich to meet in person with the responsible people of the Swiss Wealth Management Company. I met with the project manager and the CEO and I raised their attention to some of the concerns.

After some informal chit-chat, we jumped into the middle of my concerns.

- "My very first concern is on the guarantee statement in the Information Memorandum," I started. Then, I read them the clausal I found very weird.

"The fashion label will need time to access proper capital, financial and human resources: there is no guarantee that it will be able to do so properly in the future, in which case the project's development plans and survival may be affected." (Fashion Label Information Memorandum)

- "What is the problem with this?," asked the CEO. "I cannot understand the concern here."

- "Does this mean that even if the investor ensures the 10 million Euro investment fund, he/she has no guarantee that the company will survive in the first year?"

- "It could happen," came the answer.

- "The Investment Memorandum mentions a five-year period for the return of the investment, however, that present statement clearly states that there is serious risk involved from the very beginning without any escape plan or solution offered.

- "Every investment has its own risk," the project manager replied immediately.

I was so happy to see that they were proving my point, so I continued by reading page two.

- *"This document does not represent an offer or a solicitation of an investment... Any party which may be interested in a participation should conduct its own professional due diligence..."* (Fashion ILabel Information Memorandum)

- "This states that all the presented information needs to be double checked, investigated and re-calculated, which questions the credibility of the presented information," I continued. "It could also mean that an investor signing an intent, based on the presented information could be misled or misinformed without any further consequences."

- "No!," the CEO raised his voice. "It only means that you have the right to double-check everything with your own lawyer."

- "Ok, it is fair enough." I started to calm down the temperature, however I knew that we were going into sensitive areas. "So what is this "raise additional debt" part on page three?"

- *"Management reserves the right to undertake, from time to time and as it sees fit, further fundraising above and beyond those currently contemplated, and raise additional equity or debt."* (Fashion Label Information Memorandum)

At that moment, I saw that the CEO could kill with his eyes, but luckily, the project manager tried to save the situation and he continued.

- "It is just a legal formality that in case another economic crisis happens, then we are allowed to raise another equity fund for the successful continuation," he answered.

- "The Information Memorandum states that the fashion label has been created and is currently running with a structure, where 93.3% is owned by the Founders and 6.7% is owned by Patrons. Who are the people behind the current company?"

- "We cannot disclose our client's name," the project manager replied quickly.

First, it bothered me and I almost stood up and walked out from the wealth management company, but I really wanted to go into the Monaco-related statements.

- "How long has the current company been running, because the business domain of the company was registered less than 4 months ago and it still has no live content."

- "We wanted to close the full funding process first. Until then we have just secured the domain."

- "Ok, but why now and not two years ago?"

- "Because this was the phase when we decided to start. During the last years we were involved in the preparation phases as well as in the research and analysis."

I looked deeply into the guys' eyes and I saw that the CEO was already scared, however, I wanted to see how the project manager would handle it if I pushed him further, just as he pushed me with this project through his emails.

- "Why was it necessary to register the fashion label?," I started.

- "Because we are collecting the funds?," smiled the project manager.

- "For a company that has the fashion label concept, an idea that started two years ago and has owners and patrons, right?," I asked.

- "Right," he replied promptly.

- "Ok, but you know I have a small issue with this."

- "Go on."

- "Today is 16 July 2012, and we have been talking about this since May, however, the company was only registered on 5 July 2012, just eleven days ago."

I watched closely the reaction of the project manager. His face started to sweat, meanwhile the CEO's face was white like a wall.

- "If the purpose of the fund and the aim of the fashion label is to operate a business in Monaco, then why was it necessary to register an offshore company just 10 (!!!) days ago, called Fashion Label Limited instead of really starting the operation in Monaco?"

- "Because the fashion designer is from London." I received a poor answer.

- "We all know it is bullshit," I started my answer. At this point I became a little bit harsh with them because I wanted them to know that they were wasting my time. "There is a special regulation in the UK for companies, which are owned by overseas owners. Based on its company registration data, the Fashion Label Limited is considered an offshore company with its capital of one Euro. Based on the Information Memorandum the fashion label is planned to operate in Monaco in August 2012. So, when will the fashion label really operate in Monaco?"

- "We already started the first steps and are in an administration process," the project manager replied.

Interesting, because on 12 July 2012, the Monaco Economic Department stated in writing that they were never approached by the team of Fashion Label and the Monaco Economic Department never received any request for company formation with the following Object Social. Based on the law in Monaco, to operate a company, several steps have to be fulfilled before the Monaco Economic

Department approves the operation permits. The complete process takes a minimum of 3 months if the Gérant currently lives in Monaco with a valid Carte de Sejour. In all other cases, it can take up to 6 months. The question in this case is how can the fashion label operate in Monaco from August 2012 if they have not even filed for an Object Social, and the Monaco Economic Department has never approved its activity?

I started to feel the weight of the big silence, which had consumed the wealth managers. The CEO had not even spoken for ten minutes and he continuously watched the project manager to help him out. I saw that he was feeling very uncomfortable. Finally, I got my excuse.

- "We are looking to purchase an existing company. This is why you cannot double check this in Monaco." I received the answer.

I have to admit, that it was a very smart answer. The project manager guy had a very sharp mind and I imagined that he could sell anything to naive investors.

- Based on the Information Memorandum, the fashion label is planning to operate in Monaco with at least four different types of activities, such as fashion, jewellery, perfume and leather goods," I continued.

- "Yes, this is our aim to have a well-diversified portfolio."

- "Based on the law in Monaco, the Monaco Economic Department will request different approvals and probably different corporate identities for these activities. How will this affect the investment fund? Will the investment fund be split between the different activities? If yes, in which form?"

- "We will disclose this later. We have not finished the work on this yet."

It was very interesting because based on the executive summary they have already raised fifteen million Euro, but they had not thought about the way of activity diversification."

- "Okay," I continued. "Where is the headquarter planned in Monaco? Based on the law in Monaco, the Economic Department strictly forbids businesses without a physical office. This means a company with only a webshop will be automatically denied if they cannot provide an acceptable physical office for their activities. The criteria for the physical office is also provided by the Monaco Economic Department after the Object Social of the company has been approved."

- "We will use the location of the company that we will purchase."

It was a very smart answer and I felt that the project manager played it well. I decided not to force this further because we both knew the real situation. So, I started to ask about the involvement of the Princely family. It was the most interesting part for me and obviously one of the main reasons why I was ready to be involved.

- "The fashion label is using the Coat of Arms of the Grimaldi House as its company logo, which is forbidden to use for all companies. The Coat of Arms is the symbol of the Prince's family and by using it, it can involve a penalty or even a business operation ban of the fashion label. It is like signing a document with the stamp of the Prince's family."

- "Except when the Prince wants this."

- "So, it was the order of H.S.H. Prince Albert II.?," I asked.

- "Yes, he specifically requested it because this brand will be related to his wife, H.S.H. Princess Charlène."

- "Well, I see." I tried to confirm his thoughts back. "In the previous communication, it was mentioned that H.S.H. Prince Albert II. and H.S.H. Princess Charléne will support the fashion label project. However, I thought H.S.H. Prince Albert II. does not support first year activities and it is very rare that he supports Monaco-based companies, which are younger than 5 years."

- "Except if it is for his wife, as I told you," said the project manager.

Bang! He tried to knock me down and he did it very well. At this point, I started to see the life coming back in the eyes of the CEO. He almost tried to have a little smile on his face. I think he started to believe that they could convince me.

- "Based on my request in the Palace, I was informed that H.S.H. Princess Charléne has never heard about this project. If such a support of the Prince's family exists, could you please provide me the Royal letter, which is signed by the Prince's family?" I looked into the project manager's eyes and continued. "This letter does not depend on the operation, the Prince's family is always ready to sign for future projects as well if they support them. Herewith, I am presenting you with how a Royal communication should look. These documents could strengthen the credibility of the above-mentioned statement of the fashion label and all possible investors will request this. Without them, there is no credibility behind them."

At this point, I handed them a Royal letter written by H.S.H. Princess Charléne of Monaco. It was a thank you letter dedicated to me personally. The wealth managers looked at the Royal letter as if were something unique and magical, which they had obviously never seen before.

- "Again Zsolt, it is a in-house project of the Prince so why would he write this letter?" He looked at me, but immediately continued. "But I will get you a letter like this for the next week. "

- "Perfect, that would be great."

- "Ok, but then you will help us to raise funds, right?"

- "If you have the Royal letter, then I believe it will be quite easy to attract investors. So my answer is yes," I replied.

At this point they started to be very calm and the stress cloud moved away from the CEO too.

- "I have one more, very last request," I started again.

- "Go on, please," the CEO finally answered me.

- The Information Memorandum includes income sources such as Donatella Versace, Marc Jacobs or Louis Vuitton. Is it a wish or a dream to work with these brands, or are there any serious commitments available or at least a letter of intent?"

Before they could answer I put in front of them another letter from Louis Vuitton, because I got one in 2010. However, the project manager was smart, he replied fast.

- "We will get this for you too. Maybe it takes two weeks, but next week you will have the letter from Prince Albert II. for sure."

- "Thank you."

We spent some more time talking about Monaco, Switzerland, wine and other topics but I was not really convinced. Summarizing the answers, they tried to prove the point that everything is all right and on the right track, just Prince Albert II. was too busy to create the reference statements. However, I tried to see everything in a positive way, so we shook hands and I flew back to Monaco.

After two weeks, the wealth management company came back to me and they started to push me forward with the fundraising process. So, I replied them.

Just a day after my letter, suddenly I received some further communication, but it was different from the one I expected. There were a lot of new details, but without the requested credibility letters.

During the next days, we exchanged some further mails and they were eager to have funds. At one point, I closed the door and I told the wealth management company that I am still looking for the letter from H.S.H. Prince Albert II.

The project manager wrote me in a very disrespectful way and he stated that my sources in the Princely Palace are incompetent and they had no clue about this project. He also told me that if I would go to the Palace today, everybody would know about the Fashion label project. So, I did as he asked me.

The Princely Palace was shocked when they heard about the fundraising in the name of the Prince and the Princess.

After this letter, I was requested to send all the documents to the Palace of Monaco because they wanted to make a deep investigation on this matter. So, I started to receive various letters confirming my original feeling, that the whole project was a fraud.

I also received a letter from the Private Secretary for Her Serene Highness Princess Charlène. Probably this letter was the biggest proof for me, but I also got a similar response from the part of H.S.H. Prince Albert II.

At this point, I was not available for further communication with the Swiss wealth management company. I definitely closed all the communication channels with them.

However, after a few weeks I noticed on LinkedIn that the project manager changed his employment history. I saw that he had left the Swiss wealth management company. I could not refrain from asking him why. Obviously, I knew the reason, but I was very interested to hear it from him personally.

During our communication, I found out that he was forced to leave the Swiss wealth management company. Obviously, the management put all the responsibility of the project on the manager. Just as usual, possibly the Swiss wealth management company sent a sorry letter to the Palace of Monaco and they stated that they had no idea about anything, but after an inside investigation, they fired the responsible person. Almost always, the smallest item on the food-chain takes the responsibility.

During the next months, I still received some letters from the Palace and they kept me informed about the initial steps they took. I really appreciated this and I thought it was a very honourable way.

Since then, I have had no information about the status, but probably firing the poor employee was enough to avoid the responsibility. However, I hope there were serious consequences for the Swiss wealth management company to bear as well, since they already collected fifteen million Euro investment funds by the time it was reported to the Princely Palace. But it was not my business anymore. It was perfectly enough for me that the Palace thanked me for my help raising attention to this fraud.

I was really happy to see the end of the story, as well as to see how serious and prompt the Prince's Palace of Monaco is in matters such as this.

Society can be the biggest trap

Let's say that you successfully reside in the Principality of Monaco. Let's suppose that you could avoid all the fortune hunters and misleading people. So, you can almost feel complete comfort.

Close your eyes, imagine that you live in a small, tiny village where everyone knows everyone. Imagine that you have enough funds to buy everything you want for yourself without even checking the balance of your daily account. Imagine that your company is prospering well without your physical presence and you can enjoy your life.

But when everything is going perfect, what is the challenge, especially in the high society?

The small intrigues and games against each other is the answer...

I remember that in late February 2015, the owner of the AS Monaco, the Russian Billionaire Dmitry Rybolovlev sent the police to arrest his art dealer Yves Bouvier. Rybolovlev, who claims that he is the main inspiration behind the character of the successful book Fifty shades of Grey, accused Bouvier of overcharging him over the past 10 years for as many as 40 masterpieces by Picasso, Gauguin and Modigliani.

Mr Bouvier always felt that the charge of fraud and money laundering was intended to intimidate him, especially in the light that Mr Bouvier and Mr Rybolovlev did not even have a formal contract.

Later on, the same allegation involved the Monaco resident Tania Rappo, who was one of his former confidant. Also, it involved the local bank and wealth manager branch of HSBC, which has been implicated in a scheme to create a pretext for the arrest of Mr Bouvier and Tania Rappo.

On 27 February 2015, after the bank's phone call, HSBC wrote to the head of Monaco's police force to clarify that Mr Bouvier was not linked to the accounts. The bank apologized for its error, according to a copy of the letter seen by the Journal.

The attorney wrote that, "it is impossible to exclude the possibility that [HSBC's] false statement was made at the request of Mr. Rybolovlev, who is furthermore one of the biggest customers of the bank."

A few months later, there was a dramatic turn in the case, when the police contacted Mr Rybolovlev again, but this time from a different angle.

The billionaire president of Monaco Football Club has been arrested, taken into custody along with his high-profile lawyer, Tetiana Bersheda. The charge was multi-million Euro alleged art fraud.

It seemed that the Mr Rybolovlev case boiled down to a rivalry between two women working for Mr Rybolovlev. But the case was not that simple at all.

In September 2017, Monaco's Justice Minister, Philippe Narmino resigned after his "vast influence peddling" in a billion-dollar art fraud case. The French press called the scandal "Monaco-gate".

The Minister of Justice for Monaco resigned just hours after French newspaper Le Monde published text messages revealing that he worked on behalf of Russian oligarch Dmitry Rybolovlev. The official reasoning was "early retirement".

Mr. Narmino, Rybolovlev and his lawyer Tetiana Bersheda, the wife of Narmino and his son, as well as Interior Minister Paul Masseron were also charged with violating the confidentiality of the investigation and "trafficking in active and passive influence".

Just as an added fact, it was also very interesting that the arrest of Mr Bouvier took place in the same penthouse where Edmond Safra, the billionaire banker and then owner of the property, died in a mysterious fire in 1999. Coincidences like this could only happen in Monaco.

Interestingly, the Lebanese banker Edmond Safra also had a link to HSBC. Safra's bank, now HSBC Private Bank (Monaco), is located on the first four floors of the Belle Epoque building, just underneath the penthouse Safra once occupied and where Rybolovlev now lives.

So, life is never boring in the high society circle and I also have experienced this first hand. I have a goddaughter, a truly cute little angel, and her father is a society person. Since the child was outside the marriage, the father ignored any support towards her daughter, starting from his fair share towards the birth cost and even the maintenance in the first years. He knew well that paying any invoice could reveal his relation to the child, so the father even sued the mother asking for jail time for her just because she showed a family picture to close. He wanted jail time for the mother, just because she proudly showed the photo of the child, which could have uncovered the secret of the father in front of his circle.

This is why you should never underestimate the power of society, because money and power can change people, and in this transformation, they can do cruel things to each other.

Don't be fooled...

Just as in a fishpond, you can find so many advisors and possible partners in Monaco. It is always easy to find them, because everyone wants a piece of your money.

However, you have to think about your main aim, which is usually a secured transaction, a beneficial investment, the expected profit or let's say the successful application for the Carte de Residence (or Carte de Sejour). No matter your main goal, it is always better to find a decent and authorised solicitor who can back you up.

Because of the increased number of gold diggers, non-residents and businesses without an actual permit to operate under the law of the Principality, do not sign any commitment without consulting with one of the recommended lawyers. I really recommend them because even if something seems to be quite clear, there can be some unexpected surprises.

Yes, lawyers will charge you for sure. Furthermore, most of them charge fees in advance; however, they have a great overview on what's really trustable in the Principality. The recommended lawyers have the power to quickly execute all the requested permits and documents which will support your personal or business aims

People to avoid in Monaco

People to avoid in Monaco

Even if it is a closed world, there are many nice people. It would be really unfair to judge a whole community based on a few people with questionable morality.

I remember not so long ago, I met with a friend of mine, a Monegasque citizen. We talked about the services and possibilities that Monaco offers to foreign individuals. When I asked a question about things that Monaco could consider offering its wealthy residents, she promptly replied to me:

"If you do not like something over here, you can leave."

At first, I felt like this was an extremely arrogant answer. It felt to me like "we do not care about you, just bring the money because we are Monaco." However, I realised soon that she was right in many senses and obviously from different aspects.

In the Principality, you have so many benefits and potential, therefore, people are trying to protect themselves from any new or negative impact. When you are relocating to Monaco, you are welcome to enjoy its benefits, but not to reform the existing rules. When you adopt them, you can have an increased quality of life.

Again, Monaco is a small and concentrated place; the whole country is smaller than the street I live on in Berlin, Germany. So, finding a negative mentality cannot detract from the immense amounts of positive ones. However, I decided to highlight for you some personal experiences, which can be useful to consider in order to avoid any unpleasant surprises.

Socialite gold diggers

What always amazed me in Monaco besides its ultra-glamorous lifestyle is the quantity of beautiful, gorgeous women from all over the world. I have never seen so many beautiful women in one place before; it is like a Miss Universe competition throughout the day and night, and especially during summer time.

However, it was not really surprising either since I always knew that "diamonds are a girl's best friend". I think many of us remember the famous performance of Marilyn Monroe from 1953 in the film called "Gentlemen Prefer Blondes".

Spending more and more time in the French Riviera , or the Cote D'Azur, I got acquainted with the term "socialite". I never heard this term before, or I just never paid attention to it, because I have never experienced it in my own life. However, it is incredibly real.

The socialite refers to the "it girl", which is a term for a young woman who possesses the quality, "it". This is the quality of the absolute attraction and with "it", they win all men. The expression reached global attention in 1927 with the movie called "It", starring Clara Bow, however one can find early uses of "it" as well. One of the great examples can be seen in a story by Rudyard Kipling:

> "It isn't beauty, so to speak, nor good talk necessarily.
> It's just 'It'."

The writer William Donaldson observed that, having initially been coined in the 1920s the term was applied in the 1990s to describe "a young woman of noticeable 'sex appeal' who occupied herself by shoe shopping and party-going."

Nowadays, the "it girls" are commonly young females in the world of fashion or entertainment. However, in Monaco, the definition of "it girls" goes much further. Many young women come to Monaco to catch their dream husband to secure a relaxed, work-free and wealthy existence for the rest of their life. I consider these socialite women to be gold diggers, because they only date extra-wealthy partners, since their sole intention is to be beneficiaries of their wealth.

To avoid any misunderstanding, let me highlight that the socialite gold diggers are not prostitutes, they are just trophy collectors. In most cases their husbands are not able to attract them based on their sexual interests, only their wealth, business or social status.

Unfortunately, the locals often complain about the prostitutes, mainly Russian ladies living on the French border, using the key word "massage".

Interestingly, this is also the main reason why single women are usually not invited to high-caliber social events in the Principality of Monaco. In the high society, the image of a good, almost perfect family is extremely important (even if the marriage is broken behind these social curtains). The outside image is everything, therefore, the fear that a single woman will seduce someone else's husband is really high.

These women are extremely dangerous because they use their emotional cards to attract men, and as soon as they see a better option, they switch with cold blood, without any emotions involved. They are the best actresses in the real-life theatre of Monte-Carlo.

Gold diggers, the man edition

It would be unfair towards the socialite women not to mention the man edition of the gold diggers. Because some men are also involved in the quick fortune hunting in the Principality of Monaco. Interestingly, as I experienced, these men are not looking for fame as their counterpart women, but they are trying to get a big piece of cake from the ultra-rich lifestyle.

Most of these types of gold diggers aim to involve their possible partners in a financial transaction-related business. They can be intermediaries, financial advisors, wealth managers, relocating advisors, etc. The common characteristic in many of them is that they do not have any business permit from the government of Monaco to operate a business or even advise in the Principality of Monaco.

Of course, if you say that you live in Monaco and you are presenting yourself as a well-established financial advisor, who would really ask for your business permit? No one, right? This is the advantage for these gold digger crooks, because in general, we are used to believing everything we read in a Facebook comment, on an Instagram account or on a Blog. Unfortunately, our human nature is that we are scared to ask and double check when it comes to personal meetings.

The thing is that these types of people can easily mislead you stating that they are your only chance to solve your "big problem" and they are there to help you. Therefore, you really need their assistance, which is a turning point where they shift your focus towards your desperate need.

However, the truth is that you are the client, therefore, you have every right to be on the safe side, especially if you need to pay a serious amount for their services. Just ask for a business permit or double check the person through trustable sources, such as the Chambre de Développement Économique de Monaco (www.cde.mc) or the Direction Expansion Economique (www.gouv.mc).

You will experience that many of the so-called professional service providers will be outraged by your request for a business permit. They will tell you it is nonsense and that you hurt their business feelings. It is like a good theatre act. However, you will also experience that except for some outrageous replies, most of them will not be able to provide you with any business permit. This simple basic question alone can save you a lot of time and it can help you reduce the risk of a future loss.

Do not work with people in Monaco who have no business license, because otherwise, you will not be able (or it will be incredibly hard) to enforce your rights. If you are not sure about someone, then use one of the lawyers or financial advisors to get some direction and safety. It is always easier to ask someone in advance, instead of running after your money because someone has vanished with it.

The Ferrari story

Living in Monaco is a continuous learning cycle of influence, power and wealth. I had a great experience with this in the summer of 2010.

I believe that all hard work should have its rewards at the end of the day. Otherwise, why should we work so hard if no one appreciates it. In 2008, I decided to give myself a reward, so I paid a deposit for the new Ferrari California even before the first presentation car arrived at the Ferrari dealer.

During that time, the California was still very new, so I had no chance of seeing it in person; I just decided to surprise myself with it. After many months of waiting, I was invited to the Ferrari factory in Maranello, Italy where finally I could see the California in person.

Honestly, I had some doubts whether it is the right car for me or not. My problem was that the California did not represent the sporty line as the 430 did. Finally. my (ex-) wife and I decided not to take it. I believe it was a good decision regarding the California, however, my passion was still there for a Ferrari.

Monaco is packed with Ferraris and all other kinds of super sport cars. If you live in the Principality of Monaco you get used to this sooner or later. It can be considered a status symbol or just a boring car, which you can see every half an hour passing by in the streets of Monaco. For me, the Ferrari meant much more, but I was able to back away from my passion.

However, everything changed in the summer of 2010, when I first saw the new Ferrari 458 Italia. It was a stunning beauty, which immediately brought back my passion. It was like awakening a big sleeping lion ready to run out of his cave to get a meal. I was ready to finally own a Ferrari. As I walked in the sunshine one day, I decided to go for it.

I went into the first Ferrari dealer and went straight to the sales guy.

- "Hello. I would like to buy a Ferrari," I said to him, getting straight to the point.

- "You can buy one on the next corner," he replied.

I was really surprised and did not understand what this guy was talking about.

- "What do you mean by next door?," I asked him back.

- "There is a souvenir store for tourists," he answered.

I was a little bit shocked, but by that time, I started to feel that he acts like a "small king", so I accepted the rules. I pulled out my cheque book and asked him gently.

- "What if a resident wants one?"

I thought he would be more polite, but I was wrong. He just replied with an ice-cold face without the slightest sign of any emotion.

- "It takes twelve months," he replied.

I really felt that he did not care whether I bought a car from him or not. I first thought that he did not realize I was a buyer, but after some rethinking, I concluded that he probably enjoys his great salary and is not really motivated in selling more. He is working only as much as it is necessary without caring about the main aim of the dealership, which is selling the product.

- "Ok. Then I will get it from someone else by Monday," I replied and started to head out.

- "It is impossible," he said to me.

At this point, I knew that I had gotten him. I knew that he wanted the deal, but by this time, I was not sure whether I wanted to give the commission to him or the next dealer. So I pulled out my Blackberry and showed him that one can find online at least twenty Ferraris for immediate pick-up. At this point, his face changed and he asked for five minutes to make a call.

- "Sir," he started finally in a polite way. "We are able to deliver a brand-new Ferrari 458 Italia by Monday morning. It is not a problem for us."

Suddenly the impossible turned into possible. This was the point when I knew that he was just too under motivated to work. So, I looked into his eyes, but did not answer him.

- "Sir, it would be a red, beautiful Ferrari with black interior," he continued, almost praying for my confirmation.

I wanted to answer him but my mind started to work on the color. It is boring, especially in Monaco. When you see twenty-five red Ferraris that look exactly the same in front of the Hotel de Paris, the only thing that you can say is that it is boring because just one black Mercedes could stand out from the crowd.

I also had many positive thoughts related to the color red. Many of us associate the color red with courage, however, red is also and maybe most commonly associated with love and passion as well. But I could not stand to relate the color red with danger as well; just imagine the warning signs. Red is definitely a color filled with emotions. The color red also involves body reactions as well because the human eye is capable of seeing the color red in the infrared range, therefore red can be sensed as a heat source.

Once I successfully confused myself, I had to realize that red is the ultimate color for the Ferrari, but I also kept in consideration my human values regarding service. I always used to tell my friends the same old example regarding why I go to restaurants.

I am not going to the restaurant because of the food, because I can cook too. I am pretty sure that when you are hungry, you can make something nice at home. I am not going there either to meet with my friends or business partners, because I can meet with them anywhere else. It is because of the service that I go to a restaurant. The service is what really counts. I go there because I like how they seat me, how they serve me, and not to mention, those hours spent there give me the feeling that I get something special in exchange for my money.

This special feeling was not really there in the Ferrari dealer store, therefore, I asked the sales guy to send me over a written proposal;

but I knew at that point that I would probably spend my money elsewhere, with his competitor.

What I learnt from this is that in Monaco, money talks. If you are able to show the cash, you can get whatever you want. However, you need to understand the difference between service, willingness and exchanges, because small kings are all over and they are playing from their ultra-comfortable positions; they are not always there to serve you.

Small kings of Monaco

If you are able to spend more time in Monaco, you can discover very interesting human behaviours among some of the employees in the Principality. For many people, working in the Principality of Monaco means much more than a simple job, it is a lifestyle and it is also a symbol of their imagined, but never realized social status.

By watching the reactions of people, you can see that many of the employees believe that they are the small kings of Monaco, just because they work there. You can mostly observe this kind of attitude in companies handling assets and wealth.

I think it is a great quality when someone is proud to be part of a community. However, everyone needs to know his or her limits. There are lines, which are not good to cross.

Be careful with the small kings, because working in Monaco does not equal to living and having a residence permit in Monaco. The difference can be a million Euro per year.

The most common place where you can feel the effect of the small kings is the business area. When you meet someone at a company and start a communication on a managerial level, you will immediately notice that almost everyone is a decision maker. It is really amazing.

I know many business people looking to achieve their aims, who are attending various events, "networking", spending huge amount for different business lunches and dinners. These people are 100% confident that if they are networking more and meeting with more people, then based on the quantity, they will have more businesses at the end of the day. This is not working anymore, and especially not with the small kings of Monaco.

To move up in the "food chain", you need to reach the decision makers, because that is the level where the desire for results, quality and solutions are. People with eight, nine or ten-figure deals buy time, money and risk. Meanwhile, a small king has no time or money, and hates to take risks. So, you can imagine how beneficial your time, effort and energy spent will be with the small kings, because at the end of the day, you will realize that they are not on your level of decision-making.

In the past, business came down to trust. Everyone was able to make business deals based on a one-on-one personal meeting, because it was not about money, but rather about building up trust. It was a much easier way to deal with people, because the speed of business equalled speed of trust. However, nowadays, the assets and funds are handled by wealth managers and family offices, which slow down the business. It is rare to find direct access to wealthy individuals.

The thing with big organizations is, wealth managers do not allow their employees to make big budget decisions, especially not alone. Big organizations are much more complex and often have an overcomplicated budget planning and purchasing system which can destroy their efficiency when it comes to quick decisions. This makes it almost impossible to get a big deal done through the small kings.

A typical small king type of conversation would look like this:

- "May I ask you who is the decision maker?"

- "I am, of course..." replies the small king. The answer is always the same.

- "And are you able to sign this deal?"

- "Yes, I am."

And the minute when you are ready to move forward with a proposal, they will tell you that they need to run it through a higher level, or they need to talk it over with their team. At that point, you will immediately understand that you have spent valuable time with the wrong person.

Therefore, with their little "act" the small kings of Monaco are basically robbing your time as well as your enthusiasm. We all know that time is money, but they do not. All they know is that they want to be in the spotlight, they want to be seen as much more important and they really enjoy the attention that we give them. However, the result is not always what you expect.

When people overstep the Princess of Monaco

At the beginning of the book I mentioned how we delivered two artworks for the Princess of Monaco, Her Serene Highness Princess Charléne (chapter: "The craziest people to approach Monaco").

It was a wonderful achievement and I was truly honoured by all the professionalism and kindness how the Prince's Palace team helped us through the process. Even if I was not the artist, Her Serene Highness Princess Charléne of Monaco took the time to write me a personal thank you note, which felt great. I was very proud to be party of this community.

However, in the long term the story had a negative twist, which I wanted to share with you. I believe it is a good lesson for everyone who wish to create a co-operation with Monaco actors. I am not saying that this can happen with you, but we all can learn from this story.

A year after we delivered the half-side of "The Biggest Love Story" artwork to Her Serene Highness Princess Charléne of Monaco, the artist, Dodo Newman decided to auction the other half of the artwork for a good cause. In deep respect for the Princely family and respecting the official protocols, we approached well in advance the Prince's Palace and the Princess of Monaco for their approval.

Since the aim was to raise funds with the artwork for charity, the Princess of Monaco gave her blessing to the auction and in her hand-signed letter she stated "I wish you all the best for your auction". We also agreed with the Princess on the location and we got her kind approval on the 29th October 2013.

We planned the auction on the 6th December 2013 at 7pm, which was a Friday night. We invited more than 200 guests for the weekend from all around the world. Many of the friends and collectors of the artist made the trip to the Principality of Monaco, in order to support the good cause and to make a donation. But life changed our plan.

On the 5th December 2013, Nelson Mandela passed away. Due to her South African roots and her friendship with Nelson Mandela and his family, the Princess immediately left Monaco and flew to South Africa.

Despite the unforeseen circumstance and due to the fact that most of our guests already arrived to Monaco, we decided to proceed with the charity auction. Everything seemed perfect until 45 minutes before the start of the charity auction.

The auctioneer called us saying that he received an e-mail from the Princess Charléne of Monaco Foundation at 6:14pm in which the sender stated: "I would strongly advise you to cancel that auction".

The letter from the Foundation came 14 minutes after the closing time of the office of the Prince's Palace, leaving us literally no chance to contact anyone. Even if we immediately forwarded the hand-signed letter from the Princess, we had no chance to change the events.

The reason they used and referred to is, that the hand-signed letter from the Princess mentions the Princess Charléne of Monaco Foundation, which was attached to the auction lot.

you for your incredible work about the Titanic. I wish you all the best for your auction and in all your future projects.

According to their statement, the Princess's Foundation never agreed with her to raise charity funds that night. As we later understood, basically they overruled the Princess of Monaco.

Since the auctioneer had a copy of the letter from the Princess, we asked him to proceed and put the raised funds on hold util we clarify with the Princess herself upon her return to the Principality of Monaco. However, instead of proceeding the auctioneer decided to remove the lot and he sent home our over 200 guests just 45 minutes before the venue.

I can not express the magnitude of the damage that was made that night. Not just because the expected six digit fund for charity was cancelled, but also because of the reputation damage for artist.

Through my connection I could reach out to the Princess Charléne of Monaco Foundation and they replied that they are now out of working hours. When I told them that they sent out the message 14 minutes after the official hours leaving us and more importantly our guests no chance, they replied that they are open to meet first thing the following Monday.

It was clear for me that it was not a misunderstanding, because there seemed to be no intention to find a solution. As I experienced it then, it felt like a sabotage of the wish of Her Serene Highness Princess Charléne of Monaco. A typical power play and small king attitude, which I very much disapprove of in Monaco. There was nothing to do and the damage was done.

Next week when the Princess of Monaco returned from South Africa, I approached her. Her Serene Highness expressed her apologies, as on the 18th December 2013 the artist received the following e-mail:

> "Her Serene Highness Princess Charlène well received your letter and is sorry for all this misunderstood. Her Serene Highness hopes that you did not lost too much money or your reputation, and wishes you all the best in your future...".

Later on and through the secretary, the artist wished to have at least the possibility for a personal meeting with the Princess, but this was avoided at all costs. I assume the involved people tried to cover up with a different story.

After this, the artist lost her belief in Monaco, just as she lost many of her collectors thanks to the way how the "supposed to be good" cause ended. It is always a tragic loss when a country looses its advocates, the people who promote and raise awareness in a selfless way.

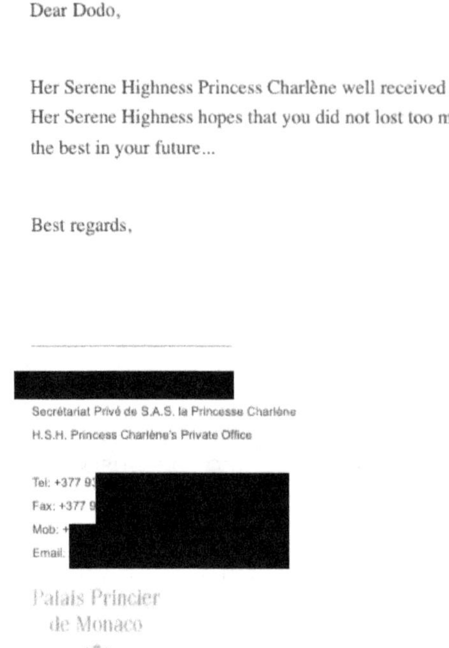

Personally I do not agree with the way, and especially with the timing how the involved people handled the issue. But that's the past and I moved on. In life even in the darkest periods we have to aim for the light and the positive future.

The lesson we learnt is that different people have different interests in the Principality of Monaco. No matter what your aim is in Monaco, it is always good to secure yourself from every angle, because unforeseen circumstances can happen.

Just to close my thoughts on a positive note, six and a half years later in April 2020, when we had the Coronavirus and the related confinement, the Principality of Monaco had a massive shortage of sanitary masks. During this period the new team of the Princess Charléne of Monaco Foundation decided to give-away free masks in Monaco, helping all the local people. I also contacted them and without any hesitation they offered me and my family protective masks. That was a very positive and uplifting experience with the Foundation. Overall, I believe the Princess Charléne of Monaco Foundation does amazing efforts to help people. My early experience was related more to personal power games.

Many people often ask me after hearing this story, why am I still promoting Monaco. The answer is quite simple. I still strongly believe that the Principality of Monaco is an amazing place. Not just because of its location, but because of its efforts in a global scale. In life sometimes we fall, but we have to stand up and move forward. I never lost my belief in the good values of the Principality, I am just more cautious with people when it comes to co-operations.

Monaco on budget

Rent in Upper Monte Carlo

Many people wish to come to the Principality of Monaco and to increase their life qualities here. It is like a dream come true. The good news is that you can realise your dream gradually as well.

I always suggest people with limited financial possibilities to start their journey in the neighbourhood of Monaco. For example, there is Beausoleil, a small city surrounding the Principality of Monaco. Even its name translates to "Beautiful Sun", which is an uplifting start.

What is very interesting and most people do not know that Beausoleil was formerly known as "Monte-Carlo-Supérieur", which translates to "Upper Monte Carlo".

Beausoleil is located on a hillside, just above the Principality and its commune is intertwined with Monaco.

The symbolic border between Beausoleil and Monaco

Also important to highlight is that the residents of the European Union can freely relocate without any VISA requirements. Furthermore, as a European Union resident one can live up to five years in Beausoleil, without applying for official residency.

Monaco on foot

The Principality of Monaco has 79 lifts, 35 escalators and 8 travelators. Thanks to its public moving walkways, the whole Principality can be travelled on foot without a great deal of effort, in less than an hour.

In order to discover how to get about on foot in the Principality, I would suggest to have a look at the Monaco Malin brochure. It is a brochure which shows you how easy it is to get about on foot in the Principality.

The leaflet shows the lifts, escalators/travelators and pedestrian walkways, as well as the electric bike stations and public transport services available in the Principality by district. Tourist attractions, hospitals and other health facilities are also included to help you find your way around.

https://en.service-public-particuliers.gouv.mc/Transport-and-mobility/Access-traffic-and-parking/Getting-around/How-to-get-about-on-foot-in-the-Principality

Mobile Data Roaming fees in Monaco

Be aware that the European roaming freedom does not apply in the Principality of Monaco. As a tourist, visiting Monaco, or if you live in the French territory, you have to expect to pay significant roaming fees.

There are thousands of tourists visiting the Principality of Monaco every day and most of them are not prepared and well-informed about the roaming charges in Monaco.

The Principality of Monaco is almost like a must-have destination for people visiting the South of France.

Unfortunately, many people falsely believe that since Monaco is part of France, therefore the European Union roaming regulations apply here too. Even so as Monaco shares the same currency with France, the widely accepted Euro.

The Roaming Regulation (EU) 2015/2120 (sometimes called the Eurotariff) regulate the imposition of roaming charges within the European Economic Area (EEA), which consists of the member states of the European Union, Iceland, Liechtenstein and Norway (but not the Principality of Monaco).

In December 2016, the representatives of the Member States voted to abolish all roaming charges by June 2017. Regulation (EU) 2017/920 eventually led to the abolition of all roaming charges for temporary roaming within the EEA as of 15 June 2017.

The Principality of Monaco is not part of the European Union. It is part of the European Union's Schengen zone and its monetary zone. Due to this reason, roaming fees apply for visiting tourists.

The majority of people do not even notice that their smartphones have automatically selected a non-French network.

Your phone will most likely connect with Monaco Telecom, as it's the strongest provider in the city state and has roaming agreements with most providers.

This effects not just the phone calls, but also data services are charged automatically, instead of the monthly data allowance being used.

One would believe that one can easily buy a Monaco pre-paid card, but the truth is that Monaco Telecom does not offer pre-paid cards anymore. In the good old times there was a possibility to buy pre-paid cards in Monaco. I think I remember the last one around 2014, but these cards are not available anymore. Instead in 2017, the Monegasque government launched via Monaco Telecom, its new Monaco WiFi service to give residents and tourists a better connectivity in the Principality.

In order to save money you can do two things with a foreign sim card.

First, you can turn off data roaming. In Monaco it's crucial that you disable international data roaming on your mobile device, which you don't need to do any more in most of Europe to avoid a high bill.

Always turn off the data roaming on your phone before you enter Monaco and select manually a French mobile network provider.

As a second solution is to buy a secondary sim card from a French provider.

If you are aiming to buy a pre-paid SIM card for your stay in Monaco, it is good to know that Monaco Telecom has a roaming agreement with Orange in France, and users of these networks can use each other's networks without surcharges. Therefore it might be a better solution to buy a French SIM card to be used in Monaco than the one from your country of origin.

If you have a choice, Orange has the best coverage through its roaming agreement with Monaco Télécom. SFR, Bouygues Télécom and Free mobile are other options too, because their antennas reach the Principality too.

It is good to know that French mobile networks don't have 3G/4G/5G signals in all areas of Monaco. Also, there are locations where only 2G signal is available for French providers.

Cheaper postal and delivery fees

One of the benefits of having an apartment in France is that many costs will be cheaper. I am not talking about the rent only, but there are significant differences in postal, courier, food delivery costs, etc.

To give you an example, the Principality of Monaco has some great food stores. However, when it comes to the big shopping most people use Carrefour Monaco, located at Centre Commercial Fontvieille, 27 Avenue Albert II, 98000 Monaco.

It is a perfect place if you have a car, however if you are on foot then you might wish to request for home delivery. Home delivery to Beausoleil is not a problem if your minimum spending exceeds the 150 Euro. Compared to this, you can request the same home delivery to your French address from 80 Euro if you do the order online. As you can see the difference is quite big.

By the way if you like pizza try out Chicken & Pizza. I honestly love and recommend that place for their pizza.

The Dog's Head

It is not really related to your budget, but visiting the Tête de Chien or the "Dog's Head" in English is a must have to do when you come to Monaco.

The Tête de Chien is a 550 m (1,804 ft) high rock promontory near the village of La Turbie and it overlooks the entire Principality of Monaco, offering a stunning view.

The way up to this marvelous viewpoint is through a breathtaking panoramic trail from the centre of Cap d'Ail or through the small streets of Beausoleil. It is among the most scenic walks you can do in the area.

To complete the walk, which is known as the Roman Way (Chemin Romain), will take more than an hour for you up hill. The trail is sometimes very tricky, often not as easy to climb the stairs. However, you will be rewarded with a breathtaking view of the entire Principality.

If you do not want to make the heavy road climbing up, you can also take the bus up to La Turbie and from there the Tête de Chien is a relatively easy walk.

To make your climb easier I would definitely suggest to utilize your Google maps navigation on your phone.

CHAPTER 20

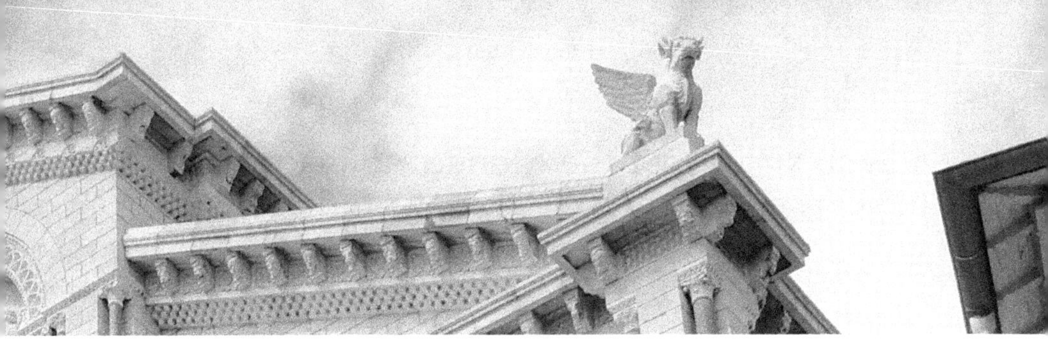

Fascinating stories & interesting facts

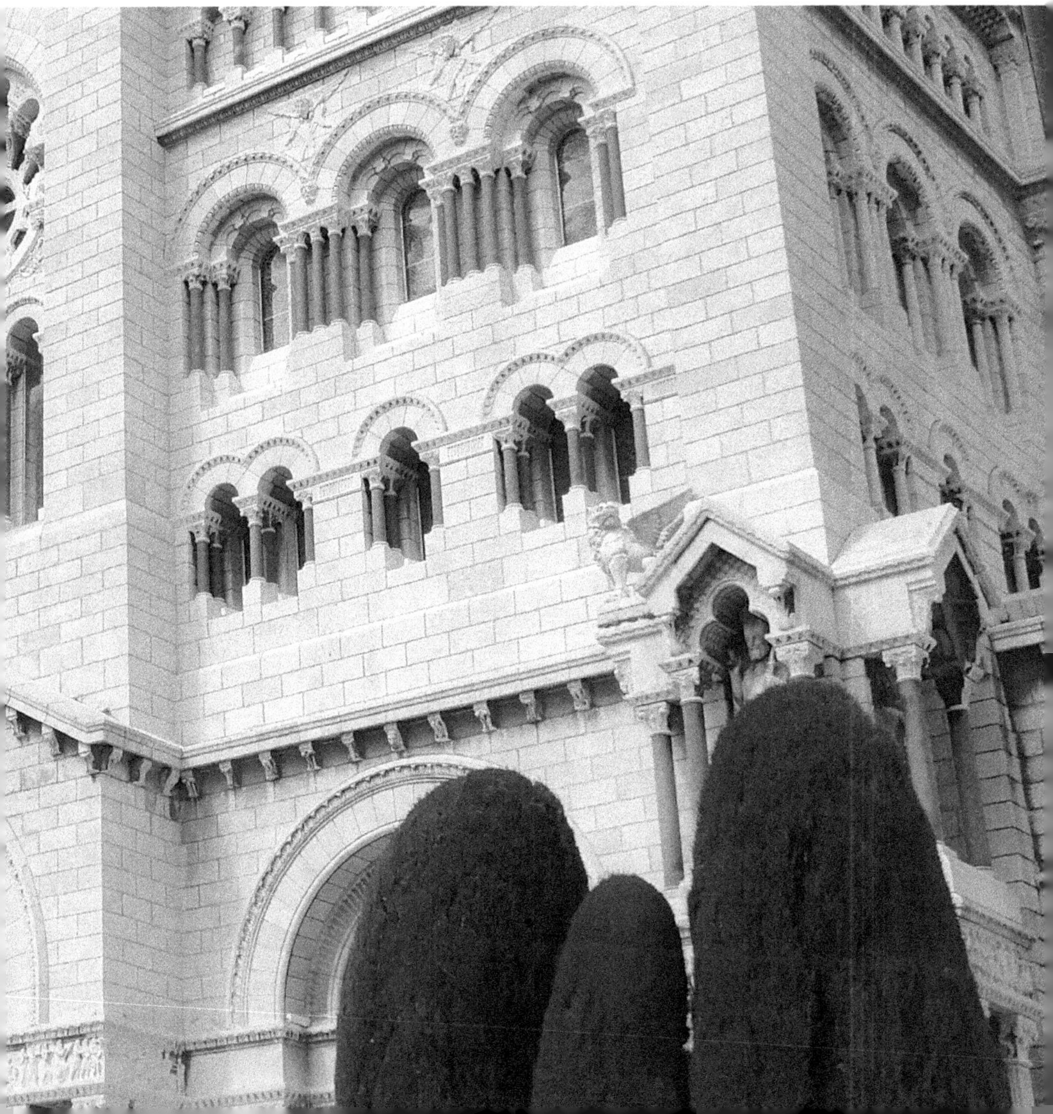

Did you know that the Monégasque language almost died?

The traditional language of the Principality is Monegù. Although nowadays Monaco's official language is French, sometimes you can also hear the traditional national Monégasque language of the Monégasque people. However, in daily life, a large number of people in the Principality of Monaco speak either French, Italian and/ or English.

This Monégasque language was threatened with extinction in the 1970s, but luckily the language is now being taught in schools and its continuance is regarded as secured.

It is a very interesting fact and a sign of safeguarding the Monégasque language, is that in the old part of Monaco the street signs are marked with Monégasque in addition to French.

There is an annual Monégasque Language Contest held on the 23rd June. This contest has been running since 1981 by Monaco's Municipality and it contains tests on Monaco's language, culture and history with both written and oral exams.

Did you know that giving birth in Monaco does not ensure automatically the Nationality, neither the passport?

It is very important to know that unlike in many countries, giving birth to a child in the territory of the Principality of Monaco does not mean that the child automatically receives Monégasque nationality.

Therefore, "birth tourism" for Monégasque passport, does not work in the Principality of Monaco. Monégasque nationality does not even apply for children born from parents who are even resident in Monaco.

Based on law the following has Monégasque nationality:

» any person born in Monaco or abroad of a Monégasque father

» any person born in Monaco or abroad of a mother born Monégasque who still had this nationality at the time of the birth and of an unknown father

» any person born in Monaco of unknown parents

Did you know that you are not allowed to walk shirtless in the Principality?

The Principality of Monaco has a very strict dress code implemented by the Monégasque law (4/VII/1940).

Outside the beach areas (meaning on the streets) no one allowed to walk bare-chested, bare-foot or wearing only a swimming costume. If anyone fails to comply with these rules can face serious police prosecution and a highly significant fine.

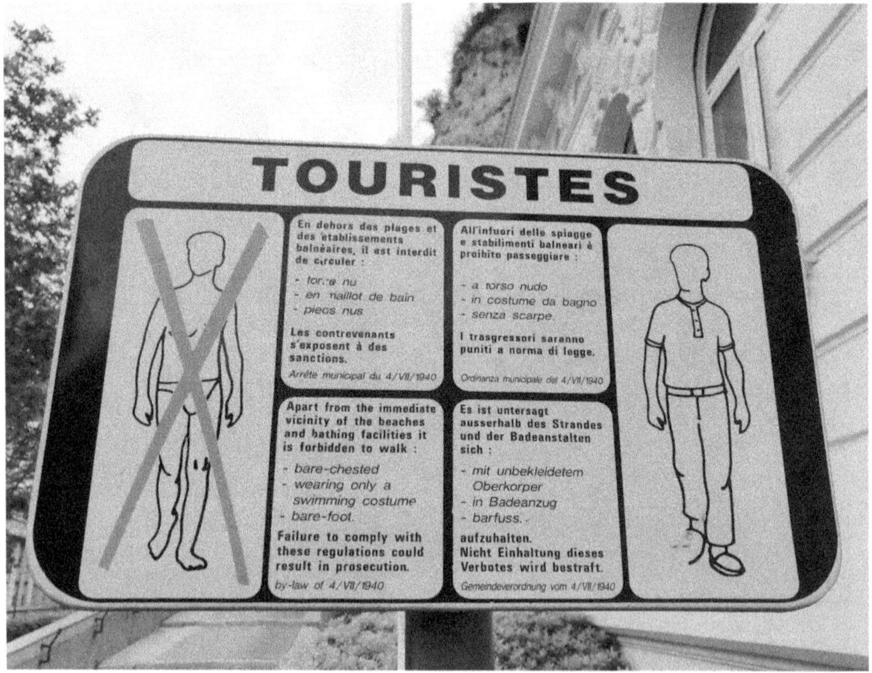

Did you know that H.S.H. Prince Albert II has four children?

Many people know that H.S.H. Prince Albert II of Monaco and his beloved wife H.S.H. Princess Charléne of Monaco are the proud parents of the Princely twins, H.S.H. Princess Gabriella Thérèse Marie and H.S.H. Prince Jacques Honoré Rainier.

However, H.S.H. Prince Albert II already had two other children with two other women.

Jazmin Grace Grimaldi was born on 4th March, 1992. Her mother is Tamara Jean Rotolo. H.S.H. Prince Albert II publicly confirmed her paternity on June 1, 2006, claiming that he had wanted to protect her identity until she was an adult. Jazmin Grace Grimaldi holds both Monegasque and American citizenships.

Alexandre Grimaldi-Coste is the son of H.S.H Prince Albert II and Nicole Coste. He was born on 24th August 24, 2003.

Since their parents have never married, neither Jazmin Grace Grimaldi or Alexandre Grimaldi-Coste in the line of succession to the Monegasque throne according to Article 10 of the Constitution of Monaco, as amended 2 April 2002 by law n°1.249, which specifies that only "direct and legitimate" descendants of Monaco's monarch (or of the monarch's siblings) may inherit the throne.

Princess Gabriella Thérèse Marie Grimaldi of Monaco, Countess of Carladès and her twin brother Jacques Honoré Rainier Grimaldi, Hereditary Prince of Monaco, Marquis of Baux was born 10 December 2014.

Even if Princess Gabriella was born first, his brother, Prince Jacques is the heir to the Monegasque throne. He also holds the title of Marquis de Baux; which all the heir apparent to the crown of Monaco have held since 1643.

Did you know that Monégasque people are not allowed to gamble in the Principality?

Even if the Principality of Monaco is among the most popular gambling destinations in Europe, the Government forbids locals from setting foot inside its luxurious casinos. The only exception is for the Monégasque people if they legally work there.

So, what is the reason behind this decision? The locals are banned from gambling due to moral reasons. Simply, The Princely Family did not want the Monégasque locals to gamble away their money.

It is important to refer back to the fact that Monaco is an independent state, therefore Monaco gambling laws do not have to conform to the ones in France. The whole casino concept in the Principality attracts gambling enthusiast foreigners. For this reason, there are passport checks at the casino entrances.

It is an interesting fact that the Monégasque law forbids the physical gambling only, therefore Monaco citizens can gamble online freely.

Did you know that Monaco has a hero from the legendary Titanic ship?

Most of the people saw James Cameron's legendary movie the Titanic, well Monaco has a forgotten hero related to the ill-fated Titanic ship. Roger Marie Léon Joseph Bricoux was one of the legendary Titanic musicians, a brave cello player who never left the sinking ship.

The 20-year-old Monaco resident Roger Marie Léon Joseph Bricoux, was not just a cello player, but a hero. He was the son of a musician and the family moved to Monaco when he was a young boy.

Bricoux was born on 1 June 1891 in rue de Donzy, Cosne-sur-Loire, France.

He was educated in various Catholic institutions in Italy and he won first prize at the Conservatory of Bologna for musical ability.

Bricoux and pianist Theodore Ronald Brailey had served together on the Cunard steamer RMS Carpathia before joining the White Star Line.

He always wanted to work as a musician; therefore, in 1912 he decided to apply for a job on the ship Titanic.

During his first trip, Bricoux became one of the legendary Titanic musicians, a cello player who never left the sinking ship and continuously played on his cello during the sinking of the Titanic.

Bricoux and his fellow band members played music to help keep the passengers calm as the crew loaded the lifeboats. Many of the survivors said that he and the band continued to play until the very end.

Bricoux was 20 years old when he died and his body, if recovered, was never identified.

Interestingly, his previous employer, the RMS Carpathiaship was the one which rescued the survivors of the Titanic disaster.

In 1913, after his apparent disappearance, he was declared a "deserter" by the French army.

It was not until 2000, that he was eventually officially registered as dead in France, mainly due to the efforts of the Association Française du Titanic (French Titanic Society).

On 2 November 2000, the same association unveiled a memorial plaque to Bricoux in Cosne-sur-Loire.

Did you know that Monaco apologized for deporting Jews in the Second World War?

Before the Second World War and the German occupation, the Principality of Monaco was home to about three-hundred Jews. It also hosted an unknown number of Jewish refugees.

The Principality of Monaco welcomed the Jews from all around, and many of those who had sought refuge from the Holocaust, thought that Monaco was a safe and neutral land. Which was actually true, because at the beginning of the war the Principality of Monaco was officially neutral. The problems started only later, when it was occupied by Italian and then German forces.

At the time, Monaco was ruled by H.S.H. Prince Louis II of Monaco, who spoke fluently German and he was also well connected to the German Aristocracy by growing up at the court of the Grand Duke of Baden.

The German Nazi regime had been aware of the advantages of an independent and neutral Monaco as a centre for German international banking and commerce. Already back in 1936, Hjalmar Schacht, the Minister for Finance for Germany visited H.S.H. Prince Louis II and started setting up companies. Before the start of the war, H.S.H. Prince Louis II suspended the constitution and reigned by decree.

Under heavy German pressure, H.S.H. Prince Louis II passed a law on 3rd July 1941, to register all Jews in Monaco.

On the night of August 27-28th 1942, the Monegasque authorities driven under pressure from Nazi collaborationist leaders in France, rounded up at least 66 Jews and they were deported to concentration camps.

Some say that in the light of the new situation, the Monegasque Government took advantage of resident Jews by taking away their wealth and assets. However, there is no actual proof supporting this theory.

In August 2015, 73 years later, the Sovereign Prince, His Serene Highness Prince Albert II publicly apologised for the Principality's role in deporting Jews to Nazi camps during World War II. He asked for forgiveness.

The Sovereign Prince also unveiled a monument at the Monaco cemetery, carved with the names of Monaco's deported Jews.

In the same year in 2015, the Monegasque Government released a report stating that there were about 90 people deported from Monaco, or Monegasque residents deported from neighbouring France, during the Second World War. From all the women, men and a child, only nine survived.

His Serene Highness Prince Albert II also acknowledged that the Monaco government has approved nine requests for compensation for property of deported Jews, seized by Monegasque authorities.

However, the truth was not complete, since the Principality was not ready to open its historic archive for historians in order to get a full picture of the country's role in World War II.

The change came only in February 2020, when His Serene Highness Prince Albert II finally agreed to open the state archive. This highly significant decision allows historians to examine state documents on the deportation of Jews to death camps. It seams, the Principality of Monaco is open now to provide some kind of closure for the relatives of the victims.

Today, an estimated number of 1000 Jews live in the Principality of Monaco. There is a Synagogue, a Chabad center, a Jewish Cultural Center of Monaco; as well as a small Jewish section in Monaco's cemetery.

Jewish Cultural Center of Monaco
3 Avenue du Berceau
98000 Monaco
Tel +377 97 70 23 62
Email: info@jccmonaco.com

Did you know that Monaco is straw-free?

All straws, with the exception of biodegradable ones, have been withdrawn from the Principality's bars. Monégasques and tourists visiting the Rocher (Monaco-Ville, also known as the Rock) are operating without plastic straws in their cocktails, since the Principality has banned these sources of pollution in bars. The new rules are also set to be extended to plastic cutlery.

The legislation banning the distribution of disposable cutlery and plastic straws is due to be introduced in 2020, but some Monaco businesses are getting ahead of the game, having already taken the decision to stop automatically offering straws to their customers.

Did you know that no drones are allowed to fly in Monaco without a permit?

According to Monaco's national aviation authority, Monaco's Civil Aviation Authority (CAA), flying a drone is legal in Monaco, but you need permission for almost all drone flights. There is only an exception for copters with a take-off weight of maximum 500 grams.

The permit may be requested from the Civil Aviation Authority (CAA), and shall be valid for three years. Moreover, one of the most important conditions is the respect of others privacy when flying your drone.

Japanese Garden / Japanese wish

The Japanese Garden is a municipal park on the Avenue Princesse Grace, next to the Grimaldi Forum Convention centre.

The garden created in 1994 and designed by Yasuo Beppu, the winner of the Flower Exhibition of Osaka 1990, is 0.7 hectares in size. It features a stylised mountain, hill, waterfall, beach, brook, and a Zen garden for meditation as well as a wish fountain.

However, many people do not know that Japanese people believe that these wishes can have very negative effects as well. For example, if you wish to lose some weight, you might have a car accident and your leg will be amputated. So, the wish may be granted in a morbid way.

It teaches us that we should make actual steps towards our aims instead of just waiting for a miracle.

Prostitution in Monaco

Prostitution in Monaco is legal, and in order to help prevent egregious human rights violations, Monaco designates a special police unit to monitor the activities of women in prostitution.

Prostitution in Monaco is legal, but organized prostitution (brothels, prostitution rings and other forms of pimping) is prohibited.

Informal red light districts form around and near hotels, clubs, and other adult establishments, especially during the Grand Prix, Monaco's largest tourist attracting event.

There are around 50 prostitutes in the country, nearly half are Brazilian, but this increases during sporting events like the Monaco Grand Prix. Most are residents of France due to the relative ease of transit and proximity.

Despite the legality of prostitution, the law states that government authorization is required in order to practice any given profession. Due to a lack of process for the formal authorization for prostitution, it falls outside the regulation of Monegasque labor laws.

Solicitation is also illegal. Forcing another person into prostitution is illegal, with penalties from six months to three years of imprisonment, plus a fine. A husband who forces his wife to engage in prostitution can be sentenced to one to five years of imprisonment, plus a fine.

In order to help prevent egregious human rights violations, Monaco designates a special police unit to monitor the activities of women in prostitution. In addition to monitoring, the security unit informs prostitutes of possible risks and resources available to them.

Cryptocurrency fail in Monaco,
The disappearing Monaco Estate (MEST) tokens

The Monaco Estate (MEST) token was initiated by Monaco Estates. This start-up had plans to launch the first ever cryptocurrency real estate investment fund with the project's token sale pegged to begin on May 1st, 2018. They even offered guaranteed buy back. However, as it seems, the concept had some major mistakes.

Everything started back in February 2018, when Monaco Estates announced the pre-sale of its cryptocurrency backed by real estate rentals in Monaco. Obviously, Monaco Estates was not licensed to make business activities in the Principality.

According to Monaco Estate's press release, 60% of rental gains was planned to go to token holders in the form of Ether and the other 40% was planned to be reinvested into the fund where it would have acted as a reserve. Additionally, another security measure was implemented to boost transparency – barring directors and shareholders from taking the company's profits.

The concept seemed perfect since Monaco's rental payments increased year by year, providing a sort of compounding effect. Therefore, Monaco Estate co-founders Daniel Golding (CEO) and Charlotte Golding (CFO) decided to leverage the good brand name of Monaco.

The Monaco Estate Token sale was also working on complying with Know Your Customer and Anti-Money Laundering regulations to ensure a smooth transition to fiat post-token sales.

The first Ethereum profit share payout to token holders was expected in December 2018.

However, as of today, the official website, the Twitter account and the official Facebook page are not available anymore. They have been all deleted!

The promise was:

"Monaco Estate is a cryptocurrency real estate investment fund focusing on high end apartment rentals in Monaco and utilizing blockchain smart contracts to allow token holders to receive a monthly profit share via Ethereum payments.

Rental payments for all properties owned by Monaco Estate will accept BTC/ETH/EUR. Making Monaco Estate the only real estate rental service in Monaco accepting cryptocurrency.

Monaco Estate is one of the best real estate agencies that know how the business works."

Did they raise any funds?

OH YES. Based on Etherscan, more than 94,000 Monaco Estate (MEST) token were traded with an estimated total value of over 61 million Euro.

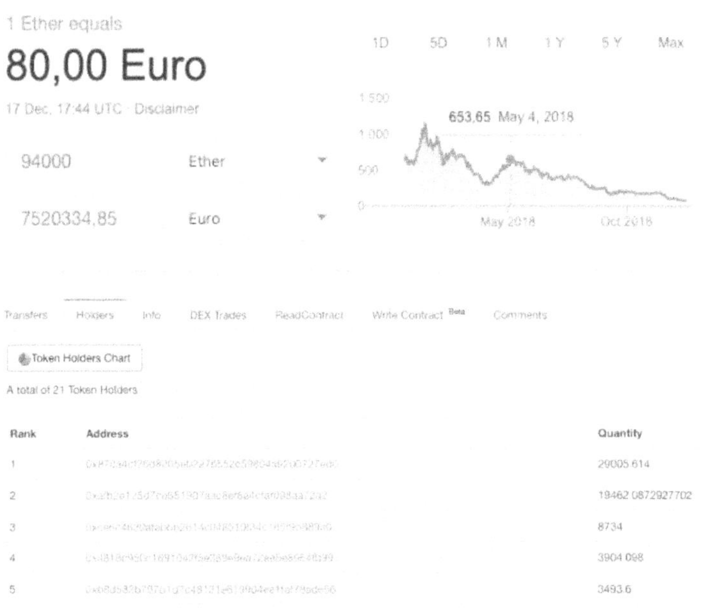

Source: Monaco Estate (MEST) Token Tracker by Etherscan

61 million Euro within a few months is a pretty impressive income for any start-up venture. One thing for sure, the name "Monaco" gained the trust of the investors.

The raised 94,000 ETH was valued at 61.5 million Euro on 4 May 2018, during the period of the Monaco Estates Token ICO.

Today the 94,000 ETH has a value of 7.5 million Euro. So, what went wrong?

Was the Monaco Estate (MEST) token reliable?

For people who only saw the brand "Monaco", yes.

However, for all those who understand the Principality of Monaco and its most basic principles, NO.

There were three major issues (at least) with the concept:

1. Since 2012 no one can use the word "Monaco" in product names. It is protected by the government of the Principality of Monaco. As a matter of fact, the Monaco Estate token was never authorised, so it was an immediate trademark infringement.

2. The concept never had a real chance to work, since in the Principality of Monaco, you need to require a government authorisation for all business activities. This authorisation process takes usually up-to 6 months. Such an application was never initiated by the founders of Monaco Estates.

3. It is OK if an ICO fails, but one should expect a small explanation. Deleting all the social media accounts is not a good one.

What went wrong?

Monaco Estates founder Daniel Golding believes that two factors played a role in the fall:

1. The timing (I would remind you that 94.000 ETH (61.5 million Euro) was raised)

2. The inexperienced young ICO buyers

Daniel Golding highlighted that ICO investors are not professional investors, and they are mostly inexperienced 18-30-year-olds who all believe the size of the team is what dictates a successful project.

"People really struggled with the concept that managing real estate properties can be done by one person or out sourced to a real estate rental agent."

– stated Daniel Golding

The team size of Monaco Estates was only 4 people: the two founders, Daniel Golding and Charlotte Golding, and two external advisors, Edwin Van den Berg and Olivier Laurent. However, we assume that Van den Berg and Laurent are both victims of this project.

It is all about the intentions.

The whole thing questions their three most basic promises:

1. Quarterly investor reports will be available detailing income/ expenditure and operating updates.
2. Transparent accounting ensures investors are fully informed on their investment finances.
3. Allegedly, a security measure was implemented to boost transparency – barring directors and shareholders from taking the company's profits.

The topic gets scarier when people realise that the LinkedIn profiles of Monaco Estates' two founding members were also deleted (Daniel Golding and Charlotte Golding).

On the positive side, by working with Monaco Wealth Management, I could reach out to Mr Olivier Laurent, one of the named advisors on the Monaco Estate (MEST) token. Mr Laurent confirmed that his trust was misused and he expressed his bitter surprise at how the Monaco Estates founder just disappeared from the online world.

"I've met the founder (Daniel Golding) in Athens in 2017 while I was meeting with my dev team for my own startup. He convinced me to be an 'advisor' to basically use my network as a share of voice. Unfortunately, I was not really informed about the evolution," said Mr Olivier Laurent

Following their meeting in Athens, Mr Laurent and Monaco Estates founder Mr Golding only communicated via e-mail.

Mr Laurent also explained that based on his opinion, Monaco Estates was specifically the kind of project for which you do not need to use blockchain. It brings no real added value in this specific case.

"I think the founder tried to surf on a trendy topic to raise funds. Most of the people who are involved in ICOs think blockchain will bring easy money. These people are real entrepreneurs, but opportunists without real business and strategic vision," remarked Mr Laurent

December 2018 was the expected date for the payments for the token holders, however, it seems someone cleared out the web.

"No single mention of Monaco Estates anymore... That speaks for itself," remarked Mr Laurent

So, we can conclude that in the Principality of Monaco, all that glitters is not gold.

It is obvious that "Monaco" and "Monte-Carlo" are names which have been a magnet for prestigious and luxury brands. However, the Principality of Monaco protects its name as a brand, therefore, it is not easy to use the word "Monaco" or "Monte-Carlo".

Notably, there was another cryptocurrency, the Monaco Token which has tried to capitalise on the Monaco brand since 2017, but based on the pressure from Monaco Brands, they had no other choice than to rebrand their token.

Important note: As mentioned before, Monaco Brands; "Brands of the State of Monaco" is a Monaco-based limited company created on 6 April 2012, for the purpose of protecting, promoting and defending the entire portfolio of brands of which it is the owner or licensee.

Verdict: Real estate is always a very attractive investment for people and Monaco is always a good place for real estate investment. Monaco Estates had a great potential, as they raised a very significant amount of funds. Yet, the founders of the Monaco Estate (MEST) Token vanished before the first token holder payouts was due. I will let you draw the conclusion.

BRASS
RESTAURANT

Chapter 21

My personal conclusion

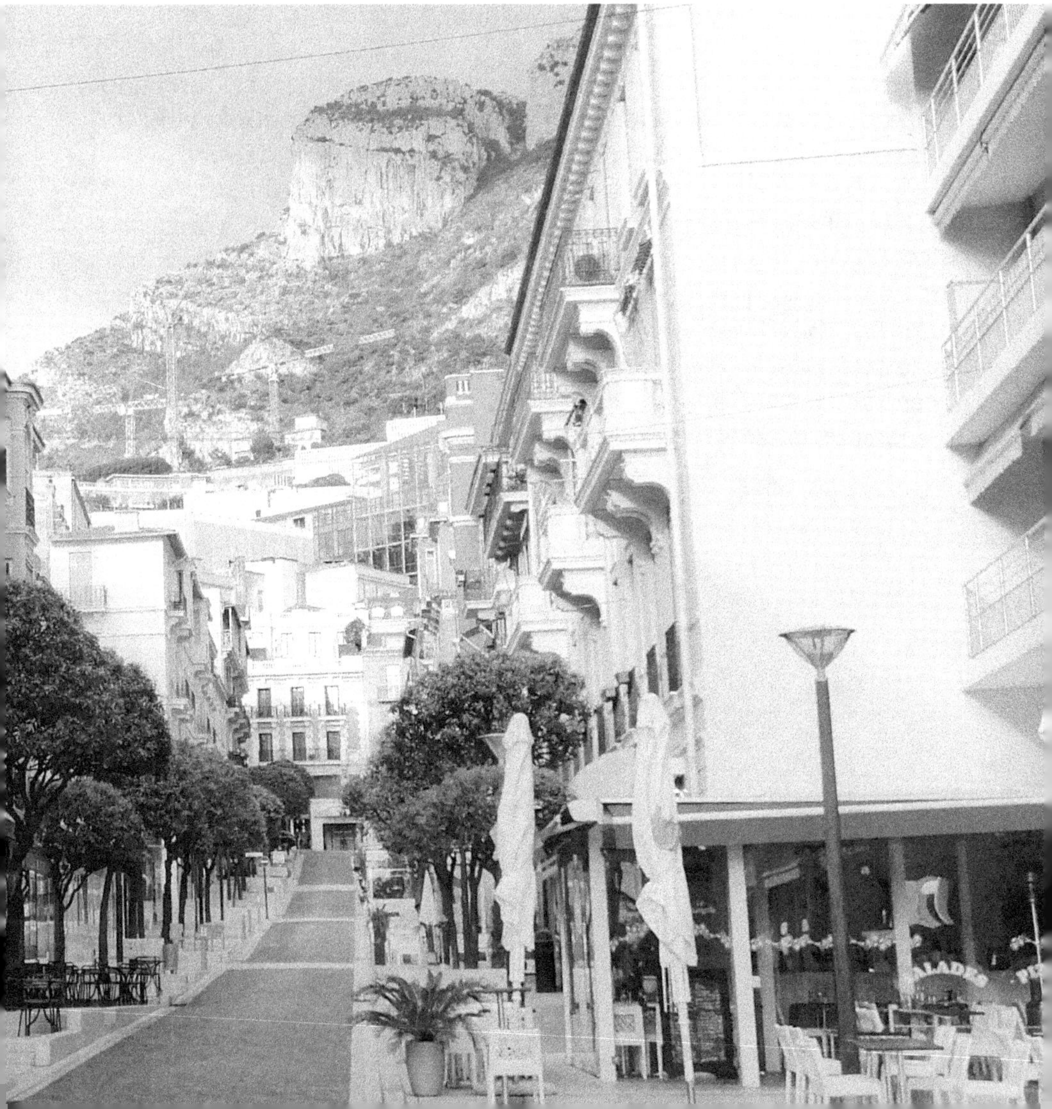

What I learnt about the country of magic

The Principality of Monaco is an exceptional place where you have many chances to increase your quality of life and potential for your business. It is a beautiful landscape with exceptional people.

Since the Principality of Monaco is a small and extremely concentrated territory you can also feel the negative effects in a more intense way. It is not a problem at all, because for example, you can find significantly more criminal activity in other countries. However, because of Monaco's concentrated territory and "small-town" feeling, if anything happens, you will feel it a hundred times more.

The Principality of Monaco is a small place with love, care and orientation towards families, as well as gossips and people who try to take advantage of the good reputation of the Principality.

You cannot hide your face because life is not a fairytale, however, life in Monaco could be an exceptionally good one for you. Obviously, not everything that shines is gold, so do not let your fascination make you blind and unprepared. But once you take your time to make smart decisions, Monaco could be your own country of Magic. It can be your Neverland where everything happens as you envision it, and your dreams become your reality.

What I learnt about the benefits of a small town

When I was a little child, I believe around 6 years old, my father left me, but I still spent many beautiful times with my grandmother. She lived in a small village with only a few thousands of inhabitants.

As a child, I sometimes felt that people knew about my family background, and they were always speaking about me behind my back. In the beginning, I did not really like to visit my grandmother because of this small and concentrated circle of people. Luckily, my grandmother showed me a different face, a small town feeling, which was the benefit of being in a closed circle.

Since the number of residents in Monaco is considerably small, you can always exchange valuable information and find a way to get introduced to the people you want. Being in a small community could be your biggest tool for networking and developing new and fruitful business and personal connections.

In a small community, you can also rely on the power of the word of mouth. Yes, there is gossip, greediness, and power plays, but there is also positive news. When you achieve something, it can be delivered to all the Monaco residents on the wings of the wind. The key is to have the capability and openness to select and question the news you hear. Soon you will know what is reliable and what is not.

When you have true human values and real intentions to improve the environment and your business, a small country like the Principality of Monaco could be a great asset for your achievements.

Look for the true things

Always look for the true things around you because those rare diamonds will guide you to the next steps.

I believe that almost every target that you set is achievable. However, there is a very important rule: achieving the targets cannot be done without replacing the basics in your head! This means that you have to be able to let new points of views into your life that lead you forward on the road towards your aims.

Do you remember my own quotation?

> "Every mountain can be climbed – you just have to find the appropriate way to do it. If you do not achieve your goal, then you have not done everything to achieve it. The secret of success is persistence!"

Being in a small town is a great possibility to learn from each other. You can make conversations and friendship with well-established and internationally respected business leaders and owners during many occasions, who can provide you with great insights.

The result is what matters

You will never find the truth on the surface, only in the results achieved, in proven track records. However, the past and the records are quickly forgotten by the brain. Sir Winston Churchill once said:

> "You have enemies? Good. That means you've stood up for something, something in your life."
>
> - Sir Winston Churchill

The result is what really matters and this is true for your personal life and your business as well. Every company or person could be introduced to different approaches. Everyone has a positive and negative side. You will realize that your competitors and haters will highlight only your failures, while your best friends, family members or business customers will never realize or care about your mistakes.

On the road towards our aims, we will undoubtedly meet obstacles. Probably, we will lose some of the battles, but it does not mean that we have to give up our aims or lose focus.

Sadly, in many cases there are unseen circumstances which can influence our decisions. Therefore, there is a big difference in the intent and the source of the possible difficulties and problems. You can always find the truth if you are ready to look under the surface.

We are able to make great decisions if we are ready to see the sources behind the symptoms. A wise business man never makes his decisions based on symptoms, he is able to see the reasons, and by discovering the sources, he is able to make decisions and rise over any kind of difficulties.

You can continuously meet with business people in the Principality of Monaco; there are many occasions that support this, and there are countless clubs and associations.

You have the ability to gain valuable information about the person you are aiming to deal with and also about his/her results. It is the benefit of a small town which can lead you to successful and mutually beneficial business opportunities.

The approach

The first days and weeks in the Principality of Monaco should be spent only by discovering the country. It is very important to wait until the pink cloud goes away from the view that you might see.

Monaco is beautiful, ultra-luxurious and the glamour is all around. These are all factors which will influence your decision. Normally, you will never make any decision based on the surface, but here you can easily make this mistake.

When people see the potential of creating a good business deal with you, most companies will invite you to nice dinners and places to show you how influential they are. They will present it to you as if no doors are closed in front of them. This could be true in some cases, but you have to be careful with these kinds of approaches.

One time, I had a dinner with a vice president of a bank, and he was so proud of his branch. It was a great sales pitch, but I had to ask one thing. I know that most of the wealth management branches have a main banking partner, so my question was obvious. Where does he keep his own income?

Usually, the answer is in the same bank. The only problem was, when he went to pay, he used a credit card issued by a different bank. A different card for a competitor bank. So, what is the meaning of this? You cannot sell me on your bank and its services while you keep your money in another one. For me, it is a question of loyalty and trust in the product or service you sell.

In some cases, the approach could be a disillusion and you always need to take your time to reconsider things. I suggest you make office visits to really get an impression about the real working environment.

Always try to utilise the benefits of a small town to get some references and first-hand impressions. Believe me, it is very easy to find existing clients or people who have dealt with specific companies.

Monaco is very small and people usually know each other. While something could be your disadvantage in any other big country, it can be your own leverage in the Principality of Monaco.

Top 5 mistakes in Monaco & How to avoid them

Most of the people dream about success and getting rich, a balanced life without financial difficulties, especially when they see the accomplished residents of the Principality of Monaco. Fame, wealth and respect are all in the air of beautiful Monaco, but can you actually achieve this on your own as well?

As I used to say, capitalization of our personal and business potential highly depends on our willingness to learn and improve.

During the past ten years, my company, Monaco Wealth Management, has helped many people to achieve their aims, however, we have also observed many people who fail because of their lack of knowledge and/or understanding of the local customs of the Principality of Monaco.

So, let's learn from their mistakes and do things better in order to achieve visible results in Monaco.

To give you some examples, I have collected the top 5 mistakes we repeatedly see from foreign brands coming to Monaco.

Mistake #1: Monaco is not a "Make a wish foundation" or a get rich program

Monaco has a strong business sector thanks to its internationally accomplished residents. Living in a zero-debt, green and wealthy country is quite a privilege. It is something which will motivate you to create and maintain a better quality of life for yourself and your beloved ones.

The Principality has the most high net worth individuals in the world; one in three people are millionaires in the country of 37,800 people.

Although, this is exactly why some people have the misconception that by simply arriving in Monaco, they can become immediately rich by gaining millions of funds from the residents. For this reason, people often bomb residents with countless "investment offers".

People in Monaco are smart and they often have earned their wealth with hard work, therefore, there is no such thing as a "get rich program" in the Principality. It also often happens that residents just ignore these emails without even taking the energy to reply or consider them. Sending your offers in advance is one of the greatest way to demolish your chances in Monaco.

A few year ago, my friend Dodo Newman held an inspirational lecture for the MBA students of the International University of Monaco where she said that usually many people think that success is a straight line, from one point to the other. It starts at point A and it ends at point B. It is straight, with logical steps, without any break or turns.

Dodo talked about the fact that many people try to reach their aims with an ideal picture in their mind without understanding the local intricacies of a luxury market such as The Principality of Monaco as well.

"Theories are only good and valid if you can really use them."

– Dodo Newman

On the positive side, you can meet influential people and learn from them; you can be inspired and you might find the right partners. But partnership in Monaco is like a marriage, it has to be based on mutual respect and appreciation towards the aims of the others.

Suggestion:

Be a part of the Monaco community, and try to get involved with as many events as you can. Build up the trust step-by-step instead of bombing people with funding requests. Once they get to know you as a person, they will be much more flexible to listen to your visions. Monaco will help you to accomplish your highest ambitions, and you will see that Monaco has some world class programs to do that. To be more precise, Monaco has more than 700 events in a year.

"The first step is to stop finding excuses and to focus on what steps we can actually take. An excuse is worse than a mistake because it effects everything around us and drains down all possible solutions. There is always a way; a wrong way ahead is much better than no way at all..."

– Dodo Newman

And if you still need some guidance, you can always contact the Monaco Welcome Office, and they will help you to find the right directions.

This was the most common mistake of foreign brands coming to Monaco, so let's see Mistake #2.

Mistake #2: Never underestimate the value of Monaco's small and niche community

In a country where there are only approximately 37,800 people, people talk. It is a friendly and closed community where 120 nationalities come together creating a platform to unite diverse interests.

When a company sends a marketing guy with a question of how many subscribers we have or how many actual residents are living in the Principality, we already know that they will fail. Dealing with the HNWI and the luxury marketing is not about the number of poeple. It is all about the Who.

Generally speaking, one person who can afford your product or service is more valuable than a million subscribers who cannot. The Principality of Monaco has a unique business society with high profile people.

In contrast to this thinking, another big mistake that brands coming to Monaco make, is expecting everything to be "discounted". For instance, working for commission is a typical request we receive every day, which gives us the following impression:

» the brand has no sufficient funds to live and breathe in the Monaco market

» the brand has no understanding about dealing with luxury clientele

Being cheap in mentality, while trying to sell products/services for ultrahigh amounts is one of the worst things you can do in this community. Trust is a very important factor in reaching Monaco's UHNWI, and many years of hard work to gain that trust comes with a price tag.

In this circle of people, if a brand or an event disappoints expectations, then the brand will automatically decrease in value. Not only does the consumer not purchase, but they will prevent others in their sphere of influence from attending either.

Suggestion:

The luxury market is expensive. It is. If you do not have the funds to bear its costs, then do not come.

Mistake #3: Lack of time to build up relationships

It often happens in Monaco that people stay for a only few days and try to do as many meetings as they can. Managing as many meetings as possible during a few days usually causes frustration and pressure.

Time and trust are the two most important factors in reaching the wealthy. The concept of "let's have a coffee and then we close the deal via e-mail" usually never works out with Monaco residents. It is also a kind of disrespectful message that you only need their money.

It is funny to see that many brands are not ready to pay for the quality marketing and professional approach, yet they expect others to pay fortunes for their products.

Suggestion:

It is very important to be prepared and focused in a meeting. Respect your companion at the level their influence requires. Do not invite someone for a quick coffee between three other meetings, instead, invite them out for a lunch or dinner and take the time to make a proper impression of yourself and your business.

Monaco is a very small place and a good impression creates a positive buzz, shortening the road to achieve your personal or business goals.

I also highly recommend companies and business professionals to contact the Monaco Government Tourist Office before they arrive in the Principality since their role is to drive more business (meaning leisure and business tourism) to the Principality. The Monaco Government Tourist Office can introduce businesses to the most appropriate local vendors in Monaco who can help them execute their program.

The Monaco Government Tourist Office is not there to represent your product or to raise funds for you, however, they can help you identify the right partners, agencies, hotels, restaurants and meeting locations. They can offer invaluable help for you to impress your targets and guests in the Principality of Monaco.

As a little bit of self-promotion, I also suggest you to discover the most iconic restaurants of the Principality for your UHNWI meetings by reading the "Signature Dishes of the Principality of Monaco" book.

Mistake #4: Dealing with the wrong partners

Monaco is a wonderful environment, which is already the base of high quality and glamour. Therefore, we always suggest a little bit of background checking to avoid "expensive" experiences. It seems like everybody lives in Monaco (but actually most of them live in France). It is amazing to see how Monaco attracts the desires of people. The glamour, the extraordinary lifestyle, the wealth and all the related benefits evoke emotions in people and everyone wants to be part of the luxurious world offered by the Principality of Monaco. It is important to be a little cautious because in Monaco "everyone knows the Prince", and one of the most used sentences is "the Prince is my best friend". Obviously, the experienced people in Monaco know that there are big differences between different events.

Companies considering the Principality of Monaco as a locale for a product launch, board of directors meeting, user conference or motivational trip will find the Monaco Government Tourist Office to be an invaluable source of information.

Do not forget that the right approach and the proper marketing and client education is much more crucial than in the mass market. It is also harder to break into the UHNW market than to the mass market.

The luxury market needs significant funds and it is far less forgiving than the mass market that allows failed products relaunch. This is typically a mistake by those people who previously worked with companies who are targeting the mass market.

Also, there are many similarities between the French and the Monegasque legal systems and a SARL company formation is not necessarily a Monegasque company.

April and May are two very interesting months in the Principality because the so-called seasonal advisors start to appear. Many fortune hunters come to Monaco during these months to advise on events, locations, investments and all other money-related topics. We call them seasonal advisors because they leave Monaco after a few months.

Many seasonal advisors are in Monaco in the hope of gaining fast money. They work for extra high fees, sometimes charging even ten times higher than any local business. Since these seasonal folks are pushing their messages in an extremely aggressive way in all kinds of social platforms, they are able to catch some small fish.

Suggestion:

It is always good to conduct a little background check on whether a business partner really exists or not in the Principality of Monaco. For this, you can use sources such as the Chambre de Développement Économique de Monaco, Direction Expansion Economique or Monaco Wealth Management.

Mistake #5: Not involving the local partners

You can find amazing local partners in Monaco to achieve your aims. No matter whether you are seeking PR, marketing, sales, event organisation, etc. help, there are multiple accomplished companies that can be at your service.

Many people believe that they can do the work themselves, however, they underestimate the value of a local partner. This is a huge and costly mistake.

In the Principality of Monaco, the up is down and the down is up. It is a unique market that requires many years of experience and massive guidance for brands.

Local businesses have a rich knowledge of possibilities, often better and discounted prices and more importantly, the social capital.

Yes, the social capital is the highest importance when you come to Monaco, because you need to target the right people. This is why my event partner's first question is always "who will invite the guests"?

Suggestion:

Having the right local partner next to you can be really costly at first sight, however, it is never as expensive as doing things in an amateur way.

Let's put it this way: working with a Monaco-based PR or marketing partner is costly because it brings you the requested result.

Everything that brings you results cannot be considered expensive. The only thing that you can call expensive are those things that do not bring you any result. A simple coffee without a business order at the end can be considered as expensive and a awaste of time and money too.

When you are aiming to plan something in Monaco, look for result-oriented solutions instead of cheap ones. There are many people who can help you from the Monaco Welcome Office or Monaco Government Tourist Office.

3 rules in the field of luxury

Finally, please let me share with you three rules from the field of luxury which are definitely applicable to the Principality of Monaco.

Over 80% of the luxury businesses coming to the Principality of Monaco fail to capitalise on their true potential. Monaco is a niche market with the most millionaires per capita in the world. In this unique field of accomplished HNWI, one event is not enough to close a deal (There are a few exceptions). Many brands organise fancy one-night events, gourmet dinners, cocktail parties and presentations, but in a country which offers over 700 official events per year and a further 3,000 private events, a one-night presentation will hardly make a difference.

The typical self-justification is: "maybe we did not grow as we expected with this campaign, but at least we strengthened our brand name in the market."

One of the major elements of the luxury market is desire. Simple putting a price tag on a product and shouting it around loudly is not enough. It is very important to remember that everyone can see the price of the product, but not its value! To accomplish this, you need time. Value has always been a relative concept, based on the personal judgement of the customer. The real luxury product never has an absolute value, a product is worth as much as the buyer is willing to pay for it.

Rule Nr. 1.: Anything can be sold to someone who wants something, but does not need it; but nothing can be sold to someone who does not want something, even if he needs it.

So how can you catch the desire of the people in Monaco? Just as in any market understanding, your target group is the key for prosperity. This is the very first step before you hold any kind of event.

There are always different types of buyers:

» some of them are only looking at the price

» some of them are looking for the best quality

» some of them are looking for the luxury or the prestige

» some of them are looking for long-term guarantees

» some of them are looking for added values

» some of them simply make their decisions based on your personality

There are different needs, but you need to know how to handle handle them. This is the main reason why it is difficult to cover various needs during a single event. It is a big mistake. In order to generate interest and convert into an actual sale, you need to aim for the long-term game. Aim for the synergy of understanding, educating, pre-qualifying, presenting, following-up and sales closing. These steps are equally important on the road of success in Monaco.

The price is only one factor, and believe it or not, the price is not the most important one, especially not in the Principality of Monaco where the average household has over 3 million Euro (and not to mention the wealth of the ultra-rich).

In life and business, one of the most important things is communication. Communication should be in both directions every time, and to establish this, you need time. Previously, I mentioned the "top 5 Mistakes in Monaco", and one of them was the "lack of time to build up relationships".

Fact: 99% of opportunities are lost by wrong and bad implementation; these are the cases when the excuse becomes the idea.

The truth is that you can capitalize on your potential by creating integrated marketing channels. And these do not need big investments. Just think about it – if a result cannot be gained from a small budget, then what kind of result can be expected from an increased budget? When your event or promotion fails, people often say that your product was not ready. Well, it is not necessarily true.

Rule Nr. 2.: The truth is that even if you know your market area well, the market is in continuous change.

Implementing brand promotion strategies in order to create value means fully understanding the behaviour of the target market. The execution is key, and for this, you need the right partners.

EXECUTIVE = latin Executor, ex: fully, sequi: monitored

In the luxury market, to think outside the box is to try to think beyond the obvious things in order to bring something new, something unique. As we all know, in many cases, success relies only on one tiny thing. It is especially interesting that 70% of people working in the luxury marketing segment do not know what luxury truly is. It is almost a trend of today that everyone is competent in everything, so that specialization has disappeared.

Real luxury marketing is catching attention and building up the desire of your well-defined target group. Learning from this, creating value in simple terms means creating products or services that people WANT! We need to show and teach the value of the product in all cases.

You will achieve success when you will are able to build campaigns to gain benefits from individual perspectives. One of the basic reasons why people immediately turn down an offer is because they do not understand its message or they simply believe that you are just one of the other 100 similar brands.

Do not fall for social media photos and fancy promises. Many events in Monaco attract the socialites, not your target group. If you want to have an event which brings you visible results, then invest in the preparation. Take your focus away from the shining photos and the celebrities and start to focus on how can you attract your prospective clients. I bet the people only looking for free champagne and dinner is not your target group.

If you want to be successful with your promotion in Monaco, you have to place your product or solution, first and foremost, in the mind of your target group, and this is a challenge in the luxury market.

Rule Nr 3.: The more comparable you are, the more boring you are in your market.

In order to achieve this, you can always aim for the continuous presence and customer education. The PR, marketing and sales functions should never be mixed up. Although, one does not exist without the other, it is necessary to separate them and to know which is responsible for what. You need to know what you are expecting the end result to be from each of them. In the Principality of Monaco, the only companies that perform in the long term are those who focus on long-term prosperity using the well-balanced combination of events and brand awareness promotions (not Instagram or Facebook).

With MonacoWealthManagement.com, we can help you by providing the right connections (9,000 members from Monaco), putting you together with the right local businesses and advisors and offering you continuous visual appearances and articles during the year in order to properly educate your target group regarding the values of your product.

Never forget that capitalization of your personal and business potential highly depends on your willingness to learn and improve. If you agree with everything I have mentioned above, then you will definitely consider joining our UHNW Business Club.

Afterwords

My first day in Monaco

Even today, one of the first topics to come up in conversations with new people is the reason why I decided to move to the Monaco area. The secret behind the choice often fascinates people. Maybe they just want to hear that I am rich and wanted to live in a tax haven. The truth is that I never decided to move to the Principality because of financial benefits. I had an entirely different reason behind my choice, driven by different values.

I still remember that it was a beautiful and sunny day in May 2010 when two of my friends and I were walking along at the Cote d'Azur. We spent a week in Cannes, France during the Cannes Film Festival, and also because of a special event related to my closest friend, the artist Dodo Newman.

It was the last day of the Film Festival and still we could not enjoy our walk at the Promenade de la Croisette because of the crowd. The city was packed with celebrities, tourists and the press. It felt as if we were sardines in a tiny aluminium box. The only thing missing was the tomato sauce on top of it on that extra hot day.

We were quite tired because of the previous night, which was devoted to the Red Cross France art auction for the Reconstruction of Haiti where Dodo's sculptural artworks on PlexiGlas were auctioned. We all helped Dodo because of our ten years of friendship (it is 19 years now) and also because the entire income of the auction was directly offered to Haiti. Yes, 100% of the income. it was a great effort to be a part of.

Our hearts were filled with happiness from the large amount raised from the auction, and yet our bodies were exhausted from the mass of people at the Promenade de la Croisette. In this bored and tired moment, my other friend Matt had an idea:

"Look guys, have you ever been to Monaco?"

"No, I have not," I answered to him.

"I have been there," Dodo indicated.

Matt saw that Dodo was quite exhausted, however, he really wanted to go and did not give up on his efforts.

"Why don't we jump over there?" He looked at Dodo with a little prayer in his eyes. "We are so close, just a few kilometres away."

"It sounds like a good idea." I nodded and Dodo also agreed with us.

I believe we all wanted something refreshing and to move away from the crowd. We did not even notice the time passing, and we were already driving on the highway towards Monaco.

I started to think in the car about what the Principality of Monaco really meant to me. I reached the conclusion after a few minutes that Monaco was always a very neutral country for me. When I tried to dig for memories in my brain, I found only two little things.

The first memory was the sad day (3 October 1990) when Caroline's, H.R.H. the Princess of Hanover's husband, Stefano Casiraghi was killed in an offshore powerboat racing accident off the coast of Monaco while defending his world offshore title. I remembered that I was in shock when I saw the live footage on TV. I really felt the loss of the Princess.

My second memory about the Principality of Monaco was a much happier one. It was a picture taken by my mother, which represented a white Lamborghini Countach. The picture captured the Lamborghini as an amazing piece of rolling art as it turned the tight Mirabeau corner driving towards the tunnel. I liked that photo because I saw the powerful rapidity of the Lamborghini depicted by all the contours of its squared chassis fading away, as the effect of the speed as it went through the Mirabeau corner. At that time, I was an insanely big fan of Lamborghini, so I will never forget that photo made by my mother. It will remain in my memory forever.

As we drew close to our highway exit towards Monaco, I started to realize that the Principality was fully packed too. However, our prayers were answered since Monaco was a little bit more relaxed than Cannes. We parked in the first spot we found and it was the perfect time to say hello to the Principality. I had no clue then that those few hours of walking and discovering Monaco would change my life forever.

The very first impression of Monaco is that it is breathtaking without any doubt. It is an incredibly small country (2.02 km2 ~ 0.78 sq mi), however, it has capitalized well on its own potential. You can find a multi-cultural environment in the Principality of Monaco made up of many nations, which makes the whole place come alive.

For first-time visitors, the Principality of Monaco is about luxury and wealth. If you just walk through the famous Formula One circle, you can notice the luxury stores, the famous Hôtel de Paris standing next to the shockingly beautiful Casino. After the Casino, the roads lead you to the Japanese garden, which I consider the most relaxing place in Monaco. Following this, just as you get out from the tunnel, you find yourself at the Port Hercule with its super-luxurious ultra-yachts.

Monaco is really small in size and yet it is so well organised to present its biggest values. Honestly, you feel this with every step you take. On almost every corner, you can see police officers safeguarding your security. Almost every building is protected by surveillance cameras, so the Principality of Monaco is without a doubt one of the most secure places in Europe. Even the celebrities who are frequent visitors in Monaco are able to walk through without their bodyguards.

A Spanish friend of mine who is a longtime resident in the Principality always says that people are coming to Monaco to capture their dreams. They come here to feel a living wonder at least for a few hours. It is a pleasant combination of Luxury, Glamour, Wealth and Elegance, which is reflected in all aspects of the Principality.

However, I discovered another side of Monaco as well, which is the very friendly Mediterranean side of the Principality. There you can find lovely small streets on the Rock or you can discover the view of endless orange trees standing in a row beside the main roads or the small chapels.

Spending one day in Monaco was enough time for me to realize the benefits of working hard in life. The Principality of Monaco was like heaven on Earth. Therefore, my number one aim was to gain this feeling. To make it permanent, I decided to convert my desire into reality. I started to visit Monaco more often. First I spent three months there in 2010, living right at the Port Hercule. Later on, I decided to relocate permanently in the surroundings of the land of dreams, the Principality of Monaco.

When I arrived, I spent my first week at the Port Palace Hotel in Monaco. Then I moved to Monaco's border, to Beausoleil. Beausoleil lies practically on the other side of the street. The right side of the street is Monaco and the left side of the street is France. It is a funny feeling that you can take 3 steps and you are in Monaco.

Spending now over ten years in and out of the Principality, I believe I have gained a bit of insight into its daily living impulse and how the country function. I have experienced some negative things, but the positive experiences outweigh them tenfold. However, the most important thing is that this book is a collection of my own experiences. Since these are my experiences, it does not mean they will be the same for you as well…

I believe in the sharing of life experiences. As I used to say, capitalization of our personal and business potential highly depends on our willingness to learn and improve. And how can we improve ourselves better than by learning from people who took the same path that is in front of us.

This book has been written for all who have a strong desire to improve the quality of their life and their businesses by relocating or utilising the benefits of the Principality of Monaco. I hope that my life experience will help you to achieve your highest ambitions!

I spent 16 years in the business as a company owner, revenue specialist and business process modeller. In 2006, I was honoured with a National Quality Prize and in 2008 I gained the Entrepreneur of the Year in the SMB (Small and Medium Businesses) category. I am also proud that I am an internationally published author with several best-selling books.

One of my most important lessons I learned on my journey was that the small things that make a real difference cannot be learned by school books, only through life experiences. This is the reason why I am proud to share with you my own life experiences.

Sometimes people take the wrong approach because of a lack of information and they often run around in unnecessary circles instead of taking the easy way. Therefore, if you really want to implement any aspect of this book into your personal life, I highly recommend you contact the professionals who can really advise you. I have to tell you that I am not an authorised advisor by the Monaco Government. There are professionals who are entitled to do that kind of service. It is also not my field of interest.

However, as I have highlighted before, I tried to collect some of the most important administration offices as reference points. They are usually very helpful no matter what your question may be.

Based on my experience, it is highly important to have a basic understanding about things before you start to pay an hourly fee for an advisor. Not to mention, you can find many so-called advisors in Monaco instead of the real ones, who are actually accepted by the Monaco Government. My advice is to always check the business license and Government authorisation of the people you work with it.

The Principality of Monaco offers various sources to protect you, but if you fail to do your homework, Monaco cannot protect you.

Would I recommend Monaco

What is my honest opinion about Monaco? Would I really recommend it after all my experiences?

Yes!

Yes!

Yes!

The Principality of Monaco is full of potentials for you, your family and your business career as well. Relocating your family to Monaco could prove to be one of the most satisfying decisions you could make for you and your family's future.

Do not forget that Monaco also has an above-average life expectancy of 89.5 years, the lengthiest in the world. Voted one of the happiest places to live on earth, an air of positivity, peace and luxury shines throughout the Principality and its culture each day.

Do not be scared by the challenges. It is an exceptional place where you can feel every impact in a very concentrated way. When you are able to deliver good things to your life, then you will feel its harmony in an extremely intense way. You can really appreciate your life in Monaco.

If you have the courage to relocate and to improve your life quality, then I am sure the Principality of Monaco will welcome you within its closed "family". I also hope that through this book you got many useful information and starting points as I tried to summarise the merits of living in Monaco.

In my personal opinion, the Principality of Monaco is not just exceptional because of its quality of life, business and taxation offers, but also because you can discover real and true people there. Hosting more than 700 events per year, Monaco offers a true cultural hub reflective of its heritage. Just dive under the fancy surface; it is like hunting for the pearls of the ocean. They are there and they are always waiting for you.

When people tell you that the Principality is only about tax evasion, money, parties and mafia, then ask yourself whether those people have really experienced this and whether they actually live in Monaco or not. And by living there, I mean for more than a weekend as a tourist...

Indeed, Monaco can be very intense the first time, but once you are in, you will become part of a very caring and protective circle. As I have always believed, in life, money comes, and goes but "family" is all that matters.

The Monaco circle is powerful, strong, protective and it provides a short cut to your aims. These are the major qualities that make the Principality of Monaco truly exceptional. The real treasure lies under the surface, so feel free to discover it for yourself.

595

Resources

Recommended resources

Monaco Government Tourism Office
www.visitmonaco.com

Monaco Welcome Office
en.gouv.mc/Government-Institutions/The-Government/Ministry-of-
Finance-and-Economy/Business-Development-Agency

Institut Monégasque de la Statistique et des Études Économiques
http://www.imsee.mc

The Office
https://www.theoffice.mc

vk*p business advisors
https://www.vkp.mc

Lanteri Partners International (Monaco)
https://www.lanteri.com.au

OMYS Monaco
http://www.omysmonaco.com

OMYS Consulting
http://www.omys-consulting.com

Monaco Villas - Ms Maya Ivdra
http://www.monaco-villas.com

Living in Monaco
https://www.livinginmonaco.com

Signature dishes of the Principality of Monaco
www.amazon.com/dp/1537484516

The Monaco Business Development Plan For Financial Actors
https://www.amazon.com/dp/B087L4M76V

Recommended partners

Lanteri Partners International (Monaco)

Lanteri Partners Group is a family owned and operated company located in Melbourne, Australia.

Lanteri Partners is regarded as one of Melbourne's most successful independent Private Wealth Management firms, offering all financial services, accounting and investment advice under the one umbrella. Lanteri Partners for over 28 years have helped executives, high net worth individuals, family offices and businesses maximize and accelerate their wealth plan with strategies to ensure their money works smarter, reduce their tax, build an investment balance sheet, and achieve long term security in retirement and beyond.

Lanteri Partners manage and advise on in excess of $1 Billion in Property and Investment Funds through its MDA Licence (the highest licence a financial services firm can obtain in Australia).

Lanteri Partners have established a consulting office in Monaco.

Lanteri Partners International (Monaco)
2, boulevard de Suisse
98000 Monaco

https://www.lanteri.com.au

OMYS Monaco

OMYS Monaco offers Strategic Consulting & Business Planning Services for corporate and individual clients worldwide.

They provide personalized guidance and support to family offices, corporations, lenders and professionals involved in managing and optimizing ownership of high-end assets.

They thrive to bring clients a better understanding of the risks and opportunities within assets such as Yachts, Real Estate, Art and Aircraft.

The purpose of the Monaco team is to build on their previous experience in the banking sector, as well their expertise developed through a successful mortgage business in France, in order to help institutions and family offices to anticipate their clients' needs and structure adaptive financial products which reconcile the strict regulations of the financial sector with the need to bring fresh options to the finance spectrum.

OMYS Monaco
14 Quai Antoine 1er
98000 Monaco

contact@omysmonaco.com
https://www.omysmonaco.com

OMYS Consulting

OMYS Monaco works in close relation with its French sister company OMYS Consulting for the specific needs of regulated mortgages and finance.

OMYS Consulting is more than a conventional mortgage broker. They strive to minimize lending costs, but this is only part of their mission. Based on their banking background and close relationship with lender's teams they are able to think ahead and defuse potential blocking points, allowing for faster credit decision.

Their teams are proud to say that their intervention has allowed on many occasions for complex transactions to meet their lending solution.

OMYS Consulting

contact@omys-consulting.com
https://www.omys-consulting.com

vk*p business advisors

vk*p (Van Klaveren & Pazzaglia) is an advisory firm that facilitates business structures (Sole traders, Limited Liability Compamies – SARL – and others) in Monaco and advises in the development of your projects through our breakthrough analysis, pragmatic approach and extensive network of contacts.

vk*p is a venture that was naturally born to address the needs of our many clients. In essence, it is the story of two young men, Pierre Van Klaveren and Aymeric Pazzaglia, who barely knew one another and who happened to work together assisting entrepreneurs and investors to manage their projects in Monaco. They were in charge of supporting these clients by assisting them to start their own businesss or developing their business activities by introducing new business resources, angel investors and/or general partners, etc.

Our collaboration soon proved to be a winning professional team, which has naturally become a friendship.

vk*p business advisors

L'Albu, 17 Avenue Albert II
c/o The Office
98000 Monaco

https://vkp.mc

The Office

The Office - Your "made to measure" business center in the Principality of Monaco.

Located in the heart of Fontvieille and close to all amenities, The Office is pleased to welcome you in two spaces with a total area of 700 m². Equipped with fully equipped offices, large co-working spaces, meeting rooms and coffee/tea rooms, The Office is the right place for your professional success.

Our team, made up of three complementary professional profiles with solid experience in various sectors such as law, economics, corporate finance and mastery of the administrative system as well as the local economic fabric, will welcome and accompany you in establishing and developing your business in Monaco.

Designed to improve your performance by promoting well-being, collaborative work and creativity, your work environment is now reinventing itself!

WE ARE THE OFFICE !
A Working Place to Redefine The Way to Work.

The Office

L'Albu, 17 Avenue Albert II
98000 Monaco

+377 97 77 62 22

contact@theoffice.mc
https://www.theoffice.mc

Monaco Villas

Monaco Villas is a Real Estate Brokerage Agency based in Monaco, offering properties for sale and to rent in the Principality and across the Cote d'Azur.

They have an extensive list of apartments and villas for sale which you can access on their website, but they also offer a comprehensive property search service through their many partners in order to find you your perfect property.

Monaco Villas proudly offer a professional and confidential service and look forward to welcoming you.

MONACO VILLAS

REAL ESTATE

Monaco Villas

2 Avenue St Laurent
98000 Monaco

https://www.monaco-villas.com

References

During the creation of present book, I found many useful and exceptionally well described pieces of information on the following public internet sites:

- »   Prince's Palace of Monaco website (www.palais.mc)
- »   The Princely Government website (en.gouv.mc)
- »   IMSEE Monaco Statistics (www.imsee.mc)
- »   Wikipedia (www.wikipedia.org)

In my book, I presented and extended topics based on my own experiences and re-phrased information that I considered to be common goods.

If you are looking for any reliable sources about the Principality of Monaco, I highly recommend you visit the above-mentioned internet sites.

I am also very thankful for Google (www.google.com) because their search engine is amazing, and it helped me a lot to find all the information I needed to compose the chapters of the latest edition of this book.

I was also inspired by various sources and publications which are not truly related to this book, but without them, I would have a less valuable view on important topics.

- »   Fondation Prince Albert II de Monaco
- »   Altana Wealth Management
- »   Art Market Monitor
- »   artnet
- »   Blue Nile
- »   Brendon Burchard: The Charge
- »   Deloitte

- » Dodo Newman: "Out of the Box Innovation"
- » Donald Trump: "Think Big: Make It Happen in Business and Life"
- » Envestors MC
- » EU Observer
- » Euronews
- » Forbes
- » Gemological Institute of America
- » Harry Winston
- » International Diamond Exchange Website (IDEX)
- » International University of Monaco
- » Investor.hu
- » InvestorPitches.com
- » J. M. Barrie: "Peter Pan"
- » Knight Frank Wealth Report
- » Life.hu
- » Malcolm Gladwell: "Blink: The Power of Thinking Without Thinking"
- » Miells & Partners
- » MonacoLife.net
- » MooringSpot.com
- » Paolo Coelho
- » Principality of Monaco - Ministre d'État
- » Rapaport Diamond Report
- » Sophia Tutino
- » Sotheby's International Realty
- » Sotheby's Mei Moses® art index
- » Starr Diamond Co.
- » The Financial Express
- » The Hollywood reporter
- » The IP Kat
- » The New York Post

» The Telegraph
» Tim Atkin
» Venturi Automobiles
» Wealth-X
» WeatherBase
» WikiPedia

Liability disclaimer

The "Living in Monaco" book by author Zsolt Szemerszky is not a substitute for independent professionals, Monaco relocation, investment or legal advice. It has been created solely with education purpose on the Principality of Monaco.

The present book serves as the author's interpretation of his personal and professional views on the Principality of Monaco, without specific advice on any personal or corporate requirements.

Use of any information from this book or any other book or web site referred to is for general information only and does not represent advice either expressed or implied. If you are interested in any part of the book, you are encouraged to seek professional advice.

Accordingly, the author, his publishers and affiliates disclaim that the information provided should not be treated as advice. Furthermore, it is a strict condition of the author that any individual reading the book recognises and accepts unreservedly that all information, process introductions, businesses, examples, or outcomes relating to past, present, or future, are provided exclusively for academic purposes and that such information must not in any way be construed as general or personal advice.

The author and/or publishers shall not be held liable for any losses, damages incurred by anyone who follows or acts on the opinions, views, processes, contents and thoughts expressed in any form in this book, on any other websites or from individuals connected.

Anyone reading this book is solely responsible for their interpretation of its contents and for their own decisions and actions. The foregoing applies also to correspondence (including private emails), to posts on other websites (including internet message boards and public discussion forums), and to articles published in other mass media.

You should make your own enquiries before entering into any decision based on the information or material on this book.

The Author of the "Living in Monaco" book is presenting the information and images inside the book with the concept of Fair Use. Copyright Disclaimer Under Section 107 of the Copyright Act 1976 grants permission to use information and images for educational purpose that might otherwise be infringing. Authors always ensures the photo credits and name of the sources.